Marxism and Real Estate Development

This book straddles two worlds and attempts to bring them together: that of Lefebvre's Marxism, on the one hand, and that of real estate development, on the other. Lefebvre has now become a household name amongst many contemporary Marxists, especially those with an interest in urban planning and certain quarters of the architectural profession; however, his work is far less well known by real estate professionals, whether investors, developers, brokers, or, indeed, policymakers.

This book has both a large scope and a very bold aim – to use an explication and analysis of the work of Henri Lefebvre not only to present a critique of development, but, also to draw these two worlds together. It therefore, first, aims to present the arguments of this increasingly well-known French Marxist philosopher, sociologist, and pioneer of urban studies; second, to situate contemporary real estate development in the light of Lefebvre's work; and third, to analyse the potential application of Lefebvre's work to each of the major components of contemporary real estate, to use Lefebvre's work in order to recommend practical action for developers, working alongside planners and architects, to influence the future of global real estate.

In addition to its direction at developers themselves, this book should be of interest to economists, real estate researchers and professionals, planners, urban studies scholars, and, of course, to those interested in the application of Lefebvre's work to real estate.

Dr Julian Roche is an international financial trainer and consultant who has taught and advised real estate developers, investors, and government agencies for over two decades; he is currently serving as Chief Economist at Cavendish Maxwell chartered surveyors as well as teaching and researching at Curtin University. He is also continuing his research into Continental Marxist philosophy commenced at Hull and Edinburgh Universities. This is his fourth book with Routledge.

Routledge Studies in International Real Estate

The Routledge Studies in International Real Estate series presents a forum for the presentation of academic research into international real estate issues. Books in the series are broad in their conceptual scope and reflect an inter-disciplinary approach to Real Estate as an academic discipline.

Delhi's Changing Built Environment
Piyush Tiwari and Jyoti Rao

Housing Policy, Wellbeing and Social Development in Asia
Edited by Rebecca L. H. Chiu and Seong-Kyu Ha

Construction and Application of Property Price Indices
Anthony Owusu-Ansah

Residential Satisfaction and Housing Policy Evolution
Clinton Aigbavboa and Wellington Thwala

International Housing Market Experience and Implications for China
Edited by Rebecca L. H. Chiu, Zhi Liu and Bertrand Renaud

Interests and Behaviours of Real Estate Market Actors in Commercial Property Valuation
Alina Nichiforeanu

New Frontiers in Real Estate Finance
The Rise of Micro Markets
Patrick Lecomte

Marxism and Real Estate Development
Taking Lefebvre for Developers Seriously
Julian Roche

For more information about this series, please visit: www.routledge.com/Routledge-Handbooks-in-Religion/book-series

Marxism and Real Estate Development

Taking Lefebvre for Developers Seriously

Julian Roche

Routledge
Taylor & Francis Group
LONDON AND NEW YORK

First published 2024
by Routledge
4 Park Square, Milton Park, Abingdon, Oxon OX14 4RN

and by Routledge
605 Third Avenue, New York, NY 10158

Routledge is an imprint of the Taylor & Francis Group, an informa business

British Library Cataloguing-in-Publication Data
A catalogue record for this book is available from the British Library

Library of Congress Cataloging-in-Publication Data
Names: Roche, Julian, author.
Title: Marxism and real estate : taking Lefebvre for developers seriously / Julian Roche.
Description: Abingdon, Oxon ; New York, NY : Routledge, 2023. | Series: Routledge studies in international real estate | Includes bibliographical references and index.
Identifiers: LCCN 2023014600 (print) | LCCN 2023014601 (ebook) | ISBN 9781032114323 (hardback) | ISBN 9781032115146 (paperback) | ISBN 9781003220244 (ebook)
Subjects: LCSH: Real estate development—Philosophy. | Communism. | Lefebvre, Henri, 1901–1991.
Classification: LCC HD1390 .R63 2023 (print) | LCC HD1390 (ebook) | DDC 333.73/15—dc23/eng/20230330
LC record available at https://lccn.loc.gov/2023014600
LC ebook record available at https://lccn.loc.gov/2023014601

ISBN: 978-1-032-11432-3 (hbk)
ISBN: 978-1-032-11514-6 (pbk)
ISBN: 978-1-003-22024-4 (ebk)

DOI: 10.1201/9781003220244

Typeset in Times
by Apex CoVantage, LLC

To my late uncle, Fred Roche (1931–1992)

Contents

Acknowledgements

I am extremely grateful to all of those who have helped me along the path towards this book. My thanks to my socialist teachers at Brockenhurst College, to my undergraduate tutors at Oxford, to my postgraduate colleagues at Exeter, Hull, and Edinburgh, and to all those who made contributions in seminars at different Australian Universities. I am especially grateful to Dr Anne Schwenkenbecher and Dr Tim Flanagan at Murdoch University for taking an interest in Lefebvre, to colleagues at Curtin University and AHURI for taking the time to suggest useful directions of housing policy research, and to Professor Kevin Cox for agreeing to read a manuscript with which he was not by any means necessarily in agreement.

I am equally grateful to those who guided me into practical involvement with real estate. To the example set by my grandfather, John Roche, who came from Ireland and created a housebuilding firm in London before World War II. To the inspiration provided by my uncle, Fred Roche, who began his career as an architect, went on to become General Manager of the Milton Keynes Development Corporation, and finished his career as a real estate developer in his own right. To all those with whom I have worked in development and letting properties. To the training companies which gave me the opportunity to participate in global real estate development and to those of my friends and colleagues in global real estate who have taken the time to comment on this book. To my colleagues at Cavendish Maxwell, where I have been able to continue my engagement with real estate at a practical level as Chief Economist. And to the architects, planners, and developers who took the time to engage in dialogue with me over the contents of this book as well as giving generously of their time for the parallel research project into developer strategy in which I am also engaged.

I am also delighted to thank Routledge, both my superb Editorial Assistant Martha Luke, who had far too much work to do on this manuscript and to whom I owe a deep debt of thanks indeed, and to my inspiring and dedicated editor Ed Needle, who not only managed the process with great efficiency but can also take credit for making the excellent suggestion that, in covering such a wide ground, I use many case studies rather than few.

My final deep appreciation goes to my family. To my late father and mother, dedicated public servants and loving parents both, and to my wife Gowri and our daughter Tabitha, who have endured my engagement with successive Continental

Marxist philosophers with tolerant good humour and support throughout, but who have heard me lament too many times in this particular case that I am engaged on bringing two ends of a chain together, success in which is beyond the capacity of any one individual. The gap between Marxism and real estate development remains extensive. If this book goes some way towards bridging it, it will have been a worthwhile endeavour.

1 Introduction

The scale of the problem

Introduction: why write this book?

Real estate development and philosophy of any sort, let alone Marxism, might not at first thought appear to be the most likely of consorts; the former is often depicted as the very epitome of capitalism in practice, whilst the latter has at its core the conviction that capitalism is transient and that it is possible to build a better world beyond it. Henri Lefebvre (1901–1991) therefore stands out as 'one of the few great 20th century European philosophers to engage directly with the urban, both in theory and in practice' (Leary-Owhin, 2018:1). So, if there is to be any kind of engagement, Lefebvre might therefore be a bridge, or at least a place to start to build one.

I must hope that developers are intrigued, rather than immediately discouraged, by the fact that despite, or possibly at least in part because of his Marxism, Lefebvre has enjoyed a posthumous 'glittering academic' shelf life across many dimensions. His reputation as an innovative urbanist, as a prototypical postmodernist, as the inventor of the concept of 'everyday life', as a giant thinker about space, as a state theorist, as a utopian architect's best friend' (Merrifield, 2009:937) has resulted in his being 'more influential than any other scholar in opening up and exploring the limitless dimensions of our social spatiality' (Soja, 1996:6). More than a decade before this book, in fact, the question had indeed already therefore been put by a reviewer: 'do we need another work on Lefebvre – is it not now time to work with Lefebvre? (Vogelpohl, 2011:216). This despite the suggestion that 'Lefebvre never intended his writing as a guide for urban planners and designers' (Read *et al.*, 2013:382), let alone real estate developers. Why then do almost exactly the opposite and write a book to try to present Lefebvre, a 20th-century Marxist philosopher of the urban, to 21st-century real estate developers?

I advance two reasons. Firstly, the slightly circular one that Lefebvre's arguments are themselves now much more accessible, appreciated, and hopefully understood by a wider spectrum of individuals and organisations than several decades ago. In part this has been the result of indefatigable proponents and cataloguers of his extensive range of his work (e.g. Hess & Weigand, 2006, Elden, 2003, 2004). So far as the Anglosphere is concerned, this is at least also partly due to the wonderful efforts of translators such as John Moore (Lefebvre, 1947, 1961, 1981 [2014]),

DOI: 10.1201/9781003220244-1

Donald Nicolson-Smith (Lefebvre, 1974 [1991]), Frank Bryant (Lefebvre, 1973 [1976]), Eleonore Kofman and Elizabeth Lebas (2000), David Fernbach (Lefebvre, 1965 [2016]), Gerald Moore, Neil Brenner, and Stuart Elden (Lefebvre, 2009), and Robert Bononno (Lefebvre, 1973a [2014]). Even those who are sceptical of his elevation to a position of successful historical futurist, for example, drawing attention to the cultural, geographical, and temporal context of 20th-century France within which his work was embedded (Schneider, 2015:556–557), recognise the way in which so many connected with the real estate professions but of progressive inclination do indeed now choose to work 'with' Lefebvre. Indeed, 'When scanning contributions to journals on architecture, planning or urban studies these days, references to Henri Lefebvre's work seem to be omnipresent' (Schneider, 2015:555), with expansive claims being made for the value of his work, no less than 'The possibility for a reconfigured approach to the planning, design and structure of the architecture and landscape of the city and the urban' (Zieleniec, 2018:5).

The second reason is almost the opposite of the first. Despite the importance of real estate developers worldwide, the application of Lefebvre's ideas appears to have halted at the border, and not gone further into the development process itself. Developers themselves are therefore probably unlikely to have engaged with Lefebvre, and so likewise unlikely to have absorbed his analytical principles, let alone precepts: this book is intended to persuade them that they should do all of those things and more.

What is real estate development?

Let us take a step back, especially if we are not real estate developers ourselves or close to the industry, to coral our subject. If 'to confront these forces we have first to understand them' (Harvey, 1973:314), then to insist upon the importance of understanding real estate developers is essential to build that connection between them and Lefebvre. So, especially for those readers with different métiers, what do we mean by real estate development, and by a real estate developer?

The process of real estate development

Development itself has been invested with many meanings, from the advance of productive forces within capitalist society, through a wider socio-economic conception, to a more normative conception reflected within the UN system (Moulaert *et al*., 2013:2–3). The specifically real estate development process and the role of the developer within it have both been well established for decades, if not equally well researched, with by comparison broad agreement about what it entails. Definitions of real estate development abound as a result, for example that of section 55(i) of the UK Town and Country Planning Act 1990:

> Development means the carrying out of building . . . or other operations in, on, over or under land, or the making of any material change in the use of any buildings or other land.
>
> (UK Government, 2023)

This definition reflects the functional characteristics of real estate development and continues to be widely used in the UK, even internationally. Alternatively, real estate development is

> a process that involves changing or intensifying the use of land to produce buildings for occupation.
>
> (Reed, 2021:2)

Definitions also include the use of the term to refer to a group of similar buildings built in an area by a particular real estate developer, and a cynical view that the real estate development process is just

> a complex, time-consuming, capital intensive, multi-disciplinary, externality-generating, public-private endeavour.
>
> (Kohlhepp, 2012:3)

The well-known approach of James Graskamp is also still widely cited, despite it now dating back more than three decades. Graskamp said:

> Unlike many mass-production industries, each real estate project is unique, and the development process is so much a creature of the political process that society has a new opportunity with each major project to negotiate, debate, and reconsider the basic issues of an enterprise economy, i.e. who pays, who benefits, who risks, and who has standing to participate in the decision process. Thus, the development process remains a high-silhouette topic for an articulate and politically sophisticated society.
>
> (Jarchow, 1991:228)

He went on to argue:

> The creation and management of space-time in earth is termed real estate development. Real estate developments range from a simple cave to complex technology of the Park Avenue skyscraper. Like a manufactured product, a real estate project is part of a larger physical system programmed to achieve long-term objectives, but each real estate project is also a small business enterprise of its own. Thus, the development process is a continuum of construction technology, financing, marketing skills, administrative controls, and rehabilitation required to operate the real estate enterprise over many years.
>
> (Graskamp, 1981:1–2)

The sheer variety of real estate development bears witness to this contention (Figure 1.1). Residential, itself divided into a multitude of different types of residence, commercial, and a host of specialisms, from hotels through an immense range of different public buildings to mixed-use developments rely for their success on a skilful blend of different types of real estate. Conversion of existing buildings is an example of a specialism: warehouse facilities constructed mainly in the 20th

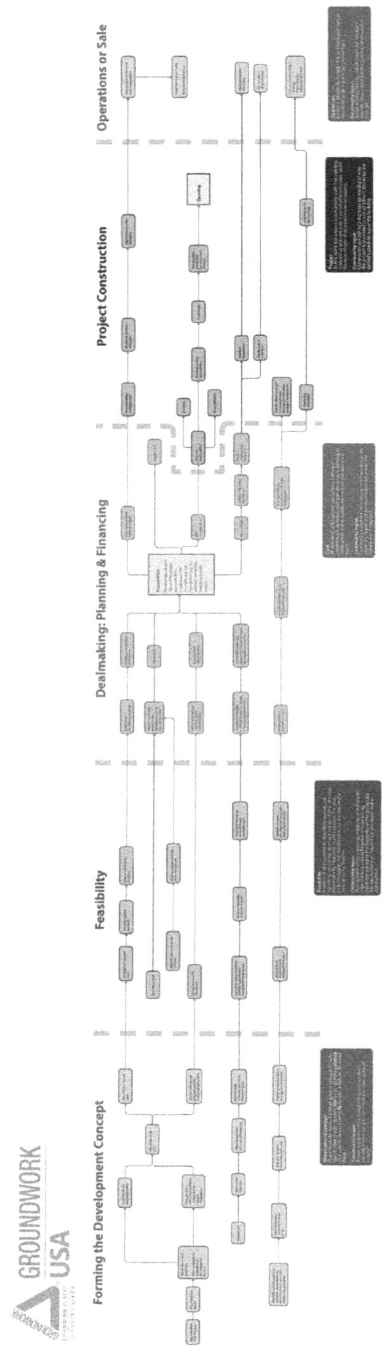

Figure 1.1 The real estate development process.

Source: Groundwork USA, 2017.

century or even 19th century have been converted to office buildings, apartments, and condominiums; more significantly in recent years, office blocks are being converted to residential use, originally in cities like London and New York, but now with the trend globalising progressively. In such work, developers – some of them specialists in conversions and renovations – take advantage of unique architectural features while remodelling existing buildings to create modern structures retaining, if they are sufficiently dexterous, something of their historical character and flavour.

Real estate development in particular, if understood as the employment of land, labour, capital, and arguably also management resources to create improvements to raw land, infrastructure, and especially buildings, with the intention of selling them, either to owner-occupiers or to investors who will lease out to tenants, ought to be distinguished from real estate investment, which can be defined as buying, or renovating already-constructed real estate, and then leasing them out, usually with a profit-making objective. Clearly, there are some organisations that do both, including building real estate which they then lease out.

Real estate development nevertheless *matters*, on that point all can surely agree. It is the second most important element, after investment, of the real estate sector as a whole, the most important store of value in the world. Housing start data in the United States, for example, are one of the most eagerly sought-after indicators of the US economy (Moody's, 2023), as they are of great importance not only to public planning but also to the entire socio-economic development of the nation.

What is equally obvious is that real estate development requires substantial quantities of resources, which in a capitalist economy means the use of capital, much of it borrowed or invested by a third party, as well as tangible resources like land, steel, and glass. Financial rates of return for real estate development not only vary widely over time, and between jurisdictions, but also depend on prevailing economic conditions (e.g. inflation, economic cycles, and the balance of local supply and demand). Whether it was ever the case that, as one of their sternest critics suggested, 'in the United States a 40 percent rate of return is not regarded as unusual' (Harvey, 1985:69), there is no doubt that real estate developers have both enjoyed great riches and experienced equally disastrous bankruptcies across different continents, sectors, and over time, a story recounted with élan several times across the decades, albeit perhaps a little less frequently than the importance of the subject might have expected to deliver (e.g. Lorimer, 1978; Marriott, 1967; Sudjic, 1992; Ross Goobey, 1992; Murphy, 2008; Brill, 2020).

Real estate developers

Whilst there are many real estate developers worldwide, a sense of perspective is required in recognising that their role, as well as associated professional disciplines such as architecture, is a severely limited and circumscribed area of work and practice in comparison to real estate ('property', as it is often termed, especially in the Anglo-Saxon use of the term, with the emphasis shifting from the physical to the legal in the process) as a whole. In most cities, most urban environments, new buildings are relatively rare. Most real estate is already built and in the process of being used or not, either commercially or more frequently as habitation. Development has, as a result, been on the fringes of the interest of the academy, especially as data has not been as plentiful as for existing real estate.

It would be fair, however, to adopt a broad definition of a real estate developer, which can include organisations as disparate as wholly or partially government-owned master developers such as those to be found in the Middle East that acquire and structure large land plots, as well as their sub-developers; fully integrated developers who own at least a substantial proportion of their own supply chain, including construction, housebuilders which aim to sell all of their product and sub-contract a great deal of their supply chain, as well as those which continue to own and lease out property that they have developed, and even pure land developers who subdivide land and put in infrastructure but do not construct buildings themselves. It is also important to recognise that far from all real estate developers are for-profit organisations. Some larger charities in a range of countries have also become involved in real estate development. Widely different in both strategy and organisation, in size, geographical reach, structure, expertise, and management, each of these organisations has a reasonable claim to be categorised as real estate developers, and there seems little merit in dicing with definitions to exclude any organisation that mobilises land, labour, capital, and other resources to create, modify, and recreate the built environment (Figure 1.2).

It is also right to recognise that real estate development is a very complex and interdisciplinary task, typically demanding a dedicated team, including people with different skill sets and expertise and the coordination of a wide range of interrelated activities. Local authorities, legal requirements, residents, and neighbours are always there to be satisfied, or at least placated; design teams and contractors are to be managed; timescales, costs, and contingencies must be monitored and controlled, whilst the requirements of lenders and the needs of other stakeholders, in particular prospective tenants and investors, must be met at the end of the process. In addition, real estate developers are often faced with considerable and constant changes in their environment and new challenges driven by the macro-economic, social, urban planning, political–legal, regulatory, environmental, and technological framework conditions, even during the course of an individual project, let alone differences across jurisdictions.

Market, risk, and analysis

Whilst it is true that many organisations undertaking real estate development, even those depicted as exclusively for-profit, have objectives that are wider than purely financial, the analysis of projects from a financial standpoint is the centre of decision-making for most development organisations and even for quasi-private developers heavily influenced by the government. Financial returns often therefore represent a 'maximise subject to' criterion – to be maximised subject to a range of other constraints. Achieving a profit depends on the developer, as for a manufacturer, on balancing costs against sale value, whether achieved before, during, or after construction.

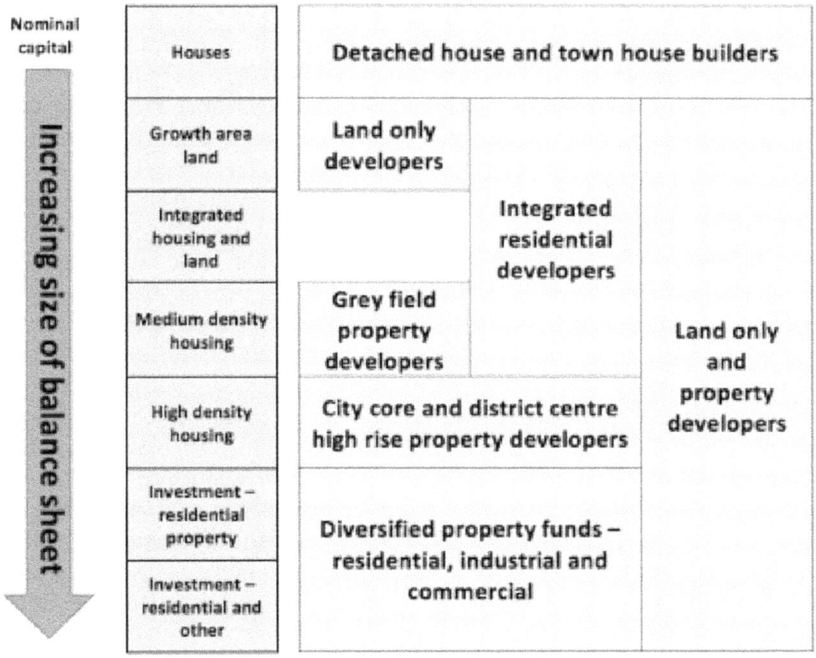

Figure 1.2 A schema of real estate developers in the early 21st century, the Australian example.

Source: Ong *et al.* (2017:53), adapted from Rowley *et al.* (2014:18).

Successful development in a capitalist economy depends, inter alia, on bringing the adequate real estate product to the market, or the future owner directly, at the right time at the right price. Critically, however, once decided upon, development has little room for manoeuvre.

This one reason why a crucial insight about development, which Graskamp does not emphasise and which many developers still do not appreciate, is that it is *riskier* than investment. Riskier in a conventional fund management sense, in that the dispersion of returns (often measured by Beta, the volatility of returns by comparison to a benchmark) will be greater; and riskier in risk management terms, in that the probability of loss over time is greater.

In view of the issue of risk, it is worth probing slightly into how developers assess project viability. A clear trend for developers over the past half-century, in common with corporate finance (Brealey *et al.*, 2022), has been to move away from more basic analysis of projects, such as payback period or accounting rate of return, towards Discounted Cash Flow Net Present Value (NPV) and Internal Rate of Return (IRR)–based analysis, requiring financial modelling and a concept of the time value of money reflected in a cost of capital (Bardet *et al.*, 2020). Many developers might query its accuracy, but financial theory suggests that the financial returns – arguably, their social returns as well – of real estate developers ought therefore, on average and over the long term, to exceed those of investors. If they do not, we can at least tentatively conclude that the market is not performing efficiently.

The complexity of development demands that, even if human factors often intervene, at least minimal market research ought to underpin the substantial investment required. If carried out as objectively as possible, the aim of such analysis is, firstly, to answer the question for the developer, 'do we want to be involved in this market at all?'; secondly, and as evidence for that answer, evidence on all the key market indicators relevant to development in that market, which will include, but may not be limited to, land prices, construction costs, debt availability and cost, rental levels, operating costs, capitalisation rates (broadly, the relationship between rental values and market prices) and market liquidity; and thirdly, to provide some guidance as to timing in relation to political risks and economic cycles. Developers have no more wish to become helpless victims of circumstance than any other economic actor; the evident fact that they often do indeed become so reflects on the inadequacy of market analysis as well as other dynamics of the market, to which as we shall have cause to note, Lefebvre himself was very alert. As a more recent observer sagely commented, 'The reality is that development happens on the margin. It's not easy to find sites and projects that make any sort of financial sense. More often than not they don't' (Donnelly, 2017). The values the variables included in market analysis take may depend in turn on economic factors, but they are also influenced by cultural and even individual preferences. That people like sea views is not a consequence of a market; how much they are prepared to pay for them is.

Highest and Best Use (HBU)

HBU plays a major part in the epistemology of developers and their relationship with capitalism. It is based on the assumption that developers, and by extension the investors to whom they sell, will seek the greatest return for the capital they invest in real estate, and will therefore select that kind of use that provides the greatest return (in IRR terms, usually) for land and the buildings on it. If that use does not accord with the current use of the land, there may be a development opportunity. HBU is not a unidirectional evaluation, however – it is more appropriate to envisage it as a series of 'gateways', of which there are at least three. Firstly, what alternative uses are physically possible, given constraints such as the size of the plot, slope, soil, drainage, overlooking buildings, access, and other factors. Secondly, what does local planning permit, in terms of zoning? Many locations are designated for specific types of development; there may be trade-offs between utilising existing zoning or attempting to change what is permitted. Finally, what makes it through the first two gateways, what provides the highest IRR, or otherwise fits the strategic purpose of the developer, funders or strategic stakeholders?

The outcome of an HBU analysis is a decision as to whether to construct a new building on a greenfield or brownfield site, the latter of which obviously entails demolishing (or at least substantially remodelling) the existing site improvements, whether then rebuilding, converting an existing building to an alternative use, or recognising that the existing site and whatever buildings are currently in situ is already HBU and therefore there is no current financially feasible development opportunity, in which case the developer may either sell the land to an investor or continue to hold and wait until circumstances are more propitious for re-development. To hold land in this fashion, especially undeveloped land, is the 'land banking' that has been roundly criticised by radical geographers and many others, and which has occasioned substantial regulatory effort to defeat it, for example the White Lands tax imposed by Riyadh in Saudi Arabia (Hariri, 2022). HBU is therefore a special target for radical critics of real estate developers: as one put it, if

> one vision of potential – what is often referred to as the 'highest and best use' – over others fails, then the space for alternative futures is left wide open and the possibility of a more democratic and sustainable definition of 'best use' can emerge.
>
> (Kallin, 2021:630)

As to *how* this might occur, radical critics are less vocal.

As for developers themselves, it would be a fair assertion that they are mostly comfortable with the idea in principle: HBU works for many of them, both as a valuation premise and a driver of development choice. The use of HBU can go some way to explaining why development occurs in some locations and not in others, and why particular locations see one kind of development rather than another. But it should be said right away that the idea of HBU being both easy to determine and uniformly applied is an unrealistic implication of a complex decision-making process that may be influenced far more by other considerations: HBU is a theory as well as a technique, and a partial one at that, not a complete explanation of the actions of developers and other real estate stakeholders such as planners and investors.

Feasibility studies

Historically, it has been said to be the case that a real estate project is 'feasible' when the real estate analyst determines that there is a reasonable likelihood of satisfying explicit objectives when a selected course of action is tested for fit to a context of specific constraints and limited resources (Graskamp, 1972:515). A feasibility analysis, which ought to come after both the market analysis and then any HBU study, should include all the relevant factors surrounding a proposed development – not only the financial analysis, but the proposed development in the round – to reach a firm conclusion as to whether it should proceed. An over-optimistic feasibility study – and there have been many – may lead to a less-than-optimal project, to failure of major project goals, whether financial or otherwise, or to negative financial outcomes such as loan defaults, project restructuring, or even bankruptcy for the participants. Too cautious a feasibility study – and there have been a few – will lead to missed opportunities.

At first glance, this process may seem abstract and unclear, even impossible, but it accurately explains the real breadth of feasibility analysis: not only the 'usual' IRR hurdle rate, and the accompanying NPV and IRR themselves, but also all the constraints posed by the physical conditions of the site, of zoning and planning permission, the local and where relevant city-wide and even national political factors that will influence the project, and what resources both financial and otherwise that the developer can, must, and should bring to the project, including any required joint venture or technical partners, and the timescale, all set in the context of the analysis of comparative risks. A feasibility study does not therefore present just one feasibility, financial, but many: physical, regulatory, legal more widely, political *and* financial. In particular, large public projects are often subject to intense scrutiny, especially in countries with active political participation, whilst even small projects can face opposition from neighbourhood or other campaigning groups. As has been observed, only developers, who have never had an angry group of residents, slow or even stop their projects and do not care about local politics (Demsas, 2022). The core of the feasibility study, however, is a financial model, usually of the Discounted Cash Flow type, which is responsible for delivering the NPV and IRR outcomes. This type of financial model incorporates, or at least should incorporate, land costs at market value, the costs of construction, and projected sales (and where the development is to be retained, net rents), all discounted (i.e. costs and benefits depreciated over time) by the developer's cost of capital, whether at a corporate level or via funding at the project level. It is crucial that the feasibility study aims at evaluation, and does not either merely repeat the market study (from which it will draw assumptions about market values such as rents, construction costs, yields, etc.) nor, worse, work backwards from a desired outcome, whether NPV, IRR, or some wider more strategic considerations. As with market studies and HBU, the value of feasibility studies derives from their independence, which in turn leads, so far as possible, to their objectivity in relation to likely outcomes, including risks and scenarios.

It is not an easy task. For example, land cost at market value is usually a significant portion of the cost of a development, so accurate land valuation is an essential and now vital part of every feasibility study, but land prices in a capitalist land market are often very volatile, even hard to ascertain due to a lack of recent comparable transactions. Another example is that there is an inevitable tension between the developer's wish to prepare an accurate feasibility study and the fact that accurate revenue and cost data will not be available until after the appointment of architects, construction contractors, and other professionals, and even for land. This is unavoidable: the developer must use their expertise to forecast as accurate as possible. It is the hallmark of an accurate feasibility study, and when repeated over time, a successful developer, to be able to carry out these forecasts accurately, as well as convincingly. For so far as potential funders are concerned, be they banks or third-party investors, as it is on the basis of the feasibility study that external funders will make their choices as to whether to support, and to what extent.

Once funded, often from a number of different sources, frequently only to a limited extent from the developer's own internal equity, and the feasibility study approved, the role of the real estate developer is either only that of a financial coordinator or, together with the role of the project manager, they are responsible for coordinating a range of different project stakeholders, including their own consultants (architects, surveyors, and many more), planners and building inspectors, the construction company, and their customers, be they prospective purchasers or tenants.

A curious silence

Real estate developers and their tasks now defined, with their process and their tools at least sketched out, the absence of any attempt to present Lefebvre's theory *to* them is all the more remarkable, especially as there has been a 'turn to empirical studies' (Stanek, 2011:xv), with efforts being made to apply Lefebvre's work empirically across a range of urban settings. As examples, early work included a case study of a shopping mall in Baltimore (Shields, 1989), analysis of the production of the abstract space of finance in London and its socio-economic consequences (Allen & Pryke, 1994), the development of post-war Glasgow (Fyfe, 1996), contested development in Malaysia (Cartier, 1997) in post-apartheid Cape Town (Dierwechter, 2002), ethnicity and development in Singapore (Sin, 2003; Sim *et al.*, 2003), public space (Mitchell, 2003); antiracist politics (McCann, 1999; Tyner, 2007); migrant rights, citizenship, and multiculturalism (Carpio *et al.*, 2011; Gilbert & Dikeç, 2008); and education (Lipman, 2011). Later studies have tended to focus more emphatically on struggle, such as place-based politics in Kuwait (al-Nakib, 2014), informal settlements in Cape Town (Huchzermeyer, 2014), street vendors in Brazil (Nogueira & Shin, 2020), refugees in Turkey and Greece (Tsavdaroglou, 2020; Tsavdaroglou & Kaika, 2022), and failures of planning and development in Sweden (Berg, 2022). Broadly, studies have also focused on 'spatial justice' (Soja, 2010; Kipfer *et al.*, 2013:128).

Lefebvre's influence does not stop there: his work has been applied to social work (Saravia, 2019), theatrical performance (Watkins, 2005), the trials of academic life (Barnett, 2010), skateboarding (Borden, 1998), an architectural video game (François & Triclot, 2020), the visual arts and theology (Soja, 2009:26–29), and works of fiction (Fischer & Bauer, 2019:8; Solak, 2022:187). Reviewing what was already an expanding field, it was suggested that Lefebvre's work has also been 'used most fruitfully' in research on transnational urbanisation, postcolonial spaces, and global restructuring of statehood (Stanek, 2011:xiii).

Certainly, in an escape from the mechanistic economic determinism that was once thought to characterise it, the reappropriation of cultural practices, of architecture, literature, theatre, and art all run deep for contemporary Marxism, whilst the academy is of obvious great importance to Marxists, both theoretically and practically. No doubt too there is value in the recognition that a fixation on the concrete materiality of spatial forms, and on formal ideas and representations of space, can overlook places, real and imagined, a cultural perspective of great and enduring worth (Soja, 1996:10–11). But others had already cautioned that 'Few writers are concerned with the implications of their analysis for planning or development, which makes their work less immediately relevant for the planning field' (Carp, 2008:131). And not merely planning. Is not the disparity between this wide application of Lefebvre's work and the absence of much application to real estate development itself worthy of note?

Most of the voices commenting on Lefebvre are thoroughly progressive, and from the academy; they will be heard throughout this book, not only for their erudition and Lefebvre scholarship, but also as representatives of the opinion that views Lefebvre as of principal importance as a theorist who has most accurately outlined the direction of urban development, change, and even revolution. It is certainly one view that the academy does not exist to make policy recommendations, that analysis and explanation may suffice, but I doubt that either Lefebvre or Marx himself would be wholly satisfied with that. It should be possible to bridge this gap, to ensure 'more rigorous recognition of how his spatial theory, analyses and approach can be adopted, adapted and applied by planning and design practitioners' (Zieleniec, 2018:6): in sum to present Lefebvre in such a way as to be useful to practitioners. As yet, however, there is only a minority seeking to apply Lefebvre's analytical categories, ethical injunctions, and political standpoint to the work of those engaged in creating, managing, and transforming the urban environment. This book aims to make a contribution in this category. In particular, the audiences to whom this book is primarily directed are real estate developers themselves, along with their advisers, as well as urban planners and policymakers more widely.

A biographical detour

Neither Marxists nor real estate developers need to be afraid of biography, nor of the contribution made by individuals in both theory and practice (Sève, 1968 [1978], 2008). Lefebvre's personal story is that of an interdisciplinary public whose intellectual interests spanned politics, literature, language, history, philosophy, planning, and, in later life, even policymaking (Kofman & Lebas, 2000:6).

Whilst several different ways to divide his long career into periods have been suggested, there is agreement that the focus on the urban dominated the years between the late 1960s and the late 1970s (Sangla, 2010:10). This is a vitally important point in relation to developers, because although it unfortunately took until 1991 for his master work on the urban, *The Production of Space*, to be translated into English, it was actually written in 1974 (Lefebvre, 1974 [1991]). In the interim, private sector, real estate developers in particular became more prominent features of the real estate landscape whilst Lefebvre had already written much that can be understood as a modification to what he originally wrote (e.g. Lefebvre, 1990, 1992 [2004]).

Another biographical point ought perhaps to be recognised, albeit perhaps reluctantly. If we are to accept that 'Lefebvre's writings on architecture and urbanism need to be understood within their specific historical condition' (Stanek, 2011:xi), we may also contend that Lefebvre was a complex and contradictory personality, most certainly of his time and place. Some examples: born in Navarrenx, a provincial town in France that was 'redolent with the history of religious wars'

(Davidson, 1992:152), despite his 'nostalgia for original community' (Trebitsch, 1991 [2014:20]), which he himself strenuously but perhaps predictably denied (Lefebvre, 1947 [2014:150]), he preferred to spend his time in the artisan quarter of Paris, and was indeed at a time 'wary of being packed off to some provincial backwater' (Trebitsch, 1991 [2014:9]). Secondly, and of note for a contemporary readership, if the worth of an individual's ideas is to be judged biographically, Lefebvre might not be an ideal candidate for any pantheon (Elden, 2004:3). Thirdly, although standards of referencing were lower than today when he and his contemporaries wrote, Lefebvre perhaps also did not acknowledge all of his philosophical debts, whether to Heidigger (Elden, 2007), Axelos (Elden, 2008), or even to Henri Bergson (Fraser, 2010). Whilst it may be tempting to overlook these flaws, it is surely likely that if Lefebvre is to offer anything to the modern world, his biography is no longer necessarily likely to inspire anyone to read his work – or to agree with him. It may be necessary to ask forbearance from a contemporary reader, no doubt very alive to the significance of personal practice, of the very different values and standards of conduct that pertained to the age in which he wrote.

A peculiar Marxist

Throughout his long career, Lefebvre always maintained that he was a committed Marxist. Developers may be tempted to jump to the conclusion that no Marxist can offer anything of interest to them. But what sort of Marxist? Lefebvre did remain in the Parti Communiste Française (PCF) for three decades until 1958, even briefly acting as the PCF's prime ideologist in its struggle with existentialism (Drake, 2010), on occasion although both the Marxist humanists and the existentialists could be said to have been 'after the same quarry' (Trebitsch, 1991 [2014:7]). Lefebvre did produce work that mirrored if not actually created the Party line in its characterisation of existentialism as self-indulgent individualism (Lefebvre, 1946:62–63). After he left the PCF, however, Lefebvre is far more easily identified with Western, even Critical Marxism, alongside other theoreticians such as Theodore Adorno, Ernst Bloch, Roger Garaudy (at least for a time), György Lukács, and Herbert Marcuse (Trebitsch, 1991 [2014:5]). Critical Marxists were far from their traditional adversaries in many ways, not least their focus on living and transforming modern capitalist societies themselves.

Little wonder therefore that the Secretary-General of the PCF, Maurice Thorez, wrote in *Pravda* in 1964 that Lefebvre had joined 'the worst kind of renegade and adventurers, degenerate elements, revisionists driven out of the Communist ranks because of their anti-Marxist views' (*Le Monde*, 30 June 1991). The same fate was to befall other leading theorists – Roger Garaudy was expelled in 1970, and eventually decades later even Lucien Sève left the PCF. What we can rest assured of is this: if Marxism is still to be defined by the views of minority Party leadership, or those in academia who reflect a similar standpoint, Lefebvre was indeed a renegade whose unorthodox views could be disregarded. Everyone may of course decide for themselves whether Lefebvre is to be considered as a Marxist. To side with Thorez, however, entails that not only Lefebvre's claim to Marxism must be set aside, but the central premise of this book must follow it into the oblivion reserved by the orthodox for such renegades, so I hope no one does.

So, we ask again, what sort of Marxist? Neither David Harvey's resolute materialism (Harvey, 1982) nor Edward Soja's poststructuralism (Soja, 1996), but rather, Lefebvre's own intertwining of materiality and representations (Elden, 2004:16; Wilson, 2013:365), for 'although Lefebvre was very much a Marxist, he was by no means an orthodox one' (Purcell, 2014:145). No text of Marx was sacred: Lefebvre believed in an end to the practice of textual hagiography that should be entirely alien to Marxism, a view with which he was sure Marx would have concurred (Lefebvre, 1980:29).

One of the characteristics of Lefebvre's work was moreover its constant reformulation in the form of many successive books and articles that together formed a patchwork quilt of theory, a term itself frequently used to express the reality of urban life itself (Kipfer *et al.*, 2013:120; Boano, 2015:26; Garrido, 2019:126). He himself was always insistent that he had no intention of building a system of any kind, any more than Marx himself (Lefebvre, 1975:10). Some themes, however, are consistent: Lefebvre was according to another leading French intellectual of the time, George Labica, always 'a warm, Dionysian Marxist' (Sangla, 2010:3), a romantic revolutionary, both by his own admission (Lefebvre, 1957, 1959) and in the view of others (Marcolini, 2007:38; Hess, 2011:13), whose approach always took 'a humanist Marxist perspective that focuses on creativity, activity, praxis, Hegelian dialectics, human essence, alienation, and the total human' (Fuchs, 2019:133). Lefebvre did share much with other Marxist humanists, in particular the conception of a human essence, albeit one that is historical and unfolds within history (Lefebvre, 1966 [1968:18]). His 'project' entertained a campaign against both the State and the Hegelian philosophical system that glorified it (Lefebvre, 1958:21) in favour of

> a Marxism that rejects the state, that maintains itself as an open and evolving project, and that comes to understand itself as more than anything a democratic project, as a struggle by people to shake off the control of capital and the state in order to manage their affairs for themselves.
>
> (Purcell, 2014:145; Lefebvre, 1975:9)

So, notwithstanding his occasional lapses, including even to deny the need for a subject (Lefebvre, 1973 [1976:7]), any claim for Lefebvre's Marxist credentials must rely on the existence of a Marxist humanism that concerns itself primarily with future freedoms after capitalism has been superseded.

This recognition of the importance of Marx in his world view is not to suggest that Lefebvre's own 'broader philosophical and political framework' (Gray, 2017:321) did not develop over his long and productive life. As he himself contended even at the moment of his maximum adherence to the Party line, in a piece of self-criticism that must have been difficult to write: 'Fresh practical problems, and their resolution, demand the enrichment and development of theory' (Lefebvre, 1949:45). There is a question, of course, about the fairness of any insistence upon the terminus of any individual thinker's intellectual trajectory. There is no law that demands adherence to the words of Henri Lefebvre at a particular time, any more than to those of Marx himself. There should be likewise, in principle, no reluctance for a radical geographer; therefore, in raiding Lefebvre's theoretical locker for his insights into the urban, although if he did disavow an earlier view later in life, it would equally only be fair for a Marxist to record that he did so.

Lefebvre scholars are fond of arguing that it is unfair, if not impossible, to analyse his work on the urban in isolation. Certainly, throughout his career, Lefebvre's philosophical interests had always been broad, and once released from the strictures of Party membership, it became quickly apparent that Lefebvre's Marxist humanism, or perhaps more accurately his position within Western Marxism, led him to be sceptical of the socialism that prevailed in the Soviet Union and other state socialist countries, the failure of which was an impulse to his own theory of space (Stanek, 2012:49). His was always – in principle at least – a thoroughly open Marxism, critical of the Soviet state socialist model, to which he counterposed the freedom that individuals, society, and the whole world will derive from surpassing capitalism. He justified this perennial confidence primarily through the Marxist concept of alienation, which 'becomes the key concept in analysing human situations since Marx' (Trebitsch, 1991 [2014:6]): 'In short, individual and social man's relation to objects is one of otherness and alienation, self-realization and loss of self' (Lefebvre, 1966 [1968:9]), especially as demonstrated in the practice of everyday life in a society that is riven by class conflict. Because economic organisation has been flawed, up to and very much including capitalism, most human existence remains alienated, controlled by elites of one form or another, highly structured, planned, and as a result creating 'quantitative' rather than 'qualitative' lives for individuals and communities. Although the distinction may seem unusual – a developer might not ask, why not simply say many are oppressed – Lefebvre was clear enough in saying that the opportunities thus denied contrasted dramatically in Lefebvre's view with a future society in which capitalism has been superseded, in which as famously expressed, 'the free development of each is the condition for the free development of all' (Marx & Engels, 1848 [2010:27]). More specifically, Lefebvre's emphasis on creative activity leads him to follow Marx (at least in his view, and to align with those of others even outside the Marxist humanist tradition such as Sève (1973 [2022]) in a persistent emphasis on the need to end *alienation* in order to liberate the creative forces of humanity, the 'way a dehumanized, brutally objective power holds sway over all social . . . alienation is constant and everyday, culminating in estrangement suffusing everyday life' in the fetishistic form – determinate 'mode of existence' of capitalist society (Lefebvre, 1947 [2014:186]). 'Bourgeois life is thus alienated because it is not only fragmented, but artificial' (Trebitsch, 1991 [2014:12]). This theme, he claimed, 'is to be found throughout Marx's entire work': ending alienation will only be possible with the ending of capitalism itself (Lefebvre, 1980:117; Goonewardena, 2011:51). His goal therefore became to 'rediscover authentic Marxism, defined as the critical knowledge of everyday life' (Trebitsch, 1991 [2014:11]).

It has therefore been suggested that 'The Marxism of Lefebvre is hence a 'classically theological discourse' conforming to a 'narrative of grace, alienation, and redemption which structures its account of the loss of significant totality, the fall into repetition, and the promise of a future advent of a life again become meaningful' (Gardiner, 2004:236). The barely veiled implied criticism is that, thanks to the then prevailing intellectual climate, there is in Lefebvre's Marxism humanism a 'patriarchal resonance' (Kelly, 1992:62). If so, it is certainly something to be guarded against, for which purpose one might expect that international, feminist, and other radical perspectives both on Lefebvre's work and on Marxism and space more generally might be useful.

Critics, with whom developers perhaps may have some sympathy, might regard these assertions regarding alienation as both too broad and too optimistic. They can point no doubt to the failures of previous socialist experiments, even those with which Lefebvre himself expressed sympathy such as Yugoslavia (Lefebvre, 1978 [2009:286]). They could also argue that readjusting the economic framework will not solve problems that are fundamentally not of an economic order. 'A cynic might recognise in Lefebvre's conception of alienation simply a concoction of all he disliked' (O'Kane, 2018a:62n). But undeterred by potential criticism of this kind, and alive to the history and contemporary reality of money, commodities, and capital, Lefebvre extended his criticism of capitalism by reference to Marx's concept of commodity fetishism, whereby 'social objects become things, fetishes, which turn upon him' (Lefebvre, 1947 [2014:198]). The idea of commodification is not Lefebvre's: it is at root a very traditional Marxist concept, aiming to capture how, for example, the pursuit of profit has increasingly determined not only what housing is constructed, but how it is used, managed, and distributed, all at the expense of wider social concerns (Harloe, 1982; Achtenberg & Marcuse, 1986; Kholodilin *et al.*, 2022), as 'the risk of investment in the production of urban space is related to the fact that this commodity is immobile but today tradable on global markets as a liquid asset' (Savini & Aalbers, 2016:880).

Even developers alert to intellectual and cultural trends may concede that this narrative, along with Western Marxist concepts such as the experience of commodity culture, fetish relationships, feelings of alienation in urban environments, and the de-professionalisation of the arts have all been absorbed into current discourse, such that 'Marxism has thus become part of a diverse intellectual inheritance that architectural theory has taken as flexibly appropriable and adaptable to the designing of buildings in the age of global capital' (Swope, 2021:3). Where Lefebvre extended the concept was through envisaging the way human individuals and groups interact with one another as a realm of shadows, 'appearances which are something more and else than mere illusions, which Lefebvre calls concrete abstractions' (Stanek, 2011:134), 'abstract' social forms which are nonetheless 'concrete' since they are constituted by social praxis' (O'Kane, 2018:258). Whatever scepticism there has been as to Lefebvre's claim to Marxism, all must admit, however, that Lefebvre himself never abandoned what he regarded as its fundamental tenet, that only through praxis in everyday social life can that alienation be even understood, let alone opposed and superseded, and that 'the imagination and production of concrete alternatives are, as Lefebvre believed, hiding out in the plain sight of the everyday' (Coleman, 2014:4).

From the late 1970s onwards, too, Lefebvre did also move closer again to the PCF, attracted by both its espousal of decentralising policies of local self-government and the more dialectical and humanist approach of its leading theorists, especially the Marxist theory of personality espoused by Sève (Kelly, 1992:63). Throughout his life, whether a Party member or not, Lefebvre never lost sight of the centrality of political concerns, even if he perhaps is less vocal at, rather than before and after, key moments of high political drama. Perhaps we should not be surprised, as an emphasis on the theoretical never appears to have troubled him: 'When Marx takes philosophers to task for interpreting the world without transforming it, he is being rather unfair. In so far as it interprets the world, all philosophy contains a certain attempt at transforming it' (Lefebvre, 1962 [1995:5]).

None of this might necessarily encourage a rejection of Lefebvre's claim, as Marxism itself is no doubt a broad church, but Marxists have traditionally insisted that it is not possible to be 'partly Marxist' – to assign Marxism to a category of human existence but to balance it with other perceptions, reflections, and philosophies, as Lefebvre undoubtedly did. Whilst in the PCF, Sève, for example, denied any possibility that Marxism can be in any sense part of a wider truth – 'Marxism is not a voice, even the bass, in the speculative polyphony of an ecumenical humanism' (Sève, 1968 [1978:126]), such a bold assertion runs aground, not least on the fact that since Marx originally wrote, his ideas have been subject to continuous change and evolution. Very broadly, the contention that there have been 'two Marxisms' was widely circulated long before even the fall of the Berlin Wall. If 'Scientific' Marxism could still be defended whilst the politics of violent revolution could still be held out as a plausible solution to the problems of capitalism, it can now be said that 'Critical' Marxism, where 'concepts exist to interpret social processes; politics is an arena for the realization of ultimate values; [and] ideology is a moral force' (Burawoy, 2020:468–469) is now at leading a prominent Marxist theoretical tradition.

Despite his alignment with this tendency in Marxism, and his insistence on Marxist categories, Lefebvre eventually made the distinction between the word Marxism, which 'no longer means very much' (Lefebvre, 1987 [2003:255]) and 'being a Marxist', which he argued was 'a tool for enlightenment. It uncovers, it brings to light, it destroys, or begins to destroy, what it drags out of the shadows, out of the world of secrets' (Lefebvre, 1987 [2003:255]), beyond 'above all, a method of analysing social practices; it is not a series of assumptions, postulates, or dogmatic propositions' (Lefebvre, 1983 [1987:30]). For Lefebvre, this necessarily involved the use of a specific method, the dialectic, refined over thousands of years since Heraclitus. And not just applying it to concepts such as alienation, surplus value, or exploitation – but an open-mindedness, of course to the eventual supersession of capitalism – but also to innovate, to explore the world and the worldwide, to suggest, in short, to invent (Lefebvre, 1987 [2003:255]). For Lefebvre, being a Marxist in the mid-20th century was always

> at one and the same time a certain way of thinking, a way of living (and behaving) and a way of being. The political position is not fundamental or

> essential – theoretical thinking regains primacy. . . . The relationship with others is now defined in terms of conflicts between realisation of the individual and the group and alienation. . . . 'To be a Marxist' is to live in this society, without letting oneself get caught by its seductions or its traps. It isn't about quoting Marx all the time – it's about life winning over death. No determinism nor ready-made meanings of history.
>
> (Lefebvre, 1987 [2003:255–257])

Yet if one mistake Marxists often make is to fail to recognise that their actions are often as damaging to the progressive cause as their words are encouraging, then another perhaps even more serious one is to dream of the future whilst abstracting themselves to existing reality. The consequence is all too often 'a relative retreat by critical intellectuals from active participation' (Merrifield & Swyngedouw, 1996:5). Such a world view has led those who would criticise Marxism from the Left to find their voice in any appropriation of Lefebvre that is not purely utopian, that does not actively seek the immediate revolutionary replacement of capitalism. They too would claim Lefebvre for their own:

> [M]any people feel and think (even if they do not say it) that Lefebvre's approach sounds 'too utopian'. But then they should at least be honest enough to leave Lefebvre alone, instead of using his words and even his name to decorate a reformist discourse and to legitimate a reformist, status quo-conforming approach to our problems.
>
> (De Souza, 2010:319)

But if I am right about the direction which Marxism has taken, or at least in which it must go, then there is, or would be, much less justification in understanding Lefevre's work as closer to 'anarcho-syndicalism or libertarian socialism than to Marxism' (Purcell, 2014:145). Marxists are no less utopian than any other voices on the Left: the difference lies, as Lefebvre stressed, in the claim to praxis. This leads to the correlate, the need for the continuous development of the relationship between Lefebvre's work and current economic and political conditions.

The importance of everyday life

It does now seem that there are underlying differences of emphasis within what might now justifiably be called 'Lefebvre studies', especially in the Anglosphere. His writings on the urban reached translation, and therefore a wider audience, before many others, but they have opened doors to the colossal body of his work, dwelling on such issues as the State and its critical role in modern capitalism (Lefebvre, 1976a, 1976b, 1977, 1978) and Marxist philosophy more widely (e.g. Lefebvre, 1959, 1975). For several decades now, critics have lamented 'the spatial bias of some recent, particularly Anglophone, interpretations' (Elden, 2004:195), stressing that Lefebvre enjoyed a range of philosophical interests, ranging across metaphysics, rural and urban sociology, critiques of fascism, memoirs, poetry, and literary criticism (Lewis, 2021), and encompassing citizenship, difference, capitalism, and globalisation.

The transformation in Marxism that Lefebvre sought was however not a resolution of the tussle between humanism and structuralism in the former's favour, as others enthusiastically sought (Garaudy, 1966), nor to explain the correct role of the individual within Marxism (Sève, 1968 [1978]), nor any other question close to the hearts of his Marxist contemporaries that he regarded as of secondary importance. Rather, it was, he said, to examine Marx's thought under three headings: 'globality or totality, critical capacity, and the power of the imagination and of images of the future (utopia)' (Lefebvre, 1980:74) – all of which bore both on everyday life and on the study of places and the creation of space, without which a proper analysis of Marxism was in Lefebvre's view simply impossible (Lefebvre, 1968 [1980:194]). 'In order to change life, we must change society, space, architecture, the city' (Lefebvre, 1980 [1987:11]).

Lefebvre himself regarded a radical, in his view Marxist, theory of 'everyday life' (Lefebvre, 1947:10) as his most important contribution (Trebitsch, 1991 [2014:23), as he found Marxism rather deficient in respect of sociology (Lefebvre, 1947, 1961, 1981 [2014]). Yet 'everyday life is the supreme court where wisdom, knowledge and power are brought to judgement' (Lefebvre, 1947 [2014:28]. Everyday life, in a sense residual, defined by 'what is left over' after all distinct, superior, specialised, structured activities have been singled out for analysis, must be defined as a totality. Considered in their specialisation and their technicality, superior activities leave a 'technical vacuum' between one another which is filled by everyday life. Everyday life is profoundly related to all activities, encompassing them with all their differences and their conflicts; it is their meeting place, their bond, their common ground. And it is in everyday life that the sum total of relations which make the human – and every human being – a whole takes its shape and its form. In it are expressed and fulfilled those relations which bring into play the totality of the real, albeit in a certain manner which is always partial and incomplete: friendship, comradeship, love, the need to communicate, play, etc. (Lefebvre, 1947 [2014:119). Indeed, the 'sphere of everyday life' and the reproductive work carried on therein have always been equally crucial and logical starting points of political practice for many, for example socialist feminists (Rose, 1983:68).

> Empowerment and creative liberation, therefore, necessitate grappling with everyday life and the rituals inscribed in urban life. . . . Daily life is the screen on which our society projects its light and its shadow, its hollows and its planes, its power and its weakness; political and social activities converge to consolidate, structure and functionalize it.
>
> (Lefebvre, 1968 [2017:64–65])

Real estate developers will be inclined to agree on the importance of the topic; for them, too, everyday life is the starting point for the realisation of the possible.

As Marxists, Lefebvre says, we must not exclude themselves from tradition, from everyday life. His attempt at a dialectic begins with a distinction between a triumphalist modernism, with its characterisation as certainty and arrogance, and the critique of questioning and critical reflection that characterises modernity (Lefebvre, 1962 [1995:2]). His hopes and perceptions did fade and erode – decades later he was of the view that the last illusions of modernity had faded away together with the misplaced hopes it had brought (Lefebvre, 1981 [2014:719]). Maybe so, but everyday life remains as important as it has always been, and Marxists owe a debt to Lefebvre for forcibly intruding that importance into their understanding of the world.

These arguments have however not gone without scrutiny. It has been suggested that if everyday life is also where to find Lefebvre's expansive notion of alienation and his romantic theory of domination reside, then it is possible to visualise Lefebvre's determination to use an account of fetishistic concrete abstractions derived from Marx as setting up 'an eclectic opposition between the quantitative forms that seek to dominate everyday life and the ways in which the qualitative human contents that are present in capitalist society resist determination' (O'Kane, 2018:9). Eclectic and perhaps doubtful, for standing behind this optimistic theorising, is the concept that capitalism is holding back the wide-ranging capacities of the 'total man', a tenet held widely and in different ways by Marxists from early Soviet psychologist onwards, albeit that 'The total man is but a figure on a distant horizon beyond our present vision. He is a limit, an idea, and not a historical fact' (Lefebvre, 1947 [2014:88]). The tantalising concept leads Lefebvre to a certain theoretical haziness; however, failing, it has been suggested,

> to differentiate between phenomena that enunciate a broad notion of alienation and romantic domination in terms of transhistorical notions of opposition between 'everyday life and festival, mass moments and exceptional moments, triviality and splendour, seriousness and play, reality and dreams, etc.', and those that provide qualitative opposition to the historically specific abstraction and reproduction of human labour in everyday life.
>
> (O'Kane, 2018:261)

In short, the principal criticism is that whilst his analysis may have been acute, Lefebvre's solution, if indeed he imagined it as such, does not seem to have anything like the capacity to solve the problem as he portrays it, and so it has proved in the decades since he wrote.

There are those too who argue but agree with Lefebvre's biographer Rémi Hess that it is the theory of moments derived from the radical Situationists which is Lefebvre's 'key progressive motif, signifying that all is not lost, that all can never be lost, not quite' (Merrifield, 2009:939). The moment is nothing other than 'the attempt to achieve the total realization of a possibility' (Lefebvre, 1961 [2014:329]). 'Those poetic moments can be seen as instances that (re)construct, and give meaning to, our life melodies' (Awad, 2021:90). What can be said about a such a 'moment'?

> It is a conjunction of temporalities, a function of the individual's history and a form that is superior to and elevates itself over repetition and reappearance. Among the 'moments' that arise from everyday life are love, games, rest,

> knowledge, poetry and justice, activities that in a temporality of rupture and spontaneity tend towards a unification of the festival and everyday life. For Lefebvre, the moment was also characterized by its orientation towards the realization of a possibility; the possibility is given, stands there to be both uncovered and achieved.
>
> (Simonsen, 2005:8)

Autogestion: a way around capitalism

As a professed Marxist, Lefebvre could hardly ignore economics altogether, including the future organisation of production. While Marx framed the withering democratic state as 'created through the act of revolution' replacing the bourgeois state (Lefebvre, 1973 [1976:85]), Lefebvre (1966 [2009:305]), writing a text on revolutions in the mid-1980s leaves the question 'where and how to realize' direct democracy unanswered: 'Is it "self-instituted"? Does it emerge from a Constitution? Or from practice, from a way of living?' Given his distaste for the capitalist state, it is little surprise to find that autogestion – self-management – forms 'a decisive, but not exclusive, aspect of Lefebvre's global project' (Lefebvre, 1973 [1976:40]). What did Lefebvre have in mind? Brenner suggests that Lefebvre did not have in mind a particular economic model, whether Yugoslav, French, or any other.

> Self-management must also face and solve the problems of the organization of the market. It does not enter into its principle or its practice to deny the law of value. We will not pretend in its name to 'transcend' the market, the profitability of companies, the laws of exchange value. Only centralising statism has had this excessive ambition.[1]
>
> (Lefebvre, 1966:67)

Rather, it is at root a political orientation through which various sectors of social life, individual organisations such as factories, farms, or universities, up to cities and regions, can be decentralised, democratised, and ultimately controlled by those most immediately associated with them (and also, in a globalised world, by those most significantly affected by them). In his conceptualisation of it, at least, autogestion entails those involved in production managing collective decisions themselves rather than surrendering those decisions to a cadre of state officials (Lefebvre, 1970 [2003:187–188]).

> Only through autogestion can the members of a free association take control over their own life, in such a way that it becomes their work [oeuvre]. This is also called appropriation, de-alienation.
>
> (Lefebvre, 1966 [2009:150])[2]

A recent review of the subject suggested:

> *Autogestion* refers in law to any social space, work or activity, which is governed directly by its actors or its producers, who establish and institute

> collectively and directly the rules, norms and institutions, refusing any hierarchy vertical, any division between rulers and ruled, employers and employees, educators and educated.
>
> (Schaepelynck & Sustam, 2018:27)[3]

Lefebvre insists that autogestion 'is not a magic formula, a system, a model, or a panacea; it is not a purely technical or rational operation; it will not solve all the workers' problems' (Brenner, 2008:240). On the contrary, 'the right to self-management has coded within it an unequivocal vision for revolutionary social change' (Purcell, 2014:148), and is a struggle in itself, 'in constant danger of degenerating, of being assimilated into considerable less radical projects of co-gestion' (it encounters countless obstacles and threats; and it is in constant danger of degenerating or being assimilated into considerably less radical projects of 'co-management' (Brenner, 2008:240). Despite these risks, Lefebvre recommends a political strategy in which *autogestion* (distinct from co-management which suggests a consistently strong state) is 'the essential element' (though 'only one element') (Lefebvre, 1966 [2009:150]) in obtaining the keys to the city (Lefebvre, 2003:150). 'The control of space has become strict'[4] (Lefebvre, 1975:229). But without it, and without 'a qualitative horizon of transforming life "in its smallest, most everyday detail" (through self-management), revolution would risk repeating the quantitative state-socialist project' (Kipfer, 2002:133), that is, 'intensifying production, cultivating new space, industrializing agriculture, building giant factories' (Lefebvre, 1974 [1991:151]).

It is therefore understandable that as his confidence in state socialism descended into outright rejection, *autogestion* assumed a progressively greater importance in his thought over time: 'Towards the end of his life Lefebvre also included the possibility of a right to autogestion as a citizenship right' (Elden, 2004:227; Purcell, 2014:148). 'Lefebvre saw his new contract of citizenship not as an end goal, but as a political awakening, a catalyst for a movement toward autogestion' (Purcell, 2014:152). Lefebvre even claims that 'associative life or grassroots democracy (*autogestion*) – must be reinstated as key priorities; they assume new meanings when applied to the urban' (Lefebvre, 1989 [2014:205]), that the city itself can be transformed into an *oeuvre* through *autogestion* (Yamamoto, 2018:109).

Lefebvre reminds us however that

> [w]e must never forget that society constitutes a whole and does not consist of a sum of elementary units. Even radicalised, an autogestion that only organized itself into partial unities, without achieving globality (*le global*), would be destined to failure [yet]. . . . Only through *autogestion* can the members of a free association take control over their own life, in such a way that it becomes their work (*oeuvre*).
>
> (Lefebvre, 1966 [2009:150])[5]

By way of explanation for this final term, the concept of *oeuvre* is a recurring theme in Lefebvre's work, and it refers to a truly free individual life, to the freedom and possibilities entailed in 'producing one's life as one creates a work' (Trebitsch,

1991 [2014:16]), and to urban life in all its aspects – communal life, public spaces and buildings, freedoms of association and access, and a vast range of other positive aspects – all of which can be distinguished by their escape from the domination of capital, of private wealth, and of its results in the landscape, and life of the urban. Critics, notably the radical Situationists such as Guy Debord, who shunned engagement with conventional politics, let alone developers, argued that Lefebvre 'was still a prisoner of the old aesthetic categories of the *oeuvre* and the genre'[6] (Marcolini, 2007:22), but the differences between them ran deeper still: Lefebvre was no anarchist, no syndicalist, and never unaware of the need for politics to play a central role in the collective *oeuvre* of the urban.

A question of levels

The problem of actualising autogestion at anything other than a global scale encapsulates the wider problem of levels or scales, a problem with which real estate developers will themselves be very familiar at the operational level. Lefebvre employs two key terms – *niveau* (level) and *échelle* (scale), the former in reference to different aspects of capitalist social reality, and the latter referring to scale in more familiar sense of land, territory, and borders:

> On the one hand, Lefebvre refers to three key 'levels' or niveaux of social reality: the global (global) level; the 'mixed' or the urban level; and the 'private' or everyday level. On the other hand, Lefebvre refers as well to multiple 'scales' or échelles: the body, the local, the urban, the regional, the national, the supranational, the worldwide (mondial) and the planetary.
>
> (Brenner, 2000:368)

So 'Lefebvre would distinguish between the global, as a level of generality, and the *mondial*, as world-scale' (Schrader, 2018:3), 'the process of becoming worldwide, the seizing and grasping of the world as a whole, comprehending it as a totality, as an event in thought' (Elden, 2008:80). Similarly, Lefebvre writes of levels of society: 'The forces of production and their component elements (nature, labour, technology, knowledge); structures (property relations); superstructures (institutions and the state itself' (Lefebvre, 1974 [1991:85]). Social space underpins the reproduction of production relations and property relations; the terms intermesh, as for Lefebvre, these are not so much scalar levels in ontological hierarchies, but rather epistemological tools with different granularity to jointly understand forces construing modern society, so that each level can be traced, for example, at the scale of the city (Golubchikov, 2016:611).

L'espace (space) and real estate

The precis of his ample views above raises the question: If Lefebvre were such a rounded scholar, with so many interests, why is it that Lefebvre's work on the urban been 'perhaps the area in which the Lefebvrian heritage has had the most influence'? (Sangla, 2010:11). The answer perhaps is straightforward – probably because it was the most radical and innovative aspect of his work: to provide a spatial balance to the traditional chronological Marxist focus, to extend Marxism into geography and the built environment whilst maintaining its – by the time he wrote, increasingly tenuous – grip on history. For Marxist urban theory, it is suggested, has been divided, on the one hand, between the study of colonial and Third World urbanism, and later the New International Division of Labour, migration, and global cities, and on the other hand, between the historical development, everyday dimensions, and politico-economic dynamics of urbanisation in 'advanced' capitalist contexts. Hence the criticism that, although radical geography more widely and the spatial turn for Marxism in particular incorporated both the metropolitan New Left and a more global anti-imperialism, successive Marxist urban theories, notably Berman (1982), Katznelson (1993), and Merrifield (2002), remained 'metropolitan' in both pejorative senses of the word: pro-big city and at home in the imperial core of world order (Kipfer & Goonewardena, 2013:5). It is a hard-hitting critique; does Lefebvre escape it?

At least partially, I suggest, he does. For many decades now, it has been recognised that Lefebvre (alongside many others) was right about the onward march of urbanisation – generated in part by global free markets for agriculture as well as manufacturing and even services – in terms of living in cities and the exodus from the countryside, even in a literal sense, with entire countries turned into urban societies (Davis, 2011; Guo *et al.*, 2022; Heinrigs, 2020). This transformation, when combined with the absence of commensurate industrialisation, has led to the observation that 'Empirically, Lefebvre is being vindicated by developments in places such as Eastern and Central Africa where urbanization and urban property development have gathered pace in the virtual absence of industrial development, and are themselves shaping economies and societies' (Goodfellow, 2017:787). Rethinking the urban as a global process has probably proved as hard for Marxists as for anyone, the origins of Marxism being buried deep in the Western tradition. Similar difficulties have persistently confronted Marxism, for example the challenge posed by the liberation theology of Latin America to the Marxist-Christian dialogue in the mid-20th century.

Urban geographers have undoubtedly recognised the immense changes that Lefebvre saw emerging, those amongst them of a Marxist inclination also now widely recognising that the changes themselves are at least integral to the fabric of global capitalism, if not actually at its root: the emergence of urban mega-regions (Soja & Kanai, 2013), the development of urbanisation on an even greater and more daunting scale, with all its attendant scars on both landscape and people, the blurring and rearticulation of urban territories through manifold processes of decentralisation and recentralisation, the disintegration of the 'hinterland', the urbanisation of the 'global rural', and the end of the 'wilderness' (Brenner & Schmid, 2011; Ghosh & Meer, 2021). What often lies beneath the surface of these theories is a commitment by Marxist (and other radical) geographers against 'neoliberal discourses in the making of real estate-based 'global city' urban development strategies' (Moulaert & Jessop, 2013:39), their dominance felt even by those nominally in control of urban development (Zanotto, 2020:123). By neoliberal, developers might wish to note, radical critics seem generally to mean a familiar clutch of policies that affect them, (1) a shift towards more entrepreneurial forms of urban governance, focused around strategies to attract capital investment, promote growth, and leverage the private sector in the form of public–private partnerships; (2) a move to reduce the role of the local state in the provision of services and amenities, in favour of purportedly more efficient privatised and market-based alternatives; and (3) the articulation of new forms of urban citizenship, emphasising notions of individual choice, family self-reliance, and personal responsibility (Jones & Popke, 2010:116). But what are these discourses? Can they be dissected in such a way that it is possible to work through a political strategy? There is a history of space, yes, between anthropology and political economy (Lefebvre, 1974 [1991:116]), not yet written, but at least for the time being, contained within the history of capitalism.

For capitalist, real estate is what underpins, drives, creates, exists, and creates Marxist exchange value within Lefebvre's '*espace*' – it combines physical, social, legal, and economic aspects into a single concept, which as we have noted above, Anglo-Saxons often refer to as *property*. It is necessary, now, not only to study it, but to make judgements and design strategies of engagement. Lefebvre described his own work as a project, whilst Marxist and radical geographers such as David Harvey and Edward Soja have been even more explicit in attempting to make a direct connection between their theoretical work and 'practical solutions to the problems of race, class, gender, and other, often closely associated, forms of human inequality and oppression' (Soja, 1996:22). But an answer to the question, 'whether or not Lefebvre's formulation, even those such as Soja, who departed from his Marxism, actually enables this political project to be achieved' (Unwin, 2000:15), depends not only on the contemporary appropriateness of the theory to the urban environment in general, but on which organisations are to be analysed, approached, and ultimately influenced.

One of Lefebvre's most fervent and radical geographical exponents held high hopes for the political consequences of this analysis. For Lefebvre, he argued, 'space holds the promise of liberation: liberation from the tyranny of time apart from anything else, but also from social repression and exploitation, from self-imprisoning categories' (Smith, 2003:xiii). He pointed to Lefebvre's earlier works, where he claimed:

> This urban life tends to turn against themselves the messages, orders and constraints coming from above. It attempts to appropriate time and space by foiling dominations, by diverting them from their goal, by deceit. It also intervenes more or less at the level of the city and the way of inhabiting. In this way the urban is more or less the *oeuvre* of its citizens instead of imposing itself upon them as a system, as an already closed book.
>
> (Lefebvre, 1968 [1996:117])

This dramatic shift in political thinking to encompass a spatialised view of the world (Smith, 2003:xiii), and even to the rise of human geography within the academy, owes much to Lefebvre, his early work on the urban, at least, suggesting that 'the possibilities of revolutionary social change that comes from the streets' (Smith, 2003:xiv). These are the pathways already laid that the current work must follow, in order for developers to come to a view about Lefebvre.

Lefebvre set in stone?

Yet it is not yet possible to proceed directly along these pathways, as there appears to be a contradiction. On the one hand, 'Lefebvre always saw his own intellectual project as a series of heuristic "approximations", never as permanent dogma to be defended against all non-believers' (Soja, 1996:9). On the other hand, it has been said before of Lefebvre that 'His work seems somewhat frozen in time' (Kingma *et al.*, 2018:6). The chorus of those who in response argue that, not so, 'Translating – modifying, even transforming – Lefebvre's work is inevitable and desirable but requires care and reflexivity' (Kipfer *et al.*, 2013:116) is loud. They suggest that taking Lefebvre's work forward requires a reappraisal of what he actually wrote and an analysis of what his work can be used for today (Elden, 2004:199). It is certainly true that 'to read Lefebvre today requires accounting for the historical continuities and ruptures between the processes of urbanization as he analyzed them and the current conditions of production of space' (Stanek, 2011:xi) But what might these be? Stanek suggests that one must come to terms with the increasing co-option of his concepts into the discourses of dominant agents of the production of space, as well as the crisis of Marxism after the end of state socialism in Central and Eastern Europe (Stanek, 2011:xi). Surely yes, and this entails not only recognising how Lefebvre wanted to go beyond the disciplinary transformation of architecture, urbanism, or sociology at the time he wrote. It may also require actually engaging with the changes in the production of space that have happened since then, using those changes not necessarily in order to reappraise Lefebvre's values, or even the concepts he employed, but what we now should do if we believe in both.

Lefebvre's interest in the city, in the urban, and his thinking around time and history (Smith, 2003:xiii) lead to this question: If Marxism itself has evolved, given the conditions under which capitalism has developed since he wrote, if the struggle to overcome it has changed, and if the history of Marxist geography to date has largely been one of analysis rather than, as he had hoped, the success of his emancipatory project, then it is surely implausible to imagine that Lefebvre's work, any more that of Marx himself, should remain in a cocoon, and certainly not enjoy any right to remain outside the challenge of theoretical change because of its own emphasis on space rather than time. In that case, we are more than ever entitled to ask 'to what extent have these engagements with Lefebvre succeeded in excavating intellectual and political impulses within his writings that resonate productively with contemporary questions, concerns and projects' (Brenner & Elden, 2001:764).

In sharp contrast, Marx's ideas were swift to emerge, adopted and transformed by active politicians who not only sought power, but obtained and then lost it, both in a spectacular fashion, and were subject throughout to repeated attempts to reform and modify them, starting with Marx himself. Yet as Chapter 2 will seek to show, Lefebvre has been treated very differently. It has almost been as if Marx had only ever remained in the shadows, criticised by the likes of Louis Althusser and perhaps during sporadic occasional acts of resistance by Bolsheviks such as Leon Trotsky, but never facing the kind of sustained, reformist trajectory that Marxism as a whole has enjoyed – or to which it has been subjected, depending on political standpoint.

There may be several reasons for this. Firstly, as Lefebvre himself believed, urban studies, though an enormous and still growing field of research in their own right, remain more siloed than politics as a whole, and it has been possible for geographers and urban theorists to engage with Lefebvre's on theoretical ground that has not encompassed all of the Marxist hinterland. By extension, his work emerged at a time when the Left was soon struggling with a resurgent capitalism, even in France, which meant that gradually Marxist theories of the State were eclipsed, even in the academy. Secondly, issues of translation have certainly also played a part in the Anglo-Saxon world. But perhaps the most important reason is that however much he criticised his fellow Marxists for their lack of spatial awareness, Lefebvre situated himself in the very Western Marxist tradition that turned on 'Scientific' Marxism, and was thereby able to travel with its critics, even – or perhaps especially – after he left the PCF. 'Lefebvre and Guterman are, therefore, central to the introduction of a new type of Marxism into France, a Marxism that had as its central text the 1844 Economic and Philosophical Manuscripts' (Elden, 2006:189), although for them both,

> [i]f the political break was obviously fundamental in allowing Lefebvre to develop his thinking in total freedom, there was no real theoretical discontinuity in his desire to construct a living Marxism, freed from dogmatism and committed to the analysis of contemporary phenomena.
>
> (Trebitsch, 2002 [2014:286–287])

This enabled him nimbly to evade the kind of challenge that Sartre posed, which he had originally himself critiqued, and that more widely Marxism faced when the Berlin Wall fell, whilst also eventually providing grounds for his rejection of the Marxist structuralism of Louis Althusser and his colleagues (Lefebvre, 1959, 1971), which he disparaged as 'nothing more than the infusion of technocratic thought into the intellectual field' (Ross, 1995:176). Perhaps even more significantly, if Lefebvre has indeed been 'born posthumously' (Elden, 2006:185), then the transhistoricity engendered as a result has surely helped his work enjoy as much vitality as Lefebvre did himself in life, largely shaking off its historical (and paradoxically, specific geographical) legacy. To this has always been the difficulty of confirming Lefebvre as fully, or solely, a Marxist; he himself was apt to place Marx in a collection of other thinkers, a point elaborated in Chapter 2. As a result, in short, Lefebvre has never faced his own Bernstein, whether to triumph in such an encounter or not.

Yet, as the editors of his key writings readily conceded, it would be hard to imagine a book entitled *The New Lefebvre*. They explained that it is because he is largely known in a very narrow way, at least in the Anglosphere: the predominant focus was on the slogan of 'the right to the city', and to a lesser extent, on everyday life, concepts that eclipsed in turn his wider concerns with the role of the State, which have fallen back into the shadows (Elden *et al.*, 2003:xi). Over succeeding decades, Lefebvre has become increasingly well known since then, at least in the academy (Revol, 2012), thanks to further translations of his work and because 'Urban theorists have done much to situate Lefebvre and build upon him, and to make him continuously relevant to contemporary debates' (Kipfer *et al.*, 2008, 2013; Merrifield, 2013; Mitchell, 2003; Purcell, 2002, 2013; Soja, 1989, 1996; Stanek, 2011)' (Pierce, 2017:3). Whilst this is certainly true, there remains I suggest a continued benefit from placing those debates, and Lefebvre's continuing contribution to them, before those actively engaged in the real estate planning, development, and investment process. My central argument is that in so doing, it may be possible to move at least some way towards bridging two very different social and economic worlds that may have much to benefit from mutual engagement.

Organisation of the book

This chapter serves as an introduction to the problem and explains its organisation. In Chapter 2, I provide my own summary of the theoretical contribution made by Lefebvre overall, but with a particular perspective on how his work may be relevant to real estate development in particular. Then, given that, as has been suggested, and as Lefebvre would certainly agree, 'Urban planning presents one of the great realms of the generalised discourse on space, closely linked to that of architecture' (Shields, 2013:91). In Chapter 3, I therefore take a view of the relationship between Lefebvre's work as a whole and the discipline of urban planning. This is paralleled by Chapter 4, which builds on the pathbreaking work of Coleman (2013, 2014) to interrogate Lefebvre's views on architecture in the context of the application of his views to the contemporary role and work of architects. In Chapters 5 and 6 which place real estate developers and Lefebvre alongside one another in the production of space within capitalism, I set out a provisional relationship between a Marxism informed by Lefebvre's insights and the contemporary reality of real estate development.

The remainder of the book is largely empirical, or applied, in nature. Chapters 7–9 are dedicated to the main areas of global real estate: residential development, commercial development, and public real estate. These chapters are all punctuated by a tentative series of case studies. They are intended only to be brief and illustrative of potential positive aspects of development. Inevitably, they are snapshots in time and therefore hostages to fortune – some may fail or be revealed as less positive than they currently appear. Pure philosophy might not need such risky examples, but such an approach did not seem likely to persuade developers, so the case studies remain despite the risks. Finally, I review the opportunities and limits to this endeavour, and draw conclusions as to how successful such an attempt to evaluate how useful Lefebvre – a Marxist theoretician of a previous century – could be to a real estate developer today.

Conclusion

If Marxism, whether Lefebvre's or any other, is to continue to have relevance, it must also have applicability – not some day in the remote future, as futurology, or even as part of the current collective conscience of humanity, but as a guide to action now and in the future, then the main purpose of analysis must be to 'translate Lefebvre's ideas into potentialities for action (which I believe he would have approved of)' (Coleman, 2014:4). It would be immensely surprising if Marxists of any stripe wanted to make themselves less relevant to contemporary society, or for their Marxism to be less applicable. But how?

> What is urban space? What is a town? How are they composed at different levels – blocks of flats, buildings, monuments – in a word, the architectural and at another level, the urbanistic? We are beginning to think that these questions, which are seemingly empirical and a matter for positive knowledge, have a secret affinity with various philosophical questions. 'What is man'? What is his relation to being? What is the relation between being and space?
>
> (Lefebvre, 1981 [2014:803])

Lefebvre's intention was not only to use spatial analysis to offer a criticism of capitalism. Spatial analysis was only ever one aspect of the analysis of the reproduction of the land–labour–capital relation, 'the constitutive trinity of capitalist society' (Lefebvre, 1973 [1976:8]). His self-effacing belief was that without spatial analysis, Marxism is theoretically incorrect at its core, and that in his own work, all Marxist concepts are taken to a higher level without any one stage in theory disappearing. 'The renewal of Marx's concepts is best effected by raking full account of space' (Lefebvre, 1974 [1991:352]). By appreciating space, by taking account of it explicitly, we pass beyond Marxian political economy without abandoning the critical approach to capitalism that Marx introduced (Gottdiener, 1993:132). Politically, taking account of space and history is also necessary to achieve the replacement of capitalism that Marxists seek.

The applied chapters of this book concern real estate developers, organisations in which agreements and conflicts over representations of space may not only no doubt be found, but where in a capitalist society that has devolved so much agency to them, they may be expected to be both significant and potentially very visible. This book therefore sets out to do two things: one theoretical, the other empirical, or at least an attempt to apply theory to practice. Theoretically, the objective is to use the example of real estate developers to contribute to an understanding as to which of Lefebvre's theoretical innovations and concepts of the urban can be adopted without change, and which may require revision in the light of the subsequent decades of economic, political, and urban development. Practically, it is to apply such a revision of Lefebvre's analytical framework to real estate developers, undoubtedly one of the most important global forms of economic organisation in relation to real estate. We may easily grant to Lefebvre immense importance in bringing the spatial to the forefront within Marxism, and more widely in the social sciences, and also to raising the significance of the everyday, and of understanding the concept of modernity and its supersession by an even less revolutionary environment (Lefebvre, 1981 [2014]). But whether his work really does offer 'the possibility for a reconfigured approach to the planning, design and structure of the architecture and landscape of the city and the urban' (Zieleniec, 2018:5) based on a distinction between a functionalist and an experiential approach is both a very different and a very circumscribed question, unless the agency behind urban transformation is to include both the public and private sectors and everywhere in between, real estate developers in particular. Mike Davis is surely right to write of 'a planet of slums', with all the deprivation and frankly, horror, that they entail (Davis, 2006). But the replacement of those slums – and in some cases, it is undeniable that there have been improvements – will in practice not be as a result exclusively of policy, planning, and performance by the public sector. Developers will be involved as well. For that reason alone, if no other, developers matter.

There are I suggest two principal concerns in such an endeavour

The first is that Lefebvre scholars have constantly, correctly, pointed out that his work encompassed so much more than his work on space and the urban and lamented that too much emphasis has been given to this area of his work by comparison to others such as his focus on the everyday, on the role of the state, or on politics. I have sought not to ignore those other areas, especially as all of Lefebvre's work is intertwined, but there may still be a claim of imbalance. I can only defend against this charge by asserting that Lefebvre's work on space and the urban is not only his most brilliant and most well-known contribution to Marxist theory – *The Production of Space* is 'his most daring and far-reaching manuscript' (Pierce, 2017:2) and 'he has come to be known for his theories of space and everyday life' (Ritzer & Stepnisky, 2011:6), as well as by reiterating the purpose of this book and the intended audience. It may be that not all of Lefebvre's world view is acceptable to all Marxists – notably his enthusiasm for certain German philosophers, but even his antagonism towards structural Marxism. For all that interpreters of Lefebvre urge us in this direction, however, it does seem possible, perhaps even desirable, that Lefebvre need not be accepted in his entirety. It is possible to examine his work on the urban independently of an in-depth study of Marxism as a whole. *Most importantly, I contend that Marxists – and others sympathetic to the cause of the eventual supersession of capitalism – should take Lefebvre's project seriously as a basis for engagement with real estate developers.*

The second very different concern is that real estate developers may find Lefebvre's language obtuse, and his concepts, even perhaps as they have already been expounded in this chapter, both unduly abstract and overly complicated. More critically still, especially when they appreciate his life story, they may regard his ideas entirely of their time and place: happier times for Marxists to which they may understandably hark back, but not relevant now, or for them. For those who have imbibed capitalism since birth and who have known not only no practical alternative, not even a glimpse, nor even a theory of one – and there are now many, including those working in real estate development – Lefebvre may at first blush seem antiquated, obscure, and irrelevant to their task in hand. At most, they might grudgingly concede some interest from outside the academy in his work by architects, or policymakers, perhaps, but their first reaction may well be a polite but firm assertion that it is not for them. It is my task to persuade them otherwise: all

I can ask of them at this point is to persevere with this text, especially through the theoretical chapter that follows this, to remain open-minded, and to reserve their judgement in the meantime as to whether they should agree that they should take Lefebvre's project seriously.

Notes

1 L'autogestion doit aussi affronter et résoudre les problèmes de l'organisation du marché. Il n'entre pas dans son principe ni dans sa practique de nier la loi de la valeur. On ne prétendra pas en son nom « transcender » le marché, la rentabilité des enterprises, les lois de la valeur d'échange. Seul l'étatisme centralisateur a eu cette ambition démesurée.
2 L'autogestion est une voie, une pratique, elle ne peut pas cesser, elle est quelque chose de perpétuelle, de perpétuellement en mouvement, de perpétuellement renouvelée. Ce n'est ni une recette ni une magie ni un mot d'ordre simple à appliquer, c'est une voie à frayer, quelque chose qui se trouve devant nous et qui doit être développée,c'est un terrain de luttes.
3 l'autogestion renvoie en droit à tout espace social, de travail ou d'activité, qui est gouverné directement par ses acteurs ou ses producteurs, qui en établissent et en instituent collectivement et directement les règles, les normes et les institutions, refusant toute hiérarchie verticale, toute division entre gouvernants et gouvernés, patrons et salariés, éducateurs et éduqués.
4 Le contrôle de l'espace est devenu strict.
5 Il ne faut jamais oublier que la société constitue un tout et ne consiste pas en une somme d'unités elémentaires. Une autogestion. même radicalisée, qui ne s'instaurerait que dans des unités partielles sans atteindre le global, se vouerait à l'échec . . . Par elle seulement les membres d'une libre association peuvent prendre en main leur propre vie, de sorte qu'elle devienne leur oeuvre. Ce qui se nomme aussi: appropriation.
6 reste prisonnier des anciennes catégories esthétiques d'*oeuvre* et de *genre*.

Bibliography

Achtenberg, E. P. and Marcuse, P. (1986). Toward the decommodification of housing. In Bratt, R. G., Hartman, C. W. and Meyerson, A. (eds.) *Critical Perspectives on Housing*. Philadelphia, Temple University Press, pp. 474–483.

Allen, J. and Pryke, M. (1994). The production of service space. *Environment and Planning D: Society and Space*, 12(4), 453–475.

Al-Nakib, F. (2014). Public space and public protest in Kuwait, 1938–2012. *City*, 18(6), 723–734.

Awad, S. H. (2021). Experiencing change: Rhythms of everyday life between continuities and disruptions. *Qualitative Studies*, 6(2), 85–107.

Bardet, F., Coulondre, A. and Shimbo, L. (2020). Financial natives: Real estate developers at work. *Competition & Change*, 24(3–4), 203–224.

Barnett, R. (2010). *Being a University*. London, Routledge.

Berg, C. (2022). *Public Planning, Neoliberal Hybridity and Local Activism in Sundbyberg: Epochal Reconfiguration of Urban Development in Greater Stockholm*. PhD thesis, Uppsala University.

Berman, M. (1982). *All That Is Solid Melts Into Air*. New York, Simon & Schuster.

Boano, C. (2015). *The Patchy Patches Practice: Stock of the Possibles in the Patchwork City*. dpusummerLab 2014. London, UCL Development Planning Unit, 26–27.

Borden, I. (1998). *Body Architecture: Skateboarding and the Creation of Super Architectural Space*. London, Routledge.

Brealey, R. A., Myers, S. C., Allen, F. and Edmans, A. (2022). *Principles of Corporate Finance*. 14th edition. New York, McGraw Hill/Iwin.

Brenner, N. (2000). The urban question: Reflections on Henri Lefebvre, urban theory and the politics of scale. *International Journal of Urban and Regional Research*, 24(2), 361–378.
———. (2008). Henri Lefebvre's critique of state productivism. In Goonewardena, K. *et al.* (eds.) *Space, Difference, Everyday Life. Reading Henri Lefebvre*. New York and Abingdon, Routledge, 245–263.
Brenner, N. and Elden, S. (2001). Henri Lefebvre in contexts: An introduction. *Antipode*, 33(5), 763–768.
Brenner, N. and Schmid, C. (2011). Planetary urbanization. In Gandy, M. (ed.) *Urban Constellations*. Berlin, Jovis, 10–13.
Brill, F. (2020). Complexity and coordination in London's Silvertown Quays: How real estate developers (re)centred themselves in the planning process. *Environment and planning A: Economy and Space*, 52(2), 362–382.
Burawoy, M. (2020). A tale of two Marxisms: Remembering Erik Olin wright (1947–2019). *Politics & Society*, 48(4), 467–494.
Carp, J. (2008). "Ground-truthing" representations of social space: Using Lefebvre's conceptual triad. *Journal of Planning Education and Research*, 28(2), 129–142.
Carpio, G., Irazábal, C. and Pulido, L. (2011). Right to the suburb? Rethinking Lefebvre and immigrant activism. *Journal of Urban Affairs*, 33(2), 185–208.
Cartier, C. L. (1997). The dead, place/space, and social activism: Constructing the nationscape in historic Melaka. *Environment and Planning D: Society and Space*, 15(3), 555–586.
Coleman, N. (2013). Utopian prospect of Henri Lefebvre. *Space and Culture*, 16(3), 349–363.
———. (2014). *Lefebvre for Architects*. New York and London, Routledge.
Davidson, A. (1992). Henri Lefebvre. *Thesis Eleven*, 33(1), 152–155.
Davis, M. (2006). *Planet of Slums*. London, Verso.
———. (2011). The prevalence of slums. In Fainstein, S. (ed.) *Readings in Urban Theory*. New York: John Wiley, 440–459.
Demsas, J. (2022). Community input is bad, actually. *The Atlantic*, 29 April. Available at: www.theatlantic.com/ideas/archive/2022/04/local-government-community-input-housing-public-transportation/629625/. [Accessed 4 January 2023].
De Souza, M. L. (2010). Which right to which city? In defence of political-strategic clarity. *Interface*, 2(1), 315–333.
Dierwechter, Y. (2002). Lefebvre's modernities: Informality, planning and space in Cape Town. In Rydin, Y. and Thornley, A. (eds.) *Planning in a Global Era*. Farnham, Ashgate, 189–210.
Donnelly, B. (2017). The impact of inclusionary zoning on development. [blog]. 23 December. Available at: https://brandondonnelly.com/2017/12/23/the-impact-of-inclusionary-zoning-on-development/. [Accessed 7 November 2021].
Drake, D. (2010). The 'Anti-existentialist offensive': The French communist party against sartre (1944–1948). *Sartre Studies International*, 16(1), 69–94.
Elden, S. (2004). *Understanding Henri Lefebvre*. London and New York, Continuum.
———. (2006). Some are born posthumously: The French afterlife of Henri Lefebvre. *Historical Materialism*, 14(4), 185–202.
———. (2007). There is a politics of space because space is political: Henri Lefebvre and the production of space. *Radical Philosophy Review*, 10(2), 101–116.
———. (2008). Mondialisation before globalization: Lefebvre and Axelos. In Goonewardena, K. *et al.* (eds.) *Space, Difference, Everyday Life. Reading Henri Lefebvre*. New York and Abingdon, Routledge, 94–107.
Fischer, R. and Bauer, C. (2019). Introducing Lefebvre. In Bauer, J. and Fischer, R. (eds.) *Perspectives on Henri Lefebvre: Theory, Practices and (re)Readings*. Berlin: De Gruyter Oldenburg, 1–16.

François, T. and Triclot, M. (2020). Expérimenter la production de l'espace urbain par la médiation de Minecraft: l'expérience Rennes. Craft. In Stiegler, B. (ed.) *Le nouveau génie urbain*. Paris, FYP Editions, 225–239.

Fraser, B. (2010). From Bergson to Lefebvre: Towards a philosophy of the urban. In Fraser, B. *Encounters With Bergson(ism) in Spain. Reconciling Philosophy, Literature, Film and Urban Space*. Chapel Hill NC, University of North Carolina Press, 243–268.

Fuchs, C. (2019). Henri Lefebvre's theory of the production of space and the critical theory of communication. *Communication Theory*, 29(2), 129–150.

Fyfe, N. R. (1996). Contested visions of a modern city: Planning and poetry in postwar Glasgow. *Environment and Planning A: Economy and Space*, 28(3), 387–403.

Garaudy, R. (1966). *Marxisme au XX siècle*. Paris, La Palatine.

Gardiner, M. (2004). Everyday utopianism: Lefebvre and his critics. *Cultural Studies*, 18(2–3), 228–254.

Garrido, M. Z. (2019). *The Patchwork City: Class, Space, and Politics in Metro Manila*. Chicago, University of Chicago Press.

Ghosh, S. and Meer, A. (2021). Extended urbanisation and the agrarian question: Convergences, divergences and openings. *Urban Studies*, 58(6), 1097–1119.

Gilbert, L. and Dikeç, M. (2008). Right to the city: Politics of citizenship. In Goonewardena, K. *et al.* (eds.) *Space, Difference, Everyday Life. Reading Henri Lefebvre*. New York and Abingdon, Routledge, 264–277.

Golubchikov, O. (2016). The urbanization of transition: Ideology and the urban experience. *Eurasian Geography and Economics*, 57(4–5), 607–623.

Goodfellow, T. (2017). Urban fortunes and skeleton cityscapes: Real estate and late urbanization in Kigali and Addis Ababa. *International Journal of Urban and Regional Research*, 41(5), 786–803.

Goonewardena, K. (2011). Henri Lefebvre. In Ritzer, G. and Stepnisky, J. (eds.) *The Wiley-Blackwell Companion to Major Social Theorists, Volume 1*. London, Wiley-Blackwell, 44–64.

Gottdiener, M. (1993). A Marx for our time: Henri Lefebvre and the production of space. *Sociological Theory*, 11(1), 129–134.

Graskamp, J. (1972). A rational approach to feasibility analysis. *The Appraisal Journal*, 40, October, 513–521.

———. (1981). *The Fundamentals of Real Estate Development*. Washington DC, Urban Land Institute.

Gray, N. (2017). Beyond the right to the city: Territorial autogestion and the take over the city movement in 1970s Italy. *Antipode*, 50(2), 319–339.

Guo, J., Yu, Z., Ma, Z., Xu, D. and Cao, S. (2022). What factors have driven urbanization in China? *Environment, Development and Sustainability*, 24(5), 6508–6526.

Hariri, M. (2022). Influence of Saudi Vision 2030 on housing-related macroeconomic variables. *International Journal of Housing Markets and Analysis*, ahead-of-print (ahead-of-print).

Harloe, M. (1982). Towards the decommodification of housing. A comment on council house sales. *Critical Social Policy*, 2, 39–42.

Harvey, D. (1973). *Social Justice and the City*. London, Edward Arnold.

———. (1982). *The Limits to Capital*. Oxford, Blackwell.

———. (1985). *The Urbanization of Capital*. Baltimore, Johns Hopkins University Press.

Heinrigs, P. (2020). Africapolis: Understanding the dynamics of urbanization in Africa. *Field Actions Science Reports*, Special Issue 22, 18–23.

Hess, R. (2011 [1957]). Présentation. In Lefebvre, H. *Vers un Romantisme Révolutionnaire*. Paris, Lignes, 7–23.

Hess, R. and Weigand, G. (2006). Henri Lefebvre et son oeuvre. *Le Journal des Chercleurs*, 1–14. Available at: www.urbain-trop-urbain.fr/wp-content/uploads/2012/02/H.-Lefebvre.pdf. [Accessed 7 May 2021].
Huchzermeyer, M. (2014). Invoking Lefebvre's 'right to the city' in South Africa today: A response to Walsh. *City*, 18(1), 41–49.
Jarchow, S. P. (1991). *The Fundamentals of Real Estate Development, Graaskamp on Real Estate*. Washington, DC, Urban Land Institute.
Jones, K. T. and Popke, J. (2010). Re-envisioning the city: Lefebvre, Hope VI, and the neoliberalization of urban space. *Urban Geography*, 31(1), 114–133.
Kallin, H. (2021). Chasing the rent gap down on Edinburgh's waterfront: State failure, devalorisation, and the enduring promise of potential. *City*, 25(5–6), 614–633.
Katznelson, I. (1993). Towards a respatialized Marxism: Lefebvre, Harvey, and Castells. In Katznelson, I. (ed.) *Marxism and the City*. Oxford, Oxford University Press, 92–140.
Kelly, M. (1992). Henri Lefebvre, 1901–1991. *Radical Philosophy*, 60, 62–63.
Kingma, S. F., Dale, K. and Wasserman, V. (eds.) (2018). *Organisational Space and Beyond: The Significance of Henri Lefebvre for Organisation Studies*. London, Routledge.
Kipfer, S. (2002). Urbanization, everyday life and the survival of capitalism: Lefebvre, gramsci and the problematic of hegemony. *Capitalism, Nature, Socialism,* 13(2), 117–149.
Kipfer, S. and Goonewardena, K. (2013). Urban Marxism and the post-colonial question: Henri Lefebvre and 'colonisation'. *Historical Materialism*, 21(2), 76–116.
Kipfer, S., Goonewardena, K., Schmid, C. and Milgrom, R. (2008). On the production of Henri Lefebvre. In Goonewardena, K. *et al.* (eds.) *Space, Difference, Everyday Life: Reading Henri Lefebvre*. New York and Abingdon, Routledge, 1–24.
Kipfer, S., Saberi, P. and Wieditz, T. (2013). Henri Lefebvre: Debates and controversies. *Progress in Human Geography*, 37(1), 115–134.
Kofman, E. and Lebas, E. (2000). Lost in transposition – time, space and the city. In Kofman, E. and Lebas, E. (eds.) *Writings on Cities – Henri Lefebvre*. 2nd edition. Oxford, Blackwell, 3–60.
Kholodilin, K. A., Kohl, S. and Müller, F. (2022). *The rise and fall of social housing? Housing decommodification in long-run perspective* (No. 22/3). MPIfG Discussion Paper.
Kohlhepp, D. B. (2012). The real estate development Matrix. Paper presented at the American real Estate Society Meetings St Petersburg, Florida. Available at: www.ccimef.org/pdf/2012-299.The-Real-Estate-Development-Matrix.4-21-12.pdf. [Accessed 4 June 2021].
Leary-Owhin, M. E. (2018). Henri Lefebvre, planning's friend or implacable critic? *Urban Planning*, 3(3), 1–4.
Lefebvre, H. (1946). *L'Existentialisme*. Paris, Éditions Sagittaire.
———. (1947). *Critique de la vie quotidienne. Volume One. Introduction.* Paris: Grasset. Translated by J. Moore (1991 [2014]) as *Critique of Everyday Life. Volume One. Introduction.* London, Verso.
———. (1949). Autocritique: Contribution a l'effort d'eclaircissement ideologique. *La Nouvelle Critique*, 4, 41–57.
———. (1957). Vers un romantisme révolutionnaire. *Nouvelle Revue française*, 58, 644–672.
———. (1958). Retour au Marx. *Cahiers Internationaux de Sociologie, Nouvelle Série*, 25, 20–37.
———. (1959). *Le Somme et le Reste*. Paris, La Nef.
———. (1961 [2014]). *Critique de la vie quotidienne. Volume Two. Fondements d'une sociologie de la quotidiennetë*. Paris, L'Arche. Translated by J. Moore (2008 [2014]) as *Critique of Everyday Life. Volume Two. Foundations for a Sociology of the Everyday.* London, Verso.

———. (1965 [2000]). *Metaphilosophie*. 2nd edition. Paris, Syllepse. Translated by D. Fernbach as Metaphilosophy. [2016]. London, Verso.
———. (1966). Henri Lefebvre ouvre le debat sur la theorie de l'autogestion. *Autogestions*, 1(1), 59–70.
———. (1966 [1968]). *Sociologie de Marx*. Paris, Presse Universitaie. Translated by N. Guterman as *The Sociology of Marx*. Harmondsworth, Penguin.
———. (1968). *Le Droit à la ville*. Paris, Anthropos. In Kofman, E. and Lebas, E. (eds.) *Writings on Cities – Henri Lefebvre*. 2nd edition. (2000). Oxford, Blackwells, 63–184.
———. (1970). *Du rural à l'urbain*. Paris, Anthropos.
———. (1970 [2003]). *La Révolution Urbaine*. Paris, Gallimard. Translated by R. Bononno as The Urban Revolution. Minneapolis, University of Minnesota Press.
———. (1971). *Au-delà du structuralisme*. Paris, Éditions Anthropos.
———. (1973 [1976]). *La Survie du capitalisme: La reproduction des rapports de production*. Paris, Anthropos. Translated by F. Bryant as *The Survival of Capitalism. Reproduction of the Relations of Production*. London, Allison & Busby.
———. (1973 [2014]). *Vers une architecture de la jouissance*. Translated by R. Bononno as *Toward an architecture of enjoyment*. Minneapolis, University of Minnesota Press.
———. (1974 [1991]). *La production de l'espace*. Paris, Anthropos. Translated by D. Nicholson-Smith as *The Production of Space*. Oxford, Blackwell.
———. (1975 [2020]). *Hegel, Marx, Nietzsche, ou le royaume des ombres*. Paris, Casterman. Translated by D. Fernbach as *Hegel, Marx, Nietzsche, or the Realm of Shadows*. London, Verso.
———. (1976a). *De l'État. Théorie marxiste de l'État de Hegel à Mao*. Volume 2. Paris, UGE.
———. (1976b). *De l'État. L'État dans le monde moderne*. Volume 1. Paris, UGE.
———. (1977). *De l'État. Le mode de reproduction étatique*. Volume 3. Paris, UGE.
———. (1978). *De l'État. Les contradictions de l'Etat moderne, La dialectique de l'Etat*. Volume 4. Paris, UGE.
———. (1980). *Une pensée devenue monde: faut-il abandonner Marx?* Paris, Fayard.
———. (1980 [1987]). Quotidien et Quotidienneté. Translated by C. Levitch as The everyday and everydayness. *Yale French Studies* (73), 7–11.
———. (1981 [2014]). *Critique de la vie quotidienne. Volume 3. De la Modernité Au* Modernisme. (Pour Une Métaphilosophie Du Quotidien). Paris, L'Arche. Translated by J. Moore (2014) as *From Modernity to Modernism (Towards a Metaphilosophy of Daily Life)*. London, Verso.
———. (1987). An interview with Henri Lefebvre. In Burgel, G., Burgel, G., & Dezes, M. G. (eds.) *Environment and Planning D: Society and Space,* 5(1), 27–38.
———. (1989 [2014]). Dissolving city, planetary metamorphosis. [Quand la ville se perd dans une métamorphose planétaire]. *Environment and planning. D, Society and Space*, 32(2), 203–205.
———. (1990). Du pacte social au contrat du citoyenneté. In Lefebvre, H. and Le Groupe de Navarrenx (eds.) *Du contrat de citoyenneté*. Paris, Editions Syllepse, 15–42.
———. (1992 [2004]). *Éléments de rythmanalyse*. Paris, Syllepse. Translated by S. Elden and G. Moore as *Elements of Rhythmanalysis*. London and New York, Continuum.
———. (2003). Key Writings. In Stuart Elden, Elizabeth Lebas and Eleonore Kofman (eds.) *Henri Lefebvre. Key Writings*. London: Continuum.
———. (2009). *State, Space, World: Selected Essays*. In Neil Brenner and Stuart Elden (eds.) Translated by Gerald Moore, Neil Brenner, and Stuart Elden. Minneapolis: University of Minnesota Press. [Article in this is Theoretical Problems of *Autogestion* (1966), pp. 138–152.]

Lewis, W. (2021). *Dialectical method: Henri Lefebvre's philosophy of science*. Available at: https://philarchive.org/archive/LEWDMH. [Accessed 7 November 2021].
Lipman, P. (2011). Contesting the city: Neoliberal urbanism and the cultural politics of education reform in Chicago. *Discourse: Studies in the Cultural Politics of Education*, 32(2), 217–234.
Lorimer, J. (1978). *The Developers*. Toronto, James Lorimer & Co.
Marcolini, P. (2007). L'Internationale situationniste et la querelle du romantisme révolutionnaire. *Noesis* (11), 31–46.
Marriott, O. (1967). *The Property Boom*. London, Hamish Hamilton.
Marx, K. and Engels, F. (1848 [2010]). *The Communist Manifesto*. CreateSpace Independent Publishing Platform.
McCann, E. J. (1999). Race, protest, and public space: Contextualizing Lefebvre in the US city. *Antipode*, 31(2), 163–184.
Merrifield, A. (2002). *Metromarxism: A Marxist Tale of the City*. New York and London, Routledge.
———. (2009). Review essay. The whole and the rest: Remi Hess and les lefebvriens français. *Environment and Planning D: Society and Space*, 27(5), 936–949.
———. (2013). The urban question under planetary urbanization. *International Journal of Urban and Regional Research*, 37(3), 909–922.
Merrifield, A. and Swyngedouw, E. (1996). *The Urbanization of Injustice*. New York, New York University Press.
Meyer, K. (1973). *Henri Lefebvre. Ein romantischer Revolutionär*. Vienna, Europa Verlags.
Mitchell, D. (2003). *The Right to the City: Social Justice and the Fight for Public Space*. London, The Guildford Press.
Moody's. (2023). *United States – residential housing starts*. Available at www.economy.com/united-states/residential-housing-starts. [Accessed 4 February 2023].
Moulaert, F. and Jessop, R. (2013). Theoretical foundations for the analysis of socioeconomic development in space. In Martinelli, F. *et al.* (eds.) *Urban and Regional Development Trajectories in Contemporary Capitalism*. London and New York, Routledge.
Moulaert, F., Novy, A. and Martinelli, F. (2013). Introduction. Fighting amnesia and recovering the scientific heritage of urban and regional analysis. In Moulaert, F. *et al.* (eds.) *Urban and Regional Development Trajectories in Contemporary Capitalism* London and New York, Routledge, 1–17.
Murphy, J. B. (2008). *Le Deal: How a Young American, in Business, in Love, and in Over His Head, Kick-Started a Multibillion Dollar Industry in Europe*. New York, St. Martin's Press.
Nogueira, M. and Shin, H. B. (2020). The right to the city centre: Political struggles of street vendors in Belo Horizonte, Brazil. *Analysis of Urban Change, Theory, Action*, 26(5–6), 1012–1028.
O'Kane, C. (2018a). Henri Lefebvre and the critical theory of society. In Bauer, J. and Fischer, R. (eds.) *Perspectives on Henri Lefebvre: Theory, Practices and (Re)Readings*. Oldenbourg, De Gruyter, 55–74.
———. (2018). Fetishistic concrete abstraction, social constitution and social domination in Henri Lefebvre's writings on everyday life, cities and space. *Capital & Class*, 42(2), 253–271.
Ong, R., Dalton, T., Gurran, N., Phelps, C., Rowley, S. and Wood, G. (2017). *Housing supply responsiveness in Australia: Distribution, drivers and institutional settings*. Available at: www.ahuri.edu.au/__data/assets/pdf_file/0012/13242/AHURI-Final-Report-281-Housing-supply-responsiveness-in-Australia-distribution-drivers-and-institutional-settings.pdf. [Accessed 20 June 2022].

Pierce, J. (2017). Henri Lefebvre, Marxist thought and the city. Book review. *Antipode*. Available at: https://antipodeonline.org/wp-content/uploads/2017/03/book-review_pierce-on-lefebvre.pdf. [Accessed 3 July 2021].

Purcell, M. (2002). Excavating Lefebvre: The right to the city and its urban politics of the inhabitant. *GeoJournal*, 58(2), 99–108.

———. (2013). Possible worlds: Henri Lefebvre and the right to the city. *Journal of Urban Affairs*, 36(1), 141–154.

Reed, R. (2021). *Property Development*. New York and London, Routledge.

Read, S., de Laat-Lukkassen, M. and Jonauskis, T. (2013). Revisiting "complexification," technology, and urban form in Lefebvre. *Space and Culture*, 16(3), 381–396.

Revol, C. (2012). Le succès de Lefebvre dans les Urban Studies anglo-saxonnes et les conditions de sa redécouverte en France. *L'Homme et la société*, 185–186(3), 105–118.

Ritzer, G. and Stepnisky, J. (eds.) (2011). *The Wiley-Blackwell Companion to Major Social Theorists*. Volume 1. London, Wiley-Blackwell.

Rose, H. (1983). Hand, brain, and heart: A feminist epistemology for the natural sciences. *Signs: Journal of Women in Culture and Society*, 9(1), 73–90.

Ross, K. (1995). *Fast Cars, Clean Bodies: Decolonization and the Rendering of French Culture*. Cambridge, MA, MIT Press.

Ross Goobey, A. (1992). *Bricks and Mortals*. London, Century Business.

Rowley, S., Costello, G., Higgins, D. and Phibbs, P. (2014). *The financing of residential development in Australia*. Available at www.ahuri.edu.au/__data/assets/pdf_file/0011/2009/AHURI_Final_Report_No219_The-financing-of-residential-development-in-Australia.pdf. [Accessed 20 June 2022].

Sangla, S. (2010). *Politique et espace chez Henri Lefebvre*. PhD. Université Paris Viii – Vincennes Saint-Denis. Available at: www.idref.fr/152262784. [Accessed 5 June 2021].

Saravia, F. (2019). Espacio e intervención en trabajo social a partir de Lefebvre. *Cinta de Moebio* (66), 281–294.

Savini, F. and Aalbers, M. B. (2016). The de-contextualisation of land use planning through financialisation: Urban redevelopment in Milan. *European urban and regional studies*, 23(4), 878–894.

Schaepelynck, V. and Sustam, E. (2018). Autogestion. *Le Télémaque*, 2(54), 27–36.

Schneider, T. (2015). Urban revolution now. Henri Lefebvre in social research and architecture. *The Journal of Architecture*, 20(3), 555–560.

Schrader, S. (2018). *Henri Lefebvre, Mao Zedong, and the global urban concept*. Available at https://globalurbanhistory.com/2018/05/01/henri-lefebvre-mao-zedong-and-the-global-urban-concept/. [Accessed 2 May 2021].

Sève, L. (1968 [1978]). *Marxisme et théorie de la personalitié*. Paris, Éditions Sociales. Translated by J. McGreal as *Man in Marxist Theory and the Psychology of Personality*. Brighton, Harvester.

———. (2008). *L'Homme (Penser avec Marx aujourd'hui, Volume 2*. Paris, La Dispute.

———. (2022). Marxist analysis of alienation (1973). *Historical Materialism*, 31(1), 245–296.

Shields, R. (1989). Social spatialization and the built environment: The West Edmonton Mall. *Environment and Planning D: Society and Space*, 7(2), 147–164.

———. (2013). Spatial questions. *Cultural Topologies and Social Spatialisations*. Los Angeles, Sage.

Sim, L. L., Yu, S. M. and Han, S. S. (2003). Public housing and ethnic integration in Singapore. *Habitat International*, 27(2), 293–307.

Simonsen, K. (2005). Bodies, sensations, space and time: The contribution from Henri Lefebvre. *Geografiska Annaler: Series B, Human* Geography, 87(1), 1–14.

Sin, C. H. (2003). The politics of ethnic integration in Singapore: Malay 'regrouping' as an ideological construct. *International Journal of Urban and Regional Research*, 27(3), 527–544.
Smith, N. (2003). Foreward. In Lefebvre, H. *The Urban Revolution*. Minneapolis, University of Minnesota Press, vii–xxiii.
Soja, E. (1989). *Postmodern Geographies: The Reassertion of Space in Critical Social Theory*. London: Verso.
———. (1996). *Thirdspace: Journeys to Los Angeles and Other Real-and-Imagined Places*. Oxford, Basil Blackwell.
———. (2009). Taking space personally. In *The Spatial Turn*. New York and London, Routledge, 27–51.
———. (2010). *Seeking Spatial Justice*. Minneapolis, University of Minnesota Press.
Soja, E. and Kanai, M. (2013). The urbanization of the world. In Brenner, N. (ed.) *Implosions/Explosions: Towards a Study of Planetary Urbanization*. Berlin and Boston, Jovis, 138–159.
Solak, S. (2022). Reading architecture, city and space in Latife Tekin's Novels Through Henri Lefebvre. *Gazi University Journal of Science Part B: Art Humanities Design and Planning*, 10(2), 185–194.
Stanek, L. (2011). *Henri Lefebvre on Space: Architecture, Urban Research, and the Production of Theory*. Minneapolis, University of Minnesota Press.
———. (2012). Architecture as space, again. Notes on the 'spatial turn'. *SpecialeZ*, 4, 48–53.
Sudjic, D. (1992). *The 100 Mile City*. London, Andre Deutsch.
Swope, C. (2021). Is Green the New Red? Marxism, Ecology, and Contemporary Architectural Theory. *Humanities*, 10(1), 45.
Trebitsch, M. (1991 [2014]). Preface. In Lefebvre, H. *Critique of Everyday Life*. London, Verso, 5–24.
———. (2002 [2014]). Preface. The moment of radical critique. In *Critique of Everyday Life*. London: Verso, 277–294.
Tsavdaroglou, C. (2020). The refugees' right to the center of the city and spatial justice: Gentrification vs commoning practices in Tarlabaşı-Istanbul. *Urban Planning*, 5(3), 230–240.
Tsavdaroglou, C. and Kaika, M. (2022). The refugees' right to the centre of the city: City branding versus city commoning in Athens. *Urban Studies*, 59(6), 1130–1147.
Tyner, J. A. (2007). Urban revolutions and the spaces of black radicalism. In McKittrick, K. and Woods, C. (eds.) *Black Geographies and the Politics of Place*. Toronto, Between the Lines, 218–232.
UK Government. (2023). *Town and country planning act 1990.1990c. 8 part III meaning of development*. Available at: www.legislation.gov.uk/ukpga/1990/8/part/III/crossheading/meaning-of-development. [Accessed 7 May 2021].
Unwin, T. (2000). A waste of space? Towards a critique of the social production of space. *Transactions of the Institute of British Geographers*, 25(1), 11–29.
Vogelpohl, A. (2011). Die urbane revolution. Henri Lefèbvres Philosophie der globalen Verstädterung. Book review. *Erkunde*, 65(2), 216–218.
Watkins, C. (2005). Representations of space, spatial practices and spaces of representation: An application of Lefebvre's spatial triad. *Culture and Organization*, 11(3), 209–220.
Wilson, J. (2013). "The devastating conquest of the lived by the conceived" the concept of abstract space in the work of Henri Lefebvre. *Space and Culture*, 16(3), 364–380.
Yamamoto, Y. (2018). Reconsidering desire and style: A lefebvrian approach to democratic orientation in planning. *Urban Planning*, 3(3), 105–111.
Zanotto, J. M. (2020). The role of discourses in enacting neoliberal urbanism: Understanding the relationship between ideology and discourse in planning. *Planning Theory*, 19(1), 104–126.
Zieleniec, A. (2018). Lefebvre's politics of space: Planning the urban as oeuvre. *Urban Planning*, 3(3), 5–15.

2 Lefebvre's argument

Introduction

This chapter is intended to present Lefebvre's work on space and the urban to a primarily real estate development audience. It has the aim of encouraging developers to adopt a radical view of their important role in the world, to challenge and encourage them to take the social responsibilities that come with that evolving role seriously, and in many cases even to provoke them to act differently. In academic terms, it also tries to fulfil the function of providing the theoretical background for the application of Lefebvre to real estate development that follows. It is worth highlighting immediately the argument that developers should not shy away, suspicious of *any* theory as they may at first believe themselves to be. Construction engineering revolves around it, and so does architecture – real estate development too can benefit from the self-reflection and understanding that thinking about the production of space within a capitalist world can bring.

Theory and politics do often travel together, though. As a result, too often, it is said, approaches to Lefebvre have started with the slogan of the *Right to the City*, or with his urban writings, and not with his politics, or with his Marxism. It would indeed be to do Lefebvre an injustice if this were to have the consequence of de-politicising his work, for, as the previous chapter sought to demonstrate, Lefebvre set out not just to understand the urban and develop a theory of space, but in so doing to contribute to a transformation of Marxism. He made this crystal clear himself in several works, analysing space and the urban over a period of decades, from *Le droit à la ville* (Lefebvre, 1968), which was published at the cusp of revolutionary optimism worldwide, not least in France where the country appeared to teeter on the brink of an actual revolution, through to the ultimately discouraging 1970s, commencing with *Du rural à l'urbain* (Lefebvre, 1970a) and *La Révolution urbaine* (Lefebvre, 1970a), but finally 'that key work' (Trebitsch, 2002 [2014:669]), his masterpiece on space, *La production de l'espace* (Lefebvre, 1974b), originally published at a time when cruel reverses for revolutionary causes worldwide, including in France, had already dashed the hopes of the Left. It is within these works that the kernel of Lefebvre's theory is to be found. And it was these works which through their intellectual innovation 'earned Lefebvre

DOI: 10.1201/9781003220244-2

recognition – strangely unconventional recognition, since it was bestowed less by philosophers and sociologists than by geographers, urbanists and architects' (Trebitsch, 2002 [2014:669]).

Marxism and the urban

Lefebvre's views on the urban may usefully be compared with those of the Founding Fathers of Marxism, and with other Marxist and other radical geographers, some more traditionally Marxist, others closer to Lefebvre's own views. For developers this may seem initially rather a tiresome diversion, even an unnecessary one, but they might wish to remind themselves that it is frequently useful to appreciate a theoretical breakthrough by understanding what the landscape looked like beforehand, or even at the same time as the new theory is developed and promulgated. It may also be worth recalling that Marxism remains important both politically and theoretically, and not only in the academy; capitalism is not a universally worshipped idol, quite the contrary, even by those who pledge public allegiance to its dictates.

It must first be acknowledged that the importance of – let us be frank and admit it – the new direction in which Lefebvre took Marxism – is reinforced by the fact that contemporary Marxist students of urban processes, as those of organisations, or even religion, have had to approach their task with little guidance from the Founding Fathers themselves. Marx's own writings on the subject are scattered throughout his work (e.g. Marx, 1852, 1857 [1972]); Engels by contrast did write more specifically about urban issues, identifying the implications of development opportunities for the English working class in the mid-19th century:

> The growth of the big modern cities gives the land in certain areas, particularly in those which are centrally situated, an artificial and often colossally increasing value; the buildings erected on these areas depress this value, instead of increasing it, because they no longer correspond to the changed circumstances. They are pulled down and replaced by others. This takes place above all with workers' houses which are situated centrally and whose rents, even with the greatest overcrowding, can never, or only very slowly, increase above a certain maximum. They are pulled down and in their stead shops, warehouses and public buildings are erected.
>
> (Engels, 1872 [2021:16–17])

Despite this clear awareness of HBU from one of the Founding Fathers, albeit with an entirely negative evaluation of the process, it is easy to concur with Lefebvre's evaluation that there was no overarching theory of the urban, neither in Marx, nor Engels, nor even that of their immediate successors, even after they had seized power in what became the Soviet Union (Feldman, 1978:136), in fact, arguably a reluctance to recognise the geographical (and physical) constraints on the historical process on which they relied to deliver urban change, amongst so many other ambitions. Lefebvre further criticised Marx and Engels for what he perceived as a geographical monolithism in the Marxist project, arguing that

> [s]pace appears to Marx only as the sum of the sites of production, as the territory of various markets. The city does not yet pose major problems, except for the problem of housing (considered by Engels).
>
> (Lefebvre, 1980a:149)

Nor did subsequent theorists and revolutionaries such as Lenin focus much wider the agrarian question in order to treat land and rent, which has left these issues open to further theoretical development (Lefebvre, 1956; Elden & Morton, 2016:59). As the absence of geographical concerns became more obvious to more observers, criticism became progressively more strident as the last century proceeded, from 'Marx's own analysis of space is not central to his work (Elden, 2001:813) to

> Marx never wrote a single word about cities, and his passionate interests in ethnography, geology and mathematics were never matched by a comparable concern with geography.
>
> (Davis, 2020:xiv)

It might be added that, as a result, Marx's sharp journalistic edge, which never omitted geographical specificity, for example in the penetrating contemporary political analysis of the *18th Brumaire of Louis Bonaparte*, whether they be railways (Marx, 1852 [2010:33]), prisons (Marx, 1852 [2010:57), or statues (Marx, 1852 [2010:67]), did not always permeate through to his later theoretical work, so 'where urbanism is considered it is treated in the light of its contribution in preparing the way for industrial capitalism' (Harvey, 1973:306). Lefebvre concurred, characterising the urban as playing a background role, just a backdrop against which the historical drama of the evolution of society from feudalism to capitalism and eventually beyond it has and will play out (Lefebvre, 1980a:149). In fairness, there may have been good reasons for what may have been a deliberate choice:

> Marx is anxious to avoid any form of direct geographical determinism (such as we find in Plekhanov) or any account in which man figures purely as an object acted upon by something else other than other men and human products. Man's relations with 'nature' for Marx is always dialectical; man shapes it as it shapes him.
>
> (Kamenka, 1969:33)

The debate over geography within Marxism has certainly been prolonged and, it should be admitted, often antagonistic (Matley, 1966; Das, 2022). It is surely unlikely to abate entirely. Lefebvre continues to play a leading role in that debate, promoting the city and the urban to a central role in Marxism. In the narrative he weaves, the political city of Ancient Greece evolved through the mercantile city of medieval Europe and then into the European and US industrial cities. Given the importance of space for contemporary capitalism, however, Lefebvre crucially considers *industrial* society itself as a necessary but now superseded period of history, now replaced by today's *urban* society. He sets himself the arduous task of reconstructing Marxism accordingly on the basis of this new but cardinal assumption (Meyer, 1973:143). His striking claims deserve further elucidation. Although Lefebvre professed to believe that 'there is not a strict correspondence between modes of production and the spaces they constitute', he argued nonetheless that 'each epoch produces its own space' (Katznelson, 1993:96), comparing the first stage of urbanism – the political city – with two later stages – the mercantile city and the industrial city (Lefebvre, 1970 [2003]; Smith, 2003:xi). So, the transformation from the political city to the commercial city reflects the evolution of urbanism itself; the city still functioned as a centripetal force, attracting politics, finance, administration, and even military control, as well as the development of ideology, but as the economics of cities developed, the city also became a centre for economic exchange – the original commodity Exchanges, for example, were established in leading cities. Later came further emphasis on industrial production, which demanded production concentration to satisfy economies of scale, of both production and distribution. Marxist geographers have emphasised these roles, even to the extent of suggesting that they came to dominate the role of the city (Harvey, 1973:305). Lefebvre however sought to advance this argument one key further step: in the 20th century, he argued,

> urbanization has superseded industrialization as the leading force shaping late capitalism. It is better therefore, he argues, to characterise the world we live in urban rather than industrial. In this world, space is no mere 'container' or an 'expression' of social relations, but a productive and constitutive element of them.
>
> (Goonewardena, 2011:55)

Production, consumption, interaction – how we live – all take place under conditions of complete urbanisation.

In sharp contrast, all that could be said of what the Founding Fathers believed for sure was as follows: 'By the logic of its own functioning, urbanization under capitalism could, Engels concluded, only ever produce inequality and impoverishment' (Merrifield, 2001:65). Fast forward more than a century from those conclusions, and even after the state socialist experiment – scientific, or perhaps more accurately, traditional – Marxists could still be found concluding that how cities developed was a function of class struggle and how the surplus value of labour was embodied in the built environment were both a largely linear, deducible function of the inevitable economic cycles of capitalism. A traditional Marxist geographer even in the later 20th century could therefore suggest that 'the spatial scale of "urban" problems as distinct from "regional"; is no more necessarily a question of consumption versus production, than the distinction between regional and local markets is' (Feldman, 1978:142) Even suburbanisation, such a characteristic urban phenomenon of the 20th century and beyond, has for traditional Marxist geographers been characterised as largely the outcome of a search for ways of controlling workers, or at least a product of capitalist wage differentials within the working class. The result, critics of the traditional Marxist approach suggested, was not only the familiar accusation of an unduly economistic analytical framework, but also a politically problematic lack of concern with issues such as the quality and delivery of urban services, the nature of urban community, the interior structure of neighbourhoods, and ethnic issues (Eisinger, 1978:665–667). Developers will likely find thus far little to recognise in this particular Marxist approach, let alone to commend, and probably much with which to disagree.

Traditional Marxist geography, which rose to prominence in the 20th century in tandem with the achievement of power by at least nominally Marxist governments in state socialist countries, should be recognised as much wider aspirations than ever confining itself to a dismissive evaluation of real estate development in developed Western jurisdictions. In particular, it aimed at applying traditional Marxist categories such as class and capital to a redefinition and understanding of the entire scope of human geography, analysing familiar concepts of place and space, differentiation, and connection whilst prioritising issues of concern to Marxists such as geographically uneven development, colonialism, and territorial struggle, and in so doing, reformulating traditional Marxist political concepts of contradictions in least partly geographical terms (Cox, 2005:2). In so doing, it reflected at least in part Lefebvre's own analysis of the politics of space, 'focused not only on state spatial strategies but also, more specifically, on state territorial strategies' (Brenner & Elden, 2009:368). So, although Marxist geographers were united in criticising the obvious and frequent failures of governments in capitalist states to provide adequate housing for working people, by comparison to the deleterious effects of land markets, and property speculation, which developers cannot fail to recognise, some also perspicaciously focused on the consequences of employing HBU as a route towards treating land and real estate as a commodity (Harvey, 2012:17).

Radical geographers further co-opted land rent theory as a mechanism of understanding patterns of urban development (Charnock, 2014; Haila, 2016; Ward, 2019), placing particular emphasis on what Neil Smith characterised as the 'rent gap' – 'the disparity between the potential ground rent level flowing from differentiated profit rates and therefore different HBUs in specific locations and the actual ground rent obtainable under the present land use' (Smith, 1979:545). The rent gap fascinates Marxists 'precisely because it contains within its neat curves the necessity of failure, crisis, stagnation and dereliction, even whilst appearing to model a process that promises cleanliness, affluence, order and economic growth' (Kallin, 2021:616). Most obviously in a developed country context, the existence of comparatively cheap land and hence low ground rent in the suburbs was held likely to encourage real estate development there, compared to potentially more problematic calculations for a Central Business District (CBD), to the extent that in this Marxist schema, how ground rents played out determined the suburban location of economic expansion (Smith, 1984).

Marxist and other radical geographers paying attention to real estate development in developed capitalist economies generally disliked what they saw as the result:

> [T]he shopping centers and the supermarkets were made possible by suburban sprawl, as were the new leisure activities (from the drive-in restaurant or cinema to the private swimming pool). But even more important was the role of the single-family house in the suburbs as the perfect design for maximizing capitalist consumption. Every household, one of the most well-known Marxist geographers observed with a mixture of exasperation and contempt, must engage in an entirely illusory self-sufficiency, from the refrigerator to the TV.
> (Castells, 1977:388)

None of this is true freedom, Marxists agree, including Lefebvre, not least because 'there can be alienation in leisure just as in work' (Lefebvre, 1947 [1991:61]). A similar critique has been proferred more recently in a developing country context, where an analogous rent gap has been observed between agricultural lands, acquired from smallholders at cheap nominal compensation rates, which can then be redeveloped as higher-value (residential, commercial, industrial) land (Labbé, 2016:152). Here throughout, of course, are likewise potential opportunities for the developer. Indeed, such a 'rent gap' forms the basis for development, as well as a way of understanding gentrification, the expulsion of traditional, poorer residents in favour of more affluent newcomers (Smith, 1996), in particular its microgeography, occurring 'in particular places at particular times' (Cox, 2005:9).

The Marxist approach was not without its own critics: although there was recognition that 'the suburbanisation of industry represented a clear weakening of agglomeration economics' (Smith, 1986), its proponents have always been much less vocal in identifying the reasons why many people in developed countries actually choose to live in the suburbs, or, beyond the demand for mass housing, how exactly governments and planners in developing countries should seek to overcome the problems inherent in rapidly growing populations in urgent need of urban housing. Where the Marxist geographers have been most insistent, and surely quite rightly so, was that Marx's concepts of exchange value and use value now applied to space, a point emphasised by Lefebvre himself (Lefebvre, 1974 [1991:287]). Now globalised, in the 21st century, Marxists see that 'the landscape gets flagged out as a pure exchange value, and activities on land conform to the "highest", if not necessarily the "best", land uses' (Merrifield, 2011:474). Consequently, a key goal of political resistance to capitalism Marxists frequently envisage is 'to reinstate the use values (actual or potential) of the land, streets, buildings, homes, parks and centres that constitute an urban community' (Slater, 2017:133).

Developers who work with the concept of HBU may even find little to cavil in this so far in principle – it is rather on the practical difficulties of ascertaining what the HBU really is, especially between a myriad of potential development choices and the perception of its ethical status as entirely negative, on which they may choose to disagree with Marxist geographers. It is worth even at this early point that a Marxist methodology for calculating use values, whether entirely based on labour or otherwise (Groll, 1980; Mehrotra, 1991; Hermann, 2021), has always been left unclear, despite its evident need for evaluating alternative uses for land, to replace HBU based on valuation; nor is the source and agency of this 'political resistance' at all clear either, both points returned to in the next chapter.

Development and the role of capital

Although Marxist geographers agreed with real estate developers that the value of land is at least frequently based on an estimation of future rents capitalised with the aid of debt to reduce the cost of capital, they argued that the land market depends on 'fictitious capital', defined as expected future value fabricated into value (Harvey, 2018), that is, 'fictitious capital in the Marxian sense of the word – money invested before it is productively realised' (Kallin, 2021:620). Unfortunately, this approach to investment value does not itself reveal any actual processes by which these estimates are forecast, or what might be done to do so in a superior way, for good or ill. Lefebvre's view was that the absence of such refinement was the cause of analytic deficiencies, for example the failure to explain why the class of real estate owners persisted in capitalism, or how best to theorise the question of land and land annuity (Stanek, 2011:161), although he no more than other Marxist geographers (or economists) came close to developing any kind of calculus to replace the forecast of future value with a more socially satisfactory solution that did not depend on the problematics inherent in state planning.

Where Lefebvre and the Marxist geographers agreed was in the importance of this process, as 'Each of the global crises of capitalism was in fact preceded by the massive movement of capital into long-term investment in the built environment as a kind of last-ditch hope for finding productive uses for rapidly overaccumulating capital' (Harvey, 1978:120). This analysis – except for the 'last-ditch hope' point, which might more accurately be described as a remarkably successful set of uses – may well be more accurate with each passing decade. The result has been the transfer of the process of creating surplus value increasingly to what Lefebvre characterised as the no-longer secondary role of urban development (Lefebvre, 1974 [1991:335]), replacing the originally primary role of industrial production (Charney, 2001; Gotham, 2006), even now in countries in the Gulf that have traditionally relied on fossil fuel production as their main source of revenue (Buckley & Hanieh, 2014) or in state-driven economies such as China, with sometimes severely adverse results (Gao, 2022). Indeed, we have probably reached a point where the term 'secondary circuit' itself (Harvey, 1978) and its associated parallel, 'alternative investments', is potentially confusing, and should be replaced with something more accurate – the urban circuit of capital formation, perhaps, or from a slightly different but certainly incisive perspective, a 'finance- *and* real estate-driven regime' (Hofman & Aalbers, 2019:90), uneven no doubt in its scale and scope, but global in its operation. If even partly true, these assertions would make the questions of how space is produced under capitalism, how its transformation may lead to the supersession of capitalism itself, notwithstanding its capacity to recuperate under pressure (Lefebvre, 1981 [2014]), and even how space might be produced beyond it of paramount importance to Marxists everywhere. 'Social change, to Lefebvre, cannot occur in a planned way without the production of a changed space' (Gottdiener, 1993:133). Developers too might be impressed to realise their own significance in this evolution of capitalism: no longer peripheral to its operation, they have now become fundamental to its success, to its survival, and potentially foremost in its replacement. Marxists might be able to assist in placing them at the political centre stage where they now belong, on the basis of the importance of their contribution to the economy, and to capitalism as a whole.

Departure from the traditional Marxist script

Perhaps the colonisation by capitalism of urban space and the tensions that it engendered (e.g. between the centre and the periphery) might also provide fresh opportunities for its supersession, even globally (Kipfer & Goonewardena, 2013:87). It seems such was Lefebvre's initial hope in his writings around the time of the May 1968 protests in France (Lefebvre, 1968, 1968a). Variously translated, Lefebvre argued:

> When we use the words 'urban revolution' we designate the total ensemble of transformations which run throughout contemporary society and which serve to bring about the change from a period in which questions of economic growth and industrialization predominate to the period in which the urban problematic becomes decisive, when research into the solutions and forms appropriate to urban society become problematic.
>
> (Lefebvre, 1970a:13) [David Harvey's translation]

It has been suggested that there are two contrasting, perhaps even competing, conceptions of revolution at play in Lefebvre's writings on the urban phenomenon. The first relates to 'the creative-destructive "implosion" of the traditional pre-industrial city . . . coupled with its scalar "explosion" in the fragmented, polycentric suburban metropolis dotted with malls and criss-crossed by highways' (Lefebvre, 1970 [2003:127–128]), while the second 'refers to the possible city yet to be achieved in a revolutionary transformation of capitalist social space' (Goonewardena, 2011:56) So, this urban revolutionary Lefebvre sees this 'implosion-explosion' – urban concentration, rural exodus, the extension of the urban fabric (a term that he never defined precisely), and the complete subordination of the agrarian to the urban – as being the necessary condition for the creation of his 'critical space' (Lefebvre, 1970 [2003:15]; Moravánszky *et al.*, 2014:2). The one may be inevitable; the other very definitely is not.

The concept of scale previously discussed surfaces in this analysis, but as one would expect with Lefebvre, in different ways as this thought develops: in his earlier urban work (Lefebvre, 1968, 1970a), the focus was primarily on scale (*le mondial*) or level (*le global*) (Elden, 2016:xi); as his interest in urban questions evolved (Lefebvre, 1972, 1973a, 1974 [1991], 1974a, 1976, 1989 [2014]), it has been suggested that he focuses more on scale as territory (Brenner, 2000:368n). It is clear, however, where his interest (and arguably, his real belief in potential political change) lies: 'the urban scale appears to have become the central institutional, political and geographical interface upon, within and through which the contradictory politics of capitalist restructuring are currently being fought out' (Brenner, 2000:374). As Brenner cites Lefebvre as arguing, 'The city and the urban sphere are thus the setting of struggle; they are also, however, the stakes of that struggle' (Lefebvre, 1974 [1991:386]). So, says Lefebvre, the urban fabric is 'a kind of biological proliferation of a net of uneven mesh, allowing more or less extended sectors to escape' (Lefebvre, 1968 [2000:71]). The result has been that 'The urban fabric can be described by using the concept of ecosystem, a coherent unity constituted around one or several cities, old and recent' (Lefebvre, 1968 [2000:72]). Social and cultural life appear not only superimposed on the economic base of the urban fabric, but wholly integrated into an apparent rationality generated and conveyed by the urban. Analytically, Lefebvre also suggested that a contemporary hyper-complex urbanism – he might have reflected that it always has the capacity to become even more complex, as continues to happen – should be examined at three levels, or dimensions – architectural (including course buildings, but also monuments, which Lefebvre was well ahead of his time in identifying as repressive but also beautiful) (Lefebvre, 1970 [2003:21), urbanism (the organisation of the city, its global role), and territorial (as part of the nation) (Lefebvre, 1978 [2009:223]).

Outside the city limits

Lefebvre agreed with Marx that whatever form capital takes, it always results in the exploitation of labour, and in turn to resistance by that exploited labour. For them both, but Lefebvre explicitly, the city dominated social life, as well as serving to provide the locations exchange of goods and services that capitalism demands can occur. But Lefebvre has been praised for recognising that there is life beyond now often arbitrary city boundaries (Purcell, 2003; Elden, 2004), even though he recognised that '[t]he rural world is a space where debilitating political and religious strictures are lived canonically and without question' (Conley, 2012:14–15). Lefebvre was not the first to advance the idea that the social boundaries of the city extended beyond its physical ones: 'The influences which cities exert upon social life are greater than the ratio of the urban population would indicate' (Wirth, 1938:2). A lively debate ensued and has persisted as to the extent to which it was accurate to conceptualise the city in terms of social behaviour (Gans, 1994; Kress, 2016). But as more radically reformulated by Lefebvre, with the urban society 'built on the ruins of the city' (Lefebvre, 1968 [2000:126]), without the fact that 'society has become completely urbanized' (Lefebvre, 1970 [2003:1]), there can be no advanced capitalism:

> This concept, the urban, which has recently entered vocabularies (science and practice), does not designate the city and life in the city. On the contrary:

> it is born with the fragmentation of the city, with the problems and the deterioration of urban life.
>
> (Lefebvre, 1986:160)

The argument continues that as cities achieve greater concentrations of property, speculation, and (post)-industrial activity, the urban centre implodes, acting as a spur to the expansion, or 'explosion', of urbanisation (Lefebvre, 1968 [2000:70–71]; Millington, 2016:479). Slightly confusingly perhaps for a developer who might well be unfamiliar with his use of the dialectic, let alone with the dialectic in general, Lefebvre suggests that both concentration and extension are dialectically intertwined moments of planetary urbanisation (Brenner & Schmid, 2014:731) Equally in accord with the key Marxist distinction between the forces of production and the social relations of production, he suggests that urbanism has now become as important to the former as they had previously been with respect to the latter. 'What does the city create? Nothing. It centralizes creation. And yet it creates everything. 'Society has become completely urbanised' (Lefebvre, 1970 [2003:1]).

> Nothing exists without exchange, without union, without proximity, that is, without relationships. The city creates a situation, the urban situation, where different things occur one after another and do not exist separately but according to their differences. The urban, which is indifferent to each difference it contains, often seems to be as indifferent as nature, but with a cruelty of its own. However, the urban is not indifferent to all differences, precisely because it unites them. In this sense, the city constructs, identifies, and delivers the essence of social relationships: the reciprocal existence and manifestation of differences arising from or resulting in conflicts. Isn't this the rational delirium known as the city, the urban?
>
> (Lefebvre, 1970 [2003:117–118])

So it was that Lefebvre had rapidly transformed his theoretical approach: from a focus on a *form*, the city itself, his perspective had shifted to a *process* – urbanisation (Schmid, 2012:45). Industrial society as analysed by the Founding Fathers has been transcended; society as a whole has moved beyond industrialisation to become urbanised, and that the traditional distinction between the city and what existed outside its boundaries no longer applies: 'The concept of the city no longer corresponds to a social object' (Lefebvre, 1970 [2003:57]). As his thought developed, 'Lefebvre's scheme hinged on a separation of the city and urbanism as theoretical and empirical constructs. The city is an arrangement of objects in space; urbanism a way of life' (Katznelson, 1993:97). As Lefebvre describes it in an oft-cited lyrical passage:

> Piles of objects and products in the warehouses, mounds of fruit in the marketplace, crowds, pedestrians, goods of various kinds, juxtaposed, superimposed, accumulated – this is what makes the urban urban.
>
> (Lefebvre, 1970 [2003:116])

To this depiction he later added locality, observing that 'The rhythms of Barcelona are not those of Venice, nor Marseille' (Lefebvre, 1986:163): undoubtedly, not. On the other hand, despite his caustic reference to 'the West's infatuation with village life and rustic homesteads' (Lefebvre, 1974 [1991:123]), it is 'hard to escape a sense of nostalgia in Lefebvre's discussion of the traditional European industrial city' (Wachsmuth & Brenner, 2014:200). Even the much more recent argument from a contemporary urbanist that 'Walkable streets are our cities' greatest asset' (Derbyshire, 2015:20) aligns more with the traditional cry of the right to the city than with global urban sprawl, although Lefebvre also recognises that capitalism has taken over the street, made it into a spectacle: 'a colonization of the urban space' (Lefebvre, 1970 [2003:21]) through the spectacle of object-become-commodities. It has even been suggested that Lefebvre's argument that the clear distinction between the urban and the rural that once existed was 'gradually fading into a set of porous spaces of uneven geographical development under the hegemonic command of capital and the state' (Harvey, 2012:19). For this reason, his suggestion is that that 'urban society' or 'urban fabric' is a better term than either cities or 'post-industrial society' because he wants to point to 'tendencies, orientations, and virtualities' – perhaps equally, interdependencies (Lefebvre, 1970 [2003:2]; Merrifield, 2014:x), illustrated by the forcible eviction of slum-dwellers in numerous developing countries as part of agricultural land clearance, but by much more, 'all manifestations of the dominance of the city over the countryside. In this sense, a vacation home, a highway, a supermarket in the countryside are all part of the urban fabric' (Lefebvre, 1970 [2003:4]), all combining to render small and midsized cities 'dependencies, partial colonies of the metropolis' (Lefebvre, 1970 [2003:4]) and to corrode the residue of agrarian life (Lefebvre, 1970 [2003:3]). No longer to be considered or examined as merely a collection of physical objects, whether buildings, streets, infrastructure, or even people, the urban is a social product (Lefebvre, 1974 [1991:331–334]), 'the concrete, local articulation of processes of more general technological, economic and regulatory change' (Kloosterman & Lambregts, 2007:54). This entails rejection of the idea of urbanism as a social practice that is fundamentally scientific and technical in nature (Lefebvre, 1970 [2003:6]), by contrast envisaging urbanisation as a 'polymorphic, variable and dynamic' historical process and contested social product constituted via the urbanisation of capital, consciousness, and social practice (Brenner & Schmid, 2014:750). So far, developers should again surely have little to cavil at in Lefebvre's insistence on the all-embracing nature of the urban – on the contrary, they ought to welcome such recognition of the integrated nature of the built and social environment, the cornerstone of successful real estate development. As yet, however, they might be forgiven for remaining unclear as to what, if any, the implications for them might be.

Mediation, centrality, and difference

For Lefebvre, these three core concepts then emerge. The urban exists between the private, everyday life, and the global market, the state, and beyond them ideology and even philosophy, enjoying a perhaps precarious, always porous, yet certainly powerful existence amongst them all, characterised under capitalism by a process of fragmentation of space, both practically and theoretically. Differences, encounter, simultaneity: these three features characterize the term 'centrality' for Lefebvre (Vogelpohl, 2011:237). Difference itself is produced by exclusion from components of space, logical systems, and hegemonic social practice (Kinkaid, 2020:169); in turn, Lefebvre implies that it produces classes and struggle. But increasingly, centrality is in flux, 'contingent, unstable, and to be sustained by historically and geographically situated social practices' (Stanek, 2011:157). Lefebvre 'put the urban on the agenda as an explicit locus and target of political organizing' (Smith, 2003:vii), for 'Lefebvre writes of space as occupation. It is not geography but practice, by which he means that is not an inert and given physical environment, but a space produced by human actions' (Prakash, 2008:9), with the following observation:

> As in Bombay, so in Buenos Aires, the elite memories of the city's past unity and harmony leave no place for hierarchy and multiplicity; they mistake the earlier class and ideological dominance of the urban space for the actual description of the past.
>
> (Prakash, 2008:6)

And to complete the moving picture, Lefebvre's dialectic implies that the forces of urbanism–suburbanism, and the tensions they produce, are in constant flux (Walks, 2013:1477), 'the qualities of urban space – difference, encounter, creativity – become part of the economic logic and of systematic exploitation of productivity gains' (Schmid, 2012:56), whilst quasi-public spaces owned and controlled by private interests are designed to 'channel urban life into commercially exploitable avenues and to prioritize market-oriented and consumption-oriented practice' (Schmid, 2012:56). Via this, and the limitation to the city centre, 'The urban center is not only transformed into a site of consumption; it also becomes an object of consumption, and is valued as such' (Lefebvre, 1989 [2014:203]). The urban is 'a model, a perpetual prototype of use value resisting the generalizations of exchange value in a capitalist economy under the authority of a homogenizing state' (Lefebvre, 1979 [2009:191]). Yet Lefebvre never abandons hope: the urban retains the potential to restore the creative production of the city as oeuvre, in opposition to tendencies towards the commodification of space (Butler, 2005:27), as 'urban space loses some of its essential elements, but especially its most important characteristic – the possibility of unexpected, unplanned encounters and interactions' (Schmid, 2012:57).

In this urban fabric, where most of us (now) live, where the old boundaries between city and countryside no longer correspond to reality, complex urban life thrives, and where it is no longer rational to conceive of either an urban proletariat or its counterpart, or the rural peasantry, as the essential components of a revolution, the active urban citizens who will take their place now dwell. But not equally: key to Lefebvre's original conception was the distinction between the centre, where privileged products, people, and symbols coalesce to maintain and multiply their power, and the periphery, where dissident or undesirable elements are peripheralised, a complex dialectical relationship that reflects the political reality and contradictions of urban space more widely (Addie, 2015:569). For Lefebvre, the urban has not – yet – lost the characteristics of centrality, although towards the end of his life he had already pointed to significant change:

> [t]he historic centre has disappeared . . . . All that remains are, on the one hand, centres for power and decision making and, on the other, fake and artificial spaces. It is true, of course, that the city endures, but only as museum and as spectacle. The urban, conceived and lived as social practice, is in the process of deteriorating and perhaps disappearing.
>
> (Lefebvre, 1989 [2014:204])

We may tentatively agree that the urban does yet possess a centre, at once both 'the convergence and combination of goods and activities' (Schmid, 2012:48) and also hope that it is also playful, 'ludic', the inspiration of spontaneous action. That in difference occurs the interaction, clash, and development of 'very different worlds and value-systems, of ethnic, cultural and social groups, activities, and knowledge' (Schmid, 2012:48), 'consequentially creating our present urban areas highly dynamic, multifaceted and distinctive spaces with different cultural settings, that is, cultural assimilation, pluralism and multiculturalism' (Saha, 2022:1). But we might also believe that the distinction between centre and periphery that featured so prominently in Lefebvre's earlier writings on the urban may now be subject to discussion and review.

Centre and periphery, Lefebvre never lost sight of the importance of concepts fundamental to Marxism such as the division of labour, but he was always inclined to envisage the city as the motor of the dialectic:

> The city usurps the managing functions, and the latter becomes more refined within the urban framework: planning, administrative supervision, political orientation, relations with other territorial groups.
>
> (Lefebvre, 1966 [1968:43])

This was a role for the urban to which Lefebvre reverted often, for example his argument that the production of *new* social relations, how capitalism will be replaced, occurs 'in the everyday, in the urban and in space' (Lefebvre, 1973 [1976:14]). Hence the importance of urban space as a place of contradictory impulses and struggles:

> It is where contradictory strategies social representations engage with each other, an active support (inducing tensions, representations, practices, because it is replete with signs and symbols, intentional or not), produced, appropriated and transformed according to different interests, with conflicting values and ideas.
>
> (Busquet, 2012:3)

Crucially, however, before we succumb to the temptation to assign Lefebvre to an optimistic time for the Left now long past, the period in which Lefebvre perceived both a utopian critique of urbanism and the rise of an 'urban practice' that would build both literally and figuratively on these contradictions (Lefebvre, 1970 [2003:5)] to a more restrained evaluation was very brief: 'I think that after a brief period of hope in urbanism, disappointment was very rapid' (Lefebvre, 1975:244). 'Lefebvre's increasing pessimism results in the concept of utopia receding into the background in his later writings' (Guelf, 2010:294), a point that should lead us to question the extent to which 'urban society' is a transductive denial of the present reality and the assertion of its potential supplanter (Vasconcelos, 2019:161). No urban revolution now, then, but what?

Space at the centre of capitalism

Lefebvre's claims went as we have already seen much further than a rebalancing of Marxism between history and geography. His principal departure from a fundamentally historical approach is the dramatic assertion that 'capitalist spatial forms also develop at least partly to reproduce capitalist control, helping maintain the class relationships prevalent in capitalist society' (Gordon, 1978:27). Lefebvre's central insight is therefore not only to point to increased urbanism in a literal sense, true as it is, nor even to expand the concept of urbanism as he did, but rather also *to place the urban at the centre of the ability of capitalism to survive.*

His evaluation, certainly close to that of many real estate developers and investors, was that the urban fabric is a giant nexus of control, communication, construction, and capital, where industrial and agricultural production both have now been rendered subservient to capital accumulation through real estate. Lefebvre denies that urbanism is merely superstructural, or floating somehow independently, with only the faintest trace of interaction with the economic base. Rather, urbanism has become a force in production, akin to science and technology: a dialectical force, naturally – space and the political organisation of space express social relationships but also react back upon them (Lefebvre, 1970a). Space has dialectics at its core, in a way that conventional Marxist (and non-Marxist) analysis rejects when it is suggested that

> [u]rban structure is firstly a spatial mirror of society and its historical and organizational principles. That is, it reflects the previous and currently prevailing operating rules – of culture, technology, economy, and social behaviour – of the society within which the city has developed.
>
> (Bourne, 1982:6)

It is here, in this reformulation of urbanism as the driving force of capitalism, that Lefebvre seeks to break and then consolidate new ground. The transformation of capitalism from reliance on production into urban society had come about via the urbanisation of capital in the form of financial and property speculation, which had given rise to a second circuit of capital which has gradually come to dominate the interests of manufacturing capital (Harvey, 1978; Gotham, 2006):

> 'Real property' (along with construction) is no longer a secondary form of circulation, no longer the auxiliary and balanced branch of industry and financial capitalism that it once was. Instead, it has a leading role, albeit it in an uneven way, for its significance is liable to vary according to country, time or circumstance. The law of unevenness of growth and development so far from being obsolete is becoming worldwide in its application – or, more precisely is presiding over the globalisation of a world market.
>
> (Lefebvre, 1974 [1991:335])

In this way, Lefebvre deftly placed real estate at the centre of capitalism. There are surely many fewer now to argue with his contention than there were when he first did so.

The production of space

This new direction for Marxism is certainly to envisage the real estate sector as 'a conceptually separate and analytically distinct circuit of capital investment' (Gotham, 2009:359), but Lefebvre went further, suggesting that the very survival and development of capitalism rests upon its successful colonisation and reproduction of space (Lefebvre, 1973 [1976:21]). The explanation is that capitalism has run out of other options, even colonisation and imperialism, and now can only exist through turning inward on itself in this way, through the continued production of space. Without this ability, Lefebvre implies, capitalism would have stumbled, at least, and may have already been overthrown. Lefebvre even insists that the spatialisation of political theory, and a reconsideration of the economy in terms of the reproduction of social space, explains the survival of capitalism, which has not only subordinated exterior and anterior sectors to itself, but also *produced* new sectors (Lefebvre, 1973 [1976:83]). It also explains the main direction of the state in the 20th century (Lefebvre, 1978a:165), which even if not completely true, could certainly not be said to be less accurate in the succeeding century. It might not even be going too far as to suggest that the success of sophisticated 21st-century states can be measured by their effectiveness in controlling not only their own social space, but that of other states, a point that, perhaps keen to avoid falling into yet another arena of debate, the question of how state power deploys internationally, Lefebvre leaves largely untouched. Certainly, in the 21st century, the role of the state in the creation and ownership of abstract space is now thoroughly internationalised, as investments made by Sovereign Wealth Funds amply demonstrate, for example in London (Ward *et al.*, 2022).

This new colonisation, of the everyday, and of space, explains how 'capitalism has held its own, has transformed itself more than we were told it would, that is, there has been a growth of productive forces' (Lefebvre, 1980:28). It is precisely for this reason that the evolution of the urban fabric is central to the future of capitalism, and, from a Marxist standpoint, to a better eventual future without capitalism altogether. So even as the revolutionary promise of the 1960s gave way to a more doubt-ridden and contemplative 1970s, Lefebvre therefore proceeded to theorise space itself, especially *the production of space* – the title of his most well-known book (Lefebvre, 1974 [1991]). He recognised, as real estate developers also do, that as the intensity of capitalist development grows, so the transformation of space and the location of activities within urban locations become increasingly commodified (Parker, 2015:20). Lefebvre's observations as to the intervention by capitalism in physical space are therefore recognisable by any developer, but Lefebvre's aim was much more encompassing than simply to point to the capitalist commercialisation of space.

He pointed in particular to the fact, taken for granted by real estate developers at least until they run across obstacles in execution, that in capitalist societies 'geographical space is "spatialised" as lots – always owned by someone. Hence a privatised notion of space anchors the understanding of property which is a central feature of all capitalist societies' (Shields, 2011:282), Lefebvre's argument went further:

> Space is divided into plots that can be bought and sold. Their prices depend on a hierarchy. In this way, even as it is homogenized, social space is also fragmented among spaces of work, nature, material production, and diverse services, and along with social classes are hierarchised as they are inscribed into space – this tendency is increasing rather than, as is often claimed, diminishing.
>
> (Lefebvre, 1989 [2014:205])

Real estate developers therefore do not just reflect social and economic stratification, or work within preordained boundaries of space and time – they can and do create it. Lefebvre's theory therefore aimed to transcend both traditional physical conceptions of space, such as size, height, or density, and legal concepts, such as plots, boundaries, and easements. Rather, the essence of the city is determined by 'the quality of active, everyday processes of interaction' (Schmid, 2012:49). Lefebvre adopts what he describes as the regressive–progressive method:

> The production of space, having attained the conceptual and linguistic level, acts retroactively upon the past, disclosing aspects and moments of it hitherto uncomprehended. The past appears in a different light, and hence the process whereby that past becomes the present also takes on another aspect.
>
> (Lefebvre, 1974 [1991:66])

It is no surprise to learn that he does not regard space as either neutral or passive; it is produced and reproduced, and in a capitalist society, divided by and into socio-economic classes, it becomes a – arguably even the central – location of conflict and struggle. Moreover, the whole range of different spatial phenomena – region, land, territory, sites, now we should say also real estate itself – should be understood as part of the same process of specific spatialisation. As Rob Shields said more than two decades ago, Lefebvre's understanding of space is moreover both holistic and inclusive: we should not, and anyway cannot, conceive of social space as some kind of object, a something that can be viewed from 'outside', still less viewed in some sense 'objectively'.

> By stressing that we are inside, partaking of the process of production of space, Lefebvre moves the analysis of space from the synchronic discourses 'on' space (such as the sociological notion of territoriality) to the analysis of the processes by which discourses 'of' space are socially produced'.
>
> (Shields, 1999:46)

Lefebvre concluded: 'Summarised: space always appears dynamic and processual; it cannot be conceived of generally, but the conceptualisation is always specific as to a time, site and society; it contains many "moments" that cannot be conflated, and emphasises the becoming, the future' (Lehtovuori, 2010:5–6).

It must however be emphasised that for Lefebvre, sceptical of the structuralist and postmodern tendencies in the contemporary French philosophy, space is not just conceptual, a product of knowledge. As a Marxist, he professes an explicitly materialist ontology (Pierce & Martin, 2015:1283), but he is also a dialectician: rejecting what has been termed the paradigm of 'containerism', which presupposes that 'space is essentially empty and static, a passive and inert vessel' (Dimendberg, 1998:19), and refuting the contention that Marxism has nothing more to say than that 'Space is a social product; society is spatially constituted' (Goonewardena, 2011:55), Lefebvre conceives of space as both produced by capitalism and in turn contributing to the shaping of capitalist relations of production: 'The production of space is not just another type of production, it adds something decisive to production, it is also the reproduction of the relations of production' (Lefebvre, 1975:227). Other radical geographers agreed that

> [t]he structure of organized space is not a separate structure with its own autonomous laws of construction and transformation, nor is it simply an expression of the class structure emerging from the social (i.e., aspatial) relations of production. It represents, instead, a dialectically defined component of the general relations of production, relations which are simultaneously social and spatial.
>
> (Soja, 1980:208)

Hence Lefebvre's assertion that 'Social relations, which are concrete abstractions, have no real existence save in and through space. Their underpinning is spatial' (Lefebvre, 1974 [1991:404]). Space similarly is a 'concrete abstraction', both a field of action and a basis of action (Lefebvre, 1974 [1991:191], and therefore bearing the same paradoxical qualities of 'being', as commodity and labour held for Marx, in that it is both an object and the condition of its creation (Stanek, 2011:145). Like Marx too, these views Lefebvre then consistently maintained, however much doubt he or others had over the agency of the urban to effect radical change. It is at this point where the signal importance of real estate development for Lefebvre becomes clear: Marxists should take it very seriously indeed.

Until now, even if they might have been surprised by the extent of his claims, real estate developers might be forgiven for thinking that Lefebvre has done little more than some much needed but relatively uncontroversial theoretical rebalancing within Marxism. They may still wonder, to be brutally honest about the matter, what it has to do with them. So far, however, Lefebvre had confined himself to space in general, but his theory will not rest there.

Bad space, good space

Much more of a leap of faith for developers will be what follows: his identification of two main interrelated frameworks. First is an at least partially teleological categorisation of space, dividing it first into jagged and intermeshing periods of absolute, sacred, historical, abstract, contradictory, and then differential space that for Lefebvre at least partially replace the traditional Marxist historical periods, feudalism, capitalism, and even socialism. What Lefebvre was attempting with this triad should not be underestimated, as it 'reconstructed the orthodox teleology of modes of production – primitive communism, slavery, feudalism, capitalism, socialism – into his evolution of space – absolute, historical, abstract and differential' (Smith, 2003:ix).

Abstract space – the silent jailor

Absolute, sacred, and historical space are associated with previous epochs: what capitalism produces – especially in the contemporary urban fabric – is abstract space.

> The state determines and congeals the decision-making centres. At the same time, space is distributed into peripheries which are hierarchised in relation to the centres; it is atomised. Colonisation, which like industrial production and consumption was formerly localised, is made general. Around the centres there are nothing but subjected, exploited and dependent spaces: neo-colonial spaces.
>
> (Lefebvre, 1973 [1976:84–85])

The important point that Lefebvre makes is that the way both the private sector and state actors think, plan, and act about space is according to (in Marxist terms) its *abstract* qualities, that is, in terms of profit rather than use (Trebitsch, 2002 [2014:673]) Abstract space is where capitalist value predominantly resides and is created, and where as a result of the inconsistency between capital and genuine humanity, truly human values such as freedom and justice are prevented from development or, in the worst case, even denied altogether. In the recent past, and notwithstanding that we should not identify it with its physical manifestations, it pervaded glistening office blocks, as depicted in the pathbreaking and well-known, yet still rare, crossover work between real estate analysis and urban theory, *Towers of Capital* (Lizieri, 2009), although it has been suggested that more recently, private expensive residences are probably its most spectacular achievements (Fernandez *et al.*, 2016; Forrest *et al.*, 2017; Goldman & Narayan, 2021).

Lefebvre also added vertebrae to the spine of his argument: both that 'there must be a concerted attempt to define the appropriate meaning of, and suitable activities that can take place within, abstract space' (McCann, 1999:169), and that 'Abstract space works in a highly complex way. It has something of a dialogue about it, in that it implies a tacit agreement, a non-aggression pact, a contract, as it were, of non-violence' (Lefebvre, 1974 [1991:56]), as well as being attempting to present itself as ahistorical, 'a space from which all previous histories have been erased' (Gregory, 1994:366) and therefore possessed of a timeless, perpetual quality, at least in its own eyes. Erased by the power of the state, Lefebvre had in mind:

> It is above all the state that represents the complex, polymorphic social spaces of modern capitalism as if they were transparent, self-evident and pregiven. By projecting this 'illusory clarity of space' throughout society as a whole, the state attempts at once to manipulate political-economic relations more effectively and to mask its own pervasive role in such interventions.
>
> (Brenner & Elden, 2009:372)

It is scarcely difficult to conceive of tensions between abstract and social space more broadly, most obviously through the creation of abstract reservoirs of value that may clash with existing social space, such as the *favelas*, or even cherished old village spaces, which create little value and may not conform with HBU. Lefebvre argued that the production of abstract space is in the dominant class interests, with the inevitable consequence that

> [m]any people, members of a variety of groups and classes, suffer (albeit unevenly) the effects of a multiplicity of reductions bearing on their capacities, ideas, 'values' and, ultimately, on their possibilities, their space and their bodies.
>
> (Lefebvre, 1974 [1991:106])

Further, Lefebvre contented, the conflict between abstract and social space is a basic one in society apart from that between classes. So, 'he departs from the Marxian perspective that holds class conflict as the basic force in the history of capitalism' (Chakrabati, 2013). Quite a claim, if true. But these are different claims: to accept the former does not entail that we should try to evade Lefebvre's belief – shared by many – that 'capitalism is the main obstacle to just and inclusive urban development because it is fundamentally extractive in character and inhibits the state from taking the bold redistributive actions required to overcome urban poverty, exclusion and inequality' (Turok & Scheba, 2019:496).

For Lefebvre, the experience of abstract space is not simply a manifestation of alienation, although he viewed the urban, and originally cities themselves as 'simultaneously, the realm in which and the means through which the alienation of the 20th century takes form' (Basta, 2017:349). *Abstract space is itself a commodity*. In so being, it at least in theory reflects the abstract and concrete aspects of labour by which it is produced, and in particular, the systems of representation and procedures by which it is quantified, divided, measured and compared (Stanek, 2011:152). This marks a clear differentiation between space and time, although the opportunity to draw parallels remains. 'For Lefebvre, space of capitalism is not just commodified, but commodification becomes the operational logics of spatial practices' (Stanek, 2011:155). 'Space-become-commodity develops the traits of commodities in space to the maximum' (Lefebvre, 1974 [1991:351]). Gone, in this vision, are, or at least should be, traditional concepts of place, replaced by homogeneous yet fragmented blocks that together form a market of space. And of course, Lefebvre and those who have sought to interpret him agree with Marxists generally, as well as many others, that 'Left unchecked, a market and for-profit system always and everywhere flourishes through the abstract conceived realm' (Lefebvre, 1974 [1991:90]). And it is the State that drives this process: Lefebvre's suggestion is that

> [the] State engenders social relations in space; it reaches still further as it unfurls; it produces a support, its own space, which is itself complex. This space regulates and organizes a disintegrating national space at the heart of a consolidating worldwide space (*l'espace mondial*).
>
> (Lefebvre, 1978 [2009:225])

'Abstract space is, in short, the political product of state spatial strategies – of administration, repression, domination and centralized power' (Brenner & Elder, 2009:359). It is violent and expansive. For Lefebvre integrationists, abstract space is in the service of the state means of production, where historically, 'The outcome has been an authoritarian and brutal spatial practice, whether Haussmann's or the later, codified versions of the Bauhaus or Le Corbusier' (Lefebvre, 1974 [1991:10]). Adding an additional category, Lefebvre suggests that the crisis of the cities is 'conflicted space': the result of an increasingly challenged abstract space facing its dissolution as a result of urbanism which he claims has become the result of a 'bureaucratic society of controlled consumption' and thus disconnected from all human needs (Lefebvre, 1970 [2003:164]). Developers might find the suggested chaos and uncertainty all too familiar.

Differential space – escape to freedom

Finally, and crucially I shall argue for real estate development, there is *differential space*, which, it was said, was Lefebvre's code for socialism (Smith, 2003:xiv), and perhaps later, at least for democracy (Purcell, 2022:3041), and in both cases at the very least is its necessary prerequisite. As recognised by Neil Smith, Lefebvre did not argue that the supersession of industrialisation by urbanisation 'marks the transitional moment from abstract to differential space' (Smith, 2003:xix) – there is nothing teleological about his approach, no inevitability and not even a tightly structured direction of travel – but what he did believe was that it created the *opportunity* for the creation of differential space, a hope shared by others (e.g. Berman, 2006). Lefebvre was insistent Marxism could or should ever be allowed to fall into the historicist trap: as the proponent of 'a heterodox and open-ended historical materialism that is committed to an embodied, passionately engaged, and politically charged form of critical knowledge' (Kipfer *et al.*, 2008:3), Lefebvre's animosity towards any historicist theory or one that attempted to impose any formal future social or even economic structure was clear; his view that Marx 'conceived of a path, not a model' (Lefebvre, 1970 [2003:110]) has been well noted (Charnock, 2010:1286).

But Lefebvre's reasoning was that abstract space necessarily contains contradictions, both theoretically, between form and content, quality and quantity, and more fundamentally on the traditional Marxist tension between use and exchange values translated into spatial terms, that is, between the homogenising and abstract character of exchange value, on the one hand, and the localised and concrete character of use-values, on the other hand, a climactic fight between good and evil that carries the potential, at least, to lead to differentiated space (Lefebvre, 1974 [1991:358]). 'The resulting "contradictory space" contains within it the seeds of a postcapitalist ("differential") space in which the debilitating divisions and homogenizations of abstract space are transcended' (Sayer, 1993:458). 'The formation of spaces of difference, or differential space, thus represents for capitalism an antagonistic and ruinous tendency' (Morton, 2018:127). No doubt, but it is worth noting that whilst Lefebvre readily admitted that a contemporary revolution would involve confrontation, especially in relation to the divided interests of multiple groups in the environment (Lefebvre, 1974 [1991:422]), he never actually said that a process of violent struggle is required in order to produce differential space, although that is specifically how he has been interpreted (McCann, 1999:181). In fact, in accordance with his view of Marxism as a whole, he left the process of how abstract space could be transcended quite open.

The wisdom of so doing is exemplified by what now appears to be a nascent debate in recent Lefebvre scholarship, where the argument for democracy is made via a proposal to revise Lefebvre's conception of differential space. No longer, it has now been suggested, should it be envisaged as a reaction to thwart the strategies, plans, and programmes of the State to create abstract space, taking the form of grassroots opposition, counter-plans, and counter-projects (Lefebvre, 1974 [1991:383]), a view to which Lefebvre scholars have largely adhered, even to the extent of formulating it diagrammatically (e.g. Leary-Owhin, 2016:7). On the contrary, heterodox Marxist thought he may be, 'this way of thinking about differential space is the product of a very orthodox and very Hegelian habit of thought that lingers in Lefebvre's political imagination' (Purcell, 2022:3049). Purcell suggests that it should be revised in favour of a positive conception of differential space, closely associated with a citizens' movement towards democracy, a 'new contract' of the kind that the later Lefebvre espoused (Lefebvre, 1990:27). Perhaps Lefebvre is to meet his Bernstein after all.

But if differential space does not merely flow from the street in a facsimile of a traditional revolution with an urban twist, we are left with important practical questions: How is differential space to be identified? Who creates it? How can it endure under capitalism? Even, what is it, beyond a formula such as 'the concentrated interaction of people, ideas and materials' (Thompson, 2017:107)? Lefebvre avoids answering these questions too, and for the same reasons.

The theory, however, extends deeper. The second aspect of Lefebvre's theory of space is an epistemological framework, the spatial triad, often held to be the core of his theory (Shields, 1999; Elden, 2004; Merrifield, 2006; Schmid, 2012) and which – developers might want to be warned – 'is cited so extensively that many scholars have a stake in defending its continued importance' (Pierce & Martin, 2015:1280). The triad is meant to convey that

> space has a complex character and enters social relations levels. It is at once a physical environment that can be perceived; a semiotic abstraction that informs both how ordinary people negotiate space (the mental maps studied by geographers) and the space of corporations, planners, politicians, and the like; and a medium through which the body lives out its life in interaction.
>
> (Gottdiener, 1993:131)

Lefebvre's response is to constitute three moments in social space that act upon each other, the conceptual, linguistic-semiotic triad of *perceived*, *conceived*, and *lived* space. Social space as a whole can be envisaged, relatively intuitively for a developer, as the interactively used space of everyday life, to be contrasted to physical and mental space more narrowly.

> The form of social space is encounter, assembly, simultaneity. But what assembles, or what is assembled? The answer is: everything that there is in space, everything that is produced either by nature or by society, either through their cooperation or through their conflicts. Everything: living beings, things, objects, works, signs, and symbols.
>
> (Lefebvre, 1974 [1991:101])

Amongst these three terms, however, the third term of lived space is balanced carefully between the two poles of conceived space (idealism) and perceived space (materialism). It embodies both elements without being reducible to either of the other two (Zhang, 2006:221). In this way, conceived, perceived, and lived spaces form a unity, overlapping, not juxtaposing, one another (Zhang, 2006:222; KIngma *et al.*, 2018:4). Lefebvre is fond of triads: this conceptual triad is then further translated into what has been described as a phenomenological triad of *spatial practices*, *representations of space*, and *spaces of representation* (Lefebvre, 1974 [1991:33–39]; Ghulyan, 2019:4; Goonewardena, 2011:57). This is where the developer might recognise parallels in their own practice.

Spatial practices include production, consumption, and the formation of capital, all set in particular locations and spatial sets associated with the development reached by each society (Unwin, 2000:16). Spatial practices range from individual and group practices to the planning system of zones and regions, where space takes on physical form, what a developer might call real space, space that is generated and used (Elden, 2004:190). Lefebvre recognised that inevitably, spatial practices are over time manifested, developed, and contested in the built environment and in the landscape. Arguably, the most significant spatial practices in a capitalist economy and society are those of property and other forms of capital, to which mobility has for many decades been recognised as an essential complement (Urry, 2004:25), and to which may now be cautiously added aspects of virtual reality. Together, they 'structure daily life and a broader urban reality' (Merrifield, 1993:524). Concretely, Lefebvre wants us to understand spatial practices as depicting and enabling us to understand the way in which people are placed and move in space: he cites the daily routine of a state-subsidised block of rental flats on a housing estate as an example of a 'modern' spatial practice produced by a capitalist society and the supposed rationality of planning (Lehtovuori, 2016) – 'This routine consists of forced movement between the home, workplace and the children's day-care centre' (Lefebvre, 1974 [1991:38])' It is not, he implies, what a truly free person would choose.

> Spatial practice, which embraces production and reproduction, and the particular locations and spatial sets characteristic of each social formation. Spatial practice ensures continuity and some degree of cohesion. In terms of social space, and of each member of a given society's relationship to that space, this cohesion implies a guaranteed level of competence and a specific level of performance.
>
> (Lefebvre, 1974 [1991:33])

As a result, 'We need to "know" space, how to navigate, be in and negotiate relations in space in a coherent and consistent way to make sense and function in the world' (Zieleniec, 2018:6).

Representations of space (Nicolson translates as 'representational spaces' but Harvey and Shields suggest the former) constitute the forms of knowledge and practices that organise and represent space, particularly through the techniques of planning and the state, for example, monuments at the heart of the city (Bevan, 2022). This is the space of savoir (knowledge) and logic, of maps, mathematics, of space as the instrumental space of social engineers and urban planners, that is, space as a mental construct, imagined space (Elden, 2004:190). These representations are not in any way neutral or merely technical: they are on the contrary tied to the relations of production and to the 'order' which those relations impose, and hence to knowledge, to signs, to codes, and to 'frontal' relations (Lefebvre, 1974 [1991:33]). For Lefebvre, these representations of space belong to 'scientists, planners, urbanists, technocratic sub-dividers and social engineers . . . the dominant space of any society (or mode of production)' (Lefebvre, 1974 [1991:38–39]), and are explicit, visual representations of conceived space, analogous to the concept of space in Euclidean geometry, for which Lefebvre holds no special respect. This is not to suggest that Lefebvre had the last word in depicting conceived space: far from it. Others who followed (Soja, 1996) portrayed it as 'the dominant space in any society' (Taylor & Helfenbein, 2009:321).

For all those who broadly subscribe to the Lefebvrian understanding of space, representational space is not politically neutral: it both encompasses and insists upon structure, stratification, and social classes. Those who create, justify, manipulate, protect, and venerate representational space are as a result accomplices in the global domination of space by capital: 'for Lefebvre, those who conceive space and represent it in maps, diagrams, plans, models, images etc., reflect how power creates dominant discourses through the ways in which space is surveyed, surveilled, controlled, delimited, delineated and organised to meet particular ends' (Zieleniec, 2018:6). Hence the assertion, for example, that 'Australian suburbia embodies both an ensemble of representations of space, imposed through the planning, administration and legal regulation of the city, and a collection of constitutive, everyday spatial practices' (Butler, 2005:13). Many of these are today embedded in computer-assisted design (CAD) and geographic information systems (GIS), both often confined to the work of specialists and therefore as hidden from public view as much or even more than their paper predecessors.

Representational space, or spaces of representation – a difference in emphasis – is the third term of the triad. These are collective (and in fact also individual) dynamic experiences of space, which Lefebvre describes as

> embodying complex symbolisms, sometimes coded, sometimes not, linked to the clandestine or underground side of social life, as also to art (which may come eventually to be defined less as a code of space than as a code of representational spaces).
>
> (Lefebvre, 1974 [1991:33])

Lefebvre argues that this is 'space as directly lived through its associations and images and symbols, and hence the space of "inhabitants" and "users"' (Lefebvre, 1974 [1991:39]). It is 'space as produced and modified over time and through its use, spaces invested with symbolism and meaning, the space of *connaissance* (less formal or more local forms of knowledge), space as both real-and-imagined' (Elden, 2004:190). It has been described as what is in effect the production of meaning: 'imaginary landscapes, and material constructs such as symbolic spaces, particular built environments, museums, etc.) that imagine new meanings or possibilities for spatial practices' (Harvey, 1989:218–219), which is perhaps a somewhat more optimistic formulation than Lefebvre's own:

> This is the dominated – and hence passively experienced – space which the imagination seeks to change and appropriate. It overlays physical space, making symbolic use of its objects.
>
> (Lefebvre, 1974 [1991:39])

Both Lefebvre and more traditional Marxist geographers agree on the crucial importance of domination and appropriation as the forms of power, and resistance to power, that produce and transform space (Lefebvre, 1974 [1991:343]). Sadly, in a capitalist society, people must live in and through space made and controlled by others (those with power to shape, form and represent to us its appropriate use) and which they then have to navigate to make 'sense' of and function in the world (Zieleniec, 2018:6). Domination and appropriation may be contradictory – a project destroying an established neighbourhood, for example – but they also depend on each other (Lefebvre, 1974 [1991:164–166]). In the opinion of one reviewer, this was a master distinction: between those who produce a space for domination and those who produce space as an appropriation to serve human need. In domination, space is put to the service of some abstract purpose (Molotch, 1993:889).

	Spatial Practice	*Representations of Space*	*Spaces of Representation*
	L'espace perçu Perceived Physical Materialist	*L'espace conçu* Conceived Mental Idealist	*L'espace veçu* Lived Social Both materialist and idealist
Subjects	Members of society, family, social classes	Experts: scientists, planners, architects, technocrats, social engineers	Inhabitants and users who both passively consume space and act to influence it
Objects	The physical world, places, and their interrelationships, urban transport routes and networks, places that relate the global to the local, commoditised spaces of everyday life, desirable and undesirable spaces	Knowledge, signs, codes, images, theory, ideology, plans, power, maps, CAD, GIS, transportation and communications systems, abstract space (privatised places, boundaries, land plots and rights, markets, spaces of labour and capital), online representations, and places of abstract space	Social life, art, culture, symbols, systems of non-verbal communication, signs, images, memories, online spaces of freedom and collaboration
Activities	Perceiving, daily routines, production, reproduction of social relations	Conceiving, calculation, planning, representation, design, construction	Living, everyday life and activities, social action, and transformation

Source: Adapted from Elden (2007:110) and Fuchs (2019:137).

To recap: Stanek very usefully summed up the way successive interpreters of Lefebvre all agreed on the core of his theory (Stanek, 2011:129). Shields defined Lefebvre's spatial practices as the 'perceived space' (*'le percu'*) of everyday social life and commonsensical perception, which blends popular action and outlook, but was often ignored in the professional, and theoretical 'conceived space' (*'le concu'*) of cartographers, urban planners, property speculators, or other experts, which were representations of space 'discourses on space'; or the discursive regimes of analysis, spatial and planning professions and expert knowledge that conceives of space (*i'espace conçu*), and finally, the spaces of representation as 'discourses of space', space as it might be, fully lived space (*l'espace veçu*), the social imaginary, in which the person who is fully human (*l'homme totale*) kept alive in large measure by the arts and literature. Others had already created a tradition of reflection on the role of 'human space', notably Bollnow (1963), but 'Lefebvre writes on the same subject from a premise that could not be more different' (Kohlmaier & Bollnow, 1963 [2011:311]), that is, an inescapably political one. For Lefebvre, this 'third' space not only transcends but has the power to refigure the balance of popular 'perceived space' and official 'conceived space' (Shields, 1999:160, 2001:230). Elden agrees, identifying perceived space with the physical, conceived with the mental and imagined, and lived as that which is modified in everyday life, in turn forming the basis for the conceptual triad of spatial practice, representations of space, and spaces of representation (Elden, 2004:190). This Lefebvrian schema sees a unity between physical, mental, and social space, and Merrifield's approach was also close, arguing that spatial practices 'secrete' society's space and have close affinities with perceived space, representations of space are conceptualisations, conceived space, and spaces of representation are the lived spaces of everyday life (Merrifield, 2006:109–110).

To these can be added Schmid's summary: 'The theory of production of space therefore includes, at core, a three-dimensional process – first, material production; second, the production of knowledge; third, the production of meaning' (Schmid, 2012:52). Schmid points to the adoption of insights, at the very least – critics called them distortions of Marxism – from different sources to assist in this theoretical rebirth of Marxism – linguistic theory (Lefebvre, 1966; Kelly, 2000:96), even debts to Sartre and beyond (Lefebvre, 1965 [2016:70]; Goonewardena, 2011:57).

It is worth observing *en passant* that Lefebvre's trifurcation of space is not the only attempt to establish a theoretical division of space. Perhaps there is only 'space per se, or contextual space, and socially based spatiality, the created space of social organization and production' (Soja, 1980:209). Or perhaps we should

> place the threefold division of absolute, relative and relational space-time up against the tripartite division of experienced, conceptualized and lived space identified by Lefebvre. The result is a three-by-three matrix within which points of intersection suggest different modalities of understanding the meanings of space (and time).
>
> (Harvey, 2006:133)

These approaches may also offer valuable perspectives for developers if they can usefully complement the identification and production of differential space.

Lefebvre's sense of history

Lefebvre considered himself a sociologist by profession, albeit others saw in him a philosopher or an urbanist, so in principle at least he sought to temper Marxist enthusiasm for radical change by applying the lessons he believed he had learned from the observation of everyday life to the production of space. His forthright condemnation of the new post-war housing estates in France, illustrated by his study of Mourenx, where, he claimed, 'the new working class' is engaged in a struggle of immense importance against the scourges of the modern world: boredom, the monotony of work, and the order of the functional, bureaucratic city (Lefebvre, 1960:201; Harvey, 2010:149–150), was derived from his ideological hostility towards state-led urbanism (Stanek, 2011:106). In Mourenx, 'objects wear their social credentials, their function. Every object has its use, and declares it' (Lefebvre, 1962 [1995:119], 1965).

> Lefebvre read the social text of the new town as a metaphor for more global transformations of capitalist modernity – the concretisation of abstract space and the colonisation of everyday life through which capitalism has achieved sustained growth, displacing its internal contradictions and ensuring its continued survival. Through this process, the symbolic richness and creative autonomy of daily life are progressively eviscerated and replaced by the homogenisation and fragmentation of a technocratic rationality projected onto reality through the planned production of space.
>
> (Wilson, 2011:997–998)

For Lefebvre, modernity was 'the abstraction which rides roughshod over everyday life' (Lefebvre, 1962 [1995:120]). He contrasted this to the 'the slow evolution, intimacy and community spirit of the historic town of Navarrenx, which was small enough to have a caring familiarity and comfort but large enough to be "urban" and therefore different from the surrounding rural areas' (Leary-Unwin, 2018:2). The aesthetic, even moral, disparity between the two shines through clearly enough in Lefebvre's contrast: but developers might then ask, what is to be done? Historic towns cannot by definition be built overnight. Later chapters will return to this Lefebvrian paradox.

Lefebvre has also been held up as an environmentalist, acutely sensitive to the ecological imperative in Marx's work that has now been elucidated so thoroughly (Saito, 2017). He 'saw the sociohistorical stage as a struggle over the creation of a space for culture-ecology independent of and transcending the driving force of accumulation – conceiving this as an issue not just of life, but of survival' (Foster *et al.*, 2020:37). Lefebvre warned repeatedly of what he described as 'terricide', the self-destruction of the Earth (Lefebvre, 1978 [2003:278]). Even towards the end of his life, he never veered from the conviction that capitalism is an alienating system that generates 'conflicting dualities of production and destruction, with increasing priority for the destructive capacity that comes at its peak and is raised to a world scale' (Lefebvre, 1992 [2004:55]). Yet he was also realistic enough to recognise consistently that to 'stop growth purely and simply? It's impossible. What is needed is to orient it by reducing it; it must be oriented towards qualitative social development' (Lefebvre, 1973b:17).

The right to the city

So, how did it all turn out in practice? To be sure, it all started with great promise. The bright Lefebvrian slogan '*The Right to the City*' (Lefebvre, 1968 [1996]) found its calling in the disruptive year of its publication, which began in France with such optimism for the Left and ended in disappointment and recriminations. Lefebvre's prose soared above the crisis:

> [T]he right to the city is like a cry and a demand. This right slowly meanders through the surprising detours of nostalgia and tourism, the return to the heart of the traditional city, and the call of existent or recently developed centralities.
>
> (Lefebvre, 1968 [1996:158])

Lefebvre's nostalgia, much in evidence, even though he claimed that the right to the city 'cannot be conceived of as a simple visiting right or as a return to traditional cities. It can only be formulated as a transformed and renewed right to urban life' (Lefebvre, 1968 [1996:158]). His Eurocentrism meshes with this conception of right, and some have even suggested that Lefebvre's notion of the right to the city, although not rooted in 19th-century metropolitan street life, relies on a strategy to rescue historical forms (Kipfer & Goonewardena, 2007), the cities of the Italian Renaissance (Harvey, 2000:183), or the festivity of rural Southern France (Meyer, 1973), where in an apparently idyllic life,

> [e]veryone brought a contribution to the communal meal. Each village constituted a community: a large family of people linked by blood, a way of life, and also by a practical discipline and a fairly strict collection organization of work.
>
> (Lefebvre, 1947 [2014:227])

Enthusiasts for the concept have suggested that the right to the city manifests itself in a range of different individual rights: to freedom, to express oneself as an individual, to insist on difference, fully to inhabit a place, almost as if capitalism, and its constraints on space no longer existed. For, as opposed to mere habitat,

> [h]abitating is therefore a more 'authentic' act of place-making, a lived experience . . . one which is not imposed by authoritarian (global) powers which implement some kind of market or statist 'urban rationality', but rather generated by the agency of individuals.
>
> (Davidson, 2007:492)

He continued to insist even when his confidence in urban revolution had been eclipsed within postmodernity, 'Occupation by financial interests and private property signify control – that is to say, the end of the freedom that is indispensable to full enjoyment' (Lefebvre, 1981 [2014:800]). Of the many claims that the right to the city encompasses, arguably the three most important claims relate to habitation (to live in the city and use its facilities), appropriation (to take full advantage of its economic opportunities), and participation (to influence its form and operation) (Lefebvre, 1968 [1996]; Purcell, 2014), but also as equality:

> On the one hand, it affirmed the right of 'users' to decide on the space and time of their activities in the urban territory; and moreover, the right to use the centre, a privileged place, instead of being dispersed, driven back into ghettos (for workers, for immigrants, for those on the margins, and even for the privileged!)
>
> (Lefebvre, 1991 [2000:34])

These rights, both collectively and individually, represent a challenge to private to property rights and serve as mechanisms for struggling against the dominance of private capital and market values over urban land. In this fashion, Lefebvre envisaged the 'right to the city' as part of the global project to dismantle capitalism, brick by brick, because of its inherent exploitative and exclusionary character, and its failure to give ordinary people a proper stake in the city. He believed that equitable cities require transforming the fundamental structures of society into a quite different, fairer system (Harvey, 2008; Marcuse *et al.* (eds.), 2009; Purcell, 2014). The right to the *oeuvre*, participation, and appropriation (clearly distinct from the right to property) are implied in the right to the city (Lefebvre, 1968 [1996:141]).

> These rights would change reality if they entered into social practice: right to work, to training and education, to health, housing, leisure, to life. Among these fights in the making features the right to the city, not to the ancient city, but to urban life, to renewed centrality, to places of encounter and exchange, to life rhythms and time uses, enabling the full and complete usage of these moments and places.
>
> (Lefebvre, 1968 [1996:179])

And for Lefebvre, 'rights are always the outcome of political struggle. They are the manifestation, the end result of collective claims made by mobilized citizens' (Purcell, 2014:146). As a result, 'For Lefebvre, the right to the city will be not achieved until city dwellers – the people – do not reappropriate an essential quality of city life: urban centrality' (Van Criekingen & Breës, 2012). We must now wonder, even if we can properly explain what this means, how will it be achieved, and by whom.

Yet Lefebvre did not envisage the right to the city as just a distant dream, as radical geographers also in practice do not, as

> this urban citizenship has a specifically spatial component: it can be attained only through action over the space devoted to the production of the city-oeuvre. Urban citizenship must be won. The right to urban citizenship can be gained only through collective and self-organized action; it is inherently active.
>
> (Chiodelli, 2013:490–491)

The 'right to the city implies nothing less than a revolutionary concept of citizenship' (Lefebvre, 1989 [2014:205]). All these are processes necessary to bring about the city, itself never static, that Lefebvre captures in the complex notion of the 'right to the city' (Huchzermeyer, 2018:635–636).

Subsequently, the right to the city has been variously theorised (Attoh, 2011), often less optimistically and frequently diluted in the process. Depending on authorial inclinations, political sympathies, and contemporary focus, it has been seen as a right to occupy and reimagine public space (Mitchell, 2003; Vasudevan, 2015), or a right to housing, interlinked with the squatting movement (Holm & Kuhn, 2011), informal settlements that potentially override legal claims to land (Bouwmeester & Hartmann, 2021:102966), or individual rights such as to public transport (Keblowski *et al.*, 2019) or natural resources such as water (e.g. Roy, 2013). Others (e.g. Mitchell & Heynen, 2009) have seen the right to the city as a right against new and multiplying forms of urban revanchism (low-hanging fruit here including police brutality and state surveillance) and as a right to the use and redistribution of urban surpluses (Harvey, 2008).

What is left of the right to the city?

It has been claimed that Lefebvre's slogans, 'urban revolution' and 'right to the city' 'endure as visionary democratic ideals' (Merrifield, 2006:xxv). But is this really so? 'His call inspired a wealth of social action to strengthen the contract between cities and citizens, and a rich debate by leading academics such as David Harvey. Nevertheless, how to implement the concept remained vague' (Brown, 2010:3). Summarising what they regard as the dismal trajectory of the concept, Tavolari (2020:483) mentions critics who have 'the right to the city was felt to have become an 'empty signifier' (Harvey, 2012:xv), 'a vague, non-specific concept' (Fainstein, 2009:27), slightly more generously a conceptual 'umbrella', (Schmid, 2012:42), a 'vortex' (Kuymulu, 2013:923), or, or most bluntly, a catchphrase (Purcell, 2002:100). For

> the World Charter for the Right to the City seems to include so many rights – to cultural memory, telecommunications, retraining, day care, the removal of architectural barriers, and so forth – that the right to the city seems to be at the same time everything and nothing.
>
> (Purcell, 2014:141)

As a result, there is still uncertainty as to what the slogan means.

> But what's behind these four words that sound like a constitutional claim? A legal right? A right for all to live in the city, to be understood as a right for all to have a home? Or a right of access to the services that the city offers? Or rather, a right for all to reclaim the city?
>
> (Inter-Environnement-Bruxelles, 2012:2)

When their voices have been heard in the debate, Marxists have emphasised that commodification objectives in the housing sector have profoundly affected the acknowledgement of the 'right to housing' (Brenner *et al.*, 2012; Harvey, 2012), but they would also agree that

> [t]he right to the city is not users claiming more access to and control over the existing capitalist city, a bigger slice of the existing pie. Instead, it is a movement to go beyond the existing city, to cultivate the urban so that it can grow and spread.
>
> (Purcell, 2014:150)

It has always been contentious: The 'freedom to make and remake our cities' (argued by David Harvey) is much more than just a right to visit or stay in the city. It inevitably challenges the right of property as the basic legal framework for urban redevelopment. Second is the proposal of 'a common rather than an individual right': This argument inevitably challenges the idea of the individual as foundation for legal rights and property (Brown, 2010:2.10).

Although the need to press further has long been recognised, especially by Marxists, the question of the right to the city however cannot be dissociated from a radical critique of the production of space, daily life, and the state (Garnier & Goldschmidt, 1978).

> [F]or Lefebvre there is a surfeit of spatial utility to distribute to members of the dispossessed working class – either unused space or unused utility of otherwise employed spaces. These are currently held hostage by urban elites and thus, were the Right to the City realized, they would be available for distribution.
>
> (Pierce, 2019:22–23)

We are left with another paradox: it may be that, as Marxists would argue, 'in all its plenitude, the right to the city cannot be exercised in the ambit of capitalist urbanization' (Santos Junior, 2014:152). But capitalist urbanisation, with all its faults, is all we currently have. As a result, contemporary interpreters of Lefebvre have challenged his slogan: the right to what city? Does not globalisation and the decentrication of cities render hopelessly archaic Lefebvre's singular demand? (Merrifield, 2011:475). None of this is meant to suggest that the right to the city does not have value as a slogan or even as part of a manifesto, although it is perhaps to suggest that as cities develop, 'the politics of the encounter' (Merrifield, 2011:478) may not entirely suffice as a replacement, notwithstanding its Lefebvrian pedigree. As ever, action revolves around the question Lenin posed: *What is to be done?*

The model of radical critique that Lefebvre developed in the 1960s was one that he gradually distanced himself from at the end of the 1970s (Trebitsch, 2002 [2014:657]). Within a matter of a few years after the events of 1968, Lefebvre suggested that in France only a splinter socialist party, the PSU, was really interested in questions of space and the urban, whilst it was to Yugoslavia that he was inclined to point as a political way forward (Lefebvre, 1975:234–235). Lefebvre himself countered that trend, arguing that

> updating the UN Declaration of the Rights of Citizens is of utmost importance so that new legal-political conditions can be created so as to affirm a notion of social citizenship that effectively expresses contemporary social relations, that is, the new relations that have been formed between individuals, within society, and between individuals and society.
>
> (Fernandes, 2007:206)

These would include 'the right to information, the rights to multiple services, the right of users to make know their ideas on the space and time of their activities in urban areas; it would also cover the right to the use of the center' (Lefebvre, 1991 [1996:34]). The term 'city' itself becomes problematic. Beyond the basic practices of community information or consultation, which Lefebvre addresses as 'self-management', the right to participation encompasses 'the right to information', the right to use 'multiple services', 'the right of users to make known their ideas on the space and time of their activities in urban areas' (Strüver *et al*., 2021:6). As Schmid notes, Lefebvre himself kept amending the term 'the right to the city' with other terms: from the rather questionable 'right to centrality', (Merrifield, 2011:475), through the very modern-sounding 'right to difference' (Lefebvre, 1974 [1991:64]), and finally just a 'right to space' (Lefebvre, 1978 [2009:248]); Schmid, 2012:49). 'The urbanization of information is now just as relevant to questions of spatial justice and the city as those which surround other historical infrastructures and commodities' (Shaw & Graham, 2017:909).

> The right to the city, in Lefebvre's understanding of it, therefore requires the appropriation of the city by its citizens, redefining citizenship and therefore indissoluably entwined with criticism of State action – a direction radically opposed to the direction in which it has been taken in Brazil, a further development of planning.
>
> (Carlos, 2012:69)

Lefebvre's recommendations eventually distilled down to this relatively modest, and notably reformist, call: 'the organisation of the urban time and space to fit the lived experience of its citizens and residents could become the focus for a renewal of direct democratic relationships in modern society' (Kelly, 1992:63). So although the objective remains the same, 'the focus today is once again on basic needs such as access to shelter, food, clean water, health, and education' (Schmid, 2012:58), not least because

> [i]t is easier to mobilize a collective subject in the name of a right in late modern, liberal-capitalist societies, such as the right to the city, to public housing, to public transit, or to food sovereignty than in the name of a more abstract political goal, such as the end of capitalism.
>
> (Haderer, 2020:8)

Criticism from all sides

Lefebvre's arguments on space have never found universal agreement. On the one hand, critical human geographers, such as Doreen Massey (2005, 2007), wholeheartedly agree with Lefebvre that 'spatial factors are crucial to an adequate understanding of social relations, particularly in light of the global transformations of social life during the decades following the Second World War' (Butler, 2009:314). Their disagreement with Lefebvre lies rather in what they perceive as a narrow-minded focus on Marxist analysis, for example its frequent exclusion of gender issues (Cox, 2021:14), and by implication revolutionary or at least essentially political solutions. Such criticism does not rest exclusively on ontological grounds: even critics sympathetic to Lefebvre often regret his polemical criticism of epistemology in *The Production of Space*, engaging in a rebalancing that terminates in 'a kind of methodological demand that researchers acknowledge the epistemological multi-dimensionality of places' (Pierce & Martin, 2015:1295). These critical human geographers have in their turn been criticised by Marxists for whilst building on what they perceive as a weak, pluralistic conception of identities, running the risk of integrating differences into diversity and slipping unobtrusively and eventually ineffectively into being merely part of the colonisation of the everyday by capital rather than any attack upon it. Urban theory in this robust rebuttal should be radicalised through difference, all part of a political struggle in an and about space (Cox, 2016). Lefebvre would surely agree. Whilst there is no tribunal to adjudicate the extent to which Lefebvre can claim to be a Marxist, real estate developers can see as clearly as any that Lefebvre set out not merely to explain capitalism, but to contribute to its replacement. If the critical human geographers do not wish to participate in the struggle, Lefebvre nor the Marxist geographers are in a position to cajole them: but it is a shame nonetheless, as Marxists will always insist on the need to place analysis at the service of action, not the other way round.

On the other hand, traditional Marxists have been no less charitable towards Lefebvre, suggesting that his work 'embodies the magic of a Marxism liberated from dogma, yet this philosophical adventurousness also makes it fairly easy to find apparent paradoxes in his work' (Smith, 2003:xxii). Manuel Castells, at the time a young Marxist geographer responding to what he regarded as an ideological distortion of Marxism, many decades away from his own abandonment of Marxism altogether, thought Lefebvre was a romantic, philosophical utopian, responding to the rich theoretical tapestry that Lefebvre had woven by attempting to unpick it – the urban is not a particular form of study, just an ideological construction, political struggle was at root about economics. Castells thought Lefebvre had moved from a Marxist analysis of urbanism to an urbanist analysis of Marxism, and he had chapter and verse to back up his contention: 'Without utopia, today as yesterday, there is no more thought' (Lefebvre, 1980a:31). So, said Castells, in language that now seems so rooted in history that the time may soon come to skate over it altogether,

> one might challenge Lefebvre's libertarian and abstract conceptions of the reign of post-historical or communist society, in which one perceives no concrete process of constructing new social relations through the revolutionary

> transformation of different economic, political, ideological agencies by means of the class struggle and, therefore, of the dictatorship of the proletariat.
>
> (Castells, 1977:89)

Castells delved into the traditional Marxist repertoire for his response – that the urban question, though undeniable, revolved around the behaviour of the capitalist state, orchestrating consumption and production, hiding behind a welter of deceptions to deflect struggles and maintain its power over the working class. There was no need for an entirely separate theory of the urban, let alone to declare an end to traditional class warfare, in which the urban was essentially a battlefield, not a weapon.

It is important to recognise that although this criticism relies on Lefebvre's disdain for the traditional Marxist methods of social transformation, the key question for Marxist geographers, at least in the last century when traditional Marxist concepts of class were still considered more relevant than hitherto, was whether the organisation of space (in the context of urbanism) was 'a separate structure with its own laws of inner transformation and construction', or 'the expression of a set of relations embedded in some broader structure (such as the social relations of production' (Soja, 1980:208). On such apparently abstruse foundations was an entire theoretical debate founded.

So, Castells' criticism, and it is one that has been shared by many Marxist critics, is that urban culture and urban-modern society or the urban ideology is a kind of idealist distortion of Marxism. Soja summarised the criticism from the Marxist geographers thus:

> The structure of organized space is not a separate structure with its own autonomous laws of construction and transformation, nor is it simply an expression of the class structure emerging from the social (i.e., aspatial) relations of production. It represents, instead, a dialectically defined component of the general relations of production, relations which are simultaneously social and spatial.
>
> (Soja, 1980:208)

To Harvey, Castells, and others to follow, Lefebvre seemed to have succumbed to what Marxists have traditionally called a 'fetishism', in this case of space – rendering it autonomous, at the expense of understanding the real driver of social relations and history, the process itself. Struggling to be serious and rigorous in their application of Marxist methods, many of those most responsible for introducing an explicit and powerful spatial interpretation to Marxism thus began to establish 'certain boundaries beyond which radical spatial analysis must not reach' (Soja, 1980:208). Hence the rather abstract argument that 'having sought to annihilate space with time, capitalism can then buy back time for itself out of the spaces it conquers' (Harvey, 1985:57), so that

> capital has to build a fixed space (or 'landscape') necessary for its own functioning at a certain point in its history only to have to destroy that space (and

> devalue much of the capital invested therein) at a later point in order to make way for a new 'spatial fix' (openings for fresh accumulation in new spaces and territories).
>
> (Harvey, 1995:6, 2001:25)

As Lefebvre's more conventionally Marxist contemporary Jean Lojkine put it, slightly differently:

> The city thus appeared as the direct effect of the need to economise on incidental operating expenses, transport costs and consumption costs in order to accelerate the rate of turnover of capital and therefore to increase the period when capital is developed.
>
> (Lojkine, 1972:130)

Marxism thereupon found itself at the mercy of an academic debate, mainly in Western geography and urban studies departments, surrounding the extent to which space in urban society enjoyed any kind of independence from the traditional Marxist categories of production, class, and time.

It would be surprising if developers took much of an interest at all in what is likely to seem a very otiose debate indeed, very much of its time and now spent. But aspects of this debate have become more lively since. Lefebvre himself also wrote at the same time as, and was well aware of, those Marxists who were not only predicting the demise of the traditional working class, but even daring to suggest that a future revolving around work, at least as traditionally understood, was increasingly unlikely (Gorz, 1982). It is a view that has been debated, and refined, ever since, for example with the debate of the theory of the precariat (Standing, 2011, 2016) and revised conceptions of class (e.g. Filgueiras *et al.*, 2020). Lefebvre himself sought to incorporate the end of traditional work in his framework of the urban.

> Urban society will somehow be a 'post-work' society in the sense that Marx hinted at in the *Grundrisse* (Marx, 1857), when we all eventually get 'suspended' from the 'immediate form of production', giving rise to a latent political constituency whose only real terrain left for struggle won't be the workplace but the urban itself.
>
> (Merrifield, 2014:9)

The urban itself – where, Lefebvre would no doubt have readily conceded, injustice and inequality run rampant, a set of circumstances for which capitalism must take the majority of the responsibility. To this it is worth comparing Lefebvre's evolution of perspective, from the observation that 'Without philosophy, the proletariat cannot know what it wants. Without the proletariat, philosophy will remain futile' (Lefebvre, 1958:25) to the frank admission that revisionism 'would not have had any effect unless the working class had in large measure approved' (Lefebvre, 1980:39). It is but a short step, traditional Marxists will worry, to the thesis of the post-political city: 'largely devoid of politics, enervated, subject to the whims of global economic forces, governed through managerial consensus-driven political systems' (Beveridge & Koch, 2017:32).

Little surprise therefore that there are now fewer who agree with the traditional Marxist view, as expressed by Castells (1977) or alternatively by Lojkine (1972, 1977) that what still matters – what has always only really mattered – is 'how capital is accumulated, how means of production are appropriated, and how labour is exploited' (Neveling, 2020:229). The urban problematic becomes a global problem. As has been summarised:

> Though there is still some diversity among scholars in this tradition, the overall arc of development has been a tendency to move beyond the relatively more economic and class reductionist arguments of the early Harvey (1973) and Castells (1977), and that development resonates with Lefebvre's avowedly holistic approach to the city.
>
> (Purcell, 2014:145)

We are back to Lefebvre, and the irony entailed in the suspension as a result of Covid-19 of an international meeting convened to examine the contemporary relevance of Lefebvre's work could surely not have been lost on potential participants. The transnational space of which Lefebvre had so eloquently written had been laid low – temporarily, no doubt – by an old-fashioned pandemic that had called an abrupt halt to globalisation and transformed space.

Meanwhile, from a social action perspective, which still implicitly envisaged Marxism as dialectical and historical materialism, came the criticism that Lefebvre's work involved a double reification, that of space and of relations of production. By embodying what ought to be only a formal and classificatory concept, space, with a determining power, with agency, the criticism alleges, Lefebvre is led to reject subjective agency in favour of a materialism which places him very close to the very geo-determinists he argues against. At the same time, Lefebvre's objections to a purely technical concept of space lead him to reject spatial considerations *tout court* despite their physical and material uses. As a result, 'Lefebvre does not solve geographers' problems' (Werlen, 1988 [1993:4]).

Lefebvre's conception of space came in for criticism 'from within' as well. Firstly, for a troubling duality in Lefebvre's own standpoint: what of 'the exploitations that made possible such lovely edifices. It is not so simple to distinguish his valued absolute spaces from his devalued abstract ones' (Molotch, 1993:893). Secondly, in a fashion rather akin to Engels' recipe for ending the housing crisis in England, Lefebvre implies, though never asserts, that those who liberate urban space will not be required to share it with its prior owners, or those who controlled it, and that there will be more than sufficient to go round, which was probably not true of London property in the 19th century, and is certainly not the case for the plight of the underprivileged urban populations of the 21st century. Thirdly, Harvey criticises Lefebvre for neither being explicit about what he means by the ensemble of transformations, nor for explaining how capitalism is transformed in this fashion, nor for being explicit in arguing that 'the proportion of global surplus formed and realized in industry declines [whilst that realised in] speculation, construction and real estate development grows' (Lefebvre, 1970a:212). Linked is the criticism that Lefebvre's concept of differential space – ill-defined, yet identifiable, but at least in his use of the term apparently undifferentiated – also seems curiously at odds with his muted advocacy of individual freedom. He may therefore also be criticised for neglecting to admit, let along how to arbitrate, differences of opinion between different elements of the new working class, which 'exists, but not as the solid, certain ground, the absolute criterion for action' (Lefebvre, 1962 [1995:40]). His differential space is not only harmonious and plentiful, but disturbingly homogeneous. He never, for example, seems to have contemplated that one person's differential space could be another's abstract space: 'Under conditions of disagreement among a polity of citadins – either disagreement about use or disagreement about who has a right to use – Lefebvre offers little to guide principles of arbitration' (Pierce, 2019:22–23).

This criticism applies to Lefebvre's cherished distinction between the industrial and the urban as well:

> The true global cities of the twenty-first century may well be those large metropolises that are simultaneously emerging as production motors not of national economies but of the global economy. Industrialization and urbanization are more, not less, interwoven, and the cities of most intense population growth are also those of greatest industrial expansion.
>
> (Smith, 2003:xx)

Two decades later, after the rise of commercial cities and centres of wealth such as Dubai and Singapore, and the possibilities of global dispersal of manufacturing capabilities, this contention may appear less solid than hitherto. But as with all challenges to Lefebvre from traditional Marxists, these criticisms will remain. Real estate developers no less than Marxists can decide the degree to which they are correct, even the extent to which they matter to them.

Finally, rights discourse has moreover never been much favoured by radical geographers, who have asserted, for example, that rights claims 'unintentionally reify the uneven power relations they aim to overcome, while routinely cauterising the hard-fought collective social force that forces social gains' (Gray, 2017:319). It is therefore surely striking that whilst much later, towards the end of his life, Lefebvre himself deployed a rights-based theoretical politics, 'not dismissive of human rights nor of litigation under existing legal frameworks' (Huchzermeyer, 2018:642), radical geographers are reluctant to follow in his footsteps. Perhaps this goes some way to explaining why radical geographers are increasingly inclined to quote Chantal Mouffe, Jacques Rancière, or Slavoj Žižek in support of a criticism of contemporary capitalist democracy, rather than Lefebvre (Swyngedouw & Wilson, 2014:11), or when they do cite Lefebvre, the theoretical text of radical choice to accompany a reflection on historical community activism often harking from an earlier time (Lefebvre, 1968 [1996], 1968a). It is worth continuing to bear in mind that a rights-based and pro-development reading of Lefebvre is to one to which

'Orthodox Marxists are very hostile . . . [perceiving it as] a corruption of Lefebvre's original intentions' (Morange & Spire, 2019:28). Codification, measurability – all these allegedly represent an entirely undesirable reformist drift away from the radicalism of Lefebvre's earlier writings on which they primarily focus. Yet for Lefebvre, formulating political claims in the language of rights served, among others, a strategic purpose, and although Lefebvre radically changed course, he never abandoned hope.

Conclusion: revising Lefebvre

To suggest that Lefebvre's work is not above criticism or that it needs revision is not to disparage it. Far from it, it is to suggest that it is of such importance that it must be updated, and that many voices – from many different perspectives – may need to be heard in the process, as much has changed since Lefebvre wrote is clear. Equally clear is that these changes pose a series of significant problems for the application of his work to urban life in contemporary capitalism (Stanek, 2011:78).

> This involves discussing Lefebvre's praise of urban centrality in the context of the exacerbating social and spatial segregation between the center of Paris and the suburbs as he experienced it in Nanterre; revising his belief in dwelling as the paradigmatic practice of production of space in view of the increasing privatization and gentrification of urban spaces modeled according to domestic interiors; challenging his theorization of difference in the face of the cultural logics of consumption as differentiation; and questioning the possibility of a politics of scale in a situation in which the traditional homologies between spatial forms and social groups are undermined by the increasing mobility of urban populations, the multiplication of modes of belonging, and the crisis of traditional political associations.
>
> (Stanek, 2011:xiv; Gromark, 2013:252)

What might be added to this already formidable list? Two things in particular, I suggest. First is the question of methods. The criticism has already been made that Lefebvre 'refuses to confront the underlying problem' (Harvey, 2000:78), essentially that of methodology: How is capitalism to be transformed without some kind of authoritarian measure? If Lefebvre leaves the question open, then he is in good company – Marxists as a whole can no longer be said to be sure either. If for Lefebvre the city was the new proletariat, then any revision of Lefebvre must take into account a change in the potential revolutionary conditions of the urban, as it was a mistake of historic proportions for Marxists to believe that contemporary cities had a revolutionary trajectory or even harboured inbuilt capacities to become 'critical zones'. Lefebvre himself lived more than long enough to recognise what other Marxists have cavilled at: 'Lefebvre comes straight out with it: the notion of the people, labour as the source of value, and the revolutionary project are at an end' (Trebitsch, 2014:674]).

Secondly, and by extension, assuming Marxists are not to abandon hope of the eventual replacement of capitalism with a better, fairer system of economic and social organisation is the range of organisations that may now be involved in the process. One circumstance that stands out as clearly changed since Lefebvre's time is the rise of private sector actors in relation to the State and to political parties. In the context of the production of space, we must draw attention to the importance of real estate developers as operating on a local, urban, and often national scale, but still rarely internationally.

If Lefebvre's theory only permitted Marxists to recognise that space, like works of art, literature, or above all economics, is not politically neutral, not an abstract principle, nor even simply a means of ideological and material control, but rather, in a variety of forms it is also the contested terrain in which everyday life and practices create meanings, values, signs, and symbols (Zieleniec, 2018:6) that would be valuable, no doubt, but would leave ample room for both interpretation and translation into action.

How much of a theoretical revolution within Marxism Lefebvre intended has been debated. He has had many followers, as the numerous references in his chapter indicate, including radical geographers such as Soja: his concept of the 'Third Space' was, he claimed, founded on this Lefebvrian version of the Marxist dialectic (Soja, 1996:60). So, 'For a while, a lot of the best urbanism was carried out by Marxists, and the best Marxism by urbanists' (Merrifield, 2002:5). The eventual results, however, even within the academy as a whole, let alone outside it, were that of Lefebvre's schemata, the first, that of 'the production of space' ended up being reluctantly accepted. The second, that of the 'triplicity of space', often repeated, nevertheless remained a source of confusion, whilst the third, that of 'the conflictuality of space', has remained for many the most problematic, because of its questioning of the spatial consensus (Martin, 2006:8). So, in succeeding decades, 'Lefebvre's explicit 1970s-era materialist epistemology (and, at times, his Marxian political agenda), however, has receded from attention' (Pierce & Martin, 2015:1282). Like Marxism itself, there is a real risk that discussion surrounding Lefebvre may focus on history, and not on the future.

It would be profoundly unfair to Lefebvre if this were so, as towards the end of his life, Lefebvre himself had already moved even further from a traditional Marxist perspective, for example, with his introduction to *Du contrat de citoyenneté* (Lefebvre, 1990), than when he commenced his sequence of works on the urban, even than when he wrote *The Production of Space* (Lefebvre, 1974 [1991]), let alone *The Urban Revolution* (Lefebvre, 1968 [2003]). He still believed that the need for dramatic economic and social transformation revolving around the urban could never be in doubt: what changed over time in his thinking was not the eventual Marxist goal of overcoming capitalism, but as the world changed around him, the method – and the timeframe. It would therefore be unjust to suggest that Lefebvre's views did not change, nor would it be appropriate to judge his contribution solely on the basis of his earlier work. In particular, concepts of urban revolution might now appear as jejune to an audience of perhaps politically jaded real estate developers, who could point out that the hopes they had engendered, as Lefebvre himself recognised, 'are fading concurrently with the last illusions of modernity' (Lefebvre, 1989 [2014:203]. They should, I suggest, instead recognise with Lefebvre that the struggle to overcome capitalism has not disappeared. Rather, it has been transformed, still fought as Lefebvre identified through the production of space, albeit in very different fashion to the last century. Still, the theoretical tools bequeathed by Lefebvre may still in updated form be relevant, and that they are themselves as developers far from exempt from the battle. How fares the fight?

Bibliography

Addie, J. (2015). Towards a city-regional politics of mobility: In-between critical mobilities and the political-economy of urban transportation. In Cidell, J. and Prytherch, D. (eds.) *Transport, Mobility, and the Production of Urban Space*. New York and Abingdon, Routledge, 187–206.

Attoh, K. A. (2011). What kind of right is the right to the city? *Progress in Human Geography*, 35(5), 669–685.

Basta, C. (2017). On Marx's human significance, Harvey's right to the city, and Nussbaum's capability approach. *Planning Theory*, 16(4), 345–363.

Berman, M. (2006). *On The Town: One Hundred Years of Spectacle in Times Square*. New York, Verso.

Bevan, R. (2022). *Monumental Lies*. London, Verso.

Beveridge, R. and Koch, P. (2017). The post-political trap? Reflections on politics, agency and the city. *Urban Studies*, 54(1), 31–43.

Bollnow, E. F. (1963 [2011]). *Mensch und Raum*. Stuttgart, Kohlhammer. Translated by C. Shuttleworth and edited by J. Kohlmaier as *Human Space*. London, Hyphen.

Bourne, L. S. (1982). *Internal Structure of the City: Readings on Urban Form, Growth, and Policy*. Oxford, Oxford University Press.

Bouwmeester, J. and Hartmann, T. (2021). Unraveling the self-made city: The spatial impact of informal real estate markets in informal settlements. *Cities*, 108, 102966.

Brenner, N. (2000). The urban question: Reflections on Henri Lefebvre, urban theory and the politics of scale. *International Journal of Urban and Regional Research*, 24(2), 361–378.

Brenner, N. and Elden, S. (2009). Henri Lefebvre on state, space, territory. *International Political Sociology*, 3(4), 353–377.

Brenner, N., Marcuse, P. and Mayer, M. (2012). Cities for people, not for profit: An introduction. In Brenner, N. *et al.* (eds.) *Cities for People, Not for Profit*. Abingdon and New York, Routledge, 1–10.

Brenner, N. and Schmid, C. (2014). The 'urban age' in question. *International Journal of Urban and Regional Research*, 38(3), 731–755.

Brown, A. (2010). *Debate 1: Taking forward the Right to the City. REPORT to UN-HABITAT*, e-Debate Moderator, Alison Brown, February. Available at: https://mirror.unhabitat.org/downloads/docs/Dialogue1.pdf. [Accessed 3 September 2021].

Buckley, M. and Hanieh, A. (2014). Diversification by urbanization: Tracing the property-finance nexus in Dubai and the gulf. *International Journal of Urban and Regional Research*, 38(1), 155–175.

Busquet, G. (2012). L'espace politique chez Henri Lefebvre: l'idéologie et l'utopie. Justice spatiale-*Spatial Justice*, 5. Available at: www. jssj. org/article/lespace-politique-chez-henri-lefebvre-lideologie-et-lutopie/. [Accessed 15 August 2021].

Butler, C. (2005). Reading the production of suburbia in post-war Australia. In Manderson, D. (ed.) *Legal Spaces. Law Text Culture, Volume 9*. Holmes Beach, Law Text Culture, 11–33.
———. (2009). Critical legal studies and the politics of space. *Social & Legal Studies*, 18(3), 313–332.
Carlos, A. F. A. (2012). Le droit à la ville comme projet de nouvelle société. *L'Homme la Société*, 2012/3–4(n° 185–186), 65–81.
Castells, M. (1972 [1977]). *La Question urbaine*. Paris, Maspero. Translated by A. Sheridan as *The Urban Question-A Marxist Approach*. London, Edward Arnold.
Chakrabati, A. (2013). *Lecture 22: Socio-spatial approach or the new urban sociology. Lecture*. Available at https://pdfslide.net/documents/module-3-theories-of-urban-sociology-lecture-22-socio-nptelacincourses109104047pdf.html. [Accessed 2 November 2021].
Charney, I. (2001). Three dimensions of capital switching within the real estate sector: A Canadian case study. *International Journal of Urban and Regional Research*, 25(4), 740–758.
Charnock, G. (2010). Challenging new state spatialities: The open Marxism of Henri Lefebvre. *Antipode*, 42(5), 1279–1303.
———. (2014). Lost in space? Lefebvre, Harvey, and the spatiality of negation. *South Atlantic Quarterly*, 113(2), 313–325.
Chiodelli, F. (2013). Planning and urban citizenship: Suggestions from the thoughts of Henri Lefebvre. *Planning Perspectives*, 28(3), 487–494.
Conley, V. A. (2012). *Spatial ecologies: Urban sites, state and world-space in French cultural theory*. Liverpool, Liverpool University Press.
Cox, K. (2005). *From Marxist geography to critical geography and back again*. Unpublished paper. Department of Geography, The Ohio State University.
———. (2016). Geographies, critical and Marxist, and lessons from South Africa. *Human Geography*, 9(3), 10–26.
———. (2021). Massey, Marx, and human geography: Disjunctures and provocations. *Human Geography*, 14(1), 5–16.
Das, R. J. (2022). What is Marxist geography today, or what is left of Marxist geography? *Human Geography*, 15(1), 33–44.
Davidson, M. (2007). Gentrification as global habitat: A process of class formation or corporate creation? *Transactions of the Institute of British Geographers*, 32(4), 490–506.
Davis, M. (2020). *Old Gods, New Enigmas. Marx's Lost Theory*. London, Verso.
Derbyshire, B. (2015). Superdensity and street life. In Murray, P. (ed.) *Super Density the Sequel*. Available at: www.pollardthomasedwards.co.uk/download/SUPERDENSITY_2015_download.pdf. [Accessed 9 June 2022], 20–24.
Dimendberg, E. (1998). Henri Lefebvre on abstract space. In Light, A. and Smith, J. M. (eds.) *The Production of Public Space*. Oxford, Rowman & Littlefield, 17–47.
Eisinger, P. K. (1978). Marxism and the metropolis: New perspectives in urban political economy. Book review. *American Political Science Review*, 73(2), 665–667.
Elden, S. (2001). Politics, philosophy, geography: Henri Lefebvre in recent Anglo-American scholarship. *Antipode*, 33(5), 809–825.
———. (2004). *Understanding Henri Lefebvre*. London and New York, Continuum.
———. (2007). There is a politics of space because space is political: Henri Lefebvre and the production of space. *Radical philosophy Review*, 10(2), 101–116.
———. (2008). Mondialisation before globalization: Lefebvre and Axelos. In Goonewardena, K. *et al.* (eds.) *Space, Difference, Everyday Life. Reading Henri Lefebvre*. New York and London, Routledge, 94–107.
———. (2016). Foreward. In Lefebvre, H. *Marxist Thought and the City*. Minneapolis, University of Minnesota Press, vii–xvi.

Elden, S. and Morton, A. D. (2016). Thinking past Henri Lefebvre: Introducing "The theory of ground rent and rural sociology". *Antipode*, 48(1), 57–66.

Engels, F. (1872 [2021]). *The Housing Question*. Paris, Foreign Languages Press. Available at: https://foreignlanguages.press/wp-content/uploads/2021/03/C13-Engels-The-Housing-Question-1st-Printing.pdf. [Accessed 4 June 2021].

Fainstein, S. S. (2009). Planning and the just city. In Marcuse, P. *et al*. (eds.) *Searching for the Just City*. New York and London, Routledge, 39–59.

Feldman, M. (1978). Manuel castells' the urban question a review essay. *Review of Radical Political Economics*, 10(3), 136–144.

Fernandes, E. (2007). Constructing the right to the city in Brazil. *Social & Legal Studies*, 16(2), 201–219.

Fernandez, R., Hofman, A. and Aalbers, M. B. (2016). London and New York as a safe deposit box for the transnational wealth elite. *Environment and Planning A: Economy and Space*, 48(12), 2443–2461.

Filgueiras, V. A. and Cavalcante, S. M. (2020). What has Changed A new farewell to the working class? *Revista Brasileira de Ciências Sociais*, 35(102), 1–22.

Forrest, R., Koh, S. Y. and Wissink, B. (eds.) (2017). *Cities and the Super-Rich: Real Estate, Elite Practices and Urban Political Economies*. London, Palgrave Macmillan.

Foster, J. B., Napoletano, B. M., Clark, B. and Urquijo, P. S. (2020). Henri Lefebvre's Marxian ecological critique: Recovering a foundational contribution to environmental sociology. *Environmental Sociology*, 6(1), 31–41.

Fuchs, C. (2019). Henri Lefebvre's theory of the production of space and the critical theory of communication. *Communication Theory*, 29(2), 129–150.

Gans, H. (1994). Urbanism and Suburbnanism as ways of life: A reevaluation of definitions. In Kasinitz, P. (Ed.), *Metropolis. Center and Symbol of our Times* New York, Doubleday, 170–194.

Gao, W. (2022). Corporate liquidity risk: A case study on the evergrande group in China. *Journal of Asia Trade and Business*, 9(2), 1–14.

Garnier, J.-P. (1978). *Le socialisme à visage urbain. Essai sur la local-démocratie*. Paris, Rupture.

Garnier, J.-P. and Goldschmidt, D. (1978). *La Comédie Urbaine*. Paris, Maspero.

Ghulyan, H. (2019). Lefebvre's production of space in the context of Turkey: A comprehensive literature survey. *SAGE Open*, 9(3), 2158244019870537.

Goldman, M. and Narayan, D. (2021). Through the optics of finance: Speculative urbanism and the transformation of markets. *International Journal of Urban and Regional Research*, 45(2), 209–231.

Goonewardena, K. (2011). Henri Lefebvre. In Ritzer, G. and Stepnisky, J. (eds.) *The Wiley-Blackwell Companion to Major Social Theorists*, 1, 44–64.

Gordon, D. (1978). Capitalist development and the history of American cities. In Tabb, W. K. and Sawers, L. (eds.) *Marxism and the Metropolis. New Perspectives in Urban Political Economy*. 2nd edition. New York, Oxford University Press, 21–53.

Gorz, A. (1982). *Farewell to the Working Class. An Essay on Post-Industrial Socialism*. London: Pluto Press.

Gotham, K. F. (2006). The secondary circuit of capital reconsidered: Globalization and the US real estate sector. *American Journal of Sociology*, 112(1), 231–275.

———. (2009). Creating liquidity out of spatial fixity: The secondary circuit of capital and the subprime mortgage crisis. *International Journal of Urban and Regional Research*, 33(2), 355–371.

Gottdiener, M. (1993). A Marx for our time: Henri Lefebvre and the production of space. *Sociological Theory*, 11(1), 129–134.

Gray, N. (2017). Beyond the right to the city: Territorial autogestion and the take over the city movement in 1970s Italy. *Antipode*, 50(2), 319–339.

Gregory, D. (1994). *Geographical Imaginations*. Oxford, Blackwell.

Groll, S. (1980). The active role of 'use value' in Marx's economic analysis. *History of Political Economy*, 12(3), 336–371.

Gromark, S. (2013). A third wave of receptions: Space as concrete abstraction, Lukasz Stanek on Henri Lefebvre. *Site*, 33, 245–252. Available at: www.sitemagazine.net/content/02-issues/23-33_2013/33.pdf. [Accessed 2 March 2021].

Guelf, F. (2010). *Die urbane Revolution. Henri Lefèbvres Philosophie der globalen Verstädterung*. Bielefeld, Verlag.

Haderer, M. (2020). Revisiting the right to the city, rethinking urban environmentalism: From lifeworld environmentalism to planetary environmentalism. *Social Sciences*, 9(2), 15.

Haila, A. (2016). *Urban Land Rent. Singapore as a Property State*. Oxford, Blackwell.

Harvey, D. (1973). *Social Justice and the City*. London, Edward Arnold.

———. (1978). The urban process under capitalism: A framework for analysis. International *Journal of Urban and Regional Research*, 2(1–3), 101–131.

———. (1985). *The Urbanization of Capital*. Baltimore, Johns Hopkins University Press.

———. (1989). *The Urban Experience*. Oxford, Blackwell.

———. (1995). Globalization in question. *Rethinking Marxism*, 8(4), 1–17.

———. (2000). *Megacities. Lecture 4, Amersfoort*. The Netherlands, Twynstra Gudde Management Consultants.

———. (2001). Globalization and the "spatial fix". *Geographische Revue: Zeitschrift für Literatur und Diskussion*, 3(2), 23–30.

———. (2006). *The Limits to Capital*. London: Verso.

———. (2008). The right to the city. *New Left Review*, 53(1), 23–40. Available at https://newleftreview.org/issues/ii53/articles/david-harvey-the-right-to-the-city. [Accessed 21 October 2021].

———. (2010). *The Enigma of Capital and the Crises of Capitalism*. New York, Oxford University Press.

———. (2012). *Rebel Cities: From the Right to the City to the Urban Revolution*. London, Verso.

———. (2018). *The Limits to Capital*. London, Verso.

Hermann, C. (2021). Rediscovering use value. In *The Critique of Commodification: Contours of a Post-Capitalist Society*. Oxford, Oxford University Press.

Hofman, A. and Aalbers, M. B. (2019). A finance- and real estate-driven regime in the United Kingdom. *Geoforum*, 100, 89–100.

Holm, A. and Kuhn, A. (2011). Squatting and urban renewal: The interaction of squatter movements and strategies of urban restructuring in Berlin. *International Journal of Urban and Regional Research*, 35(3), 644–658.

Huchzermeyer, M. (2018). The legal meaning of Lefebvre's the right to the city: Addressing the gap between global campaign and scholarly debate. *GeoJournal*, 83(3), 631–644.

Inter-Environnement-Bruxelles. (2012). Le droit à la ville. Et quoi? *Bruxelles en mouvement*, 3, 259–260. Available at www.ieb.be/-Bem-259-260-. [Accessed 6 July 2021].

Kallin, H. (2021). Chasing the rent gap down on Edinburgh's waterfront: State failure, devalorisation, and the enduring promise of potential. *City*, 25(5–6), 614–633.

Kamenka, E. (1969). *Marxism and Ethics*. London, Palgrave Macmillan.

Katznelson, I. (1993). Towards a Respatialized Marxism: Lefebvre, Harvey, and Castells. In Katznelson, I. *Marxism and the City*. Oxford, Oxford University Press, 92–140.

Kębłowski, W., Van Criekingen, M. and Bassens, D. (2019). Moving past the sustainable perspectives on transport: An attempt to mobilise critical urban transport studies with the right to the city. *Transport Policy*, 81, 24–34.

Kelly, M. (1992). Heori Lefebvre, 1901–1991 *Radical Philosophy*, 60, 62–63.

Kelly, M. (2000). Demystification: A dialogue between Barthes and Lefebvre. *Yale French Studies* (98), 79–97.

Kingma, S. F., Dale, K. and Wasserman, V. (eds.) (2018). *Organisational Space and Beyond: The Significance of Henri Lefebvre for Organisation Studies*. New York and London, Taylor & Francis.

Kinkaid, E. (2020). Re-encountering Lefebvre: Toward a critical phenomenology of social space. *Environment and Planning D: Society and Space*, 38(1), 167–186.

Kipfer, S. and Goonewardena, K. (2007). Colonization and the new imperialism: On the meaning of urbicide today. *Theory and Event*, 10(2).

———. (2013). Urban Marxism and the post-colonial question: Henri Lefebvre and 'colonisation'. *Historical Materialism*, 21(2), 76–116.

Kipfer, S., Goonewardena, K., Schmid, C. and Milgrom, R. (2008). On the production of Henri Lefebvre. In Kipfer, S. *et al.* (eds.) *Space, Difference, Everyday Life: Reading Henri Lefebvre*. New York and Abingdon, Routledge, 1–24.

Kloosterman, R. C. and Lambregts, B. (2007). Between accumulation and concentration of capital: Toward a framework for comparing long-term trajectories of urban systems. *Urban Geography*, 28(1), 54–73.

Kohlmaier, J. and Bollnow, E. F. (1963 [2011]). *Mensch und Raum*. Stuttgart, Kohlhammer. Translated by C. Shuttleworth and edited by J. Kohlmaier as *Human Space*. London, Hyphen, 310–315.

Kress, C. (2016). Urban ruralities or the new urban-rural paradigm-introduction. The 17th International Planning History Society Conference – Delft, July 2016. *International Planning History Society Proceedings*, 17(4), 319–331.

Kuymulu, M. B. (2013). The vortex of rights: 'Right to the city' at a crossroads. *International Journal of Urban and Regional Research*, 37(3), 923–940.

Labbé, M. (2016). Quelle ville voulons-nous? Des pathologies urbaines au droit de la ville. *Cahiers philosophiques* (3), 61–81.

Leary-Owhin, M. E. (2016). *Ideas for Going Beyond Lefebvre: Producing Differential Space*. Unpublished paper. Available at: www.academia.edu/30256589/Ideas_for_Going_Beyond_Lefebvre_Producing_Differential_Space. [Accessed 8 February 2021].

———. (2018). Henri Lefebvre, planning's friend or implacable critic? *Urban Planning*, 3(3), 1–4.

Lefebvre, H. (1947). *Critique de la vie quotidienne. Volume One. Introduction*. Paris: Grasset. Translated by J. Moore (1991 [2014]) as *Critique of Everyday Life. Volume One. Introduction*. London, Verso.

———. (1956). Théorie de la rente foncière et sociologie rurale. *Transactions of the Third World Congress of Sociology*, II, 244–250.

———. (1958). Retour au Marx. *Cahiers Internationaux de Sociologie*, Nouvelle Série 25, 20–37.

———. (1960). Les nouveaux ensembles urbains (un cas concret: Lacq-Mourenx et les problèmes urbains de la nouvelle classe ouvrière). *La Revue Francaise de sociologie*, 1(1–2), 186–201.

———. (1962 [1995]). *Introduction à la modernite*. Paris, Minuit. Translated by J. Moore as *Introduction to Modernity*. London, Verso.

———. (1965 [2000]). *Metaphilosophie*. 2nd edition. Paris, Syllepse. Translated by D. Fernbach as Metaphilosophy. [2016]. London, Verso.
———. (1966). *La Langage et la Société*. Paris, Gallimard.
———. (1966 [1968]). *Sociologie de Marx*. Paris, Presse Universitaie. Translated by N. Guterman as *The Sociology of Marx*. Harmondsworth, Penguin.
———. (1968 [1996]). *Le Droit à la ville*. Paris, Anthropos. In Kofman, E. and Lebas, E. (eds.) *Henri Lefebvre. Writings on Cities*. Oxford, Blackwells, 63–184.
———. (1968a). *L'Irruption de Nanterre au sommet*. Paris, Anthropos. Translated by A. Ehrenfeld as *The Explosion: Marxism and the French Upheaval*. New York, Monthly Review Press.
———. (1970 [2003]). *La Révolution Urbaine*. Paris, Gallimard. Translated by R. Bononno as *The Urban Revolution*. Minneapolis, University of Minnesota Press.
———. (1970a). *Du rural à l'urbain*. Paris, Anthropos.
———. (1972). *La pensée marxiste et la ville*. Paris, Casterman. Translated by R. Bononno (2016) as *Marxist Thought and the City*. Minneapolis, University of Minnesota Press.
———. (1973 [1976]). *La Survie du capitalisme: La reproduction des rapports de production*. Paris, Anthropos. Translated by F. Bryant as *The Survival of Capitalism. Reproduction of the Relations of Production*. London, Allison & Busby.
———. (1973a [2000]). *Espace et politique*. Anthropos, Paris. In Kofman, E. and Lebas, E. (eds.) *Writings on Cities – Henri Lefebvre*. 2nd edition. Oxford, Blackwells, 185–204.
———. (1973b). Les idéologies de la croissance. *L'Homme et la société*, 27, 3–17.
———. (1974a). La production de l'espace. *L'Homme et la société*, 31–32, 15–32.
———. (1974b). *La production de l'espace*. Paris, Anthropos. Translated by D. Nicholson-Smith as *The Production of Space*. Oxford, Blackwell.
———. (1975). *Le temps des méprises: entretiens avec Claude Glayman*. Paris, Stock.
———. (1976). *De l'État. Volume One L'État dans le monde moderne*. Paris, UGE.
———. (1978 [2009]). Space and the state. In Elden, S. and Brenner, N. (eds.) *State, Space, World: Selected Essays*. Translated by G. Moore. Minneapolis, University of Minnesota Press, 223–253.
———. (1978a). *De l'État. Les contradictions de l'Etat moderne, La dialectique de l'Etat*. Volume 4. Paris, UGE.
———. (1979 [2009]). Space: Social product and use value. In Elden, S. and Brenner, N. (eds.) *State, Space, World: Selected Essays*. Translated by G. Moore. Minneapolis, University of Minnesota Press, 185–195.
———. (1980 [2009]). Space and mode of production. In Elden, S. and Brenner, N. (eds.) *State, Space, World: Selected Essays*. Translated by G. Moore. Minneapolis, University of Minnesota Press, 201–222.
———. (1980a). Une pensée devenue monde: faut-il abandonner Marx? Paris, Fayard.
———. (1980b). Marxism Exploded. *Review (Fernand Braudel Center)*, 4(1), 19–32.
———. (1981 [2014]). *Critique de la vie quotidienne. Volume 3. De la Modernité Au* Modernisme. (Pour Une Métaphilosophie Du Quotidien) Paris, L'Arche. Translated by J. Moore (2014) as *From Modernity to Modernism (Towards a Metaphilosophy of Daily Life)*. London, Verso.
———. (1986). *Le retour de la dialectique*. Paris, Messidor.
———. (1989 [2014]). Dissolving City, Planetary Metamorphosis. [Quand la ville se perd dans une métamorphose planétaire]. *Environment and planning D: Society & Space*, 32(2), 203–205.
———. (1990). Du pacte social au contrat du citoyenneté. In Lefebvre, H. and Le Groupe de Navarrenx (eds.) *Du contrat de citoyenneté*. Paris, Editions Syllepse, 15–42.

———. (1991). Les illusions de la modernité. *Manieres de voir 13, Le Monde Diplomatique*, October, pp. 14–17. Available at: www.monde-diplomatique.fr/mav/13/. [Accessed 17 February 2023]. Extract Translated in Kofman, E. and Lebas, E. (eds.) *Henri Lefebvre. Writings on Cities*. Oxford, Blackwells, 34.
———. (1992 [2004]). *Éléments de rythmanalyse*. Paris, Syllepse. Translated by S. Elden and G. Moore as *Elements of Rhythmanalysis*. London and New York, Continuum.
———. (2000). *Espace et politique: Le droit à la ville II*. Paris, Anthropos.
Lehtovuori, P. (2010). *Experience and Conflict: The Production of Urban Space*. Farnham, Ashgate.
———. (2003). *The urban revolution*: University of Minnesota Press. Translated by R. Bononno. Original is *La Révolution urbaine,* 1970 Editions Gallimard.
———. (2016). *Experience and Conflict: The Production of Urban Space*. London: Routledge.
Lizieri, C. (2009). *Towers of Capital: Office Markets and International Financial Services*. Oxford, Wiley-Blackwell.
Lojkine, J. (1972). Contribution à une théorie marxiste de l'urbanisation capitaliste. *Cahiers Internationaux de Sociologie*, 52, 123–146.
———. (1977). *Le marxisme, l'État et la question urbaine*. Paris, Presse Universitaire de France.
Marcuse, P., Connolly, J., Novy, J., Olivo, I., Potter, C. and Steil, J. (2009). *Searching for the Just City: Debates in Urban Theory and Practice*. London, Routledge.
Martin, J.-Y. (2006). Une géographie critique de l'espace du quotidien. L'actualité mondialisée de la pensée spatiale d'Henri Lefebvre. *Articulo-Journal of Urban Research (2) Social Dimensions of Economy*. Available at: https://journals.openedition.org/articulo/897. [Accessed 5 June 2021].
Marx, K. (1852). *The 18th Brumaire of Louis Bonaparte*. Available at www.marxists.org/archive/marx/works/download/pdf/18th-Brumaire.pdf. [Accessed 3 June 2021].
———. (1857 [1982]). *Grundrisse: Foundations of the Critique of Political Economy*. New York: Penguin.
Massey, D. (2005). *For Space*. London, Sage.
———. (2007). *Global City*. Cambridge, Polity Press.
Matley, I. M. (1966). The Marxist approach to the geographical environment. Annals of the *Association of American Geographers*, 56(1), 97–111.
McCann, E. J. (1999). Race, protest, and public space: Contextualizing Lefebvre in the US city. *Antipode*, 31(2), 163–184.
Mehrotra, S. (1991). On the social specifications of use value in Marx's capital. *Social Scientist*, 19(8/9), 72–77.
Merrifield, A. (1993). Place and space: A lefebvrian reconciliation. *Transactions of the Institute of British Geographers*, 18(4), 516–531.
———. (2001). Metro Marxism, or old and young Marx in the city. *Socialism and Democracy*, 15(2), 63–84.
———. (2002). *Metromarxism: A Marxist Tale of the City*. New York and London, Routledge.
———. (2006). *Henri Lefebvre: A Critical Introduction*. London, Taylor & Francis.
———. (2011). The right to the city and beyond: Notes on a Lefebvrian re-conceptualization. *City*, 15(3–4), 473–481.
———. (2014). *The New Urban Question*. London, Pluto Press.
Meyer, K. (1973). *Henri Lefebvre. Ein romantischer Revolutionär*. Vienna, Europa Verlags.

Millington, G. (2016). The cosmopolitan contradictions of planetary urbanization. *The British Journal of Sociology*, 67(3), 476–496.
Mitchell, D. (2003). *The Right to the City: Social Justice and the Fight for Public Space*. London, The Guildford Press.
Mitchell, D. and Heynen, N. (2009). The geography of survival and the right to the city: Speculations on surveillance, legal innovation, and the criminalization of intervention. *Urban Geography*, 30(6), 611–632.
Molotch, H. (1993). The space of Lefebvre. *Theory and Society*, 22(6), 887–895.
Morange, M. and Spire, A. (2019). The right to the city in the Global South. Perspectives from Africa. *Cybergeo: European Journal of Geography*, 895. Available at: http://journals.openedition.org/cybergeo/32217. [Accessed 8 March 2021].
Moravánszky, Á., Schmid, C. and Stanek, L. (2014). *Urban Revolution Now: Henri Lefebvre in Social Research and Architecture*. Farnham, Ashgate Publishing, Ltd.
Morton, A. D. (2018). The architecture of 'passive revolution': Society, state and space in modern Mexico. *Journal of Latin American Studies*, 50(1), 117–152.
Neveling, P. (2020). De-escalating the centre. urban futures and special economic zones beyond poststructuralism's neoliberal imaginations. In Bach, J. and Murawski, M. (eds.) *Re-Centring the City*. London, UCL Press, 224–231.
Parker, S. (2015). *Urban Theory and the Urban Experience: Encountering the City*. 2nd edition. Abingdon, Routledge.
Pierce, J. (2019). How can we share space? Ontologies of spatial pluralism in Lefebvre, Butler, and Massey. *Space and Culture*, 1206331219863314.
Pierce, J. and Martin, D. G. (2015). Placing Lefebvre. *Antipode*, 47(5), 1279–1299.
Prakash, G. (2008). Introduction. In Prakash, G. and Kruse, K. (eds.) *The Spaces of the Modern City. Imaginaries, Politics and Everyday Life*. Princeton, Princeton University Press, 1–18.
Purcell, M. (2002). Excavating Lefebvre: The right to the city and its urban politics of the inhabitant. *GeoJournal*, 58(2), 99–108.
———. (2003). Citizenship and the right to the global city: Reimagining the capitalist world order. *International Journal of Urban and Regional Research*, 27, 564–590.
———. (2014). Possible worlds: Henri Lefebvre and the right to the city. *Journal of Urban Affairs*, 36(1), 141–154.
———. (2022). Theorising democratic space with and beyond Henri Lefebvre. *Urban Studies*, 59(15), 3041–3059.
Roy, D. (2013). Negotiating marginalities: Right to water in Delhi. *Urban Water Journal*, 10(2), 97–104.
Saha, A. (2022). Sustaining multicultural places from gentrified homogenisation of cities. *Cities*, 120, 103433.
Saito, K. (2017). *Karl Marx's Ecosocialism*. New York: Monthly Review Press.
Santos Junior, O. (2014). Urban common space, heterotopia and the right to the city: Reflections on the ideas of Henri Lefebvre and David Harvey. *urbe. Revista Brasileira de Gestão Urbana*, 6(2), 146–157.
Sayer, A. (1993). Review: Henri Lefebvre's the production of space. *International Journal of Urban and Regional Research*, 17(3), 458–459.
Schmid, C. (2012). Henri Lefebvre, the right to the city, and the new metropolitan mainstream. In Brenner, N. *et al.* (eds.) *Cities for People, Not for Profit*. New York and Abingdon, Routledge, 42–62.
Shaw, J. and Graham, M. (2017). An informational right to the city? Code, content, control, and the urbanization of information. *Antipode*, 49(4), 907–927.

Shields, R. (1999). *Lefebvre, Love, and Struggle: Spatial Dialectic*. London, Routledge.
———. (2001). Henri Lefebvre. In Elliott, A. and Turner, B. S. (eds.) *Profiles in Contemporary Social Theory*. London, Sage, 226–237.
———. (2011). Henri Lefebvre. In Hubbard, P. and Kitchin, R. (eds.) *Key Thinkers on Space and Place*. 2nd edition. Los Angeles, Sage, 279–285.
Slater, T. (2017). Planetary rent gaps. *Antipode*, 49, 114–137.
Smith, N. (1979). Toward a theory of gentrification: A back to the city movement by capital not people. *Journal of the American Planning Association*, 45(4), 538–548.
———. (1984). *Uneven Development: Nature, Capital and the Production of Space*. Oxford, Blackwell.
———. (1986). Gentrification, the frontier and the restructuring of urban space. In Smith, N. and Williams, P. (eds.) *Gentrification of the City* (pp. 15–34). Boston: Allen & Unwin, 15–34.
———. (1996). Of rent gaps and radical idealism: A reply to Steven Bourassa. *Urban Studies*, 33(7), 1199–1203.
———. (2003). Foreword. In *The Urban Revolution*. Minneapolis: University of Minnesota Press, pp. vii–xxiii.
Soja, E. W. (1980). The socio-spatial dialectic. *Annals of the Association of American Geographers*, 70(2), 207–225.
———. (1996). *Thirdspace: Journeys to Los Angeles and Other Real-and-Imagined Places*. Oxford, Basil Blackwell.
Standing, G. (2011). *The Precariat – The New Dangerous Class*. London, Bloomsbury.
———. 2016). The precariat, class and progressive politics: A response. *Global Labour Journal*, 7(2), 189–200.
Stanek, L. (2011). *Henri Lefebvre on Space: Architecture, Urban Research, and the Production of Theory*. Minneapolis, University of Minnesota Press.
Strüver, A., Saltiel, R., Schlitz, N., Hohmann, B., Höflehner, T. and Grabher, B. (2021). A smart right to the city – grounding corporate storytelling and questioning smart urbanism. *Sustainability*, 13(17), 9590.
Swyngedouw, E. and Wilson, J. (2014). Seeds of Dystopia: Post-politics and the return of the political. In Swyngedouw, E. and Wilson, J. (eds.) *The Post-Political and Its Discontents: Spaces of Depoliticisation, Spectres of Radical Politics*. Edinburgh University Press. Edinburgh, 1–24.
Tavolari, B. (2020). The right to the city: Conceptual transformations and urban struggles. *Revista Direito e Práxis*, 11, 470–492.
Taylor, L. H. and Helfenbein, R. J. (2009). Mapping everyday: Gender, blackness, and discourse in urban contexts. *Educational Studies*, 45(3), 319–329.
Thompson, M. (2017). LIFE in a ZOO: Henri Lefebvre and the (social) production of (abstract) space in Liverpool. *City*, 21(2), 104–126.
Trebitsch, M. (2002 [2014]). Preface. In *Critique of Everyday Life*. London, Verso.
Turok, I. and Scheba, A. (2019). 'Right to the city' and the New Urban Agenda: Learning from the right to housing. *Territory, Politics, Governance*, 7(4), 494–510.
Unwin, T. (2000). A waste of space? Towards a critique of the social production of space. *Transactions of the Institute of British Geographers*, 25(1), 11–29.
Urry, J. (2004). The 'system' of automobility. *Theory, Culture & Society*, 21(4–5), 25–39.
Van Criekingen, M. and Breës, G. (2012). Réapproprier les espaces publics: Pour mieux dominer? *Bruxelles en mouvement*, 259, 16–18.
Vasconcelos, T. (2019). Urbanism and urban planning following the thoughts of Henri Lefebvre. *WIT Transactions on Ecology and the Environment*, 217, 157–164.

Vasudevan, A. (2015). The autonomous city: Towards a critical geography of occupation. *Progress in Human Geography*, 39(3), 316–337.
Vogelpohl, A. (2011). Städte und die beginnende Urbanisierung. Henri Lefebvre in der aktuellen Stadtforschung. *Raumforschung und Raumordnung*, 69(4), 233–243.
Wachsmuth, D. and Brenner, N. (2014). Introduction to Henri Lefebvre's "Dissolving city, planetary metamorphosis". *Environment and planning. D, Society & Space*, 32(2), 199–202.
Walks, A. (2013). Suburbanism as a way of life, slight return. *Urban Studies*, 50(8), 1471–1488.
Ward, C. (2019). *The Mobilisation of land as a financial asset: The politics of urban rent production in post-industrial Manchester and Antwerp*. PhD. University of Ku Leuven.
Ward, C., Brill, F. and Raco, M. (2022). State capitalism, capitalist statism: Sovereign wealth funds and the geopolitics of London's real estate market. *Environment and Planning A: Economy and Space*, 0308518X221102157.
Werlen, C. (1988 [1993]). *Society, Action and Space*. London, Routledge.
Wilson, J. (2011). Notes on the rural city: Henri Lefebvre and the transformation of everyday life in Chiapas, Mexico. *Environment and Planning D Society and Space*, 29, 993–1009.
Wirth, L. (1938). Urbanism as a way of life. *American Journal of Sociology*, 44(1), 1–24.
Zhang, Z. (2006). What is lived space? *ephemera*, 6(2), 219–223.
Zieleniec, A. (2018). Lefebvre's politics of space: Planning the urban as oeuvre. *Urban Planning*, 3(3), 5–15.

3 Real estate developers and the production of space

Introduction: the turn to practice

Urban planning has frequently been portrayed as an optimistic, future-oriented activity, promising a better future for a city and its population (Abram & Weszkalnys, 2013). Hence the observation:

> In developing cities, spatial planning and development systems are generally used to enhance the integration between sectors such as housing, spatial justice, transport, energy and industry, and improve people's quality of life.
>
> (Tabane *et al.*, 2021:77)

There has long been a corollary belief that the whole tradition of planning is progressive in the sense that the planner's commitment to the ideology of social harmony – unless it is perverted or corrupted in some way – always puts the planner in the role of 'righter of wrongs', 'corrector of imbalances', and 'defender of the public interest' (Harvey, 1985:177). Constrained by capitalism, then, but we should see planners as heroes, nonetheless. And heroes of course require villains, a role to which Marxist geography has often allotted real estate developers, amongst others. This strict allocation of roles is flawed on both sides. In practical terms:

> Planning and architecture have historically not always taken the right path. In the USA, notably, 'Street grid design, one-way streets, the absence of sidewalks and crosswalks, the location of highways and transit stops, and even residential parking permit requirements can shape the demographics of a city and isolate a neighborhood from those surrounding it, often intentionally'.
>
> (Schindler, 2015:1939)

Developers will recognise the admission that the promises of planning often go unfulfilled, are not fulfilled in ways that had been expected, or come with unanticipated downsides as they collide with people's identities, life trajectories, and aspirations (Kolling & Koster, 2019:436). And why? Lefebvre's answer was that urban planning serves an important function in the urban stage of capitalism, masking the process of the secondary circuit of capital, what we should now perhaps call

DOI: 10.1201/9781003220244-3

the real estate economy (Hofman & Aalbers, 2019), serving to conceal both how urban phenomena actually work and what opportunities may exist to improve how the city works. In this way, planning functions as 'the state's strategic instrument for the manipulation of fragmented urban reality and the production of controlled space' (Lefebvre, 1973 [1976:15]). Marxist geographers took an equally antipathetic view of the planning process, at least under capitalism: amidst the continuous spatial displacement of capital 'creatively' destroying and restructuring the built environment (Harvey, 1982), 'State and public authorities enjoy a querulous agency at best: they are important because (inter)national legislation and urban planning are mechanisms, and selective social technologies, which support a particular materialisation of cities' (Jauhiainen, 2006:186). From neither analysis does planning emerge unscathed.

Lefebvre himself was certainly not averse to criticism of planning in any of its forms; he argued that 'The argument made here is that strategic planning processes – and the documents they produce – deal with necessarily abstract planning concepts' (Lefebvre, 1974 [1991:37–39]), and shared in different ways by many others that 'urbanism is based on a misconception: making the production of the city similar to the industrial production of objects' (Vasconcelos, 2019:157). His criticism of the 'order, discipline and infrastructure' of the planning approach has been echoed many times thereafter: 'Their abstract nature conceals a lack of conceptual resolution that is only fully revealed when the concepts are applied to situated, material places (particular neighbourhoods, streets, properties, etc.)' (van den Nouwelant, 2015:2).

Urban planning and socialism

Before developers query this close association of planning failure with capitalism, it is worth stepping back to take a historical perspective of planning history. Lefebvre's polemics against 'the homogenizing, destructive, and anti-social consequences' of post-war planning for urban renewal (Brenner *et al.*, 2012:2) should be balanced against the fact that much of this planning was undertaken either in state socialist systems or in the name, at least, of socialism. Memories have rapidly faded, but even in a state socialist system, where the limitations imposed on land values by HBU considerations had theoretically been minimised, strenuous efforts had to be made to limit the growth of large cities and restrict and order urban spatial development. In Soviet cities, 'industry and housing were interspersed to a degree rarely if ever found in modern market economies' (Becker *et al.*, 2012:48), whilst city peripheries were dominated by high-rise housing (Bertaud & Renaud, 1997). These efforts, it is important to recall, ultimately foundered on contemporary logics of industrial concentration and economies of scale (Sawers, 1978:340). True, removal of inherited differentials in urban-amenity standards was a major cost variable facing socialist urban planners (Hamilton, 1979:225), but importantly, there never emerged in Soviet or other state socialist publications any broad theoretical framework for analysing urban land and the location of activities comparable to the models of Isard, the land economists, or HBU (Reiner & Wilson, 1979:53). Rather, attempts were made to overcome 'irrational urban land uses which have been created through the use of norms' (Bater, 1977:202) through subjective allocations of values to produce non-market land valuation solutions. This complicated the adoption of local planning, and the experimentation with micro-districts, and aggregations of them, neither of which 'did little to promote social interaction among their residents' (Sawers, 1978:351). Reliance on public transport actually led to *fewer* streets, with the land released for more parks as a result (Reiner & Wilson, 1979:64), but this did not serve to alleviate the litany of complaints raised by Soviet citizens, including at core the inadequate quality of their residential accommodation, but also long commutes caused by waiting lists, which also extended to housing or holiday accommodation, queues at shops and for public transport, and lengthy searches for consumer goods (Hamilton & Burnett, 1979:266), all redoubled by high population density, combined with monotony-reinforced concrete construction to produce a 'dull monotony' (Gilev, 2020:67) often constant to the outskirts of newly planned cities (French & Hamilton, 1979:79–88).

Planning however there was aplenty. If 'Master plans are the practical blueprints for the future socialist city' (French & Hamilton, 1979:20), by the 1970s these plans already incorporated decentralisation of industrial activity, zoning, and the need for an efficient communication network. Even when the urban planning system started to depoliticise, with claims then made that urban life in the Soviet Union was eventually destined to differ little from that experienced under capitalism (Frolic, 1970), inertia continued to rule until the eventual collapse of the state socialist system. Where even moderately successful developments occurred, they owed much to spirited debates ignited by local architects, as well as the influence of different national legacy space and planning arrangements (Ruoppila, 2004:6–7), and even the realisation that Soviet planning structures could on occasion be creatively interpreted (Metspalu & Hess, 2018:348). These are uncomfortable lessons for Marxists now, as they were even for some of the original protagonists (Kopp, 1981), but they must not be forgotten, albeit that Lefebvre and other Western Marxists had long disassociated themselves with the doomed venture of state socialism:

> Since the 1960s Lefebvre described the post-Stalinist socialist states in the same way as he described capitalist states: as bureaucratic regimes of controlled consumption, oriented toward economic growth, and differing from the individualist Western model in their emphasis on collective consumption.
> (Stanek, 2011:64)

More recently, in contrast with the Philippines, where 'real estate developers have acquired an unusual level of autonomy' (Mouton & Shatkin, 2020:410), China in particular has assigned significant agency to public sector institutions for real estate development projects, and 'Joint ventures facilitated specialization and cooperation between transcalar state agencies based on market benefits and returns' (Shen *et al.*, 2020:1652), with the result that 'private developers did not have much autonomy regarding what was to be built' (Shen *et al.*, 2020:1648). This too has ended largely badly, in particular with over-construction, failed mega-projects, and ultimately in development default, with serious adverse consequences for the Chinese economy as a whole, such that 'Restructuring in the property development sector is likely to be a significant drag on China's economic growth and place additional strains on local government finances for some time' (Hendy, 2022:67). Lefebvre would not, one suspects, be very surprised at this outcome. The many failures of strategic urban planning, including new cities that never eventuated, partly caused by planning overconfidence and an unwillingness to follow the dictates of market research, bears witness to the importance of both understanding why this has happened. One possible role for developers, amongst others, one might be tempted to conclude, is to try to influence the planning process to avoid the seemingly inevitable, and sometimes colossal, waste of resources that result from its failure.

Urban politics and capitalism: the politics of resistance

In place of the planners or other technocrats subjected to his criticism, Lefebvre was more inclined to take seriously those created by the elite, some artists and perhaps of those, such as a few writers and philosophers, who describe and aspire to do no more than describe (Lefebvre, 1974 [1991:39]), who are

> striving to change life and to transcend obsolescent political institutions and parties. The philosopher establishes an opposition between commerce, the state and intellectuals or artists that parallels another between need and desire, between things rational and irrational, technocratic and artistic.
>
> (Conley, 2012:23)

It is a predilection that has resonated over the decades: 'The sources of resistance generally depend, however, on the initiatives of highly motivated individuals and take place outside the formal institutional frameworks, mostly restricted to progressive neighborhoods or specific urban subcultures' (Apostol, 2015:171). There rests an echo of traditional Marxist reliance on the elite of the past, the Party – which Lefebvre eventually rejected – in these suggestions. But does this fresh elite that Lefebvre identified – which may or may not correspond to those engaged in the politics of resistance, and which may or may not be in some way 'underwritten' by a theory of the production of space (Lefebvre, 1973 [1976:17]) – represent a new and potentially successful way to combat capitalism? And if so, why has it not either been utilised over the past half-century, or, if it has, why has it not been successful? Or should we simply admit defeat and recognise wistfully that

> Lefebvre ties his humanist interpretation of Marx to a romantic humanist and expansive conception of alienation that problematically conflates a myriad of quantitative types of domination whilst promoting an eclectic array of humane types of resistance.
>
> (O'Kane, 2019:57)

Can Marxists rest content with that? The inclusion of geographical concepts into Marxist political strategy alongside its incorporation into theoretical analysis has no doubt more than a modicum of practical utility. But to respond to this failure by assimilating Lefebvre exclusively within a politics of resistance that reaches back to a syndicalist and even anarchist past before Marx, however, is very far from an inevitable response to the failure of Leninist politics and state socialism. It is, however, a hallmark of much radical urban geography. Examples abound, and it is worth taking a detour at this point to investigate characterisations of this resistance, as it is of great concern and interest to all real estate actors, from planners to developers and investors, and in what such 'engagement' consists – a term in frequent use in relation to planning, for example the observation that the planning and design disciplines need 'to adequately engage with the compound forms of inequality that will inevitably arise through climate change in the future' (Howe, 2022:391).

More history not to be forgotten. In part responding to Lefebvre, Manuel Castells, in his initial strongly Marxist guise, identified what he believed was a new political subject: urban social movements: urban social movements as powerful cross-class alliances, gathered around issues of collective consumption. In subsequent decades, these urban values spread to broader social strata, the beginning of the long rediscovery of the urban by Marxists as well as international attempts at 'urban renaissance' (Porter & Shaw, 2013). And certainly, in those decades, urban social movements sprang up in continental Europe – as elsewhere – contesting the state and demanding more investment in collective consumption, in working people and their lives. For example:

> In Brazil, there ensued a combination of apparently largely irreconcilable conceptions: an amalgam between Lefebvre's right to the city and the notion, developed by Castells, of urban social movements' struggles for access to urban facilities for collective consumption.
>
> (Tavolari, 2020:478)

They are

> fighting for urban services and housing, but also projecting a new city as the expression of a new society. These movements had been largely misunderstood by Marxist theory (although not ignored by the practice of Marxists) because of the obsession of folding all conflicts into class struggle.
>
> (Castells, 2021:2).

They have been described as micro-spatial urban practices, and claimed that they are reshaping urban practices, as under their banner has been included a diverse range of actions and places:

> [G]uerrilla and community gardening; housing and retail cooperatives; flash mobbing and other shock tactics; social economies and bartering schemes, 'empty spaces' movements to occupy abandoned buildings for a range of purposes; subcultural practices like graffiti/street art, skateboarding and parkour; and more.
>
> (Iveson, 2013:941)

That resistance is often surely admirable, is certainly sincere, and has been capable of participating in achievements ought to be beyond doubt. With the experience of many decades after Lefebvre's identification of resistance and geography, it is however now surely time to measure the impact of these diverse politics of resistance, a request that is now more than a decade old (Zeiger, 2011), to determine to what extent have they succeeded in what Lefebvre himself called for:

> [R]evolutionizing the space–time relationship, for a kind of authentically lived experience that is no longer bounded and appropriated by capitalism and divided into measurable, quantifiable units that are constantly being counted down.
>
> (Newman, 2011:353)

For linking Lefebvre to the global Occupy movement would surely be desirable, if the movement were understood to have made a measurable contribution to the overthrow of capitalism (Engler & Engler, 2016). There are certainly those who argue just that, as summarised by the title of a Guardian article: *Occupy Wall Street swept the world and achieved a lot, even if it may not feel like it* (Olla, 2021). But is this a sustainable assertion? Certainly, in response to the dismal prospect of the continuation of the global urban morass as it stands in the early 21st century, there is always hope for the return of the prodigal political offspring, but radical theorists site it theoretically in 'the excess, the remainder, that which cannot be fully accounted for by a process of institutionalisation and depoliticisation' (Swyngedouw, 2017:59), or in 'how the urban poor as part of subordinate classes challenge the hegemony of private property rights' (Shin, 2018:3):

> By appropriating and caring for places portrayed as dangerous or decaying, such as parking lots, incomplete sidewalks, or public schoolyards, they [the dispossesed] engage in the urban development plans in ways that enable them to endure the urban transformations and uncertainty of future displacement they produce.
>
> (Kolling & Koster, 2019:334)

Or:

> Urban social movements have resisted the transformation and modernization of their cities, fought against commercialization and displacement, and demanded old and new forms of urbanity, mixed districts in the city centers, street life, and public spaces. At the same time, they have created many kinds of concrete urban spaces and alternative, oppositional everyday practices.
>
> (Schmid, 2012:53)

It has even been claimed that if only on a very small scale, 'Working from the grassroots, civil society actors are creating alternative systems of production and consumption or 'grassroots innovations for sustainability' (Seyfang & Smith, 2007; Nicolosi, 2020:59). In such conceptualisations, the original hope encapsulated within Castells' concept of the urban social movement never appears to be far from the surface: the Indignados in Spain and the global Occupy Movement are the 'new modes and practices of collective political organisation . . . provisionally materialised in these localised insurrectional events' (Swyngedouw, 2017:59). For the urban poor, 'Facilitated by a broader cross-class alliance, fights for the collective consumption such as housing have a direct potential to make this [the just city] possible' (Shin, 2018:26).

No doubt that, as Lefebvre wistfully observed, 'Countless revolutionaries have vainly believed, and still believe, that a spark would be enough to engulf the world' (Lefebvre, 1973 [1976:13]). The trail of these beliefs so far as urbanism is concerned now forms an enthusiastically chronicled political archaeology in itself:

> [N]ow resurrected in France with the 'zadiste' green left which for example succeeded in preventing the construction of a new airport at Notre-Dame-des-Landes in France, this ZAD being part of a broader activist space against the 'airport world', one that, in the wake of the movement against the Keystone XL Pipeline, has come to be referred to as 'Blockadia', which Naomi Klein describes as 'not a specific location on a map but rather a roving transnational conflict zone that is cropping up with increasing frequency and intensity'.
> (Armstrong, 2021:98)

Against entrepreneurs, yes (Lachaud, 2017), but also, it must be admitted, an alliance itself of eco-activists *and farmers* (Armstrong, 2021:95, my emphasis). If there ever had been a solid class analysis of such movements, it would be ever harder to undertake with the passing decades. As one Polish study observed, 'the category of urban social movement is an umbrella term, often concealing both formal and informal entities that vary greatly in their organization, ideology, social platform, praxis and strategies' (Pluciński, 2018:655). As such, Marxists must recognise that they are not necessarily all progressive, let alone components of a coherent strategy to supersede capitalism. Already decades ago, a cloud was noted over whether such movements could represent an inveterate hopefulness and openness towards the future (Smith, 2003:viii), which has rained on progressive hopes subsequently, such that overlapping housing and refugee crises have in many instances led to a right-wing populism (Rossi, 2018:1428), not an emancipatory movement, a sobering reflection on why the globalisation of everything, as Lefebvre might have put it, cannot possibly succeed.

It is true that with their demands for affordable housing and more participation and dialogue to shape what happens in urban space, and in their protest marches against inner-city gentrification, some of these movements of varied types do sometimes refer to Lefebvre's earlier texts, even if this is not always directly evident from their websites and protest signs. Lefebvre is, indeed, to be found prayed in aid of these movements, explicit references to be found in statements made by the intellectual leaders of the movements and in social science research on recent urban social movements (Rau, 2019:xiv). His 'experimental utopia' is identified with them (Iveson, 2013:942), and often in the same breath as insistence upon the need to encounter Lefebvre's thought as a whole, and not in part, but in fact to do just the opposite:

> An antiglobalization movement that wanted to build a new anticapitalist internationalism could take a lot of inspiration from the ferment in Russia in its pre-Stalinist days, but it could also, it was claimed, learn a lot from Lefebvre's insistence on urban revolution and the prospect of a globalized creativity, urban and otherwise, delinked from the effects of a ubiquitous economic and ideological slavery that Lefebvre understood as so deadening, but which he knew could never win.
>
> (Smith, 2003:xxiii)

Admission of the fact that Lefebvre's enthusiasm for urban revolution waned markedly after the failure of the 1968 uprising in Paris and the increasingly obvious sclerosis of the Communist Bloc is not very evident in these assimilations. Aside from the many criticisms of Occupy and equivalent movements, however, and in the absence of a political strategy based on them, which Lefebvre failed however understandably to provide, radical geographers who perceive only street politics of resistance appear to be asking Marxists to make a difficult choice, between engaging in radical street opposition and resigning themselves to a retreat to the academy at best, or at worst to do nothing at all. Lefebvre would surely have completely agreed that 'capitalist cities have long served as space for envisioning, and indeed mobilizing towards, alternatives to capitalism' (Brenner *et al.*, 2012:1–2). No doubt too, there is significant resistance to the commodification of space in profit-driven urbanisation. In a projection where Marxists might seek more explanation of process, and even think of some longer-term objectives, it is asserted that 'Collective protests can grow into social movements that use a citizenship discourse in order to resist planned interventions' (Kolling & Koster, 2019:340). Unfortunately, that they can does not mean they will. It must now be considered doubtful even that the hope that 'A spatial approach might bring to light neglected opportunities for political advantage' (Shields, 1999:151) will transpire, at least within the immediate future.

It is worth remembering that Castells himself first retreated from his initial views, firstly to one much closer to that of Lefebvre (Castells, 1983) and then progressively from Marxism altogether in favour of a postmodernism that, whilst still of the Left, led him to remark wistfully that because he had, in memorable words that have often now been cited:

> I have seen so much misled sacrifice, so many dead ends induced by ideology, and such horrors provoked by artificial paradises of dogmatic politics that I want to convey a salutary reaction against trying to frame political practice in accordance with social theory, or, for that matter, with ideology.
>
> (Castells, 1998 [2010:395])

This in turn occasioned the observation that 'It is also interesting to note how Manuel Castells went from this hypercritical attitude [towards Lefebvre] to an unbridled postmodernism, falling into all the failings for which he had formerly unfairly reproached Lefebvre' (Sangla, 2011:2). So, without wishing to follow Castells' world-weary hindsight, yet never willing to abandon hope or tumbling into a postmodernist quietude, Marxists may recognise that the politics of street resistance may be exciting, even momentarily uplifting, but it is not only strategically but also politically problematic. If 'the utopian framing that customarily informs urban visioning requires reversal to a temporal sequence centered on imagining concrete spatio-temporal utopias as immediately necessary, and realisable' (Swyngedouw, 2014:186), then this might equally entail some very difficult choices. In particular, the hard realisation that there is a value in some, but not all, of street resistance.

What might a developer conclude from this? Certainly that, for radical geographers, spaces of representation may emerge as counterspaces, 'spaces of resistance to the dominant order arising precisely from their subordinate, peripheral or marginalized positioning' (Soja, 1996:68). But also, the tough reality that must be conceded, that what results may be temporarily *disruptive* space, but not *differential* space. Like many Marxists before and after him, radical geographers have been optimistic as to the direction of disruption, but as with the potentially disturbing implicit connection of ethical with socially developed psychological characteristics (Sève, 1968 [1978]), the possibility of a negative direction for disruption is never investigated.

Nor necessarily therefore do Marxists wish to focus exclusively on resistance in ever-fewer traditional streets; if the seeds of the destruction of capitalism that they seek may only be found in urban social movements born and bred in such streets, then prospects for capitalism look very bright. Indeed, in a world in which, as Lefebvre himself recognised, for over a century class relations have become less stark than when Marx wrote, and when the history of such movements has already demonstrated their sporadic qualities, Marxists might question the presumption that they can be found in them *at all*.

Fortunately, there are many intermediate positions that might be of value, for example the work of Occupy Philadelphia Housing Authority, which successfully campaigned to make the city of Philadelphia to agree to establish a community land trust and permanent low-income housing (Rinde, 2022). But even harder: Marxists might just have to accept that these protests are not necessarily 'implicit utopian glimpses into a different, post-capitalist urban world' (Kipfer, 2002:117), and, hardest of all, that they might have to look elsewhere for examples of what a future after capitalism has been superseded may resemble – even perhaps to the space produced by some, at least, real estate developers – which entails interaction with the planning system.

Back to planning

The result of the concentration by radical geographers on urban political resistance and the focus on the admittedly obvious and widespread negative aspects of planning is that there appears to be an unbridgeable gulf between theory and practice, to the extent that by the second decade of the 21st century, there may even be some suggestion that the spatial turn has lost its way. The problem certainly remains that whilst it may be clear that 'the work on the urban was a result of earlier studies of the rural, and that *The Production of Space* is a theoretical summation of all this research' (Elden, 2006:192), neither Lefebvre himself, writing at a time when the Communist Party itself was still a powerful electoral force in France, nor his interpreters have left firm guidelines as to how his work should be used in practice beyond sympathy with the dispossessed. Worse, although the *Production of Space* (Lefebvre, 1974 [1991]) has been described, surely rightly, as a key analytic that empowers geographers to think critically about the various economic, cultural, class, gender, and racial processes that shape Lefebvrian space, one suspects that they can think, survive, and even flourish well enough outside Lefebvrian categories themselves. To be useful, the concept ought to deliver more: it should be possible to lever the Lefebvrian schema of space for urban political praxis (Pierce & Martin, 2015:1279). But how?

At the global scale, this does seem a daunting task, especially as 'Planning and design do not typically address the scale of "urbanization" – a process that transforms society and space into a practically planetary-wide network' (Howe, 2022:391). Lefebvre also warns in no uncertain terms that there is violence, hidden perhaps but nevertheless intrinsic to such abstraction: 'the "plan" . . . does not remain innocently on paper. On the ground, the bulldozer realizes "plans"' (Lefebvre, 1996:191; Charnock, 2018:1455). In the past, critics of urban planning have employed the concept of a 'logic of visualisation' (Lefebvre, 1974 [1991:285]) which takes the readability of space for granted and conceals the condensation of power relations hidden in space (Butler, 2005:22), 'As for representations of the relations of production, which subsume power relations, these too occur in space' (Lefebvre, 1974 [1991:33]), for example in two-dimensional planning models of cartography (Johnson, 1997:60; Gleeson & Low, 2000), and now, presumably, nD models as well, merging physical dimensions with time, space, and cost. The dangers of this focus on representations of space are now clear. Interactive models and 'walk-throughs' – noticeable absent unwelcome intrusions such as the homeless – do not necessarily deliver socio-economic awareness. In terms of critique, then, Lefebvre is certain that 'to clear a path, we have to destroy the models' (Lefebvre, 1970 [2003:163]), as 'Every town planning scheme conceals a programme for everyday life. Explicitly or not, it refers to an overall conception of man, of life and of the world' (Lefebvre, 1961 [2014:373]). One key radical objection to the planning process under capitalism, on which Lefebvre was firm, is simply that it betrays the marginalised and disenfranchised. At best, it can be described as pandering to the majority, and at worst, aiming at a loosely defined elite at the expense of others: sometimes *all* others, and sometimes only those who are specifically excluded, most obviously the inhabitants of *favelas* and their equivalents worldwide (Davis, 2006:174). Marxists will surely agree that Lefebvre was right to draw attention to the abstractness of planning, representation, and ideology otherwise (Lefebvre, 1974 [1991:129]). His polemics against 'the homogenizing, destructive, and antisocial consequences' of post-war planning for urban renewal (Brenner *et al.*, 2012:2) reflect the fact that there are many ways in which even successful cities have been no doubt fairly claimed to be failing their poorer inhabitants, notably wage growth stagnation and resultant cost of living pressures, congestion, and inner-city crime (Evans, 2014:136), accompanied by continued suburban gentrification (Florida, 2017), generating what has been described as 'social apartheid' on a global scale, state-led, or at least state-enabled (Lees, 2019:8). In the midst of this enormous policy pressure, and whilst not absolving local government of responsibility, the extent to which there is any capacity for individual cities and their administrations to reduce these inequalities and remove spatial injustices is certainly in doubt, important as the task of trying undoubtedly continues to be (Glaeser, 2020:216). For planning does, or at least certainly can, not only conceal but embody the strategies of contemporary capitalism. Their human agents might well therefore be expected to defend themselves, and not retire meekly from the field. In that sense, planning is a battlefield that for Marxists must remain contested space.

Gentrification and residential developers

Loaded with negative connotations by Marxist geographers, described as the outcome of government regeneration processes in inner-city areas and more widely the consequences of economic restructuring, gentrification is a well-known example of such contested space. It has been explained as a function of the gap between existing and potential rent, created through a failure to make sufficient investment, a means of increasing ground rent and thence capitalising on the locational advantage of land that is currently 'underused' in terms of its capital accumulation potential, gentrification being the result – one held entirely undesirable by Marxist geographers (Smith, 1986, 2005).

In the United States, criticism of planners, and the developers they enable, has therefore significantly revolved around the anti-gentrification argument:

> High-income earners, like the tech workers who can afford market-rate housing, are effectively displacing communities and small businesses that depend on lower-income inclusionary housing and land-use policies, such as rent control that offer protection from unregulated market forces; protections won because of decades of grassroots activism by working class communities of color.
>
> (Szeto & Meronek, 2017)

And that, in this process, now for many decades worldwide, 'New-build gentrification is made up of large, newly constructed apartment complexes and luxury residential estates where the gentrification has been conducted by a developer' (Davidson & Lees, 2005:1169).

Amidst this apparent radical consensus, it is worth recalling four broad points. Firstly, Marxists have long tussled over equality, but where there has been general agreement is that a simplistic insistence on equality in the short term at the expense of either social development generally or advances that threaten capitalism is not to be incorporated into any Marxist political programme.

Secondly, the underlying economics of gentrification ought to be distinguished from the social and economic relations that are implicit in its residential aspects.

Even those broadly sympathetic to Marxist models of urban development regret that this approach pays virtually no attention to the processes behind the demographic and lifestyle profiles of gentrifiers – the people in front of the economic forces (Rose, 1983:61). Lefebvre will always encourage us to ask: What does it take to create a dwelling, a development, a village, a new town, even an entire city that is in accord with peoples' actual preferences? Radical geographers may assert that these preferences are themselves socially conditioned, and Lefebvre certainly agreed, which may suggest that future residential housing in a world where capitalism has been superseded may move away from the suburban or even the high-rise apartment model in favour of more communal living arrangements, at least to some extent, but all must agree that this must remain conjecture, and that the evidence to date provides little support, including for Marx's own radical contention regarding the family, the collapse of which has been long heralded but in practice much more complex than was predicted even half a century ago (Zaretsky, 1976), albeit that consequences in terms of space have been felt in many urban environments (Kinkaid, 2020).

Thirdly, Marxists have long recognised that political change cannot flow from a minority underclass. Whatever dramatic changes have occurred to the structure of social classes worldwide, there cannot be any expectation that the demise of capitalism will be led or even driven only by those on the fringes of society. Lefebvre himself implicitly recognised exactly this, so there is no need for any reform of his position here. Political change may have to follow in the wake of a project which is driven by urban transformation, not lead it, as in Marx's time (Lefebvre, 1973 [1976:91).

Fourthly, but perhaps most importantly, anti-gentrification arguments often focus not on the responsibility of government and planners for compensation, inclusion, or even phasing in relation to those actually or potentially displaced, but rather on

> institution-based, preventive measures against displacement, e.g., tenant protection, commercial spaces dedicated to local businesses or alternative planning tools, [that] can be interpreted as organised, 'political' visible forms of resistance.
>
> (Friesenecker & Lagendijk, 2021:701)

Concepts such as the 'planetary rent-gap' (Slater, 2017) and 'neo-Haussmannization' (Merrifield, 2014:xii) have been brought into play to support the contention by radical geographers that gentrification, which it has been recognised has been enabled if not encouraged by planners and a lack of will by government (Kern, 2022:163), has become a worldwide strategy (López-Morales, 2010; Lees *et al.*, 2015). In stressing the significance of the way in which temporary settlements and poorer residents are moved on from land subject to redevelopment, sometimes even forcibly, the argument is made that 'The theft of space from labor and its conversion into spaces of profit is achieved through displacement and resettlement' (Chatterjee, 2014:21), one voice amongst many. The issue may not be quite so clear-cut as all that, since 'several empirical studies of gentrification have failed to find substantial evidence of displacement, leading some to suggest that gentrification can sometimes generate benefits with minimal displacement' (Derakhti & Baeten, 2020:4), but the responsibility for effective resettlement of residents displaced by development is undeniable. In the Global South, there is widespread recognition that 'Formal planning has failed to address the complexity of diverse cities, and particularly their informal and unplanned nature, leading to a proliferation of informal settlements with limited or no social services and public utilities' (Andres *et al.*, 2021:33).

What for now?

And this is where Lefebvre finds himself placed, entirely equivocal as to the alleged benefits of planning in respect of such issues as gentrification. *The Production of Space* (Lefebvre, 1974 [1991]) is often referenced by numerous studies that both aim at and succeed in demonstrating how urban planning can and does violate many residents' right to the city by excluding them from a life in the city (e.g. Banerjee-Guha, 2010; Endres, 2014, 2019; Lanari, 2019; Kolling, 2019). For Lefebvre, and those who have followed in his footsteps (e.g. Leary, 2009; Lehtovuori, 2010; Thompson, 2017; Lennon & Moore, 2019), planning has only ever masqueraded as a rational process, conceiving of space as 'a fungible resource that can be changed and exchanged relative to the needs of capital accumulation, irrespective of the social dynamics which currently sustain and are sustained by it' (Lennon & Moore, 2019:119). Others have already cautioned that whilst it is relatively easy to agree in the broadest terms that 'From capital's point of view, the diffusion of entrepreneurial governance and the neoliberal city can be viewed as processes of creating isotopias, of commodifying urban common spaces and subordinating them to the logic of capital' (Santos Junior, 2014:155), there remains the problem that 'few writers are concerned with the implications of their analysis for planning or development, which makes their work less immediately relevant for the planning field' (Carp, 2008:131).

But this is where the planner who wishes to take Lefebvre on board needs most assistance. So far as the planning process is concerned, even under capitalism, it is far from certain that it should in its entirety should be dismissed as the irretrievable servant of capital. On the contrary, the open-mindedness that Lefebvre argued ought to characterise Marxists should lead them to recognise that the goal of the insurgent planner, the entryist into the planning system, or even the planner with a social conscience, must be to side with Lefebvre in the attempt to make use of technical resources and means, citizens' political participation, and a renewal in the art of 'making the city' with 'work' (*oeuvre*) and 'use value' prevailing over production for the market and 'exchange value' (Vasconcelos, 2019:164). For Lefebvre's ideas to gain traction within planning, it must not be the case that 'market forces are inexorable' (Wang, 1996:314). Resistance to market forces, whether *described* as 'insurgent planning', 'radical planning' or not, forms the central core of any effort by planners to create differential space, even in the midst of and despite global capitalism.

The task of such a 'differential planner' – to add another term to a growing list – is therefore to unmask the hypocrisy, inconsistency, and ontological inaccuracy of their own discipline. The starting point must be that some kind of urban planning is required. That this should have to be justified will no doubt seem incredible to a practising urban planner, but in the light of critical analysis, the justification evidently still needs rehearsing.

That urban planning is here to stay is surely beyond doubt. The observation is as follows:

> More urgent than transductive reasoning about future urban plans is the need to confront current reality: urban planning is with us to stay for the foreseeable future, its hypothetical function in a society freed from the demands of capital overlaid by its role as a bureaucratic contribution to the process of social reproduction and an instrument of compromise and coordination between different components of the capitalist economy.
>
> (Harvey, 1985:175)

This remains as true now as when it was written. However, if urban planning is required, and almost certain to continue both now and when capitalism is eventually superseded, what should it be? How can it be used, even under capitalism, to create differential space, or at least promote the reassertion of use rather than exchange values? Lefebvre himself is notoriously silent on all of these points, implicitly relying on a cornucopia of vastly improved social relations for success, of which we can all easily conceive – for example, genuinely rational appreciation of the long-term implications of planning decisions (notably environmental externalities, but also for communities), greatly improved dispersion of accurate information, but above all a far greater degree of social homogeneity and shared interests, which for Marxists can only be completely achieved after the alienation flowing from capitalism has subsided. What, however, should we make of the problem *now*?

Problems with legacies

Lefebvre has already shown us why there is such extreme difficulty in developing a theory of the production of differential space under capitalism. A comparison with psychology may help illustrate why. Sève and others argued that although the individual personality is so heavily determined by social relations that the end of capitalism will inevitably bring about a change, there is no 'Marxist psychology' – just Marxist psychologists (Sève, 1968 [1978:21]). Marxism is not a replacement for scientific endeavour. In the case of the built environment, however, its very existence has been a function of and now a dominant component of capitalism itself. Whereas medicine after capitalism has been superseded, for example, can be expected to be better distributed and therefore more effective overall, although it will still depend on legacy hospitals, for example, and for that matter a generation of legacy surgeons and nurses, space after capitalism in general must necessarily start with its predecessor, in which physical space has been twisted and contorted into abstract space to fit the requirements of capitalism, but which now in that deformed state be put to the service of a just world and only slowly altered the work of many generations. Real estate development has long-lasting effects, as 'the city you say goodnight to is still, for the most part, still there in the morning' (Borden, 2003:116). In Lefebvrian terms, there can be few maximal differences. 'Lefebvre's point is that the right to the city is unlikely to be realized in our inherited urban centres' (Garbin & Millington, 2018:141): a street after capitalism has been superseded will, as Lefebvre says, look superficially similar. We may term this 'legacy space' a vital category of space with which the utopian and architect-manqué in Lefebvre was uncomfortable. And we can be certain that this existence of specialised, parcelled-out, neocolonial space – by past developers, certainly, but not only by them – poses a massive problem for the creation of differential space. We could wish that Lefebvre had spent more time grappling with the problem, but whilst he dwells on how failing to focus on the relations of production can lead to an exaggerated sense of the power of ideology and a reluctance to admit of modifications to the capitalist mode of production (Lefebvre, 1973 [1976:68]), the assurance that 'the reproduction of the relations of production cannot be localised in the enterprise' (Lefebvre, 1973 [1976:81]) leads only to the recognition of the production of space, and not to confrontation with produced, legacy space.

Legacy space has a number of components – the complex reality of existing land use and the built environment: constructed real estate, buildings under construction now and in the planning stage, and current and likely future technology, including of construction and architecture, all of which represent its raw material. As with Lefebvrian categories themselves, legacy space should not however be understood simply as physical space, but rather as an analytical category that can be applied to the urban fabric as a whole. There are practical examples of this that even Engels glimpsed, but refused to consider, employing the convenient mantra that to do so is mere utopianism. Now, worldwide, from suburbs to slums, legacy space would control what could happen for many centuries at the very least. The principles underlying legacy space have already been explored in a very different context, that of the imposition of socialist planning in already long-established cities. It is a scarcely encouraging vista.

Not everything about legacy space is however necessarily objectionable. Far from it, the post-capitalist world will have been bequeathed not only architecture of breath-taking beauty, but also a series of public spaces and communal facilities – some very dated, it must be conceded – of immense value. Hospitals, schools, concert halls and theatres, civic buildings and meeting places, parks, and the infrastructure of transport, production, and distribution would all be at the better service of such a world. Unfortunately, as we all know, neither planners nor those for whom they plan, including developers, do not inhabit that world. No doubt there are 'complex and provisional hierarchies between places, with their evolution depending on social actors' (Viala & Keerle, 2020:7). Yet all too often,

> [t]he top-down approach of placemaking is driven by city officials and developers to sterilise the image of the city to attract economic and cultural

> investment. This approach often treats the land as a resource and excludes marginalised communities who have their history, memory, and symbolism embedded in the land.
>
> (Gonsalves *et al.*, 2021:238)

In practice, these two approaches intertwine and may both be seen in operation concurrently and even in the same place. In part, this is because a top-down approach is often self-defeating: successful placemaking needs 'organizational and discursive strategies that are designed to build voice, to foster a sense of common benefit, to develop confidence among disempowered groups, and to arbitrate when disputes arise' (Friedmann, 2010:161).

Lefebvre does not always help here, as his epistemology remains opaque, even confusing, if not hidden, whilst his insistence on a holistic approach to imagining and possibly to creating social space seems to allow little room for nuance, different perspectives, or conflict, even though from a 21st-century perspective, the assertion that 'competing place-frames articulate different spaces' (Pierce & Martin, 2015:1294) seems on solid ground, if not even now part of a global consensus. Not least, as Marxists focused on psychology such as Sève would have been no doubt quick to point out, the importance of recognising the impact of individual biography on the moment, the perception of place, and even the conceptualisation of space. Places themselves combine legacies, the present and the future, stretched between humans and the natural world, interacting to produce inspiration, loyalty, and a host of other emotions and actions. Preferably, measures supported by Marxists will allow placemaking itself to contribute to the overcoming of capitalism and at the same time leave legacy space as suitable for a world after capitalism as possible, even though the full contours of that world are notoriously difficult to ascertain, let alone delineate or even describe in detail, so much so that Marx and Engels themselves largely foreswore such utopian thinking. The incorporation of placemaking and legacy space into a Lefebvrian Marxist perspective is a difficult path to tread, but it is one that must be followed – in this case, there really is no alternative.

Insurgent planning

No doubt scepticism towards the various more conventional planning movements that have enjoyed prominence across successive decades would be entirely appropriate for a Lefebvrian perspective on planning that intended to identify and promote use values. Whether New Urbanism, Traditional Neighborhood Design, Transit-Oriented Development, or Smart Growth (Kim, 2022; Kim *et al.*, 2022), all refuse to confront the central issue Marxists wish to raise, that of the dominance of capitalism within the planning process, and none solves the demands that it imposes on real estate development and the misuse of urban space that Lefebvre identified it has entailed. Even if there are elements of merit in each, Lefebvre would surely insist that Marxists cannot rely on any of them uniquely. If they are to have any value as part of the creation of differential space, it must surely be together, each as facets of an essentially *political* whole.

There is additional potential support. In contrast to conceptions of planning within capitalism as inevitably oppressive in content, if deceptive in form, there are also now a range of potentially valuable approaches, often assembled under the rubric of radical or 'insurgent citizenship' (Holston, 2009) and 'insurgent participation' (Hilbrandt, 2017) that notwithstanding important differences between them, in particular that insurgent planning (Sandercock, 1998; Miraftab, 2009; Basta, 2022) is grounded in political society, leans more on the agency, and epistemic privilege of marginalised social groups, and takes practice as the unit of analysis (Huq, 2020:375) that might incline a Marxist taking Lefebvre seriously to view the latter even more favourably than the former.

Insurgent planning practices are instigated by mobilised communities, acting as planners for themselves, largely dispossessed people working outside formal planning practices to plan against and despite spatial injustice (Miraftab, 2009, 2017; Friendly, 2022). There are many potential examples, including residents' roles in producing urban space as modes of urbanisation, for example the role of women in contesting traditionally male urban spaces (Sletto, 2021), even in ways in which people can work within formal planning systems to 'make themselves into citizens and political agents, become fluent in rights talk, and claim the cities as their own' (Caldeira, 2017:3). A linked concept is that of decoloniality: in a developing country context, an indigenous planning system which breaks free from the legacy of colonialism and elitism can potentially use *decentralised* commercial and public services within the urban to transcend difficulties of access (Muzorewa *et al.*, 2018). This is a standpoint that may sit awkwardly, it must be admitted, with the early Lefebvrian focus on the 'centre', but it is one that recognises the impact of change and the need for an open approach, and therefore one that a revised Lefebvrian approach could cautiously welcome, if carefully and consistently applied with the principles of the 'right to the city' constantly in view. Insurgent planning will always have its limitations, no doubt – but as with all other positive contributions to planning, it will have a role in the creation of differential space. Developers might want to consider how they can best be of use to the marginalised communities that seek to adopt it.

Planning as conflictual space

Answering the question of how to lever Lefebvrian theoretical categories in respect of planning is also complicated by the obvious fact that it is rare to identify a direct linear connection between a capitalist economy and a particular set of local planning regulations. As has been observed in relation to transportation in particular:

> Whether to promote existing patterns of automobility or enable healthier modes of active transport, whether to build light rail systems or high-speed rail, to extend metro lines or change local zoning codes, to disinvest from public transit or privatize bus systems – these are all political decisions framed by competing constituencies exposed to different costs and benefits, and more or less excluded from decision-making.
>
> (Sheller, 2015:14)

Lefebvre's displayed an antagonism, even more familiar today than when he wrote, towards 'the invasion of the automobile and the pressure of the automobile lobby' destroyed the complex functionality of streets and were 'harmful to urban and social life' (Lefebvre, 1970 [2003:18]). In response, however, the conflictual space of planning reality worldwide is that there have been many city-wide initiatives in place to spur public transport for decades, and they have become progressively more ambitious, that is to say, stricter. Increasing density, at least up to a point, reducing travel times, encouraging public transport, promoting environmentally sensitive construction, including where possible pedestrian and cycle access to facilities, are all different aspects of the creation of true differential space, which must push back against financial bargaining power in the production of space, whether its creation, structuring, or ultimately the use of space itself. It is through the retrospective assessment of relative collective and even individual bargaining power that the outcome of a particular development planning process might reveal how something of a world in which capitalism has been superseded has been achieved – including its contribution to a better environment and the direction of the revenues from its sale or leasing that constitute the criteria by which a Lefebvrian Marxist may seek to judge the outcome of a planning process.

Urban sprawl – a legacy problem

One specific legacy problem is urban sprawl, which, to give credit where it is due, the New Urban Principles, discussed below, set out to challenge is the formless suburban sprawl that has characterised American, Australian, and many other countries' residential developments since the mid-20th century, and which has now become almost the dominant form of residential real estate development worldwide. Criticism of urban sprawl is so widespread that it can certainly not be regarded as confined even to radical geographers or urban planners, let alone to Marxists. Significant elements of public administration and government have sought to contain it for decades, with varying degrees of success (Lindstrom & Bartley, 2003). Sprawl is now considered responsible for the significant fiscal cost for infrastructure provider agencies from both public and private sectors. Sometimes, it is even considered responsible for unbalanced public health services. Many of the negative externalities generated by urban sprawl are not born either by the developers or by the residents of the suburbs (Arbury, 2005).

The response of 'progressive planning' has been to suggest a Lefebvrian return to the traditional street, a warm vista of mixed land-uses, retail and varied residential settings that encourage mutual recognition and embed social interaction. In this dreamy vision of space, schools, day care, and play areas for children should all be close by, whilst the streets themselves should be narrow and generally unfriendly to automobiles. Where possible, natural features and drainage are to be preserved in order to have the minimal environmental impact, and infrastructure and services are designed so as to minimise waste and maximise energy efficiency (Parker, 2015:66). All this is surely highly desirable differential space to be produced in the future, but it fails to address the existing urban sprawl, which will remain problematic legacy space for generations.

Nor does it address the fact that despite its many obviously unappealing aspects, urban sprawl has helped many parts of the population access less expensive, single-family homes on large lots while giving residents greater freedom of movement, whereas highway systems have been expanded (Shawly, 2022:5). An oft-cited (though now decades-old) study of urban sprawl concluded that it is a consumer preference, and people prefer living in sprawl areas over a more compact and 'crowded' urban environment, not least because 'a key environmental driver of stress is noise' (Evans, 2014:122). Planners, even those with the most sincere intentions to create differential space, and even armed with significant powers to control sprawl, must recognise these limitations on what can be achieved. Even the supersession of capitalism will not eliminate noise, nor of itself create lasting communities: what it may do is encourage more, though not all, people to live in closer mutual proximity, which may make the task of planners easier in encouraging higher density developments.

None of this should suggest that there is not merit in the maintenance of public claims to urban space, which may form the basis for evaluation of planning proposals. From the setbacks and stalemates that confront activists in their demands worldwide, Marxism may try to reclaim some aspects of international, state, and city proclamations of the right to the city,

> to the extent that streets and squares of large cities have become established as centre stage for recent social struggles, the right to the city will continue to be at the centre of grassroots demands and to figure both as an analytical category and a horizon of emancipation.
>
> (Tavolari, 2020:487–488)

But it is to say that caution is needed here, just as it is in relation to urban sprawl, as it is only three decades ago that the claim that 'a city can truly be called a city only when its streets belong to the people' (Friedman, 1993:139) seemed reasonable to make. Now, the rise of cities without streets, especially in the Middle East, would suggest that it is planning itself that needs to belong to the people, not the streets themselves. The cultural ties that bound Lefebvre to the West, to Europe in particular, are starkly illustrated by his view of the urban. As he exalts, in language strongly reminiscent of his erstwhile allies, the Situationists:

> The urban is defined as the place where people walk around, find themselves standing before and inside piles of objects, experience the intertwining of the

threads of their activities until they become unrecognisable, entangle situations in such a way that they engender unexpected situations.

(Lefebvre, 1970 [2003:39])

Moreover, many of the festivals that Lefebvre celebrated are now far from spontaneous or ludic: they now form part of the competitive relationship between cities that characterises contemporary capitalism. They are therefore now businesses, the province of capital, and the domain of city administration. The critics Friedman cited were surely right in this, that the co-option by international, state, and city agencies of the right to the city in the service of modest reforms of the status quo has at the very least severely constrained its capacity to serve in the capacity Lefebvre originally intended, as a successful rallying cry against the capitalism of the urban. But its legacy has surely not been entirely negative: many of the young activists who read and admired '*The Right to the City*' went on to become influential architects, planners, politicians, and academics (Parker, 2015:20). What can *their* role be in creating that better future?

Not all rights to the city are progressive

Critics of neoliberal housing policies and planning argue that 'neighbourhood cohesion as privilege involves acknowledgement of a central aspect as the basis of this cumulative disposition, namely the possibility of and comfort with the exercise of choice' (Méndez *et al.*, 2021:1698). So whilst it may be tempting for Marxists to believe that the right to the city, 'some kind of shaping power over the processes of urbanization' (Harvey, 2012:5), is in some sense inevitably radical, the social cohesion that generates NIMBY demonstrates that this is not so. The unfortunate fact is that the ways in which individuals, families, and groups seek to help shape that urbanisation is frequently based on individual or localised collective self-interest, rendered especially prominent under any economic system that does not effectively restrain or reduce self-interest as a whole. 'In Vancouver, people often fought high-rise buildings because they would obstruct views of the sea and the mountains' (Lorimer, 1978:136). Lefebvre himself did recognise this, but suggested a division between, on the one hand, those he called reactors, who 'oppose a particular project in order to protect their own privileged space, their gardens and parks, their nature, their greenery, sometimes their comfortable old homes' (Lefebvre, 1974 [1991:381], and, on the other hand, 'liberals' or 'radicals' who will 'oppose the same project on the grounds that it represents a seizure of the space concerned by capitalism in a general sense, or by specific financial interests, or by a particular developer' (Lefebvre, 1974 [1991:381].

Given such a complex outcome, there is a strong possibility that a conflict can develop: on the one side, politicians, often those on the Left, and the developers they seek to encourage and whose developments they seek to permit, whilst on the other side, local residents, often privileged, with advantages entrenched for many decades, sometimes in alliance with radical opponents of development, notably on environmental grounds. Marxists must recognise that certainly under capitalism, and to some lesser extent once it has been superseded, 'People's ability to re-interpret and creatively misuse planned spaces' (Zhang *et al.*, 2008:904) is not necessarily positive (Kingma *et al.*, 2018:11). It is a story unfortunately repeated worldwide, not least through disparate and potentially conflicting values, a problem specifically pointed to in recent discussion of Lefebvrian conceptions of 'continuously socially produced and relational space' (Herzog *et al.*, 2022:2).

With such obstacles, and notable failures of planning, it has been suggested that responsibility and the focus of interest should lie elsewhere, notably with the importance of action at the community level (Bednarska-Olejniczak *et al.*, 2019; Belausteguigoiti, 2019). For example, by the end of the last century, it was widely recognised that official agencies with responsibility for housing have in the past carried out some policies which are now generally acknowledged to have been at the very least badly misconceived, largely as a result of apparent, or even wilful, ignorance of the interaction in traditional communities between housing and community life that Lefebvre so cherished. Replacement of 'slums' with drab and monotonous high-rise apartment blocks is the usual target of such criticism, aimed principally at local government housing policy, for example, in the UK (McCall & Mooney, 2018), not private sector developer initiatives aimed at a different market sector. More recently, amidst the gentrification of some high-rise and increasingly positive evaluations of their potential contribution to solving planning problems, for example, in Germany (Altrock, 2022), criticism has changed focus, from the built environment itself to governance, to 'the blurred mass of quangos which are replacing democratically elected local government' (Minton, 2012:xxvii). Developers have found themselves caught in the resultant policy confusion.

Competing visions of the right to the beach – Scarborough in Western Australia

3 Oceans, a Chinese developer, initially proposed two towers, one of 43 storeys and the other of 35, to include 346 apartments and 158 hotel rooms. There was a determined and high-profile campaign of opposition by local residents, stressing that the Scarborough Master Plan Design Guidelines agreed by the public in 2016 entailed maximum heights between 2–12 storeys. 'We didn't ask for skyscrapers, wind tunnels, shadows on our beach and we don't want them at Scarborough Beach' was one local comment. The Metropolitan Redevelopment Authority (MRA), responsible for planning at city level, rejected the proposal in December 2017 over concerns that it was a significant overdevelopment at the site, but accepted a revised proposal in June 2018, taller than the original site, with fewer apartments and hotel rooms, but also featuring a hundred public parking bays, an observation deck with an art gallery and restaurant/cafe, and retail and food outlets covering almost 3,000 m^2. The combination of persistent local opposition and a sluggish market led to the project being put on hold in 2019, but by 2021 it had been revived.

The State Premier, Mark McGowan, with ultimate planning responsibility, then said he had liked the developer's proposal and he would support another high-density project on the site. His comments were reported as follows:

> You've got to remember that the Government has invested around $100 million in infrastructure there at the Scarborough foreshore, with the swimming pool and the redevelopment, the skate park and all of those things, and you want lots of people to use it. . . . Having greater density in an apartment complex like that, you have more people, more life, more vitality, you have the businesses with people in there, buying coffees, buying meals, you have activity and life, which is exactly what precincts like Scarborough need. . . . It's an easy political thing for people to do to say, 'We don't want high-rise, we don't want this or that', but I do support that sort of development, because for some people, particularly those who are retired, that's what they want.
>
> (Carmody, 2019)

If from a Marxist perspective one wished to present a class analysis of the conflict, there can be little doubt that the more privileged, at least, have been those opposing the development, not those supporting it. The developer has been caught in the middle, and it has no doubt been an expensive trap in which to be caught.

High rise and density

It is true that density does not demand skyscrapers or even high-rise, at least for the immediate future. Many of the densest areas of European cities have little high-rise real estate. It might well be possible for the same number of people to be accommodated by the plot without building so high – but only at the expense of another vaunted and now largely private amenity, the sea view. None of this is to decry 'the role played by mobilising opposition to state authority in the production of spaces more responsive to the experiential desires of communities, rather than the capital control and accumulation agendas of elites' (Lennon & Moore, 2019:117). Rather, it is to suggest first, recognising that this opposition may in part lie within developers themselves, as opposed to a more conventional radical narrative that tends to place planners, together with the local community, and developers, with their financial backers, on opposite sides of a supposed moral compass, and second, that when communities express their opposition to particular developments, their experiential desires may be entirely in conformity with class and other social relations that are fully aligned with capitalism, not in opposition to it. Planners, including those of an insurgent inclination, must wrestle with these dilemmas – quite possibly, even after capitalism itself has been superseded, as even Lefebvre never categorically asserted that *all* problems associated with space could be directly traced to capitalism itself.

Planners, producers of differential space?

Lefebvre had little patience with an intellectual division of labour with which he himself refused to be bound. He criticised the social role of 'techniques, technicians, technocrats, epistemology, and the research of a purely technical or epistemological order' (Lefebvre, 1970a [2009:175]), who sought to use the production of space to divide rather than unite human social praxis, and compartmentalise the spheres or activities of everyday life, with the effect of entrenching privilege and power, and denying difference. 'The rationalist will establish or re-establish coherence into a chaotic reality which he observes and which offers itself up to his action' (Lefebvre, 1968 [1996:83]). Each specialist will no doubt reply in turn that it is simply impossible for any one person, even any one organisation, to retain all the information, knowledge, and expertise to manage every aspect of real estate development, even if they have the most holistic of intentions and the widest of perspectives. Some degree of specialisation is inevitable.

A key task then becomes the analysis of the role of different categories of organisations in the creation of abstract and differential space, their interrelationships, and mutual dependencies. Is it just that 'the creation of differential spaces [is] characterised by alternate modes of land use, organisation and social engagement to that normally recognised by the bureaucracy of planning' (Lennon & Moore, 2019:123)? The answer to this question can help us to understand how might Lefebvre expect Marxists to treat key participants in urban planning many decades on from his own work, and, now of crucial importance for the real estate market, in the development process, as planners, architects, developers, surveyors, and many other professionals. I am sure that Lefebvre did not mean to suggest that there should not be surgeons, not be nurses. His concern was for how organisations and the people who work for them are structured, how they manage information, what is their intention, and how they manipulate and are manipulated in the creation of abstract space under capitalism. What stands out now is that planners may be in a markedly inferior position to other participants in the process, especially developers, whose entire work consists of gathering resources and managing disparate interests, in respect of their ability to 'unite human praxis'.

Lefebvre demanded that whoever 'owns and makes space through planning and design must also provide opportunities for play, for festival, for the imaginative use of the public and social spaces of the city' (Zieleniec, 2018:5). Must? Or simply as Zieleniec goes on more meekly to suggest, can and should? For a developer, Lefebvre presents as much a theory of business ethics as a depiction of the future. Every plan, every Request for Proposal, contains within it a detailed 'second map' – of inequalities, spatial injustices, and opportunities for capitalism to flourish; but that same 'second map' may also contain steps, however small, to reduce inequalities, remedy injustices, and curb the excesses of capitalism or even replace it. A plan for a public square, the inclusion of a public health clinic or a cultural museum in a proposed zone redevelopment, changes to density rules to allow lower-income groups to live in areas previously denied to them, requirements for old-age accommodation, access to public transport, facilities for the less able – all these may become examples of those small steps. Whatever his traditional Marxist reluctance to engage in ethical discussion, what Lefebvre says amounts to the argument that planners have an ethical responsibility to fight for them. But how are they to be categorised, analysed, and weighed off against one another? And what might be satisfactory policies that planners can and should adopt that will maximise the opportunity for the creation, largely by developers, of differential space in a capitalist economy, watched over by an equally capitalist state?

Global policy agenda – no panacea

Neither principles of urban development nor planning itself is a direct route to the supersession of capitalism, that much is evident. But that is no reason necessarily to reject them outright, for example those included in the original New Urban Agenda (Garde, 2004:498), even if its message has now become eroded, even mundane, and 'the debate on New Urbanism now focuses on barriers to implementing the normative ideals of the movement and not on its relevance to the field' (Garde, 2020:455). There can be, in principle, little objection to such sustainable real estate development, to at least many of the elements of participatory planning and decision-making, to integrated urban planning, transparent accountability, and knowledge- and information-sharing, or to mechanisms such as cross-subsidies, social protection, and gender balance to ensure an adequate standard of living to the most economically disadvantaged and vulnerable population. The New Urban Agenda still points to ways in which the global reliance on real estate investment to finance 'the urban' can be counteracted, 'highlighting the need for regulations and taxation schemes that prevent speculation and land value capture which would only benefit speculators' (Robin & Brill, 2018:3), for example, the control of proliferating free zones (Mogielnicki, 2021). A manifesto that proclaims fine words such as these is surely admirable as far as it goes:

> We will promote the development of adequate and enforceable regulations in the housing sector, including, as applicable, resilient building codes, standards, development permits, land use by-laws and ordinances, and planning regulations, combating and preventing speculation, displacement, homelessness and arbitrary forced evictions and ensuring sustainability, quality, affordability, health, safety, accessibility, energy and resource efficiency, and resilience.
>
> (United Nations, 2017:28)

But what is obvious is that none of this is now remotely new. For over two decades now, the UN has promoted the 'Inclusive City', a place where everyone, regardless of wealth, gender, race, or religion, can participate in the (social, economic, and political) opportunities throughout the urban fabric. The 2030 Sustainable Development Agenda and its Sustainable Development Goals (SDGs), in particular SDG 11 – the urban target – calls for a cities and human settlements to be inclusive, safe, resilient, and sustainable. This includes improving the management of human settlements; promoting sustainable land-use planning and management; promoting sustainable energy and transport systems in human settlements; and promoting sustainable construction industry activities, all of which are connected to urban regeneration. SDG 11 makes room for urban regeneration to become part of urban transformations in order to promote inclusivity and sustainability (United Nations, 2021:11). The UN is hardly alone amongst international NGOs in promoting this type of agenda. Marxists can at the same time agree with them in principle, whilst at the same time pointing out that laudable goals such as geographical and social mobility, resilience to global, environmental, and socio-economic shocks and threats, and mechanisms to ensure the sustainable use of a city's resources are in many such agendas seamlessly linked to business environment and pro-poor financing services that attract capital investment and enable everybody to undertake economic activities (Asian Development Bank, 2023).

A summary – one of many – of the problems involved in global planning, especially for housing, delivered this accurate but entirely predictable analysis a decade ago. Explicitly spatial plans were required, with best practice oriented towards poverty alleviation strategies at a regional level, towards working with community organisations, and specifically aimed at building assets of the poor and upgrading slums as an alternative to disruptive redevelopment or as part of more limited redevelopments (Belsky *et al.*, 2013:21). These criteria, and their variants, to which many more can be added, such as access to housing, safe drinking water and sanitation, action against pollution, more renewable energy, better and greener public transport, sustainably manage their natural resources nutritious food, healthcare and family planning, education, culture, and access to communication technologies, and, as the New Urban Agenda also promotes, the requirement to take into account the needs of women, youth, and children, people with disabilities, marginalised groups, older persons, indigenous people, among other groups ought to be essential parts of how planners assess and judge the outcome of real estate development. The demands are many, they will change, but they can certainly form the basis for a set of interrogatory political engagements by planners with developers, whether by individuals, groups, or even political parties.

This all makes for a wish list of which it is hard to disapprove, albeit that if it is not pursued systematically, many of the benefits will accrue only to those who already enjoy a high standard of living, and vastly fewer to those who do not. The task of the differential planner, inspired by Lefebvre, is to interfere with the inequalities that capitalism inherently generates, and to interact with developers in such a way as to promote all of the laudable goals identified in the New Urban Agenda and many more.

Marxists may wish to go further, starting to consider how to balance competing and even conflicting concerns, a task that Lefebvre seems almost deliberately to have eschewed. Concerns around urban greening are an example, as this now often forms part of a new form of growth machine supported by planners and elected officials (DuPuis & Greenberg, 2019; Gould & Lewis, 2018; Loughran, 2020). How to resist? García-Lamarca *et al.* (2022) cite a number of policies of resistance that might be of potential interest to developers, including ambitious social and affordable housing targets, as in some European cities (Euro Cities, 2018), although the question of implementation obviously remains paramount, of concern to developers as much as to planners.

An activity to which, in the co-option of Lefebvre to this agenda, 'the right to the city' has been counterposed (Inter-Environnement-Bruxelles, 2012:2), the suggestion being made that it has become defanged as a result – worse, even aligned with a capitalist agenda (Harvey, 2010:179). Marxists recognise that 'There is an important distinction between a radical political interpretation implying fundamental systemic change through collective mobilization and a reformist approach aimed at securing specific human rights in cities through legislation and related mechanisms linked mainly to state action' (Turok & Scheba, 2019:496). On the Left, the reformist mobilisation of the right to the city discourse (Gray, 2017:320) has been greeted with predictable outrage. Radical fury has been vented against those politicians, urban planners, or developers, who (notably in France itself) attempted to co-opt the concept of 'change the city in order to change life' in order to do with it precisely the opposite of what it originally meant – to use architecture and planning to manage disorder and prevent the imposition of society (Inter-Environnement-Bruxelles, 2012:3). For Harvey and other radical geographers the right to the city is always, and sometimes it seems only, a right to a future city, from which capitalism has been excised: as he himself recounted in relation to the UN 5th Urban Forum: 'When I mentioned that the Right to the City is something that cannot work within a capitalist system during the debate I participated in today, the entire panel went silent' (Action Aid, 2010).

More than a decade after David Harvey's uncomfortable observation, the UN 11th Forum declared that the undeniably urban future of humanity raised some key questions about the future of cities. What kind of cities are needed to support the future of humanity? How do we envisage and reimagine the future of cities? What do we want our cities to look like? (United Nations, 2022:xv). Whilst Marxists might recognise that at a fundamental level Harvey is right, they ought also to recognise that capitalism has shown no immediate sign of collapse in the intervening now more than a decade – quite the contrary. The need to answer the questions posed by UN Habitat remains as pressing as before.

Can planning policies create differential space?

None of the UN Habitat policies, in principle, ought to conflict with any Lefebvrian perspective. The devolution of planning authority is one particular aspect that ought to meet with Marxist approval. The real issue is in application; as has been asked: Is this a recipe for the creation of differential space by developers, or a manifesto of gentrification, which is not only a movement or urban strategy of capital reproduction on a global scale, now analysed from a multitude of different directions (Wu *et al.*, 2017:662; Wu, 2020:981), but also now proven to be a contributor to poor outcomes for collective interests such as public health? (Romero & Jaramillo, 2022). Marxists will be quick to point out that there are often huge divergences between what planners promise and what they end up delivering, and on the ground, implementation has always been less satisfactory. New Urbanist principles encouraging parks and gardens, for example, found easier favour with developers than the creation of neighbourhoods and districts that provide affordable housing and incorporate ethnic diversity.

> Even the incoherent, bland, and monotonous suburban tract development that continues to dominate in many areas, now gets its antidote in a 'new urbanism' movement that touts the sale of community and a boutique lifestyle as a developer product to fulfill urban dreams.
>
> (Harvey, 2012:14)

Another set of policies proclaimed within the New Urban Agenda, which has received much attention, has been zoning. Lawyers sympathetic to Lefebvre have suggested that zoning, for example, 'both codifies dominant representations of space and helps to reproduce their dominance by inscribing them in the physical uses of land' (Butler, 2005:21), and is therefore a crucial, indeed essential, component of the mechanism within capitalist society for the reproduction of abstract space. 'Absolute spaces, created by human practices, are essential, it seems, to the realization of class-monopoly rent' (Harvey, 1985:79). It is quite a step to conclude from this that zoning is, was, and must be entirely a tool at the service of abstract space, however, especially if by zoning is also included policies directed at social inclusion, that

> policymakers should use the various tools used in IH [inclusionary housing] programs, such as cost offsets and alternative contribution options, to 'soften' the transition between IH covered market sectors and unregulated market sectors and reduce the incentive for developers to divert investment.
>
> (Li & Guo, 2022:12)

The results can be positive:

> Absent federal leadership, some [cities] responded on their own, either by adopting inclusionary housing laws which require developers to include a percentage of affordable units in their market-rate projects, or by upzoning neighborhoods to accommodate higher-density housing and mixed-use development. In a notable example of this second strategy, Minneapolis recently announced that it would effectively eliminate single-family-only zoning, removing a significant barrier to apartments and condominium construction.
>
> (Landis, 2020:3)

Marxist geographers have suggested that the attempts of the local state to achieve affordable housing are 'negated by the dynamics of property capital, which are neither understood nor controlled by the state' (Gough & Das, 2016:7). Certainly – but to what extent? And does zoning, at least of certain types, make a measurable difference, to the extent that Marxists should in fact support it, at least in principle?

There are many different approaches to inclusionary zoning, for example density bonuses (allowing more houses per lot) to developers in exchange for supplying more affordable housing (Ryan & Enderle, 2012; Shenvi & Slangen, 2018), zoning variances (forgiving parking requirements or other exceptions), and/or expedited permitting (reducing costs by helping a project move more quickly) are all regulatory concessions aimed at offsetting developers' cost of renting or selling a mandated percentage of their newly constructed units at prices that would otherwise tend to reduce their IRR, even to a level that would prevent them from committing to the project (Yan *et al.*, 2021:2). Since inclusionary units are integrated with market-rate units, inclusionary zoning ensures not only the production of affordable units, but also the spatial distribution of affordable units across a jurisdiction. As has been observed in a developing country context:

> The current measures of government to provide affordable housing for low-income households in Kathmandu are also inadequate. There are barriers of limited resources for grants, funds, or financial schemes and little control over land. Small-scale projects of detached houses showed the limit in matching the increasing needs for affordable housing. Considering the domination of private developers in the housing market in Kathmandu, an inducement policy on the private sector focusing on the distribution of development gain is one of the options available.
>
> (Karn & Park, 2022:315)

There are evidently plenty of possible approaches to judgement, and to the offer of support where they promise positive outcomes. There is no suggestion that inclusionary zoning is any kind of panacea: in China, for example, the suggestion has been made that poor governance has placed undue costs on developers whilst concurrently allowing local government to reap the benefit of increased land values (Yan *et al.*, 2021:12).

Inclusionary zoning requires that a percentage of housing units in new residential developments be rented or sold for prices that are affordable to low- and moderate-income households. Inclusionary zoning can become a central component of a community's affordable-housing toolbox, because it can help meet multiple housing goals, including diversity. It is also fair to observe that not all protagonists for affordable housing are convinced the inclusionary zoning model is always the right one. The obvious point is that it can only meet these goals if the affordable component of the development *stays* affordable. There are many potential ways to achieve this, ranging from a development agreement to actual transfer of the units to a non-profit, combined with either controlled rents or various versions of shared-equity homeownership structures (Housing Enterprise Foundation, 2022). It seems clear that inclusionary housing is just one example of a differential approach to planning: workable solutions vary internationally, even across individual cities.

Another example of a planning policy that may – not necessarily, but may – help create differential space is the rather more contentious policy of incentive zoning: originally implemented in the United States, the idea of negotiating with developers, exchanging permissions to exceed height and floor-to-area ratio restrictions in their provision of community benefits, initially public spaces (Kayden, 1991). 'Since then, many jurisdictions have adopted the planning tool and broadened its use to include a range of community amenities, including design improvements, affordable housing, and sustainability. Incentive zoning is used worldwide (Qian *et al.*, 2016; Homsy & Kang, 2023). Lefebvre would surely be in agreement that rules and regulations should never stand in the way of a socially just outcome, especially perhaps those generated by the planning system, but equally, there is no guarantee that relaxing zoning restrictions will automatically lead to desirable outcomes for less economically and socially advantaged future residents. It is what developers do with their freedom that matters.

More obvious tools that may help create differential space, difficult as it will always be for planners to estimate, include enacting rent controls to ensure that excessive rents are not seized by new green rental housing developers; and the development of approaches to combine affordable housing and green open space options, offering public sector recommendations to make these possible (Yee *et al.*, 2019:11). 'While these are all important initiatives and actions to fight for, dominant development dynamics and (green) growth strategies often overturn or outmaneuver them' (García-Lamarca *et al.*, 2022:8). From these suggestions, the conclusion to be reached is that if 'green grabbing' by developers is a problem, the solutions that have been advocated to improve housing outcomes solutions lie once again within the planning system (Oscilowicz *et al.*, 2021). What is striking about these proposed initiatives and actions is the way in which the developer features so passively in them all: driven entirely by short-term profit motives, on the one hand, yet able to incorporate remarkably sophisticated strategies of appropriation and 'green grabbing' on the other. It is this implicit characterisation of developers that subsequent chapters aim to challenge.

This is not to suggest that there is no truth in the assertion that if developers are to realise class-monopoly rents (or simply, be profitable at all), they must make significant investments in the political process of planning and zoning. One need not be a Marxist to understand that the level of profit developers reach will depend on their relative bargaining power by comparison to their customers, as well as the efficiency with which the planning system operates and their ability to bend it in their favour (Harvey, 1985:68). What must be recognised, however, is that the relationship between developers and the planning system is two-way, indeed a complex dialectic that has as its result the production of space in capitalist society. Many developers, especially those at the smaller end of the spectrum, experience planning regulations as a largely immovable external set of constraints within which they must seek to operate profitably, not as a game to play and win. Others, notably large publicly owned developers, have much more control over the planning process but are not constituted to earn private monopoly rents from it. The problem here, of course, is that the cloaking of developers in one-size-fits-all class clothes can disguise the degree to which the size, structure, and indeed geopolitical location of developers interacts with the actual process of development.

Fast cities, clean property rights

Smart cities, it is said, leave little room for the technologically illiterate, the poor, the elderly, persons with disabilities, and generally those who are traditionally marginalised in the city discourse and decision-making processes. Serious urban problems like inequality, marginalisation, and poverty, it has been said, are largely absent from the smart city discussion (Hollands, 2015), contributing to the establishment of what have been described as 'functionally sophisticated enclaves' (Anttiroiko, 2013:503) amidst the urban. These retain the evident capacity to amplify, not reduce, social polarisation in cities, even decades after the problem had originally been identified (Reuter, 2019:9). This reinforces the importance for the differential planner of ensuring the gender inequalities that have been inscribed in the urban design of neighbourhoods, communities, and the home (Vestbro & Horelli, 2012) are *actually* reduced.

Critics, although they differ in emphasis, recognise the sustained critiques of those in the Marxist and associated radical tradition of geographers who suggest that in practice, 'networked cities engaged in the articulation and governance of cross-border economic activities' (Parnreiter, 2013:15) represent 'fundamental power in the 21st century is communication power' (Castells, 2021) and lead to conclusions about gender issues as well as many others that are as realistic as they are glum. This swift and vast influx of population to cities in the absence of a process of planning that could transcend global neoliberalism (Haneef *et al.*, 2021:186) has in many cases overwhelmed them, resulting in severe problems in terms of both atrocious urban living conditions (Davis, 2006), now well-researched for many decades (Panori *et al.*, 2019), and the peripheralisation of poor citizens (Caldeira, 2017), the growth of an enormous informal economy (Chen, 2016), and environmental damage (Harvey, 2005:5), the fortification of the rich in the Global South (Glebbeek & Koonings, 2016) or commentary on sprawling, sometimes gated communities and fortified enclaves (Brenner & Theodore, 2002; Harvey, 2001).

> The globalisation of urbanization leads to universal forms of spatial segregation; it seems today that the separation is much more accentuated and is at the point of creating methods of isolation that descend to all levels of society and that, in certain cases, creates something akin to 'microstates'.
>
> (Costes, 2011:96)

Sadly, the reality is that growth has been largely on the periphery of larger cities, whether as planned suburban developments, business parks, or all too often as favelas and occupation, with all its attendant complexities. We are led to believe that the 'smart, sustainable character of informal settlements stems from their polycentric political structure' (Geyer, 2022). But at the same time, informal settlements are 'unable to adequately regulate the social costs of certain externalities, including policing open spaces and public areas, littering, sewerage and refuse removal, fires, and environmental degradation' (Geyer, 2022). What was said of one Algerian town, that 'The inadequacy of urban planning and management tools has generated illicit developments that mitigate the deficiencies of the planned city, absorb growth, but consolidate a heterogeneous and discontinuous extension on the outskirts of the city' (Hayet, 2012:27), has been said of so many worldwide.

Planned developments on occasion also do provide a glimmer of light, but they are admittedly rare.

Magarpatta: a smart township in Pune, India

Magarpatta is a privately owned community located at Hadapsar in the city of Pune, India. Magarpatta City has a residential area, central parks, schools, shopping complex, and security services. Through its sustainable development model, Magarpatta City has introduced eco-friendly development and has green spaces that make up for 30% of the area. Almost 30% area of Magarpatta had been reserved for greenery. About 120 acers area had a natural green cover. In Magarpatta, eco-friendly practices have been implemented such as solar water heating, rainwater collecting, garbage segregation and waste management, biogas plant, vermiculture, and solar water heating: arrangement that created a self-sustainable framework and assist improvement of the environment. The recreational spaces are ordinarily found distant off in any city, but at Magarpatta City, they can be found in many locations around the city, including social, retail, and entertainment centres (Figure 3.1). Finally, the transport infrastructure is designed in accordance with international procedures (Patel & Padhya, 2021:31).

The new township policy retained the provisions of earlier policy proposals, including the reservation of 20% of the residential built-up space to be reserved for social housing comprising smaller units for low-income and economically weaker sections (Nallathiga *et al.*, 2021:90):

(i) *Walk-to-Work/Walk-to-School:* Designed as an integrated township development, all city-level amenities and features are integrated into the area; all these facilities are easily accessible, easily walkable. This forms a crucial planning parameter to Magarpatta City's success. As more than 90% of the daily trips made from home are for work and school/college, by placing these units in the vicinity, a greater amount of valuable travel time can be saved resulting in a better social and family life. Magarpatta City has been planned in such a way. Offices are about 10 minutes walking distance away from any residential sector. The City Public School is placed so that students can walk or cycle from their home in a safe and secure pedestrian priority walkway, a couple of minutes away

Figure 3.1 Magarpatta City.
Source: Associated Space (2023).

from their residence. Great design emphasis has been laid on the design of these roadside pedestrian walkways; it also incorporates barrier-free design concepts. This ensures better and more effective use of footpaths in Magarpatta City, comfortable for young, old, able, and disabled.

(ii) *Affordable Housing Options:* A significant percentage of the total housing stock is reserved for smaller flats, priced in an affordable range (Nallathiga *et al.*, 2021:92).

Environmental sustainability is a major concern for any city; and in Magarpatta, the issues of energy and waste infrastructure are claimed to be well taken care of. Solar water heating systems are used; green spaces consist around 30% of the township. Residents have also implemented a waste management system, segregating garbage at source on a monthly basis, dividing it into biodegradable waste for vermiculture and bio-composting and non-biodegradable waste for recycling. As for transportation, most residents do not have to commute to nearby urban centres for work as is typical of satellite towns. In Magarpatta, many commercial spaces are conveniently located within the township itself, thus promoting the philosophy of 'walk to school, walk to work' (Salamah, 2021:141).

The treatment of property rights in the United States, with possible global application, is another example. Under capitalism, it has been said, 'A property rights regime works to separate the land from the surrounding community of users, and it abstracts the land from its role in the web of urban social connections' (Purcell, 2014:149). In principle, yes; even for the majority, most probably. But in practice, property rights can never escape intense debate, and are never absolute, even under capitalism, where planning regulations constrain and regulate the externalities that the property rights regime does inevitably generate, rendering them inevitably only partial. The creation of a Justice Easement is a case in point, it being

> a negative easement that allows the holder to enforce affordability restrictions on the burdened property. These restrictions may include limits on the sale price, a cap on rent that can be charged, and income restrictions on whom the property can be sold or rented to. The easement may also provide the grantee with a perpetual right of first refusal that gives them the opportunity to purchase the property at an affordable price when the owner wishes to sell.
>
> (Fernandes & Orsi, 2020:5)

Others include Community Land Trusts, which can serve as a model for decommodifying land, albeit with problems of scalability (DeFilippis *et al.*, 2019). Another is a land-value tax, an oft-touted interim measure designed to curb land speculation (Fainstein, 2010). There are many more potential pro-poor planning mechanisms and tenure securities for land beyond innovative land taxation models, including redistribution of the ground rent, flexible land tenure, indigenous, customary, and other informal land use rights, all of which can eventually be combined with leasehold rights or usufruct in order to achieve the balance with the formal legal system (Thiel, 2012:12).

Planning and developers

That may be conceded, and guarded against, but nonetheless, the reality upon which Lefebvre insisted, and that Marxists should recognise, is that planning has at times served to segregate and marginalise, delimit, and exclude as much as it has opened up avenue for an enhanced and expanded social life (Zieleniec, 2018:13). Serving power, money, and capital, in this view, leads to the construction of abstract space, including acting as the instrument of segregation and discrimination.

It is interesting to compare concept of direct transmission with Fainstein's use of the concept of fragmentation (Fainstein & Fainstein, 1982; Fainstein, 2010), which in principle takes into account the funding and organisational and operational complexity of developers, recognising divisions both among capitalists and within the state that create opportunities for social movements to apply pressure and initiate change. This is a departure from an orthodox Marxist view of capital as a unitary interest, of envisaging 'developers and their allies in the state who recast the city as a locus of exchange value and capital accumulation' (Kuymulu, 2014:161), but the concept was restricted to conflicting interests between sectors of the economy, amongst which the state could act as a referee in a world where 'the local, municipal state takes on a crucial role in mediating between capital and citizens' (Shields, 2013:345). There looks to be a choice, as to whether on this basis Marxists must surely argue that the role of planning must be strengthened, even if the eventual goal is for the state to wither away (Mitchell, 2003) or to criticise 'the powers of developers backed by finance, corporate capital, and an increasingly entrepreneurially minded local state apparatus' (Harvey, 2012:9).

One other point that might usefully be made at this point is that the influence of developers on planners is not a one-way street by any means. The many failures of strategic planning, including new cities that never eventuated, bear witness to the importance of both understanding why this has happened and what to do as a developer to avoid the inevitable waste of resources (notwithstanding any learning process or synergies involved). Developers clearly do, perhaps partially in response, influence urban planning, for example in relation to density. One survey suggested that they actually dominate it (Cooper & Boyko, 2012:23). Certainly, if developers work exclusively to the objectives of financial investors, as traditional Marxists argued, then it is certainly reasonable to question the extent to which urban planners and city governments can resist (Guironnet *et al.*, 2016:1444). Evidence is plentiful that urban policy has become a financial instrument (Lake, 2015), or at any rate some urban policies are turned into financial instruments (Aalbers, 2020:597). This view is typified by the remark that

> city governments in Canada are strongly and directly tied to the property investment and land development industry, with the strongest links being the arrangement which puts a hard core of small-time property industry people like contractors, real estate agents, architects, developers, and real estate lawyers on city councils.
>
> (Lorimer, 1978:68)

On the other hand, it is important to present a balanced picture, especially when considering the potential roles of both planners and developers in the creation of differential space. The influence of developers on planners is not a one-way street by any means. On the contrary, from my own experience in detailed conversations with developers as part of university research, they identify the planning system and the role of planners as a key factor in their strategy. The active role of planners in influencing developer strategy is crucial in understanding what agency they possess.

How then does it work out in practice? What kind of response should Marxists make to the interrelationship between planners and developers in a world in which real estate capital plays an increasing role? Unfortunately,

> Harvey and Lefebvre encourage grassroots communities to effect change but both scholars fail to provide a detailed account of community engagement. Neoliberal policies appear to have affected the access to land at local level as community members are excluded from the process of loss of land as a resource and the planning of land distribution.
>
> (Bidandi & Williams, 2020:3)

Not to say that it cannot have some effect: in Brazil, for example, 'direct participation organised the participants into class-based groupings' (Caldeira & Holston, 2015:2010). But this represents such a stark contrast to a highly developed environment, where, for example, 'Between 2001 and 2006, all Australian cities developed strategic plans. All were based on sustainability principles, and all were participatory, vision-building processes' (Newman & Jennings, 2008:13). Alienation is not, however, a one-way street whereby the more progressive the policy, the less alienation the result. Unfortunately, capitalism is more tenacious than that. A good example is rail transport. It may be accurate to describe Perth's rail system as 'a partnership of community, government and business for a more sustainable city' (Newman & Jennings, 2008:177) but it is also right to recognise its limitations. Even in a thoroughly developed and wealthy economy such as Australia,

> [t]ransport infrastructure is a major form of capital investment, and recent decades have seen new arrangements for coordinating and financing major transport infrastructure projects. Governments continue to face budgetary pressures that generate demand for new ways to obtain public value from projects through innovative funding and financing arrangements.
>
> (Dodson *et al.*, 2021:65)

These include value capture and developer contribution programmes which force private developers to give up part of their planning gain to fund infrastructure, including social infrastructure projects such as schools and hospitals as well as transportation. As a tool of public policy, value capture has had wide international application, including contributing land for public services, providing those services themselves or through taxation structures, such as the Community Infrastructure Levy in the UK and developer contributions in Australia, and contributing to both infrastructure development and public services such as schools, clinics, and sports facilities. Politically, the challenge is to ensure that the full extent of value capture is displayed transparently, and the opportunities that it provides to create and improve public services are promoted and campaigned for. What developers are less well-placed to do, however, is provide financial or management assistance for public services once completed, which of necessity remains a planning and budgeting issue for the public sector.

> We will promote best practices to capture and share the increase in land and property value generated as a result of urban development processes, infrastructure projects, and public investments. Measures could be put in place, as appropriate, to prevent its solely private capture as well as land and real estate speculations, such as gains – related fiscal policies. We will reinforce the link among fiscal systems, urban planning, as well as urban management tools, including land market regulations. (United Nations, 2017:34) The New Urban Agenda will require new urban rules and regulations, improved urban planning and design, and municipal finance, among other things.
>
> (United Nations, 2021)

Critics of UN policies draw attention to the fact that their recipients are primarily public sector institutions, local government in particular, interested in implementing the principles of good governance and employing management tools such as participatory budgets, transparent management methods, and participative decision-making. Although certainly useful if properly used, the tools themselves do not confront capitalism directly. Moreover, as Mayer (2009) observed, the problem with their general category of urban residents is that it assumes the existence of a relatively cohesive civil sphere that requires protection against the effects of liberal policies. It suppresses the class divisions and differences in levels of agency within those affected by urban policies. In other words, the definition of right to the city popularised by transnational organisations effectively calls for more inclusion within the existing system, without offering a vision of changing the current development model (Domaradzka, 2018:614).

Value capture and its *dirigiste* subsidiary, planning gain, are half of a story that unfolds across a relationship between developers and the public sector that is often inscribed in planning law and which in practice includes debate, valuations, negotiation, and eventually, more often than not, agreement upon a detailed plan for the sharing of benefits. The resultant developer contributions include cash payment requirements to sell a proportion of housing to non-market housing providers at discounted prices and direct provision of in-kind facilities (open space, playgrounds, health care facilities, transport infrastructure etc.) (McAllister *et al.*, 2018:318). For example, in China, the government insists on a minimum amount of sport-space per household needs be designed into the public space of residential parks (Zhang, 2018). The issue remains contested, and not all of these are created equal: cash payments to the public sector in lieu of actual construction of affordable housing has, for example, attracted significant criticism, both as to whether the replacement construction actually occurs and what rent it attracts (35% Campaign, 2022). Campaigning by developers for zoning changes constitutes a major contributor to developer profits, of that there is no doubt. It follows therefore that until the market is removed entirely from development decisions, the role of public authorities in transferring at least some of the benefit developers obtain in this manner to a wider group of stakeholders is something with which Marxists should concur. The extent to which developers have been forced to give up a proportion of their land value gain varies widely, both between jurisdictions and over time, but there is ample evidence of the use of this policy tool by planning authorities to facilitate infrastructure development as well as on pure grounds of equity. In London, for example, 'approximately half the 'no developer contributions' land value has been captured, mainly via nonmarket housing provision' (McAllister *et al.*, 2018:324). The trend is not necessarily positive, however, and Marxists will be first to recognise that much remains to be done to divert surplus value to the community.

The problem of residual land calculations in the UK

Developers have the capacity to deliver more affordable housing, but only at the expense of their financial returns. They can if they wish use financial viability assessments (FVAs) to challenge their obligations to provide affordable housing. The FVA produces a market-based residual land value, which depends on the buoyancy of the housing market, and which therefore renders affordable housing dependent on market conditions. Planners at local authorities then compare the residual land value to an administratively set benchmark land value. If the former does not exceed the latter, the developer can potentially avoid S.106 (developer contribution) obligations. The planning authority can dispute the FVA, and produce its own, but FVAs require technical expertise in financial modelling which planning authorities – despite the obvious need for it – do not appear to have acquired. Local planning authorities are often also reluctant to adjust their affordable housing policies geographically to take advantage of higher house prices in certain areas to press for more affordable housing there. Despite these difficulties and obstacles, S.106 agreements provided the financial resources to construct almost half of the UK's affordable housing in recent years (UK Government, 2022).

In reviewing the opportunities and challenges for affordable housing in the UK, Hill pointed to a number of innovative approaches by local planning authorities that can lead to improved outcomes, including geographical sculpting, a 'clawback' mechanism to S.106 agreements to ensure that financial outperformance is diverted to affordable housing construction, the enforcement of universal affordable housing requirements, or offering developers a fast track through the planning system if their scheme can demonstrate compliance, in the case of London by providing 35% affordable housing (Hill, 2022).

Conclusion: scarcely heroes

The less than perfect history and current roles Lefebvre identifies for planning worldwide suggest that Marxists cannot, must not, create artificial ethical hierarchies amidst ideological distinctions between the public and private sectors of a capitalist economy in relation to the production of space. For now, however, there is still cause for some hope: perhaps Lefebvre's revelation of the production of space has had more of an impact on the struggle against capitalism than has been recognised after all. Not in the obvious sense of resistance on the streets, in 'moments' that all too often evaporate without any lasting impact – but rather, in the way that public planning, investors – and developers too – have themselves developed responses to the capitalist strategies they see before them that have challenged the dominance of purely financial criteria in the city and even begun to alter the capitalist orientation of the organisations themselves. That the struggle has become the everyday, exactly as Lefebvre foretold.

As to the future, any society that supersedes capitalism will be confronted with a huge legacy space as well as a continued need to control real estate development, to prevent it falling into chaos and catastrophe (Harvey, 1985:68). The subtle concatenation of economies of scale with markets (Harvey, 1985:131) or criticism of 'the gospel of efficiency' as an excuse for planners to evade social responsibility (Harvey, 1985:184) cannot serve as justification for the wholescale rejection of either, as future planners will surely discover, even if a future society can succeed in driving down more production to a local level and meeting real social needs rather than manufactured individual ones to a far greater extent than hitherto.

Were he here to consult, however, Lefebvre might be less than optimistic about the ability of the planning system within *any* geographical territory, capitalist or otherwise, to succeed completely in ensuring the equitable development of urban green space, for example, any more than of itself creating a complete capacity to provide high-quality residential accommodation to those in need. Urban planning represents a prime location for 'wicked problems' (Rittel & Webber, 1973), compounded by 'hidden values – unexamined, incomplete' (Lynch, 1981:38). Transcending capitalism itself cannot – will not – remove them all, and certainly not immediately. But the responsibility for real estate development cannot lie on the shoulders of planners alone, even if they are encouraged and supported by a range of political movements and actions. For them to gain agency in urban renewal, in promoting the right to the city, they need at least two more important allies – architects, and, perhaps the most challenging to mobilise in the service of the creation of differential space, real estate developers themselves. To them both – convinced of their continuing importance, and very much hoping they are still with us – I therefore turn.

Bibliography

35% Campaign. (2022). *Southwark developments that fail to deliver real social rent*, 7 December. Available at: www.35percent.org/posts/southwarks-new-developments-that-fail-to-deliver-social-rent/. [Accessed 9 December 2022].

Aalbers, M. B. (2020). Financial geography III: The financialization of the city. *Progress in Human Geography*, 44(3), 595–607.

Abram, S. and Weszkalnys, G. (2013). *Elusive Promises: Planning in the Contemporary World*. New York, Berghahn Books.

Action Aid. (2010). *Can the Right to the City Work Within a Capitalism System?* 10 March. Available at: https://usf2010.wordpress.com/2010/03/25/can-right-to-the-city-work-within-a-capitalism-system/. [Accessed 6 July 2022].

Altrock, U. (2022). Housing in Germany and the Rebirth of the high-rise in post-modern urban design. *Urban Planning*, 7(4), 298–312.

Andres, L., Bakare, H., Bryson, J. R., Khaemba, W., Melgaço, L. and Mwaniki, G. R. (2021). Planning, temporary urbanism and citizen-led alternative-substitute place-making in the Global South. *Regional Studies*, 55(1), 29–39.

Anttiroiko, A. V. (2013). U-cities reshaping our future: Reflections on ubiquitous infrastructure as an enabler of smart urban development. *AI & Society*, 28, 491–507.

Apostol, I. (2015). Urbanity and the right to difference. *sITA – studii de Istoria şi Teoria Arhitecturii* (3), 160–173.

Arbury, J. (2005). *From Urban Sprawl to Compact City: An Analysis of Urban Growth Management in Auckland*. Auckland, University of Auckland.

Armstrong, J. (2021). Against the airport and its world: The ZAD and frontiers. *Contemporary French and Francophone Studies*, 25(1), 95–105.

Asian Development Bank. (2023). *Urban development*. Available at: www.adb.org/what-we-do/themes/urban-development/overview#solutions. [Accessed 19 February 2023].

Banerjee-Guha, S. (ed.) (2010). *Accumulation by Dispossession: Transformative Cities in the New Global Order*. New Delhi, SAGE Publications India.

Basta, C. (2022). Are radical and insurgent planning (truly) at odds with a nonviolent conception of liberal planning? *Planning Theory (London, England)*, 21(2), 212–218. doi:10.1177/14730952221089749

Bater, J. H. (1977). Soviet town planning: Theory and practice in the 1970s. *Progress in Human Geography*, 1(2), 177–207.

Becker, C., Mendelsohn, S. J. and Benderskaya, K. (2012). *Russian Urbanization in the Soviet and Post-Soviet Eras*. London, International Institute for Economic Development. Available at: www.iied.org/10613iied. [Accessed 4 September 2021].

Bednarska-Olejniczak, D., Olejniczak, J. and Svobodová, L. (2019). Towards a smart and sustainable city with the involvement of public participation – The case of Wroclaw. *Sustainability*, 11(2), 332.

Belausteguigoitia, J. (2019). Inclusive urbanism, sustainable design and community engagement: A holistic approach. *WIT Transactions on Ecology and the Environment*, 238, 131–141.

Belsky, E. S., DuBroff, N., McCue, D., Harris, C., McCartney, S. and Molinsky, J. (2013). *Advancing Inclusive and Sustainable Urban Development: Correcting Planning Failures and Connecting Communities to Capital*. Cambridge, MA, Joint Center for Housing Studies of Harvard University.

Bertaud, A. and Renaud, B. (1997). Socialist cities without land markets. *Journal of Urban Economics*, 41(1), 137–151.

Bidandi, F. and Williams, J. J. (2020). Understanding urban land, politics, and planning: A critical appraisal of Kampala's urban sprawl. *Cities*, 106, 10285.

Borden, I. (2003). What is radical architecture. In Hall, T. and Miles, M. (eds.) *Urban Futures Critical Commentaries on shaping Cities*. London, Routledge, 111–121.

Boyko, C. T. and Cooper, R. (2012). High dwelling density as sustainability solution in Lancaster. *Proceedings of the Institution of Civil Engineers-Engineering Sustainability* 165(1), 81–88.

Brenner, N., Marcuse, P. and Mayer, M. (2012). Cities for people, not for profit: An introduction. In *Cities for People, Not for Profit*. Abingdon and New York, Routledge, 1–10.

Brenner, N. and Theodore, N. (2002). Cities and the geographies of "actually existing neoliberalism". *Antipode*, 34(3), 349–379.

Butler, C. (2005). Reading the production of suburbia in post-war Australia. *Law Text Culture*, 9, 11–33.

Caldeira, T. P. (2017). Peripheral urbanization: Autoconstruction, transversal logics, and politics in cities of the global south. *Environment and Planning D: Society and Space*, 35(1), 3–20.

Caldeira, T. P. and Holston, J. (2015). Participatory urban planning in Brazil. *Urban Studies*, 52(11), 2001–2017.

Carp, J. (2008). "Ground-truthing" representations of social space: Using Lefebvre's conceptual triad. *Journal of Planning Education and Research*, 28(2), 129–142.

Carmody, J. (2019). *Scarborough Beach twin towers development on hold as 3 Oceans explores other options*. Available at: www.abc.net.au/news/2019-04-18/scarborough-beach-twin-towers-development-on-hold/11028156. [Accessed 3 September 2021].

Castells, M. (1983). *The City and the Grassroots: A Cross-Cultural Theory of Urban Social Movements*. Los Angeles, University of California Press.
———. (1998 [2010]). *End of Millennium. Vol. III of The Information Age. Economy, Society and Culture*. 2nd edition. Oxford, Blackwell.
———. (2021). From cities to networks: Power rules. *Journal of Classical Sociology*, 21(3–4), 260–262.
Charnock, G. (2018). Space, form, and urbanity. In Best, B. *et al*. (eds.) *The SAGE Handbook of Frankfurt School Critical Theory*, 1450–1456. California, LA, Sage.
Chatterjee, I. (2014). *Displacement, Revolution, and the New Urban Condition: Theories and Case Studies*. New Delhi, SAGE Publications India.
Chen, M. A. (2016). The informal economy: Recent trends, future directions. New solutions: A *Journal of Environmental and Occupational Health Policy*, 26(2), 155–172.
Conley, V. A. (2012). *Spatial Ecologies: Urban Sites, State and World-Space in French Cultural Theory*. Liverpool, Liverpool University Press.
Cooper, R. and Boyko, C. (2012). *The Little Book of Density: A Guide to Density in Urban Environments*. Lancaster, Imagination Lancaster.
Costes, L. (2011). Del" derecho a la Ciudad" de Henri Lefebvre a la universalidad de la urbanizaci6n moderna. *Urban* (2), 89–100.
Davidson, M. and Lees, L. (2005). New-Build 'Gentrification' and London's riverside renaissance. *Environment and Planning A: Economy and Space*, 37(7), 1165–1190.
Davis, M. (2006). *Planet of Slums*. London, Verso.
DeFilippis, J., Williams, O. R., Pierce, J., Martin, D. G., Kruger, R. and Esfahani, A. H. (2019). On the transformative potential of community land trusts in the United States. *Antipode*, 51(3), 795–817.
Derakhti, L. and Baeten, G. (2020). Contradictions of transit-oriented development in low-income neighborhoods: The case study of Rosengård in Malmö, Sweden. *Urban Science*, 4(2), 20.
Dodson, J., Curtis, C., Ashmore, D., Woodcock, I. and Kovacs, S. (2021). *Innovative Responses to Urban Transportation: Current Practice in Australian Cities*. AHURI Final Report 360. Melbourne, Australian Housing and Urban Research Institute.
Domaradzka, A. (2018). Urban social movements and the right to the city: An introduction to the special issue on urban mobilization. *Voluntas: International Journal of Voluntary and Nonprofit Organizations*, 29(4), 607–620.
DuPuis, E. M. and Greenberg, M. (2019). The right to the resilient city: Progressive politics and the green growth machine in New York City. *Journal of Environmental Studies and Sciences*, 9, 352–363.
Elden, S. (2006). Some are born posthumously: The French afterlife of Henri Lefebvre. *Historical Materialism*, 14(4), 185–202.
Endres, K. W. (2014). Downgraded by upgrading: Small-scale traders, urban transformation and spatial reconfiguration in post-reform Vietnam. *The Cambridge Journal of Anthropology*, 32(2), 97–111.
———. (2019). Traders versus the state: Negotiating urban renewal in Lào Cai City, Vietnam. *City & Society*, 31(3), 341–364.
Engler, M. and Engler, P. (2016). *This Is an Uprising: How Nonviolent Revolt is Shaping the Twenty-First Century*. New York, Bold Type Books.
Euro Cities. (2018). *European Pillar of Social Rights. Cities Delivering Social Rights Equal Opportunities and Access to the Labour Market in Cities in Europe*. Brussels, Euro Cities. Available at: https://eurocities.eu/wp-content/uploads/2020/08/EUROCITIES_report_Cities_delivering_Social_Rights-1.pdf. [Accessed 19 February 2023].

Evans, G. (2014). Living in the city: Mixed use and quality of life. In Cooper, R., Burton, E. and Cooper, C. (eds.) *Wellbeing and the Environment: Wellbeing: A Complete Reference Guide, Volume II*. Oxford, Wiley-Blackwell, 119–146.
Fainstein, S. S. (2010). *The Just City*. Ithaca, Cornell University Press.
Fainstein, N. I. and Fainstein, S. S. (Eds.). (1982). *Urban Policy Under Capitalism*. Beverly Hills, Sage Publications.
Fernandes, J. and Orsi, J. (2020). Housing justice easements: A tool to combat the housing crisis. *California Real Property Journal*, 38. Available at: https://ssrn.com/abstract=3730840. [Accessed 6 January 2023].
Florida, R. (2017). *The New Urban Crisis: How Our Cities Are Increasing Inequality, Deepening Segregation, and Failing the Middle Class – and What We Can Do about it*. New York, Basic Books.
French, R. A. and Hamilton, F. E. I. (1979). Is there a socialist city. In [same authors]), *The Socialist City: Spatial Structure and Urban Policy*. Chichester, John Wiley, 1–22.
Friedmann, J. (1993). The right to the city. In Morse, R. M. and Hardoy, J. (eds.) *Rethinking the Latin American City*. Baltimore, Johns Hopkins University Press, 135–151.
———. (2010). Place and place-making in cities: A global perspective. *Planning Theory & Practice*, 11(2), 149–165.
Friendly, A. (2022). Insurgent planning in pandemic times: The case of Rio de Janeiro. *International Journal of Urban and Regional Research*, 46(1), 115–125.
Friesenecker, M. and Lagendijk, A. (2021). Commercial gentrification in Arnhem and Vienna: The local enactment of, and resistance towards 'globally' circulating creative neighbourhood policies. *City*, 25(5–6), 698–719.
Frolic, B. M. (1970). The Soviet study of Soviet cities. *The Journal of Politics*, 32(3), 675–695.
Garbin, D. and Millington, G. (2018). 'Central London under siege': Diaspora, 'race' and the right to the (global) city. *The Sociological Review*, 66(1), 138–154.
García-Lamarca, M., Anguelovski, I., Cole, H. V., Connolly, J. J., Pérez-del-Pulgar, C., Shokry, G. and Triguero-Mas, M. (2022). Urban green grabbing: Residential real estate developers discourse and practice in gentrifying Global North neighborhoods. *Geoforum*, 128, 1–10.
Garde, A. (2004). New Urbanism as sustainable growth? A supply side story and its implications for public policy. *Journal of Planning Education and Research*, 24(2), 154–170.
———. (2020). New urbanism: Past, present, and future. *Urban Planning*, 5(4), 453–463.
Geyer, H. S. (2022). Can informality help create smart, sustainable cities? The vibrancy of self-organised informal settlements in Cape Town. *GeoJournal*, 1–19.
Gilev, S. (2020). Architectural problems of implementation of residential development in Voronezh (issues of urban development). *Russian Journal of Building Construction and Architecture* (4), 64–75.
Glaeser, E. L. (2020). Urbanization and its discontents. *Eastern Economic Journal*, 46(2), 191–218.
Glebbeek, M. L. and Koonings, K. (2016). Between Morro and Asfalto. Violence, insecurity and socio-spatial segregation in Latin American cities. *Habitat International*, 54, 3–9.
Gleeson, B. and Low, N. (2000). Australian urban planning, new challenges, new agendas. Book review. *Environment and Planning A: Economy and Space*, 32(10), 1893–1894.
Gonsalves, K., Foth, M., Caldwell, G. and Jenek, W. (2021). Radical placemaking: An immersive, experiential and activist approach for marginalised communities. In Griffin, H. (ed.) *Connections: Exploring Heritage, Architecture, Cities, Art, Media. Vol. 20.1*. Canterbury, AMPS (Architecture, Media, Politics, Society, 237–252.

Gough, J. and Das, R. (2016). Human geography special issue: Marxist geography. *Human Geography*, 9(3), 1–9.
Gould, K. A. and Lewis, T. L. (2018). From green gentrification to resilience gentrification: An example from Brooklyn. *City & Community* 17(1), 12–15.
Gray, N. (2017). Beyond the right to the city: Territorial autogestion and the take over the city movement in 1970s Italy. *Antipode,* 50(2), 319–339.
Guironnet, A., Attuyer, K. and Halbert, L. (2016). Building cities on financial assets: The financialisation of property markets and its implications for city governments in the Paris city-region. *Urban Studies*, 53(7), 1442–1464.
Hamilton, F. E. I. (1979). Spatial structure in East European cities. In French, R. A. and Hamilton, F. E. I. (eds.) *The Socialist City: Spatial Structure and Urban Policy*. Chichester, John Willey & Sons, 195–261.
Hamilton, F. E. I. and Burnett, A. D. (1979). Social processes and residential structure. In French, R. A. and Hamilton, F. E. I. (eds.) *The Socialist City: Spatial Structure and Urban Policy*. Chichester, John Willey & Sons, 263–304.
Haneef, M., Alta, S. and Sulaiman, M. (2021). Inequities in urban development global North Versus South. *City University Research Journal*, 11(1), 182–193.
Harvey, D. (1982). *The Limits to Capital*. Oxford, Blackwell.
———. (1985). *The Urbanization of Capital*. Baltimore, Johns Hopkins University Press.
———. (2001). Globalization and the "spatial fix". *Geographische Revue: Zeitschrift für Literatur und Diskussion*, 3(2), 23–30.
———. (2005). *A Brief History of Neoliberalism*. Oxford, Oxford University Press.
———. (2010). *The Enigma of Capital and the Crises of Capitalism*. New York, Oxford University Press.
———. (2012). *Rebel Cities: From the Right to the City to the Urban Revolution*. London, Verso Books.
Hayet, M. (2012). De l'eclatement urbain a la fragmentation de l'espace annabi. Des instruments de gestion urbaine en question? *Sciences & Technologie. D, Sciences de la terre* (36), 21–27.
Hendy, P. (2022). *Evolving Financial Stress in China's Property Development Sector*. Canberra, Reserve Bank of Australia. Available at: www.rba.gov.au/publications/bulletin/2022/sep/evolving-financial-stress-in-chinas-property-development-sector.html. [Accessed 6 September 2022].
Herzog, R. H., Gonçalves, J. E., Slingerland, G., Kleinhans, R., Prang, H., Brazier, F. and Verma, T. (2022). Identifying public values and spatial conflicts in urban planning. *arXiv* preprint arXiv:2207.04719.
Hilbrandt, H. (2017). Insurgent participation: Consensus and contestation in planning the redevelopment of Berlin-Tempelhof airport. *Urban Geography*, 38(4), 537–556.
Hill, S. (2022). Taking back affordable housing. *New Economics*, 22 February. Available at: https://neweconomics.org/2022/02/taking-back-affordable-housing. [Accessed 5 September 2022].
Hofman, A. and Aalbers, M. B. (2019). A finance- and real estate-driven regime in the United Kingdom. *Geoforum*, 100, 89–100.
Hollands, R. G. (2015). Critical interventions into the corporate smart city. *Cambridge Journal of Regions, Economy and Society*, 8(1), 61–77.
Holston, J. (2009). Insurgent citizenship in an era of global urban peripheries. *City & Society*, 21(2), 245–267.
Homsy, G. C. and Kang, K. E. (2023). Zoning incentives: Exploring a market-based land use planning tool. *Journal of the American Planning Association*, 89(1), 61–71.

Housing Enterprise Foundation. (2022). *Housing affordability in Australia. Tackling a wicked problem. Sydney, housing enterprise foundation*. Available at: https://vfhousing.org.au/wp-content/uploads/2022/04/VF_Housing-AffordabilityReport_Web.pdf. [Accessed 19 February 2023].

Howe, L. B. (2022). Towards a cooperative urbanism? An alternative conceptualization of urban development for Johannesburg's mining belt. *Environment and Urbanization*, 34(2), 391–412.

Huq, E. (2020). Seeing the insurgent in transformative planning practices. *Planning Theory*, 19(4), 371–391.

Inter-Environnement-Bruxelles. (2012). Le droit à la ville. Et quoi ? *Bruxelles en mouvement, 259–260*, 3. Available at: https://www.ieb.be/-Bem-259-260

Iveson, K. (2013). Cities within the city: Do-it-yourself urbanism and the right to the city. *International Journal of Urban and Regional Research*, 37(3), 941–956.

Jauhiainen, J. S. (2006). Urbanisation, capital and land-use in cities. Place and Location. *Studies in Environmental Aesthetics and Semiotics*, 5, 179–193.

Johnson, L. (1997). Feral suburbia. In Grace, H. *et al*. (eds.) *Home/World: Space, Community and Marginality in Sydney's West*. Annandale, Pluto Press, 31–65.

Karn, P. L. and Park, J. (2022). Affordable housing for low-income households through floor area ratio incentive: The case of Manohara settlement in Kathmandu, Nepal. *International Journal of Urban Sustainable Development*, 14(1), 304–318.

Kayden, J. S. (1991). Zoning for dollars: New rules for an old game: Comments on the municipal art society and Nollan cases. *Washington University Journal of Urban and Contemporary Law*, 39, 3–52.

Kern, L. (2022). *Gentrification Is Inevitable and Other Lies*. London, Verso Books.

Kim, J. (2022). Smart city trends: A focus on 5 countries and 15 companies. *Cities*, 123, 103551.

Kim, S.-C., Hong, P., Lee, T., Lee, A. and Park, S.-H. (2022). Determining strategic priorities for smart city development: Case studies of south Korean and international smart cities. *Sustainability*, 14(16), 10001.

Kingma, S. F., Dale, K. and Wasserman, V. (2018). *Organisational Space and Beyond: The Significance of Henri Lefebvre for Organisation Studies*. New York and London, Taylor & Francis.

Kinkaid, E. (2020). Re-encountering Lefebvre: Toward a critical phenomenology of social space. *Environment and Planning D: Society and Space*, 38(1), 167–186.

Kipfer, S. (2002). Urbanization, everyday life and the survival of capitalism: Lefebvre, Gramsci and the problematic of hegemony. *Capitalism, Nature, Socialism*, 13(2), 117–149.

Kolling, M. (2019). Becoming favela: Forced resettlement and reverse transitions of urban space in Brazil. *City & Society*, 31(3), 413–435.

Kolling, M. and Koster, M. (2019). Introduction: Betrayal and urban development across the globe. *City and Society*, 31(3), 436–440.

Kopp, A. (1981). *Housing for the masses*. Paper presented at Conference on The Origins of Soviet Culture. Kennan Institute for Advanced Russian Studies, The Wilson Center, 18–19 May. Available at: www.wilsoncenter.org/sites/default/files/media/documents/publication/op149_housing_for_the_masses_kopp_1981.pdf. [Accessed 3 December 2022].

Kuymulu, M. B. (2014). *Claiming the Right to the City: Towards the Production of Space from Below*. PhD City University of New York. https://academicworks.cuny.edu/gc_etds/439/

Lachaud, G. (2017). *L'entrepreneur et le" zadiste". Logiques discursives et conflit de légitimité des acteurs de l'espace public sociétal*. Paper presented at Colloque International GRESEC Université Grenoble Alpes Information-Communication publique ET espaces publics sociétaux: Interactions et tensions. Grenoble, 12–13 October.

Lake, R. W. (2015). The financialization of urban policy in the age of Obama. *Journal of Urban Affairs*, 37(1), 75–78.

Lanari, E. (2019). Envisioning a new city center: Time, displacement, and Atlanta's suburban futures. *City & Society*, 31(3), 365–391.

Landis, J. D. (2020). *A Housing Plan Both Parties Can Support*. Penn Institute for Urban Research, January. Available at: https://penniur.upenn.edu/uploads/media/A_Housing_Plan_Both_Parties_Can_Support.pdf. [Accessed 3 June 2021].

Leary, M. E. (2009). The production of space through a shrine and vendetta in Manchester: Lefebvre's spatial triad and the regeneration of a place renamed Castlefield. *Planning Theory & Practice*, 10(2), 189–212.

Lees, L. (2019). Planetary gentrification and urban (re)development. *Urban Development Issues* 61, 5–13.

Lees, L., Shin, H. B. and Morales, E. L. (eds.) (2015). *Global Gentrifications: Uneven Development and Displacement*. Bristol, Policy Press.

Lefebvre, H. (1961 [2014]). *Critique de la vie quotidienne. Volume Two. Fondements d'une sociologie de la quotidiennetë*. Paris, L'Arche. Translated by J. Moore (2008 [2014]) as *Critique of Everyday Life. Volume Two. Foundations for a Sociology of the Everyday*. London, Verso.

———. (1968 [1996]). *Le Droit à la ville*. Paris, Anthropos. In Kofman, E. and Lebas, E. (eds.) *Henri Lefebvre. Writings on Cities*. Oxford, Blackwells, 63–184.

———. (1970 [2003]). *La Révolution Urbaine*. Paris, Gallimard. Translated by R. Bononno as *The Urban Revolution*. Minneapolis, University of Minnesotta Press.

———. (1970a [2009]). Reflections on the politics of space. In Elden, S. and Brenner, N. (eds.) *State, Space, World: Selected Essays*. Translated by G. Moore. Minneapolis, University of Minnesota Press, 167–184.

———. (1973 [1976]). *La Survie du capitalisme: La reproduction des rapports de production*. Paris, Anthropos. Translated by F. Bryant as *The Survival of Capitalism. Reproduction of the Relations of Production*. London, Allison & Busby.

———. (1973a [2000]). *Espace et politique*. Anthropos, Paris. In Kofman, E. and Lebas, E. (eds.) *Writings on Cities – Henri Lefebvre*. 2nd edition. Oxford, Blackwells, 185–204.

———. (1974 [1991]). *La production de l'espace*. Paris, Anthropos. Translated by D. Nicholson-Smith as *The Production of Space*. Oxford, Blackwell.

Lehtovuori, P. (2010). *Experience and Conflict: The Production of Urban Space*. Farnham, Ashgate.

Lennon, M. and Moore, D. (2019). Planning, 'politics' and the production of space: The formulation and application of a framework for examining the micropolitics of community place-making. *Journal of Environmental Policy & Planning*, 21(2), 117–133.

Li, F. and Guo, Z. (2022). How does an expansion of mandatory inclusionary housing affect housing supply? Evidence from London (UK). *Journal of the American Planning Association*, 88(1), 83–96.

Lindstrom, M. J. and Bartley, H. (eds.) (2003). *Suburban Sprawl. Culture, Theory and Politics*. Lanham, Rowman & Littlefield.

López-Morales, E. J. (2010). Real estate market, state-entrepreneurialism and urban policy in the' gentrification by ground rent dispossession' of Santiago de Chile. *Journal of Latin American Geography*, 9(1), 145–173.

Lorimer, J. (1978). *The Developers*. Toronto: James Lorimer & Co.

Loughran, K. (2020). Urban parks and urban problems: An historical perspective on green space development as a cultural fix. *Urban Studies*, 57(11), 2321–2338.

Lynch, K. (1981). *Good City Form*. Cambridge, MA, MIT Press.

Mayer, M. (2009). Shifting mottos of urban social movements. *City*, 13, 362–374.

McAllister, P., Shepherd, E. and Wyatt, P. (2018). Policy shifts, developer contributions and land value capture in London 2005–2017. *Land Use Policy*, 78, 316–326.

McCall, V. and Mooney, G. (2018). The repoliticization of high-rise social housing in the UK and the classed politics of demolition. *Built Environment*, 43(4), 637–652.

Méndez, M. L., Otero, G., Link, F., Lopez Morales, E. and Gayo, M. (2021). Neighbourhood cohesion as a form of privilege. *Urban Studies*, 58(8), 1691–1711.

Merrifield, A. (2014). *The New Urban question*. London, Pluto Press.

Metspalu, P. and Hess, D. B. (2018). Revisiting the role of architects in planning large-scale housing in the USSR: The birth of socialist residential districts in Tallinn, Estonia, 1957–1979. *Planning Perspectives*, 33(3), 335–361.

Minton, A. (2012). *Ground Control: Fear and Happiness in the Twenty-First-Century City*. London, Penguin.

Miraftab, F. (2009). Insurgent planning: Situating radical planning in the Global South. *Planning Theory*, 8(1), 32–50.

———. (2017). Insurgent practices and decolonization of future (s). In Gunder, M. (ed.) *The Routledge Handbook of Planning Theory*. London, Routledge, 276–288.

Mitchell, D. (2003). *The Right to the City: Social Justice and the Fight for Public Space*. London, The Guildford Press.

Mogielnicki, R. (2021). Elite embeddedness in free zone development. In Mogielnicki, R. (ed.) *A Political Economy of Free Zones in Gulf Arab States*. Cham, Springer, 133–164.

Mouton, M. and Shatkin, G. (2020). Strategizing the for-profit city: The state, developers, and urban production in Mega Manila. *Environment and Planning A: Economy and Space*, 52(2), 403–422.

Muzorewa, T. T., Nyawo, V. Z. and Nyandoro, M. (2018). Decolonising urban space: Observations from history in urban planning in Ruwa town, Zimbabwe, 1986–2015. *New Contree*, 81, 114–137.

Nallathiga, R., Tewari, K., Saboo, A. and Varghese, S. (2021). From satellite townships to smart townships. *Theoretical and Empirical Researches in Urban Management*, 16(1), 86–106.

Newman, P. and Jennings, I. (2008). *Cities as Sustainable Ecosystems: Principles and Practices*. Washington, DC, Island Press.

Newman, S. (2011). Postanarchism and space: Revolutionary fantasies and autonomous zones. *Planning Theory*, 10(4), 344–365.

Nicolosi, E. (2020). Counterspaces against the odds? The production and emancipatory potential of alternative spaces. *Geoforum*, 108, 59–69.

O'Kane, C. (2019). Henri Lefebvre and the critical theory of society. In Bauer, J. and Fischer, R. (eds.) *Perspectives on Henri Lefebvre. Theory, Practices and (Re)Readings*. Berlin, De Gruyter, 55–76.

Olla, A. (2021). Occupy Wall Street swept the world and achieved a lot, even if it may not feel like it. *Guardian*, 6 October. Available at: www.theguardian.com/commentisfree/2021/oct/06/occupy-wall-street-achieved-a-lot-even-if-it-may-not-feel-like-it. [Accessed 2 March 2022].

Oscilowicz, E., Hajtmarova, S. and Anguelovski, I. (2021). Enacting just urban green futures: Promising policy and planning tools and regulations for Europe and North America. In Anguelovski, I. and Connolly, J. J. (eds.) *The Green City and Social Injustice*. New York and London, Routledge, 295–310.

Panori, A., Mora, L. and Reid, A. (2019). Five decades of research on urban poverty: Main research communities, core knowledge producers, and emerging thematic areas. *Journal of Cleaner Production*, 237, 117850.

Parker, S. (2015). *Urban theory and the Urban Experience: Encountering the City*. 2nd edition. Abingdon, Routledge.
Parnreiter, C. (2013). The global city tradition. In Acuto, M. and Steele, W. (eds.) *Global City Challenges. Debating a Concept, Improving the Practice*. Basingstoke, Palgrave-Macmillan, 15–32.
Patel, M. and Padhya, H. (2021). The neighbourhood planning in India: A case study of Magarpatta City. *International Journal of Research in Engineering and Science*, 9(1), 29–33.
Pierce, J. and Martin, D. G. (2015). Placing Lefebvre. *Antipode*, 47(5), 1279–1299.
Pluciński, P. (2018). Forces of altermodernization: Urban social movements and the new urban question in contemporary Poland. *VOLUNTAS: International Journal of Voluntary and Nonprofit Organizations*, 29(4), 653–669.
Pluciński, P. (2020). Henri Lefevbre's second life. The real utopia of the right to the city in contemporary Poland. *History of European Ideas*, 46(8), 1107–1121.
Porter, L. and Shaw, K. (eds.). (2013). *Whose Urban Renaissance? An International Comparison of Urban Regeneration Strategies*. London: Routledge.
Purcell, M. (2014). Possible worlds: Henri Lefebvre and the right to the city. *Journal of Urban Affairs*, 36(1), 141–154.
Qian, Q. K., Fan, K. and Chan, E. H. (2016). Regulatory incentives for green buildings: Gross floor area concessions. *Building Research & Information*, 44(5–6), 675–693.
Rau, S. (2019). Preface. In Bauer, J. and Fischer, R. (eds.) *Perspectives on Henri Lefebvre. Theory, Practices and (Re)Readings*. Berlin, De Gruyter, vii–xv.
Reiner, T. A. and. Wilson, R. H. (1979). Planning and decision-making in the Soviet city: Rent, land and urban form. In French, R. A. and Hamilton, F. E. I. (eds.) *The Socialist City. Spatial Structure and Urban Policy*. Chichester: John Wiley, 49–71.
Reuter, T. (2019). *Human Rights and the Smart City. Social Practice of Human Rights Conference*. Dayton, OH, 1–4 October. Available at: https://ecommons.udayton.edu/human_rights/2019/events/55/. [Accessed 3 September 2021].
Rinde, M. (2022). New Philly land trust was promised dozens of homes; How's it going? *Shelterforce*, 25 October. Available at: https://shelterforce.org/2022/10/25/new-philly-land-trust-was-promised-dozens-of-homes-hows-it-going/. [Accessed 12 January 2023].
Rittel, H. W. and Webber, M. M. (1973). Dilemmas in a general theory of planning. *Policy Sciences*, 4(2), 155–169.
Robin, E. and Brill, F. (2018). The global politics of an urban age: Creating cities for all'in the age of financialisation. *Palgrave Communications*, 4(1), 1–5.
Romero, F. S. and Jaramillo, P. A. (2022). Can gentrification battles promote civic health? A case study analysis in San Antonio, Texas. *Housing Policy Debate*, 1–18.
Rose, H. (1983). Hand, brain, and heart: A feminist epistemology for the natural sciences. *Signs: Journal of Women in Culture and Society*, 9(1), 73–90.
Rossi, U. (2018). The populist eruption and the urban question. *Urban Geography*, 39(9), 1425–1430.
Ruoppila, S. (2004). Processes of residential differentiation in socialist cities: Literature review on the cases of Budapest, Prague, Tallinn and Warsaw. *European Journal of Spatial Development*, 2(1), 1–24.
Ryan, S. and Enderle, B. E. (2012). Examining spatial patterns in affordable housing: The case of California density bonus implementation. *Journal of Housing and the Built Environment*, 27, 413–425.
Salamah, A. (2021). Participatory urban development in India: A tale of Two townships. *Environment and Urbanization Asia*, 12(1), 136–147.

Sandercock, L (1998). *Towards Cosmopolis: Planning for Multicultural Cities*. Chichester, Wiley.
Sangla, S. (2011). Politique et espace chez Henri Lefebvre. *Appareil*, 28 March. Available at: http://journals.openedition.org/appareil/1185. [Accessed 3 July 2021].
Santos Junior, O. (2014). Urban common space, heterotopia and the right to the city: Reflections on the ideas of Henri Lefebvre and David Harvey. *urbe. Revista Brasileira de Gestão Urbana*, 6(2), 146–157.
Sawers, L. (1978). Cities and countryside in the Soviet Union and China. In Tabb, W. K. and Sawers, L. (eds.) *Marxism and the Metropolis. New Perspectives in Urban Political Economy*. 2nd edition. New York, Oxford University Press, 338–364.
Schindler, S. (2015). Architectural exclusion: Discrimination and segregation through physical design of the built environment. *The Yale Law Journal*, 124(6), 1836–2201.
Schmid, C. (2012). Henri Lefebvre, the right to the city, and the new metropolitan mainstream. In Brenner, N. *et al.* (eds.) *Cities for People, Not for Profit*. Abingdon and New York, Routledge, 42–62.
Sève, L. (1968 [1978]). *Marxisme et théorie de la personalitié*. Paris, Éditions Sociales. Translated by J. McGreal as *Man in Marxist Theory and the Psychology of Personality*. Brighton, Harvester.
Seyfang, G. and Smith, A. (2007). Grassroots innovations for sustainable development: Towards a new research and policy agenda. *Environmental Politics*, 16(4), 584–603.
Shawly, H. (2022). Evaluating compact city model implementation as a sustainable urban development tool to control urban sprawl in the city of Jeddah. *Sustainability*, 14(20), 13218.
Sheller, M. (2015). Foreword 2: Mobilizing transportation, transporting mobilities. In Cidell, J. and Prytherch, D. (eds.) *Transport, Mobility, and the Production of Urban Space*. New York and Abingdon, Routledge, 12–18.
Shen, J., Luo, X. and Wu, F. (2020). Assembling mega-urban projects through state-guided governance innovation: The development of Lingang in Shanghai. *Regional Studies*, 54(12), 1644–1654.
Shenvi, A. and Slangen, R. H. (2018). *Enabling smart urban redevelopment in India through floor area ratio incentives*. ADB Working Paper Series, 58. July. Available at: www.think-asia.org/bitstream/handle/11540/8520/swp-058-smart-urban-redevelopment-india.pdf?sequence=1. [Accessed 3 March 2022].
Shields, R. (1999). *Lefebvre, Love, and Struggle: Spatial Dialectic*. London, Routledge.
———. (2013). Lefebvre and the right to the open city? *Space and Culture*, 16(3), 345–348.
Shin, H. B. (2018). Urban movements and the genealogy of urban rights discourses: The case of urban protesters against redevelopment and displacement in Seoul, South Korea. *Annals of the American Association of Geographers*, 108(2), 356–369.
Slater, T. (2017). Planetary rent gaps. *Antipode*, 49, 114–137.
Sletto, B. (2021). Informal landscapes and the performative placing of insurgent planning. *Planning Theory*, 20(2), 157–174.
Smith, N. (1986). Gentrification, the frontier and the restructuring of urban space. In Smith, N. and Williams, P. (eds.). *Gentrification of the City* (pp. 15–34). Boston, Allen & Unwin, 15–34.
———. (2003). Foreward. In *The Urban Revolution* (pp. vii–xxiii). Minneapolis, University of Minnesota Press.
———. (2005). *The New Urban Frontier: Gentrification and the Revanchist City*. Abingdon, Routledge.
Soja, E. W. (1996). *Thirdspace: Journeys to Los Angeles and Other Real-and-Imagined Places*. Oxford, Basil Bakcwell.

Standing, G. (2016). The precariat, class and progressive politics: A response. *Global Labour Journal*, 7(2), 189–200.

Stanek, L. (2011). *Henri Lefebvre on Space: Architecture, Urban Research, and the Production of Theory*. Minneapolis, University of Minnesota Press.

Swyngedouw, E. (2014). Insurgent architects, radical cities and the promise of the political. In Swyngedouw, E. and Wilson, J. (eds.) *The Post-Political and Its Discontents: Spaces of Depoliticisation, Spectres of Radical Politics*. Edinburgh, Edinburgh University Press, 169–187.

———. (2017). Unlocking the mind-trap: Politicising urban theory and practice. *Urban Studies*, 54(1), 55–61.

Szeto, A. and Meronek, T. (2017). YIMBYs: The darlings of the real estate industry. *truth-out*. May 10. Available at: https://truthout.org/articles/yimbys-the-alt-right-darlings-of-the-real-estate-industry/. [Accessed 5 July 2021].

Tabane, I. T., Gumbo, T., Musakwa, W., Moyo, T. and Mbinza, Z. (2021). *Assessing the efficacy of spatial planning and development system in improving living conditions of the society*. l. Proceedings of REAL CORP 2021, 26th International Conference on Urban Development, Regional Planning and Information Society, 77–87. Available at: https://repository.corp.at/736/. [Accessed 20 July 2022].

Tavolari, B. (2020). The right to the city: Conceptual transformations and urban struggles. *Revista Direito e Práxis*, 11, 470–492.

Thiel, F. (2012). *Real estate development for poverty reduction – A new paradigm for legal and financial cooperation in Africa and Asia?* AfRES afres2012_136. African Real Estate Society. Available at: https://ideas.repec.org/p/afr/wpaper/afres2012_136.html [Accessed 14 July 2022].

Thompson, M. (2017). LIFE in a ZOO: Henri Lefebvre and the (social) production of (abstract) space in Liverpool. *City*, 21(2), 104–126.

Turok, I. and Scheba, A. (2019). 'Right to the city' and the New Urban Agenda: Learning from the right to housing. *Territory, Politics, Governance*, 7(4), 494–510.

UK Government. (2022). *Affordable housing supply in England: 2021 to 2022*, 17 November. Available at: www.gov.uk/government/collections/affordable-housing-supply. [Accessed 15 December 2022].

United Nations. (2017). *New urban agenda*. Available at: https://habitat3.org/wp-content/uploads/NUA-English.pdf. [Accessed 4 September 2022].

———. (2021). *Urban regeneration as a tool for inclusive and sustainable recovery*. Available at: https://unhabitat.org/sites/default/files/2022/05/report_egm_urban_regeneration.pdf. [Accessed 6 October 2022].

———. (2022). *UN-HABITAT. world cities report 2022*. Available at: https://unhabitat.org/sites/default/files/2022/06/wcr_2022.pdf. [Accessed 7 January 2023].

Van Den Nouwelant, R. (2015). *Does strategic planning provide the clarity it claims? Framing land-use conflict as competing interpretations of the same planning concept: The case of the 'mixed-use neighbourhood'*. Paper presented at the State of Australian Cities Conference 2015: Refereed Proceedings, 9–11 December 2015, Gold Coast, Queensland. Available at: https://apo.org.au/node/63260. [Accessed 3 July 2021].

Vasconcelos, T. (2019). Urbanism and urban planning following the thoughts of Henri Lefebvre. *WIT Transactions on Ecology and the Environment*, 217, 157–164.

Vestbro, D. U. and Horelli, L. (2012). Design for gender equality: The history of co-housing ideas and realities. *Built Environment*, 38(3), 315–335.

Viala, L. and Keerle, R. (2020). Centralité(s), métropolisation et territoires: pour un fondement métaterritorial de l'équité. *JSSJ*, 15. Available at: www.jssj.org/article/

centralites-metropolisation-et-petites-villes-pour-un-fondement-meta-territorial-de-lequite-2/. [Accessed 18 February 2023].

Wang, V. (1996). Mixed use: The answer to the successful urban environment. *Built Environment*, 22(4), 312–314.

Wu, Q., Zhang, X. and Waley, P. (2017). When Neil Smith met Pierre Bourdieu in Nanjing, China: Bringing cultural capital into rent gap theory. *Housing Studies*, 32(5), 659–677.

Wu, F. (2020). Scripting Indian and Chinese urban spatial transformation: Adding new narratives to gentrification and suburbanisation research. *Environment and Planning C: Politics and Space*, 38(6), 980–997.

Yan, J., Haffner, M. and Elsinga, M. (2021). Inclusionary housing: An evaluation of a new public rental housing governance instrument in China. *Land*, 10(3), 305.

Yee, T., Trinh, S. and Zappella, N. (2019). *Pathway to Parks & Affordable Housing Joint Development*. Los Angeles, La Thrives & La Rosah. Available at: www.sparcchub.org/wp-content/uploads/2019/08/Pathway-to-Parks-and-Affordable-Housing.pdf. [Accessed 4 September 2021].

Zaretsky, E. (1976). *Capitalism, the Family and Personal Life*. London, Pluto Books.

Zeiger, M. (2011). *The Interventionist's Toolkit, Part 3: Our Cities, Ourselves*. New York, Design Observer.

Zhang, Z. (2018). Exploring the spatial dynamics of the city: A case study in China. In Kingma, S. *et al.* (eds.) *Organisational Space and Beyond: The Significance of Henri Lefebvre for Organisation Studies*. New York and London, Taylor & Francis, 237–260.

Zhang, Z., Spicer, A. and Hancock, P. (2008). Hyper-organizational space in the work of JG Ballard. *Organization*, 15(6), 889–910.

Zieleniec, A. (2018). Lefebvre's politics of space: Planning the urban as oeuvre. *Urban Planning*, 3(3), 5–15.

4 Scarcely heroes

Urban planning and real estate development

Introduction

The purpose of this chapter is twofold. Firstly, to provide some indication – primarily for developers – of how Lefebvre envisaged the role of architecture, both within capitalist society and as a vehicle for its supersession. Secondly, to compare and contrast Lefebvre's publicly expressed view of the architect's role in the creation of differential space to the unexplored view he may have taken of developers, had he witnessed their rise in importance in the development process. And to do this primarily because, to paraphrase David Harvey, who suggested that 'the question of space is too important to be left to geographers. Social theorists of all stripes and persuasions should take it seriously' (Harvey, 1985:xi), perhaps the question of space is also too important to be left to them either. Architects, planners, and real estate developers all need to take space seriously as well, especially as they are actively involved in its creation on a daily basis.

They will only do so if they are prepared to allow their window of perception to open at least a chink to allow in some theory, to accept the benefit of applying thinkers from beyond the discipline (Coleman, 2014:4). Lefebvre's belief, we may say trust, in philosophy may be of some comfort to philosophers everywhere, as it no doubt was a comfort to Lefebvre himself, as no Marxist could be content with merely *understanding* the experience, the consequences, as well as the survival of capitalism (Zieleniec, 2018:6), any more than a developer would content themselves with understanding real estate, rather than creating it. But however useful Lefebvre's appreciation of space is, and however important understanding is to formulating practical responses and programmes of action, what Marxists really seek in Lefebvre's epistemological expansionism is a contribution to a programme of action. If Marxist philosophy cannot issue into actual politics, and if conversely the actions of those who produce space do not contain some philosophical underpinning, both ethical and political, there is for Marxists surely something seriously amiss. In that sense, Lefebvre's contribution must be at least partly prescriptive, or by Marxist criteria, it will fail its most important test. And at this point, we must admit that despite the translation of many of his key works into English and other languages, and notwithstanding the enthusiastic adoption of his analytical framework by a significant proportion of the academy, 'his influence on the actual

DOI: 10.1201/9781003220244-4

production of space, on architecture and the city, has been less pronounced' (Coleman, 2014:1). What could be done about that?

The role of architecture

The starting point for both Lefebvre himself and his subsequent interpreters, as well as his more traditional Marxist critics, must certainly that so long as capitalism endures – and perhaps even afterwards – architects, and by extension, developers, will work under severe constraints. Without some remaining agency, however, Lefebvre would have had to accept the entirely pessimistic arguments that architecture has been almost completely captured by capitalism, that what has been created is what the utopian Marxist philosopher Ernst Bloch – who could fine hope in virtually any quarter – called merely a 'hollow space' within it (Bloch, 1988:187), which as Coleman notes would imply that under capitalism the 'true architecture' (and urbanism) is impossible (Coleman, 2013b:351). But it was Manfred Tafuri's critique of Lefebvre in particular (Tafuri, 1976) that was attuned most closely to the views of traditional Marxists: that architectural practice is unable to transcend its position within the capitalist division of labour, and that therefore a truly revolutionary architecture was impossible – all that could be hoped for was to burnish skills and visions appropriate to the future architecture of revolution, as 'the history of architecture can be read on the basis of historiographical parameters that are relative to both the vicissitudes of intellectual labor and to the development of the modes and relations of production' (Tafuri, 1987:14). Urban forms created through architecture are subsumed into consumerism, with the fulmination of those in agreement with Lefebvre against 'the premium on newness, on differential status, on enjoyment not only through one-upmanship but also through planned obsolescence' (Tabb & Sawers, 1978a:18).

It would not be too difficult to make a plausible argument that in the wake of successive deployments of capital into the urban fabric, the negative aspects of architecture's intense relationship with capitalism are even more apparent decades later. In a detailed (and, it must be conceded, highly persuasive) 21st-century rendition of the argument suggesting that architecture has now been produced by finance capitalism, and that architects have now been subsumed into the production of space to such an extent that 'architecture can be described as a primary medium of financialization' (Soules, 2021:38), the depth of the integration process is illustrated through five global architectural types: iceberg homes (homes for the very wealthy with large underground spaces), exurban investment mats (housing for the less wealthy on the periphery of the existing urban fabric), superpodiums (towers placed on podia, creating new 'ground' levels), ultra-thin (or at least very slender) pencil towers, and financial icons (Soules, 2021). Many of them empty or underused, these forms of capitalist excess are 'designed and used to suit the logics of finance capitalism' (Soules, 2021:39). In summary:

> The architecture of finance capital has five broad characteristics:
>
> 1. It is inherently unstable and creates spaces of crisis.
> 2. It increasingly functions as speculative wealth storage.

3. It is the means of uneven development and heightened inequality.
4. It has a simultaneously propensity for highly iconic and extremely standardized spaces.
5. It increases liquidity.

(Soules, 2021:40)

If this devastating litany of criticisms not only be accurate, but be the only tale of 21st-century architecture worth telling, 'Can any more be said than that architects are part of the manufacturing process of abstract space? (Harvey, 1985:6, 2006:232–235). That, paralysed by this invasive process of capture, architecture and development can never do much more than repetitively and compulsively reinscribe alienation into the built environment (Coleman, 2014:5), the role of architects, and by extension other professionals such as chartered and quantity surveyors, and by extension the developers with whom they frequently work, all reduced to mere hired technicians of capitalist development, from which repeated calls are made in vain for them to escape (Pugalis & Giddings, 2011:284–285). Marxists can only take heart from believing that these successive spaces of crisis will eventually produce a cataclysmic counter-reaction – a revolution – that will transform and somehow *rationalise* the production of space, and lead to the future replacement of exchange value with use value.

Is there any degree of influence over the process possible – even to alter its course? Yes, Lefebvre says, for example in the manuscript on '*The Architecture of Enjoyment*' (Lefebvre, 1973 [2014]) that had lain unseen for many decades until brought to light by Łukasz Stanek. A forthright statement,

> what does ring out of it is an implicit dismissal of the 'Venice school' of Marxian architectural historiography that Tafuri led, and a determination to avoid 'the incessant repetition of the idea that there is nothing to be done, nothing to be thought . . . because capitalism rules and co-opts everything'.
>
> (Hatherley, 2015, n.p.)

At the time, Lefebvre's focus therein was on the increased leisure time that was emerging as a feature of capitalist (and even state socialist) society, and the hopeful, public architecture it brought in its wake. But as we proceed, we must now be very careful to take account of social, cultural, technological, and political changes since he wrote, very much including those that bear on architecture. For example, when Lefebvre doubts whether a differential space of leisure and self-realisation is really possible in a capitalist economy at large, 'in the architecture of enjoyment, Lefebvre identifies an opportunity to challenge and evade modernism's deterministic model of spatial production' (Touloumi, 2016:114), we may ask, in a postmodernist world, what though does such enjoyment now consist? Is a contemporary architecture of enjoyment necessarily so public as in Lefebvre's time? The easy association of leisure with public space in which he revels, let alone his contention that 'Only the people – the humiliated, the oppressed, the exploited – retain a vital, explosive energy, the energy of enjoyment – expended in festivals and revolutions' (Lefebvre, 1973 [2014:70]), may both need some rethinking, at the very least. Similarly, a masterly eye cast over 'socialist worldmaking' (Stanek, 2020) is also surely sufficient to appreciate that the principles and practice of state socialist architecture more generally in an international context is also very much of its time, serving as a further warning against Marxism as a lost future past.

Fortunately, the principle that Lefebvre applied to the architecture of leisure is capable of much wider application, for as against Tafuri's blanket negativity, Lefebvre counterposed a more nuanced and selective theory of a duel between an insurgent autonomy and capitalist recuperation (Lefebvre, 1989 [2014]). Reflecting Lefebvre's own recognition of the urban, although the city demands design, requires architecture, it at the same time thwarts its success (Cuff & Sherman, 2011), resisting it at almost every turn, the solid legacy of the built environment and the spatial limitations often placed on architecture militating against its success as a creator of differential space – even of abstract space. Yet it is not beyond the capacity of Marxists in turn to subvert. But how can – should – they do so?

Lefebvre's own starting point was similar to his critics, also highly critical of architecture as having any stand-alone capacity to deliver change. A major consequence, in this view, was the homogeneity of styles that had been created and was now reinforced by globalisation:

> [I]n the domain of architecture, a variety of local, regional, and national architectural styles has given way to 'architectural urbanism', a universalizing system of structures and functions in supposedly rational geometric forms.
>
> (Lefebvre, 1980 [1987:8])

If true, these arguments would imply standardisation of those architectural

> [p]oints, moving through space and defining lines, lines defining planes, planes defining volumes of form and space. Beyond these visual functions, these elements, by their relationships to one another and the nature of their organization, also communicate notions of domain and place, entry and path of movement, hierarchy and order.
>
> (Ching, 2007:406)

And not just standardisation: Lefebvre's underlying message is that 'architectural urbanism' enables – the verb we choose to follow matters here – architects to reflect in their work the least potentially oppressive physical structures that underpin capitalism, rather than attempting at least a contribution to the struggle for precisely their replacement. It is a point of conjuncture between Lefebvre and traditional Marxist geographers that despite this opportunity, most architects, planners, and designers tend to take a relatively passive role in the production of space, as technocratic 'doctors of space' (Lefebvre, 1974 [1991:99]).

> When architectural urban space responds to the 'social commission' of developers and the authorities, it is contributing actively and openly to the

> reproduction of the social relations [*i.e.* to the continuation of capitalism]. It is programmed space.
>
> (Lefebvre, 1973 [1976:88])

The architect has for so long attempted to combat *nature*, Lefebvre claims, broadly in line with Foucault (Fontana-Giusti, 2013), that their social role in protecting space against *power* has become defanged. As a result, they work in an *Alice Through the Looking Glass* world, their efforts to protect social space and defend against power not only thwarted, but frequently resulting in the opposite, the dilapidation of social space and its replacement by abstract space that ultimately serves to reinforce social relations of dominance and oppression. As Lefebvre puts it:

> The graphic elements involved (in drawings, sections, elevations, visual tableaux with silhouettes or figures, etc.), which are familiar to architects, serve as reducers of the reality they claim to represent – reality that is in any case no more than a modality of an accepted (i.e., imposed) 'lifestyle' in a particular type of housing (suburban villa, highrise, etc.). A 'normal' lifestyle means a normalized lifestyle.
>
> (Lefebvre, 1974 [1991:338])

If Lefebvre privileged the role of the architect, he therefore did not exonerate the profession from criticism altogether – far from it. Bereft of utopian vision, depoliticised in the worst, ironic sense of the term, infected both by the idea of planning as science and by the zeal of communication and advocacy planning, architecture always ran the risk of divorcing itself from the everyday (Borden, 2012:163), and becoming a series of castles in the air, inhabited by talented men – almost always, men – who

> believe themselves to be at the centre of knowledge and experience whereas they remain at the centre of systems of writing, projections on paper, visualizations. Architects tending on their part towards a system of significations which they often call 'planning', it is not impossible for analysts of urban reality, grouping together their piecemeal facts, to constitute a somewhat different system of significations that they can also baptize planning while they leave its programming to machines.
>
> (Lefebvre, 1968 [1996:117])

In this fashion, Lefebvre claimed that architects often fell into the dogmatic acceptance of function, form, and structure in the guise of their ideological counterparts – functionalism, formalism, and structuralism, the last of which he believed inevitably evolved into an attempt at a reformist functionalism (Stanek, 2011:121). This meant that architects behaved too often like unsophisticated sociologists – seeing the world in mechanistic terms without appreciating 'the significations perceived and lived by those who inhabit' it (Lefebvre, 1968 [1996:152]). Even the most market-oriented developer might express concern at commissioning architecture from such a mirror of a market, and a rear-view mirror at that.

But Lefebvre was targeting the ability of architecture operating independently to achieve social transformation, not working in collaboration, and the same argument could no doubt be extended to developers themselves. Although architects were intimately connected to all the complex concepts of space that he theorised, he recognised that control over the production of space rested with many actors, unfortunately often 'amongst which architects tend to have the least influence' (Stanek, 2011:147).

Much later Lefebvre still pointed with deliberate indecision to a debate between two 'schools of thought', which envisaged the future of the urban differently. For some,

> architecture and the architect have a decisive role; they produce, they make, they create urban life. It is therefore at this level that the invention must intervene today or tomorrow, which will have repercussions on the other 'levels'. It is the field of initiatives, including that of knowledge.
>
> (Lefebvre, 1986:168)

Yet, for others,

> architecture follows in the wake of the idea of urban space, which is decisive.
>
> (Lefebvre, 1986:168)

Lefebvre has evident sympathy for both arguments. On the one hand, he says, the great architects of the past have delivered their own style, an art of building that has influenced the environment – the arrangement of squares and streets in the historical cities of Italy and Spain owe their existence, structure and role to architects – the creative geniuses, people of great importance, quasi-demiurges. On the other hand, that because architectural initiatives are always situated in a social context, architects can only express the desires and wishes of the structure of social and economic power, merely serving to execute and transmit this impulse. 'Architects have come under pressure from interests, authorities, banks, promoters, after those of the most prestigious sovereigns and princes' (Lefebvre, 1986:168). Lefebvre still at this point questions the importance of this obvious fact. But given this assessment, how much agency do architects indeed possess in terms of the creation of differential space? And in any case, whatever the extent of that agency, what should architects do?

Lefebvre proffers some hope, at least theoretically, from the distinction he drew between 'architectural space' and the 'space of architects'. As Lefebvre put it:

> Architects have a trade. They raise the question of architecture's 'specificity' because they want to establish that trade's claim to legitimacy. Some of them then draw the conclusion that there are such things as 'architectural space' and 'architectural production' (specific, of course). Whereupon they close their case.
>
> (Lefebvre, 1974 [1991:104])

The latter, by virtue of the experience that people have of it, is one of the means through which social space is produced (Forty, 2000:272). Unfortunately, this social space runs the risk, at least, of becoming indistinguishable from the space of planners, politicians, and administrators, whereas architectural space, despite its social character, can interact dialectically with the mental space of architects to preserve some degree of autonomy, some independence from the dictates of capitalism (Koch, 2018:71; Lefebvre, 1974 [1991:300]).

Inspired at least in part by Lefebvre, there *are* radical (we may call them differential) architects (and, I would add, developers) who adopt a critical position towards capitalism and the state-led urbanism that Lefebvre persistently rejected. They retain hope of architectural (and developer) autonomy, even of actual achievements. They do not believe that their sometimes very modest creations are the unexceptional standardisation that must necessarily accompany architectural excess. They must tread a difficult path, at the same time both realistic enough to seek 'not to enact a total, all-or-nothing revolution but to make a radical difference' (Borden, 2003:118), mindful of Lefebvre's admonitions about the futility of entirely independent efforts to strike out, and also acutely aware of the risks, in particular, the devaluation of the 'right to the city' into an exclusive concern with physical space, as 'if such tactical moves come at the expense of a broad, transformational perspective, they may become cases of misplaced concreteness' (Kipfer *et al.*, 2013:129). Developers seeking to follow the same or an equivalent path should likewise heed such warnings.

Transductive thinking for architects

'The notion of transduction, which builds a virtual object using information, and which uses givens to arrive at a solution. We can also say that transduction goes from the (given) real to the possible' (Lefebvre, 1961 [2014:412]), creating and building a theoretical object, a possible object, based on information about reality, as well as a question raised about that reality, and then developing a feedback loop between the conceptual framework and empirical observations.

> Transduction is the term Lefebvre uses to describe the process of constructing a theoretical object (such as a new city) on the basis not only of information relating to (say) current urban reality, but by the problematic posed by existing urban realities. As new theoretical imaginings are given concrete form, the feedback mechanism ensures that subsequent projections/projects are informed by this newly altered reality in an endless loop of speculation – investigation – critique-implementation.
>
> (Parker, 2015:21)

Hence,

> the work of speculation not only takes place through the activities of builders and developers, but it also circulates through other forms of cultural activity

> and representational practice as well, specifically those forms and representations that lay claim to the future.
>
> (Boucher *et al.*, 2008:1001)

Transduction might be useful for architects, but not, therefore, on the basis of the description above, a form of thought limited to architects so far as the production of space is concerned. There is no reason why the advantages of creating and thinking constructively about a future city could not equally employed by developers: in fact, I would suggest that they already are, encapsulated – for good or ill – in the surely overworked term 'vision' in the context of real estate developments. The issue though is *what* is being thought transductively, how architects and developers pose the urban realities and perceive solutions to them. Marxists may hope that it reflects a world that has superseded capitalism, but that vision may have to compete with others.

Lefebvre's second proposal in the right to the city, experimental utopia, was premised on the idea that any urban planner of genuine worth in the late 20th century should consider herself or himself a utopian. However, utopianism that aimed at the creation of an ideal community required the study of everyday life in actual urban settings, hence the importance of the everyday for the discipline of architecture itself (Upton, 2002). By studying what made for good, happy, and playful urban dwellers, Lefebvre believed that the city of tomorrow could be built from the dreams of today (Lefebvre, 1968 [1996:152]). Intrigued by the prospects of a practical, or least experimental approach to utopia on the part of architects, he actually called for detailed, grounded, empirical analysis of what the consequences were in term of actual practice, what worked, what did not, and why, 'the times and rhythms of daily life which are inscribed and prescribed in these "successful" spaces favourable to happiness', these practical utopias (Lefebvre, 1968 [1996:151]; Coleman, 2013a). 'In this and much more, Lefebvre was informed by his close involvement with a range of urban and architectural institutions, networks and practitioners' (Pinder, 2013:37). There is little for a 21st-century differential architect to disagree with here – or a developer.

Utopian architecture

To where, though, should practitioners look for guidance? At the time he worked and wrote, whereas some architects drove him almost to despair, others served to provide Lefebvre with both inspiration and confidence, in particular those architects such as the CoBrA Group who held the definite goal 'to create an architecture that would *itself* instigate the creation of new situations' (Ross & Lefebvre, 1983 [1997:71], my italics). It is worth observing in this respect the difference between Lefebvre and the Situationist radicals, whose claimed political position was to the left of Marxists of any stripe, over the meaning of the term utopia itself – in response to what he came to regard as their abstract utopianism, Lefebvre asked almost rhetorically, 'Is experimenting with a different kind of city a concrete utopia that already forms part of the revolution? Or does it remain at the level of architectural designs?' (Lefebvre, 1961 [2014]; Trebitsch, 2002 [2014:291]).

If architecture is to participate in Lefebvre's project, then architects themselves cannot be exonerated from the ethical imperative to create differential space. At worst, then, this is all that could be rescued: intention, hope, and motive. We can after all easily contrast this set of objectives with the at least partially profit-driven motives that drive the contemporary celebrity architect worldwide: to provide one example amongst many, in Turkey, where 'Private real estate developers have worked only with a handful of big-name architects, stifling competition and innovation in the organisation of urban space' (Gülhan, 2022:1455). Marxists can contribute through not only pointing out the flaws inherent in the star architect model itself, denouncing the fact that

> [t]he competitive nature of 'signature architect' office construction and design reflects the influence of individual decision-makers, even if the outcomes have a common flavour – the desire to outdo rivals in terms of size and striking design produces competition within and across cities.
>
> (Lizieri, 2009:141)

It can also contribute by promoting the fairer, more egalitarian selection of architects across more numerous, usually smaller projects. In turn, fairer architecture aimed at the creation of many differential spaces requires plentiful real estate developers with a range of different approaches to development.

Whether good intentions or based on virtue, ethics in general were for Lefebvre however never enough, as his critical view of those architects who championed planned cities amply demonstrated; many of their claims to revolutionary status could be safely swept aside, he believed. Lefebvre delivered specific criticism of one particular project, for example – a proposed new city in the Furttal Valley in Switzerland – that in his view assumed isomorphism between social and spatial entities. He extended his criticism to their contemporaries in the Soviet Union and other state socialist countries, who were in Lefebvre's eyes, after a promising start (Lohtaja, 2021), then dramatically halted, later attempting sterile work that could not be identified as socialist, no better or even different than was being created in capitalist countries (Lefebvre, 1974 [1991:54]).

It is worth recalling that Lefebvre was fighting battles that today either no longer need to be fought or at least are less fundamental to contemporary real estate development. The struggle he waged against architecture and urban planning as the fulfilment of 'needs' is one obvious example (Stanek, 2011:100). Many of the criticisms Lefebvre levelled against modernist architecture in particular were founded on the accusation of a simplified understanding of needs and functions, ultimately traceable back to the theory of the hierarchy of needs (Maslow, 1943, 1954), that was not likely to enjoy success once it encountered real people, a concept that Lefebvre persistently held, especially given his sympathy with the idea that capitalism itself manufactured these alleged 'needs'. Le Corbusier never quite went so far as to claim that everyone had the same needs, but Lefebvre had no patience with the concept of 'need' as understood outside Marxism: like Marx, he saw needs as at least largely a product of history and therefore of class, or at least of marketing in capitalist economies. Where Lefebvre conceded the existence of needs at all, it was only in the context of a dialectical, social set of needs (Lefebvre, 1967 [1970:195]).

The claims of functionist architects may have been extensive – 'Bauhaus people aimed to transform life: the architect, then, was the demiurge, the transformer of social relations' (Lefebvre, 1975:19) – but in his view their achievements in this direction were meagre, if not indeed the opposite of what they had set out to achieve: 'It is certainly arguable that the writings and works of the Bauhaus, of Mies van der Rohe among others, outlined, formulated and helped realize that particular space' (Lefebvre, 1974 [1991:126]). And this at a time when revolutionary optimism was arguably at its height, with a widespread conviction that architecture of this bleak and ultimately conformist set of styles could play a significant role in ameliorating 'human nature' and contributing to the construction of a more equal and just society. How much worse the situation now, when such optimism has been entirely occluded, and when the failures of state socialism in the architectural sphere as so many others have become so obvious? Whatever Lefebvre's utopian architecture was to be – and however developers are to be involved with it – it cannot be a return to the vision of the Bauhaus.

Looking back over the critique, the response by architects to design apartments, complete with cultural centres and clubs, in order to foster social relationships was – or at least was very likely to be – in Lefebvre's view as utopian in a negative sense as Le Corbusier's (Smith, 2002). He was, as a result, sharply critical, one of his leading interpreters presenting his view as that 'The analysis of dwelling as an ensemble of practices rather than a set of isolated needs is a more convincing response to functionalist discourse' (Stanek, 2011:103). For Lefebvre, although he was never quite prepared to dismiss the Bauhaus altogether, he did overall view their vision as a misconception of utopia, and a potentially disastrous one at that. So, although there were undoubted individual successes, and mass housing did succeed in putting roofs over heads, in some cases improving peoples' lives immensely, worldwide there was criticism, including the role of developers:

> When his [Corbusier's] prototypes were translated into the harsh commercial reality of constructed buildings in Canadian cities, however, there was little evidence of Le Corbusier's humanism. What was bold and exhilarating about high-rise apartments was not the accommodation they provided, but rather the dramatic new scale of operation they permitted apartment developers.
>
> (Lorimer, 1978:131)

And not only the role of private sector developers was under criticism, but also the public sector was in many countries at the forefront of the process. The critique was as consistent as it was widely shared, from Lefebvre's initial savage denunciation:

> In the new housing estates, objects with aesthetic pretensions appear ridiculous, and indeed they are, because they have been added on in an intentional

> and clumsy manner; there is nothing surprising about them, except perhaps the surprise of uneasiness they afford.
>
> (Lefebvre, 1961 [2014:373])

It is now a well-established view in retrospect that

> [n]o matter that the city of dwellers liked their own front doors, and a patch of garden; acres of small, and undoubtedly substandard, Georgian and Victorian housing were swept away in the name of Le Corbusier and blocks of high-rise flats built in their place.
>
> (Ross Goobey, 1992:29)

However, in an earlier age, Le Corbusier, one of the earliest star architects, had his proponents defending him from 'Criticisms from the English journalists, architects and historians – bitter and ill-informed' (Gardiner, 1974:14), as 'his imitators copied his outlines and ignored the underlying principles from which these outlines evolved' (Gardiner, 1974:116–117), with hindsight what was once a radical contention, that mass housing in the style of Le Corbusier was a giant mistake, is now an entirely familiar one. We now understand that 'With very few exceptions, usually lived in by the wealthy and childless, such as the Barbican Centre [especially in its initial decades], large multi-storey estates are nearly universally shunned by those who can afford to choose' (Smith & Morton, 2013:5). And that, therefore, even supporters of relatively dense urban development suggest that 'there should be a presumption against "hyper-dense" developments, often presumed to be those of over 350 homes per hectare, which should be confined to exceptional locations and subject to exceptional justification' (Murray, 2015:10). Institutions dedicated to the promotion of this part of the Lefebvrian vision of the city, at least, exist aplenty, albeit not necessarily the remainder.

Where Lefebvre and Le Corbusier silently agreed, however it should be recognised, was on the importance of centrality, exemplified by developments like the Barbican. Subsequent positive commentary on social housing architecture has largely concurred:

> [B]y centrality we mean the easy relation with the city, fuelling urban life, enabling benefit from it in a useful and healthy way. It may not be a strictly architectural decision (it is more related to political and economic issues), but it has, undoubtedly, huge repercussion on its architecture.
>
> (Rodrigues, 2018:30)

We may have to alter this emphasis, in a world where physical centrality may not demonstrate the same allure in the future as it has in the past.

If not the Bauhaus, then what?

We are probably entitled to conclude that Lefebvre did not want to see more mass housing along functionist lines. His conception of successful architecture was always on a more human scale.

The City of Space – a utopian vision

Lefebvre pointed to this project which the Ricardo Bofill tried to construct in Madrid (Figure 4.1) (Faura, 2014) as 'an attempt at utopia in real life' (Lefebvre, 1975:246). This project certainly did embody a strong element of purely utopian thinking, but claims have been made for its real-world plausibility, in particular through the proposed use of a plausible light prefabricated system allowing for the further growth of the complex over time, a concept to which developers may yet return in force as the rise of prefabricated housing gathers pace in the subsequent century. Streets, squares, and arcades were to be introduced on several elevated levels, while the ground floor was occupied by services and parking spaces, concepts that might still be of use, but equally may no longer be required. The complex would have provided a mixture of functions on all levels and would be managed by a cooperative, at least of a kind (Fabrizi, 2016). The project remained unbuilt, although Bofill did finish other somewhat similar projects, Walden 7 being the closest to his original ideas. A sobering reflection on this particular utopian approach is nevertheless served by the fact that Bofill himself rejected it after his first project in Paris, *La Pétite Cathedrale*, instead embracing neoclassical post-modernism (Hidden Architecture, 2016).

Figure 4.1 The City of Space.

Source: Bofill Office (2016).

This is just one example of a utopian architectural project: Stanek (2011) provides numerous others, such as CoBrA's Constant Nieuwenhuys' New Babylon to which Lefebvre made approving reference (Ross & Lefebvre, 1997:70), although most remained as architectural designs. But as Marxists, we just as much as practitioners must be careful not to slide into the analysis of futures past. Moreover, if architecture were to be destined to make a contribution to the creation of differential space only on this haphazard, occasional basis, even ultimately in the case of the City of Space disowned by its own progenitors, there might be grounds for considering the representations of differential space created by architecture to be sporadic, and certainly ineffectual in broad political terms. Is there more on offer? Yes, in Lefebvre's view, though first, there are more caveats to be entered.

Some potential contradictions

Reimagining the urban is a perennial pursuit. No doubt that as Emily Talen has consistently argued (Talen, 2008; Talen & Lee, 2018), there is a reciprocal relationship of great importance between urban forms and social diversity, which in turn demands actual tools for architects. Authors, especially in the United States, have suggested several characteristics of 'community-generating neighborhoods', whether they be stores, parks, plazas, and civic buildings that bring people together, including being a suitable size for a neighbourhood-based community organisation; comprising houses and spaces that are arranged to facilitate social interaction; and having the appearance of a community (Brower (2020; Tatian *et al.*, 2012). If none of this now seems remotely surprising or original, this is no reason for Marxists not to embrace these architectural elements of New Urbanism, albeit cautiously. They will however place special emphasis on the less privileged members of the community, for example the close relationship between the built environment and community health (Mukhija & Takahashi, 2022). They will also recognise uncomfortable truths – for example, that superseding capitalism will not bring an end to all urban problems, nor will it permit global uniformity of solutions, as some architectural achievements do not travel well, and what may flourish in developed urban economies in largely temperate climates does not necessarily do so elsewhere.

Nevertheless, architectural utopia might be considered across a number of dimensions. One of them – with which Lefebvre had great sympathy – is the environmental aspect of building. This subject has been examined exhaustively, especially over the past two decades: in temperate climates and in developed countries at least. Justified concerns about the potential obscuring of social impact should not themselves prevent recognition and approval of the environmental benefits of genuinely environmentally sensitive architecture, as the creation of differential space is not a linear process that can be expected to achieve results on all fronts simultaneously. What remains unclear, however, despite this intense and prolonged attention, is the expenditure of vast resources of time and money, and considerable success in purely environmental terms is the extent to which much green building represents a genuine liberation, the creation of differential space, or whether it ought to be considered under a quite different risk management rubric. Architects may be able to use whatever autonomy they possess, and work with other participants in the development process to achieve environmental goals without sacrificing equivalent benefits in terms of living quality or even financial return. Whilst this may not be of direct benefit to occupiers, or owners, such an outcome should also without much controversy be considered differential, in that the building will contribute to wider social goals. Where problems arise, they are in potential trade-offs between social and environmental goals, a complexity that in his uniform and homogeneous concept of differential space Lefebvre did not pause to consider, any more than did Engels in his proposed resolution of the London housing crisis (Engels, 1872 [2021]). Of equal concern to doubts about New Urbanism, therefore, is the possibility that the incorporation of environmental design features as part of a global drive towards net zero real estate may actually reinforce the existence of abstract space, a possibility that Lefebvre did not consider. The conclusion is a clear need for active political engagement with architects, one which demands a reconsideration of Lefebvre's characteristic distaste for quantification.

Measuring ESG impact for architects

A leading US architectural practice known for its progressive approach observed that, at least at present, companies seeking to incorporate ESG principles in their buildings and spaces look to a set of traditional features, including green certification rating systems like LEED, straightforward building upgrades like high-efficiency lighting retrofits, and neighbourhood assessments like Walk Score. By comparison, Gensler set out to measure, and eventually incorporate into architectural design, the ESG value of no fewer than 70 metrics – from the thermal performance of outdoor space, to optimising how the public accesses amenities, to low-carbon construction materials, looking beyond the building itself to how a project can benefit the surrounding neighbourhood as well (Brower *et al.*, 2022).

Some more home truths

Although there are still Marxists, Lefebvre included, who have never been comfortable with the domestic, the private, the personal, or even the psychological, as a sociologist, Lefebvre himself was rather generous to the *pavillon*, despite his evident contempt for its attendant social mores. At the same time, Lefebvre had little respect for their preferences, the very stuff of alienated lives:

> Their owners' superficiality oozes forth in an abundance of ridiculous details, china animals on the roofs, glass globes and well-pruned shrubs along the miniature paths, plaques adorned with mottos, self-important pediments.
>
> (Lefebvre, 1947 [2014:65])

But there is a tension in his thought with which we should all sympathise, as he admits that modern man can 'dwell poetically' in a *pavillon*, in a 'small-minded way', and noted that empirically, the vast majority of the French population, at least, would prefer to inhabit a *pavillon* than an apartment (Lefebvre, 1966). Studies stretching across decades support this assertion: a Vancouver study now five decades old, echoed by a much later UK study (Dunse *et al.*, 2013), identified the housing features people considered desirable: privacy, adequate space, a private yard, private parking, and quiet (Bell & Constantinescu, 1974), 'None of these features is usually available to the high-rise tenant' (Lorimer, 1978:136). Lefebvre explained why quite precisely:

> The space in which he is able to organize it according to his own tastes and patterns is somewhat malleable. It lends itself to rearrangement. This is not so with the space provided for tenants or co-owners on an estate; that space is rigid, inflexible. It is difficult, often impossible (and almost always prohibited) to convert it. Space in a detached home allows the family group and its individual members to appropriate to some extent the conditions of their own existence. They can alter, add or subtract, superimpose their own ideas (symbols, organization) on what is provided. Their environment thus acquires meaning for them: there is a system of signification, even a double system: semantic and semiological, in words and in objects.
>
> (Lefebvre, 1966)

It was not therefore surprising that he viewed Boudron's critical analysis of Le Corbusier's early experiment, the *Quartiers Modernes Frugès* at Pessac – now fashionable apartments, but at the time a rationalist experiment viewed with suspicion by the workers who were intended to inhabit them – with both interest and sympathy. Those who did move in adapted and changed the conformist, linear, modernist, style of their new homes: 'Instead of inserting themselves into this receptacle and passively adapting to it, they have to some extent actively inhabited it' (Lefebvre, 1969:ix), behaviour that has found echoes in a different time and at the other end of Europe (Figure 4.2) (Saifi *et al.*, 2012; Fernandes, 2014).

Assigning to this the philosophical categories of the universal and the singular, Lefebvre viewed the actions of the inhabitants of the *Quartiers Modernes Frugès* as a process in which the abstract space created by modernist architecture was transformed at least in part to a differential space through the appropriation of space and the creation of literal and figurative differences by the inhabitants themselves.

This is not only a warning of the difficulties facing mass housing, but evidence that differential space need not necessarily emerge purely as the result of dialectical struggle, that it is perhaps too easy to coral differences as arising or enduring only 'on the margins of the homogenized realm, through resistances to the agendas of land developers, urban planners, and the State, and through the production of heterotopias and "heterologies"' (Stewart, 1995:615). In fact, the pursuit of heterotopic spaces of appropriation may well only ever be an intermediary practice towards differential space (Gallico, 2016:295). For Lefebvre, 'diversion and vacant spaces are left by him as merely tactical, as insignificant residuals though deemed

Figure 4.2 Cité Frugès in the 21st century.

Source: Photo by Fred Romero (2023), https://www.flickr.com/photos/129231073@N06/sets/72157670256603596.

of great importance' (Lilliendahl Larsen & Brandt, 2018:56). It is remarkable how much attention has been devoted to them despite agreement on this point – and how little to undoubtedly less visually exciting, but arguably more socially important architecture.

Architects can, on the other hand, produce elegant and sophisticated designs of great practicality and value that can be described, if a mixing of the triads can be permitted, to be representations of differential space. For example, Mel Malik and Max Engel Wight produced a series of renders of housing typologies for affordable housing in Vietnam, Cambodia, Bangladesh, Nepal, Myanmar, and Fiji. There are housing options for small to large families, and they are as varied as the cultures they are made for (Habitat for Humanity, 2022). They may not have a spectacular appearance, but differential design need not necessarily mean spectacular design. It may just mean design that, once built, dramatically improves the lives of the less advantaged people who now live there (Figure 4.3).

Figure 4.3 Affordable housing for the Asia-Pacific.

Source: Habitat for Humanity (2021).

It is hard to see why Lefebvre would not have approved, although it is perhaps to be regretted that he did not focus much more on this kind of architectural achievement – outside Paris, even outside Europe altogether for the most part.

Participatory design

It was a leading British politician of the Left who once observed that whilst people do not necessarily want socialism, they do want democracy (Benn, 1981). No accident, then, that recognising that underlying aspiration,

> active involvement in the field of participatory design was a challenge pursued by many other architects and planners, with notable experiences, such as the intervention by Ralph Erskine in Byker Wall in Newcastle upon Tyne, England, and in other projects undertaken by Team X.
>
> (de la Cal, 2018:167)

More democracy in architecture, especially at a local level, does not however *necessarily* result in better building or more differential space – it may not result in any construction at all, or it may result in inegalitarian and exclusive development. Marxists must therefore be careful in their support: Lefebvre himself was doubtful about the benefits to be delivered by, for example, Yona Friedman's portable structures that can be joined together to create ephemeral groupings – Air BnB is the reality of this, the use of financial structures to replace physical ones, in order to 'generalize and democratize the luxury life of millionaires, who move from home to home, villa to villa, or yacht to yacht' (Lefebvre, 1970 [2003:95]). Nevertheless, there can be clear benefits, especially where entire communities are involved and the projects themselves are aimed at improvements in low-income areas without the displacement that accompanies gentrification.

A contemporary role for architecture

Can architecture still assist, at least, in liberating the potential for the division of labour and the dominance of private property? (de Stefani, 2015:92). Lefebvre appears to suggest that architecture can potentially enjoy a privileged space, methodologically isolated from the structures of state and capital (Wilson, 2014). So when Lefebvre on one occasion compares himself with architects, he conceives of them as intellectuals of architecture and urban transformations, and Stanek concludes, 'this statement pointed to a shift in architectural culture, with the architects claiming the position of intellectuals' (Stanek, 2011:xi; Gromark, 2013:249). All this might be worth querying, for several reasons. Firstly, it has been suggested that Lefebvre lacked 'fieldwork experience, direct knowledge of the terrain and sufficiently deep exchange with architects' (Chombart De Lauwe, 1996:94–95; Stanek, 2011:viii). We must also recognise that the urban is not what it was, and that Lefebvre's concern with architecture was of its time. When he developed his theory of space, the production process for what we now describe as real estate was very different.

Architect as cultural globaliser

The scale of the challenges in urban design and masterplanning has vastly increased along with the rapid global trend towards greater urbanisation. Each increasing factor of population, energy consumption, transport needs, pollution, and required prosperity must be taken into account on a scale not seen before. Some developers, seeking to draw on their experience globally, in a way that would conceivably be more difficult for an organisation with a local focus, have taken the view that vertical mixed-use developments are the right way forward.

In Asia, the chairman of an architectural practice that operates there observed: 'They are used to high rise, high density, truly mixed-use developments – having everything on one site, so you can live, work and play without ever leaving the building. We think that's the way London needs to densify' (Wainwright, 2014).

No doubt these developments have their problems. They certainly have their critics. But what is surely hard to argue against is that if plans and projects of this kind are to be put forward for consideration by local planning authorities in cities such as London, even Paris or Perth, where high-rise is even less popular than in London, the designs that are submitted draw on both cultural and physical differences between locations (Kalantari & Shepley, 2021) and the best possible international experience, for example, which features of green buildings contributed to health perceptions (e.g. Xue *et al.*, 2016), with all the lessons learned now over several decades.

Lefebvre's manifesto for architecture was for the adoption of new experimental approaches involving spatial forms and urban time that will allow 'urban society' to fully emerge, but it is not at all clear how this might encompass the transfer of architectural information worldwide. He believed that even under late capitalism, the rural-agrarian world still limited and stifled the potential for a genuine urban society that is free of rural and 'natural' dominant features (and these were the essentially negative ones of a rigid, hierarchical social order, high levels of surveillance and social control, anti-intellectualism, and anticosmopolitanism (Parker, 2015:21) And there is no doubt that utopia always played a more sophisticated role in Lefebvre's thought than the mere reversion to pre-Marxist thinking portrayed by his more strident traditional Marxist critics (Castells, 1977:89). Architecture and design, bringing forward utopia, 'sketching out' part of the future in design, technology, and, above all, in construction, these are key to how utopia can still play an important *practical* role for Marxists when confronting and responding to the urban. But importantly for the overall thesis of this book, if it is necessary to retain both a romantic and a utopian vision in order to 'think with Lefebvre' (Coleman, 2014:1), then why are not these others also capable of that vision? Surely, *they are*.

Hence the important quote with which Coleman begins his book and on which it is now necessary to reflect and question:

> The architect occupies an especially uncomfortable position. As a scientist and technician, obliged to produce within a specified framework, he has to depend on repetition. In his search for inspiration as an artist, and as someone sensitive to use and to the 'user', however, he has a stake in difference. He is located willy-nilly within this painful contradiction, forever being shuttled from one of its poles to the other. His is the difficult task of bridging the gap between product and work, and he is fated to live out the conflicts that arise as he desperately seeks to close the ever-widening gulf between knowledge and creativity.
>
> (Lefebvre, 1974 [1991:396])

Control over design in the 21st century largely rests with the collection of stakeholders that empower, direct, and manage real estate developers. If, as Stanek suggests, the role of the architect is to proceed transductively, which whilst the domain of architects in the 1960s is now what developers also – and perhaps more so – do. Not least because amidst a wide variety of development funding and management structures, some architectural practice has for many decades converged on acting as developers themselves, a popular subject for architectural theses in particular (Benkert, 2010; Funari, 2013; Owens, 2015; Gondaliya, 2020). Architects may also now work within developers themselves, for them, or as them, and have in the process inevitably therefore heeded the advice to 'consider collaborating with financiers in a manner that is similar to how they currently work with engineers' (Soules, 2021:210). As a result of these changes, we can surely no longer accept as broad and yet as narrow a definition of architecture as 'the production of space at a specific level, ranging from furniture to gardens and parks and even landscapes' (Lefebvre, 1973 [2014:3]) without, at least, recognising that the borders of the profession have become fuzzier, that the role of the architect may now encompass that of project manager, in some cases even verging on developer themselves. Architectural autonomy is under these circumstances not what actually happens. 'The section of space assigned to the architect – perhaps by "developers", perhaps by government agencies – is affected by calculations that he may have some intimation of but with which he is certainly not well acquainted' (Lefebvre, 1974 [1991:360]). That acquaintance has certainly deepened since then: there is a tense relationship between architecture, marketing, sales, and leasing: sometimes productive, sometimes not, but never entirely neutral. Architects now claim project management space, and many have substantial financial understanding. What we can conclude is that the closer that architects edge into the realm of work hitherto thought reserved for developers, and the more their work overlaps with them, the more that must lose any especially privileged status within a lexicon of actors capable of creating differential space.

None of this is to suggest that acting in the capacity of project managers, architects cannot achieve the creation of differential space – they can.

Competing pathways – pedestrianisation in Cairo

Their names are as plentiful as the spaces themselves – passageways, laneways, lorongs, and many more – and cities such as Cairo abound in them, 'spaces between buildings that connect the main streets that located off the main channels of traffic and operate as hubs for competing interests and claims to space' (Ashour & Braker, 2018:138). Rejuvenating one of them in particular, the Kodak passageway, is a task that in Cairo initially began with a private–public partnership between CLUSTER (Cairo Laboratory for Urban Studies, Training and Environmental Research), CKU (Center for Culture and Development), and DEDI (the Danish Egyptian Dialogue Institute). The work was sponsored and funded by DEDI and CKU, in collaboration with the

Cairo Governorate, with additional support by a consortium of community members, including a real estate investor, law firm, and retail (Nagati, 2023).

Kodak Passage itself is a linear space flanked by a U-shape building that is empty as many of the surrounding shops either are empty or have low street traffic. It is a linear passage that connects Adly Street to Abdel Khaleq Tharwat Street. The indoor spaces flanking Kodak offer an opportunity for pilot art and cultural programmes that may potentially spill over the passage integrating all premises and engaging these programmes with a wider public (Ashour & Braker, 2018; Danish Egyptian Dialogue Initiative, 2022). Covering an area of 636 m^2 (width: 9.5 m, length: 80 m), the redeveloped Kodak Passage became a park, with benches, trees for shading, soft lighting, and the facades along both its sides were renovated. Its activities now vary according to the time of day and day of the week; this new public space can, the creators claimed, be considered a 'cultural park', as it hosts different intellectual events, art exhibitions, film screenings, book fairs, and performances. For every season, it claimed, the street changes its decorations to embrace the occasion. As an attempt to create a 'hybrid equilibrium of urban design and art manifestation' in the northern part of Downtown Cairo, its creators argued that it highlighted the existing and emerging initiatives in a way that would help activate other underutilised public spaces in the area – more diverse, safer, and environmentally enhanced experience in the passageways (Figure 4.4).

Figure 4.4 Kodak passageway.

Source: Cluster Mapping Initiative (2015).

These approaches, with their embedded extensive processes of seeking information, consulting, and negotiating with local stakeholders (Nagati & Stryker, 2016; Kamvasinou & Akl, 2019), have been contrasted with 'out-of-touch proposals characteristic of those of central government' (Abdelaal *et al.*, 2021:52). Moreover, they can serve as models for local government to follow, as was the case in Cairo where other nearby passageways were renovated, based on the Kodak precedent – notably Al Alfi Bey (Abdelaal *et al.*, 2021:52n6.). Reviewing the project after eight years, the Principal of CLUSTER observed:

> Kodak Passageway was developed as a pilot for an alternative framework to reimagine downtown and the city from the inside out, working within its fissures and interstices, both geographically and politically. The project was designed and implemented through an innovative participatory approach – we dubbed as "urban diplomacy" – to renegotiate a common ground between the competing interests of stakeholders. This experiment of local urban governance should be viewed in the context of the absence of elected city councils in Cairo since 2011.
>
> (Nagati, 2023)

Success stories of this kind are fortunately not unique. But the logical consequence of such examples is also that no longer can we join with Lefebvre in seeing the main ideological opponents to the creation of differential space as the 'the planning state and postwar functionalist urbanism' (Stanek, 2011:ix), as it has to a significant degree evaporated into a capitalism that has transferred much of this functionality to at least nominally non-state actors, including architects, especially in their project management role. So, whereas it has been suggested that the most promising avenue of research for 'reimagining, rethinking and revaluing architecture (and the city)' is to be found within the discipline of architecture itself (Coleman, 2014:4), the application of a parallel principle to developers has not been attempted and the same requirement exits for developers. Yet there are those within developers who are equally capable of speaking on behalf of urban space as do architects, and often do so within a much broader perspective than the architects they employ.

Conclusion

Architects, like developers, are responsive to a range of ethical and political demands stretching far beyond their contribution to the private profitability of individual organisations. Or at least, according to Lefebvrian principles, they ought to be. These include widely promoted and increasingly now effectively regulated environmental pressures, a set of quite conventional and widespread principles of governance and fairness as to the operation of their organisations, and also a social responsibility for what they design to contribute to achieving the replacement of abstract by differential space. At a project and even an organisational level, they therefore can and should be engaged in the creation of differential space.

Yet architects, again no more than developers, evidently do not work in isolation, so the responsibility cannot rest on their shoulders alone however supported and encouraged outside the development process by urban social movements, or active politics of any kind.

> [T]he understanding of space as materially transformed, represented and experienced requires an attention to the variety of actors with whom the architect engages, thus moving beyond the bipolar, 1960s image of the architectural practice overshadowed by its dark other: 'the market' or 'the state'.
> (Stanek, 2011:51)

If so, then the further passage of time and the transformation of the institutional actors involved in the creation of space within capitalist society globally demand a rebalancing of that privileged independent position of architects that Lefebvre consciously promoted. We may now legitimately ask in relation to the pessimistic evaluation of architecture by David Harvey cited above, who does the hiring? Who does the manufacturing? Who provides the finance? Two further sets of actors therefore demand immediate inclusion: urban planners and real estate developers themselves. To these professions we must now turn.

Bibliography

Abdelaal, A., Awatta, H., Nagati, O., Salman, S. and Shykhon, M. (2021). Centralised urban governance in the Greater Cairo City Region: A critical understanding of key challenges and responses. In Bekker, S., Croese, S. and Pieterse, E. (eds.) *Refractions of the National, the Popular and the Global in African Cities*. Burlington, African Minds, 41–58.

Ashour, S. and Braker, B. (2020). Private initiatives versus state interventions in downtown Cairo: An on-going debate questioning the sustainability of newly pedestrianized streets. the cases of kodak and Al-Alfi passageways. In Mateev, M. and Nightingale, J. (eds.) *Sustainable Development and Social Responsibility – Volume 1. Proceedings of the 2nd American University in the Emirates International Research Conference, AUEIRC'18 – Dubai, UAE 2018*, 131–147. Cham, Springer.

Bell, L. and Constantinescu, J. (1974). *The Housing Game: A Survey of Consumer Preferences in Medium-Density Housing the Greater Vancouver Region: Survey Period, Fall, 1972*. Vancouver, United Way of Greater Vancouver. Social Policy and Research Department.

Benkert, M. (2010). *Architect as developer: A model for triple top line development*. University of Cincinnat, Master's Thesis. Available at: OhioLINK Electronic Theses and Dissertations Center. http://rave.ohiolink.edu/etdc/view?acc_num=ucin1275664157 [Accessed 3 February 2022].

Benn, T. (1981). *Arguments for Democracy*. London, Jonathan Cape.

Bloch, E. (1988). Building in empty spaces. In *The Utopian Function of Art and Literature: Selected Essays*. Cambridge, MA, MIT Press, 186–199.

Borden, I. (2003). What is radical architecture. In Hall, T. and Miles, M. (eds.) *Urban Futures Critical Commentaries on Shaping Cities*. London, Routledge, 111–121.
———. (2012). Beyond space: The ideas of Henri Lefebvre in relation to architecture and cities. *Journal of Chinese Urban Science*, 3(1), 156–193.
Brower, A., Handelman, A. and Olson, S. (2022). *The future of ESG in architecture*. Available at: www.gensler.com/blog/measurable-impact-the-future-of-esg-in-architecture-design. [Accessed 8 August 2022].
Brower, S. (2020). *Neighbors & Neighborhoods: Elements of Successful Community Design*. New York and London, Routledge.
Boucher, N., Cavalcanti, M., Kipfer, S., Pieterse, E., Rao, V. and Smith, N. (2008). Writing the lines of connection: Unveiling the strange language of urbanization. *International Journal of Urban and Regional Research*, 32(4), 989–1027.
Castells, M. (1972 [1977]). *La Question urbaine*. Paris, Maspero. Translated by A. Sheridan as *The Urban Question – A Marxist Approach*. London: Edward Arnold.
Ching, F. D. K. (2007). *Architecture. Form, Space and Order*. 3rd edition. New York, Wiley.
Chombart De Lauwe, P-H. (1996). *Un anthropologue dans le siècle*. Paris, Descartes et Cie.
Coleman, N. (2013a). Utopian prospect of Henri Lefebvre. *Space and Culture*, 16(3), 349–363.
———. (2013b). Building in empty spaces': Is architecture a 'degenerate utopia'? *The Journal of Architecture*, 18(2), 135–166.
———. (2014). *Lefebvre for Architects*. New York and London, Routledge.
Cuff, D. and Sherman, R. (2011). *Fast-Forward Urbanism. Rethinking Architecture's Engagement With the City*. New York, Princeton Architectural Press.
Danish Egyptian Dialogue Initiative. (2022). *Cairo downtown passages – kodak passage*. Available at: https://dedi.org.eg/cairo-downtown-passages-kodak-passage/. [Accessed 4 September 2022].
De la Cal, P. (2018). Citizen participation. Urban development for and by the people. In Medina, C. D. and Monclús, J. (eds.) *Urban Visions. From Planning Culture to Landscape Urbanism*. Cham, Springer, 165–174.
De Stefani, P. (2015). La producción social de la arquitectura en Lefebvre. In Gasic, I., Narváez, A. and Quiroz, R. (eds.) *Reapropiaciones de Henri Lefebvre: Crí tica, Espacio y Sociedad Urbana*. Santiago, Editorial Triángulo, 72–95.
Dunse, N., Thanos, S. and Bramley, G. (2013). Planning policy, housing density and consumer preferences. *Journal of Property Research*, 30(3), 221–238.
Engels. (1872) [2021]. *The Housing Question*. Paris, Foreign Languages Press. Available at: https://foreignlanguages.press/wp-content/uploads/2021/03/C13-Engels-The-Housing-Question-1st-Printing.pdf [Accessed 12 May 2021].
Fabrizi, M. (2006). The city in the space by Ricardo Bofill and Taller de Arquitectura (1970). *Socks* [blog], 8 December 2016. Available at https://socks-studio.com/2016/12/08/the-city-in-the-space-by-ricardo-bofill-and-taller-de-arquitectura-1970/. [Accessed 4 July 2022].
Faura, R. (Writer). (2014). Ricardo Bofill en Madrid: la Ciudad en el Espacio (1970). In *Escola Tècnica Superior d'Arquitectura de Barcelona*. Spain. Available at: https://upcommons.upc.edu/handle/2099.2/3837
Fernandes, E. (2014). *Life versus Architecture. Rationalist ideals facing popular taste, from Pessac to Malagueira*. Paper presented at the 20th Century New Towns. Archetypes and Uncertainties, Oporto.
Fontana-Giusti, G. (2013). *Foucault for Architects*. London, Routledge.
Forty, A. (2000). *Words and Buildings: A Vocabulary of Modern Architecture*. London, Thames & Hudson.

Funari, S. D. (2013). *The Architect as Developer*. Master of Architecture. University of Tennessee. Available at: https://trace.tennessee.edu/utk_gradthes/1618/. [Accessed 3 November 2021].

Gallico, T. (2016). *Urban space interventions, appropriation and the creation of differential space: An analysis of Berlin*. PhD. University of New South Wales. Available at: http://handle.unsw.edu.au/1959.4/57835. [Accessed 2 September 2021].

Gardiner, S. (1974). *Le Corbusier*. London, Fontana.

Gondaliya, H. (2020). *Architectural Agency Through Real Estate Development*. Available at: https://scholarworks.umass.edu/masters_theses_2/922/. [Accessed 10 February 2023].

Gromark, S. (2013). A third wave of receptions: Space as concrete abstraction, Lukasz Stanek on Henri Lefebvre. *Site*, 33, 245–252. Available at: www.sitemagazine.net/content/02-issues/23-33_2013/33.pdf. [Accessed 2 March 2022].

Gülhan, S. T. (2022). Neoliberalism and neo-dirigisme in action: The state – corporate alliance and the great housing rush of the 2000s in Istanbul, Turkey. *Urban Studies*, 59(7), 1443–1458.

Habitat for Humanity. (2021). *Building Houses That Are Affordable, Sustainable and Resilient to Climate Change*, 13 October 2021. Available at: https://habitat.org.au/building-houses-for-apac/. [Accessed 3 March 2022].

———. (2022). *Habitat and TIST Join Forces to Help Tonga Rebuild After Disaster*, 10 August 2022. Available at: https://habitat.org.nz/habitat-and-tist-join-forces-to-provide-education-and-hands-on-experience-to-help-tonga-rebuild/. [Accessed 5 March 2022].

Harvey, D. (1985). *The Urbanization of Capital*. Baltimore, Johns Hopkins University Press.

———. (2006). *The Limits to Capital*. London, Verso.

Hatherley, O. (2015). *Socialism at the Seaside: The Holiday Architecture of the Left*, 11 March 2015. Available at: www.architectural-review.com/essays/books/socialism-at-the-seaside-the-holiday-architecture-of-the-left. [Accessed 4 April 2022].

Hidden Architecture. (2016). *City in the Space*. Available at: https://hiddenarchitecture.net/city-in-space/. [Accessed 24 May 2022].

Kalantari, S. and Shepley, M. (2021). Psychological and social impacts of high-rise buildings: A review of the post-occupancy evaluation literature. *Housing Studies*, 36(8), 1147–1176.

Kamvasinou, K. and Akl, A. 2019. *Alternative Urbanism in the Historic City Centre: A Transnational Perspective on Theory and Practice*. AESOP Annual Congress Venice 2019. IUAV Venice, Italy 9–13 July 2019 Universita IUAV di Venezia, 3237–3248.

Kipfer, S., Saberi, P. and Wieditz, T. (2013). Henri Lefebvre: Debates and controversies. *Progress in Human Geography*, 37(1), 115–134.

Koch, D. (2018). On architectural space and modes of subjectivity: Producing the material conditions for creative-productive activity. *Urban Planning*, 3(3), 70–82.

Larsen, H. G., Hansen, A. L., MacLeod, G. and Slater, T. (2016). Introduction: The housing question revisited. *ACME: An International Journal for Critical Geographies*, 15(3), 580–589.

Lefebvre, H. (1947). *Critique de la vie quotidienne. Volume One. Introduction*. Paris: Grasset. Translated by J. Moore (1991 [2014]) as *Critique of Everyday Life. Volume One. Introduction*. London, Verso.

———. (1962 [1995]). *Introduction à la modernite*. Paris, Minuit. Translated by J. Moore as *Introduction to Modernity*. London, Verso.

———. (1966). Préface. In Antoine Haumont, N. H. *et al.* (eds.) *L'habitat pavillonnaire*. Paris, Centre de recherche d'urbanisme.

———. (1967 [1970]). Propositions pour un nouvel urbanisme. In *Du rural à l'urbain*. Paris, Gallomard, 183–195.

———. (1968 [1996]). *Le Droit à la ville*. Paris, Anthropos. In Kofman, E. and Lebas, E. (eds.) *Henri Lefebvre. Writings on Cities*. Oxford, Blackwells, 63–184.
———. (1969). Préface. In Boudon, P. (ed.) *Pessac de Le Corbusier*. Paris, Dunod, ix–x.
———. (1970 [2003]). *La Révolution Urbaine*. Paris, Gallimard. Translated by R. Bononno as *The Urban Revolution*. Minneapolis, University of Minnesotta Press.
———. (1973 [2014]). *Vers une architecture de la jouissance*. Translated by R. Bononno as *Toward an architecture of enjoyment*. Minnesota, University of Minnesota Press.
———. (1973a [1976]). *La Survie du capitalisme: La reproduction des rapports de production*. Paris, Anthropos. Translated by F. Bryant as *The Survival of Capitalism. Reproduction of the Relations of Production*. London, Allison & Busby.
———. (1974 [1991]). *La production de l'espace*. Paris, Anthropos. Translated by D. Nicholson-Smith as *The Production of Space*. Oxford, Blackwell.
———. (1975). *Le temps des méprises: entretiens avec Claude Glayman*. Paris, Stock.
———. (1980 [1987]). Quotidien et Quotidienneté. Translated by C. Levitch as The everyday and everydayness. *Yale French Studies* (73), 7–11.
———. (1986). *Le retour de la dialectique*. Paris, Messidor.
———. (1989 [2014]). Dissolving city, planetary metamorphosis. *Environment and Planning D: Society & Space*, 32(2), 203–205.
Lilliendahl Larsen, J. and Brandt, J. (2018). Critique, creativity and the co-optation of the urban: A case of blind fields and vague spaces in Lefebvre, Copenhagen and current perceptions of the urban. *Urban Planning*, 3(3), 52–69.
Lizieri, C. (2009). *Towers of Capital. Office Markets and International Financial Services*. London, Wiley.
Lohtaja, A. (2021). Henri Lefebvre's lessons from the Bauhaus. *The Journal of Architecture*, 26(4), 499–515.
Lorimer, J. (1978). *The Developers*. Toronto, James Lorimer & Co.
Maslow, A. (1943). A theory of human motivation. *Psychological Review*, 50(4), 370–396.
———. (1954). *Motivation and Personality*. New York, Harper & Row.
Mukhija, V. and Takahashi, L. M. (2022). Enhancing sharing capabilities: Housing and neighborhood planning opportunities for improving health. *Journal of the American Planning Association*, 30 June 2022.
Murray, P. (2015). Foreward. In *Super Density the Sequel*. Available at: www.pollardthomasedwards.co.uk/download/SUPERDENSITY_2015_download.pdf. [Accessed 9 June 2022].
Nagati, O. (2023). *Kodak Passageway*. [e-mail]. 24 February.
Nagati, O. and Stryker, B. (2016). Cairo downtown passageways: A framework for urban regeneration. In Nagati, O. and Stryker, B. (eds.) *Creative Cities: Reframing Downtown Cairo*. Proceedings of an International Symposium, 31 October–1 November 2015, AUC Tahrir Campus, Cairo. Cairo, CLUSTER and the American University in Cairo, 177–187.
Owens, C. A. (2015). *The Role of The Architect in the Process of Development*. Master's Thesis, University of Tennessee. Available at: https://trace.tennessee.edu/utk_gradthes/3497/. [Accessed 3 November 2021].
Parker, S. (2015). *Urban Theory and the Urban Experience: Encountering the City*. 2nd edition. London, Routledge.
Pinder, D. (2013). Reconstituting the possible: Lefebvre, utopia and the urban question. *International Journal of Urban and Regional Research*, 39(1), 28–45.
Pugalis, L. and Giddings, B. (2011). A renewed right to urban life: A twenty-first century engagement with Lefebvre's initial "cry". *Architectural Theory Review*, 16(3), 278–295.
Rodrigues, A. L. (2018). *In pursuit of a healthy city: Bouça Housing Complex by Álvaro Siza (1977), a lesson to retain*. Paper presented at the AMPS Conference Health: The Design,

Planning and Politics of How and Where We Live. AMPS, Architecture_MPS; University of the West of England, 25–26 January. Available at: http://repositorium.sdum.uminho.pt/handle/1822/51184. [Accessed 4 November 2021].

Ross Goobey, A. (1992). *Bricks & Mortals*. London, Century Business.

Ross, K. and Lefebvre, H. (1983 [1997]). Lefebvre on the situationists: An interview. *October*, (79), 69–83.

Saifi, Y., Yuceer, H. and Bilge, B. (2012). Flexible social housing as an alternative to mass-produced housing in the Walled City of Famagusta. *Journal of Applied Sciences*, 12(17), 1869–1881.

Smith, M. (2002). Ethical difference (s): A response to Maycroft on Le Corbusier and Lefebvre. *Ethics, Place & Environment*, 5(3), 260–269.

Smith, N. B. and Morton, A. (2013). *Create Streets: Not Just Multi-Storey Estates*. London, Policy Exchange.

Soules, M. (2021). *Icebergs, Zombies, and the Ultra-Thin: Architecture and Capitalism in the 21st Century*. San Francisco, Chronicle Books.

Stanek, L. (2011). *Henri Lefebvre on Space: Architecture, Urban Research, and the Production of Theory*. Minnesota, University of Minnesota Press.

———. (2020). *Architecture in Global Socialism: Eastern Europe, West Africa, and the Middle East in the Cold War*. Princeton, Princeton University Press.

Stewart, L. (1995). Bodies, visions, and spatial politics: A review essay on Henri Lefebvre's the production of space. *Environment and Planning D: Society and Space*, 13(5), 609–618.

Tabb, W. K. and Sawyers, L. (1978a). Introduction. In Tabb, W. K. and Sawers, L. (eds.) *Marxism and the Metropolis. New Perspectives in Urban Political Economy*. New York, Oxford University Press, 3–24.

Tabb, W. K. and Sawers, L. (1978b). New perspectives on the urban political economy. In Tabb, W. K. and Sawers, L. (eds.) *Marxism and the Metropolis. New Perspectives in Urban Political Economy*. 2nd edition. New York, Oxford University Press, 3–20.

Tafuri, M. (1976). *Architecture and Utopia. Design and Capitalist Development*. Cambridge, MA, MIT Press.

———. (1987). *The Sphere and the Labyrinth. Avant-Gardes and Architecture from Piranesi to the 1970's*. Cambridge, MA, MIT Press.

Talen, E. (2008). Beyond the front porch: Regionalist ideals in the new urbanist movement. *Journal of Planning History*, 7(1), 20–47.

Talen, E. and Lee, S. (2018). *Design for Social Diversity*. London, Routledge.

Tatian, P. A., Kingsley, G. T., Parilla, J. and Pendall, R. (2012). *Building Successful Neighborhoods*. Urban Institute. Available at: www.urban.org/research/publication/building-successful-neighborhoods. [Accessed 7 May 2021].

Thiel, F. (2012). *Real estate development for poverty reduction – A new paradigm for legal and financial cooperation in Africa and Asia?* AfRES afres2012_136. African Real Estate Society. Available at: https://ideas.repec.org/p/afr/wpaper/afres2012_136.html [Accessed 14 July 2022].

Touloumi, O. (2016). Henri Lefebvre. Toward an architecture of enjoyment. Book review. *Buildings and Landscapes*, 23(1), 112–114.

Trebitsch, M. (2002 [2014]). Preface. In Lefebvre, H. *Critique of Everyday Life*. London, Verso.

Upton, D. (2002). Architecture in everyday life. *New Literary History*, 33(4), 707–723.

Wainwright, O. (2014). China town: Meet the architecture giant with Asian designs on London. *Guardian*, 15 July. Available at: www.theguardian.com/artanddesign/architecture-design-blog/2014/jul/15/china-town-aedas-architecture-giant-london. [Accessed 4 December 2022].

Wilson, J. (2014). Henri Lefebvre: Toward an architecture of enjoyment. *Antipode on-line*. Available at: https://antipodeonline.org/wp-content/uploads/2014/10/book-review_wilson-on-lefebvre.pdf. [Accessed 9 November 2021].

Xue, F., Gou, Z. and Lau, S. S. Y. (2016). Human factors in green office building design: The impact of workplace green features on health perceptions in high-rise high-density Asian cities. *Sustainability*, 8(11), 1095.

Zieleniec, A. (2018). Lefebvre's politics of space: Planning the urban as oeuvre. *Urban Planning*, 3(3), 5–15.

5 Hardly villains

Real estate developers and differential space

Introduction: the relevant future

Marxists have now been forced by massive setbacks to recognise that their original timescales for the supersession of capitalism, and even what form its successors should take, have been proven both overly optimistic and unduly linear. No more is this obvious than in surveying the urban fabric. Although rays of optimism still shine through Lefebvre's urban theory – that despite the fragmentation of space, there is the ability to produce space on a global and even greater scale for the growing global population (Lefebvre, 1973 [1976:19]), decades on from when he wrote, the actual result has been 'the proliferation of overflowing, apparently indistinguishable urban landscape' (Schmid, 2012:47), riven with inequalities in the opportunity to create or experience space.

Such revisions in the trajectory of the future, and the ways in which capitalism may be eventually overcome, have become necessarily ingrained throughout Marxist thoughts, words, and deeds. What most Marxists will now surely admit, at least in private, is that despite enormous pressures, capitalism is not set to collapse from its internal contradictions in the short term, and very definitely not in the immediate timeframe in which real estate development occurs after decisions have been made. The *relevant future* of real estate stakeholders globally therefore unfortunately remains capitalist, so Marxists must respond and adapt to that inimical reality, whilst at the same time never giving up hope and never relenting in the development of means to overcome capitalism beyond that relevant future.

Marxism and the developers

No doubt green design, sustainable buildings, and entire cities are an urgent need. Lefebvre noted in relation to the importance of ecological questions, 'it is correct to assert that the milieu of life and the quality of the environment have acquired an urgent, politically central status' (Lefebvre, 1989 [2014:205]). The extent of the problem suggests that social and environmental needs alone justify real estate development, and on a substantial scale. Given their current and most likely future importance in directing and managing the process of creating real estate, it is therefore of importance to reflect on how Marxist geographers and other radical

DOI: 10.1201/9781003220244-5

urban theorists refer to real estate developers in capitalist economies. The record shows that in the past, Marxists tended to regard them as mere ontological 'property capital', denoting those business interests engaged in the process of remaking space to capture rents (Lamarche, 1976; Molotch, 1979), though key to facilitating the switching of global capital into the built environment (Harvey, 2006, 2010; Kaika & Ruggiero, 2015). Hence, for example, the observation that 'The realization of a class-monopoly rent depends, however, on the existence of a class of speculative-developers who have the power to capture it' (Harvey, 1985:67) And what is this class?

> The term speculative-developer is here used generically to refer to all those individuals and institutions that operate in the land and property markets with a view to realising gains through ultimate sale or change in land use. In practice there may be considerable division of labor in this activity, while different institutions operate under different constraints. See, for example the difference between entrepreneurs and the relics of the feudal order – the crown, the church.
>
> (Counter-Information Services, 1973:1)

Some critics have assigned developers such a negative, destructive, one might even say starkly evil role that it must surely be difficult for many of those convinced by their arguments to envisage them as anything other than one-dimensional pantomime villains (Lofland, 2004):

> The perverse rationality of real estate capitalism means that building owners and developers garner a double reward for milking properties and destroying buildings. First, they pocket the money that should have gone to repairs and upkeep; second, having effectively destroyed the building and established a rent gap, they have produced for themselves the conditions and opportunity for a whole new round of capital reinvestment. Having produced a scarcity of capital in the name of profit they now flood the neighborhood for the same purpose, portraying themselves all along as civic-minded heroes, pioneers taking a risk where no one else would venture, builders of a new city for the worthy populace.
>
> (Smith, 2005:21)

It is striking that developers have also frequently been represented as capitalism personified, which then extends to an identification of what drives their actions: 'the developer's entrepreneurial instinct was to maximise potential profits by pushing the upper end of the property market at central locations' (Tian & Wong, 2007:227). For Marxist geographers, the consequences of their actions were frequently described in collective and unsurprisingly also uniformly negative terms:

> The produced geographical landscape constituted by fixed and immobile capital is both the crowning glory of past capitalist development and a prison

> that inhibits the further progress of accumulation precisely because it creates spatial barriers where there were none before.
>
> (Harvey, 1985:43)

Amongst a raft of other criticisms of developers, critics also pointed to the negative consequences of developmental trajectories that bypass industrialisation, channelling capital instead to a very uneven urban transformation that leaves the poor behind, especially in jurisdictions in developing countries where 'most real estate development is untaxed . . . the developmental benefits of real estate development are not clear' (Behuria & Goodfellow, 2019:588), for example when 'the costs associated with these resettlements [from development projects in Luanda] were often not imputed to the developer, translating into public subsidization of these projects' (Dias, 2021:317).

There is an ambiguity in the criticism of developers here that should be highlighted: Is this 'leapfrogging' (Behuria & Goodfellow, 2019) to be considered entirely negatively – the whole direction of Lefebvre's thought after all was to suggest the inevitability of global urbanisation – or is the implicit criticism of avoidable inadequate industrialisation and failed development implicit in a traditional Marxist critique justified? (Harvey, 2006). Perhaps it is both – but we lack tools to be able to analyse to what extent real estate developers have extracted resources that would otherwise have proceeded to productive investment in other areas, and we must surely recognise that even if real estate development is no guarantee of social improvement, improvements in city landscapes are far from incompatible with the domestic and foreign investment that is required for industrialisation.

Critics also suggest that as agents of often international capital, the role of developers 'threatens the objectives of inclusion and the creation of "cities for all"' (Robin & Brill, 2018:2). Supporting evidence has been plentiful over the decades: an early example was that an ostensibly bohemian artists' quarter that had grown up among the abandoned garment warehouses of Manhattan was destroyed by property redevelopers, who profited from the expropriation of a cultural 'scene' which was then used to price-out the very artists who have created it (Zukin, 1987), a standpoint that has informed much debate about gentrification since (e.g. Brown-Saracino, 2013). Impelled by capitalist logic, unlike, at least on occasion, the planning system, developers have had little need of explication, let alone investigation. In the past, where light has been shone onto developers, it is often simply to identify what pattern of development is followed, and not a favourable one, as

> developers such as Robert Moses in New York City were able to follow Le Corbusier's masterplan by driving expressways through the heart of long-established urban communities in the cause of 'rational planning' with devastating effects on local neighbourhoods.
>
> (Berman, 1982:290–312; Parker, 2015:61)

It was only gradually, whether in France or elsewhere, that Marxists even grew to empathise with Lefebvre in appreciating the importance of the locality

(Preteceille & Briquet, 1989:26). Some analysts still simply removed developers from development altogether, advancing a strikingly circumscribed milieu confined to 'research centres, think tanks, policy institutions and political activists' (Moulaert *et al.*, 2013:13). Or banishing developers differently, through the assertion that urban experience and social needs

> can be understood by looking at everyday life on the streets, at its specific and diverse qualities, at the meanings it might have for those who live it, and in particular at the complex tensions which arise between different needs, different meanings and different users in spaces.
>
> (Stevens, 2007:7).

In part, this omission was surely deliberate, owing much to the persistent perspective that government, whether at local or other levels, is or ought to be preserved as the principal actor in space, enmeshed with developers to project power. Even the riposte of urban regime theory, emphasising that the struggles of urban politics 'should not be reduced to urban growth strategies, solely driven by property developers' (Oosterlynck & Swyngedouw, 2013:89), has by the 21st century already been deemed insufficient by radical geographers, and as requiring reformulation in the safer, or at least less granular, territory of a broader political–economic context (Jessop, 1997). It is surely consistent with this perspective that where individual names are mentioned in such a perspective, they are generally those of politicians, not developers, who remain in the shadows both epistemologically and ethically. What could developers be expected to make of this, except that they are not invited to the party?

They might also worry that efforts to understand socio-economic development as an integral process (Novy *et al.*, 2013:57) does surely run the risk of gliding over the actions of individual developers, just as at a more comprehensive level ignoring the existence and biographies of individuals threatens the intellectual appeal of Marxism as a whole (Sève, 1968 [1978]). The consequence of this analytical gulf that has existed between Marxist – to be fair, not only Marxist – geographers, and organisational theorists, who are often relatively dismissive of 'institutional' approaches (e.g. Smith, 1996), is that real estate developers have remained largely as black boxes in Marxist analysis. Only more recently has radical geography begun to engage much more closely with developers themselves, a surely welcome alteration of trajectory towards a 'focus on the constitutive spatialities of urban territories and of the actors involved in urbanisation processes, including their transnational reach and flows, institutional formations and lived experiences' (Robinson, 2022:1718) that no doubt owes much to the unavoidable recognition of their contemporary importance in the creation of urban space. Yet for now, the gulf between this reality of real estate development as practised within capitalist economies and the perspective of Marxist and other radical geographers remains undeniably – in my own view, in all senses, tragically – wide. But is it unbridgeable? And to what extent could Lefebvre help provide us to cross such a bridge, notwithstanding that in fairness, he has been criticised similarly, even by radical geographers themselves: 'his philosophical insistence on the openness of space allows little hint at all about how that differentiation of space is made and remade' (Smith, 2003:xiv).

Unfortunately, Lefebvre's engagement with all of these categories, it must be conceded, is also entirely at the abstract level – not one entity, let alone one individual developer is ever mentioned in his text, even though places proliferate. In his defence, the overwhelming majority of his work was conducted towards in a different era, before the many contemporary methods of privatising space that Marxists have consistently decried. When Lefebvre wrote, large-scale public provision of housing in particular was the norm, with the many adverse consequences as yet only beginning to be revealed; city and local authorities also took a major role in the post-war redevelopment of city centres throughout Europe; Asia-Pacific countries such as Singapore and Malaysia had created major public sector agencies to manage idiosyncratic yet in many cases successful forms of housing development and ownership. There was therefore good reason for Lefebvre, as well as others, if not to identify real estate development as an integral activity with policy and construction, then at least to engage in a balanced critique that focused significantly on criticism of public sector agencies (e.g. Williams, 1976:81), whilst treating construction itself as the output of planning processes directed by the public sector, even if it was actually undertaken by private sector entities.

In the 21st century, what presents itself for analysis and a possible political response is quite different. Marxists must surely find it problematic, on the one hand, to recognise that 'Only when politics focuses on the production and reproduction of urban life as the central labor process out of which revolutionary struggles arise will be possible to mobilise anti-capitalist struggles capable of radically transforming daily life' (Harvey, 2012:5), and then, on the other hand, exhibit a relative indifference to crafting strategies of engagement with particular institutions that are instrumental in precisely this process of production and reproduction, that is, real estate developers and their stakeholders. For if Harvey is right – and I believe he is, with the caveat that the process is as he would surely readily concede much more than a process of *only* labour, and that labour may be difficult to coral, even define, in the context of the work of real estate developers – then exactly the opposite is required: the importance of real estate developers now demands active critical and political engagement by those taking Lefebvre seriously with developers themselves. As those who have studied them argue:

> [R]eal estate developers constitute a relevant object of analysis for exploring the conjuncture between forces operating at different scales in the production of urban space. The nature of their activity requires them to be 'relational actors' that are able to mobilize numerous resources and interact with a myriad of institutions and organizations in order to materialize their projects.
>
> (Mouton & Shatkin, 2020:418)

Their jurisdiction of interest is the Philippines, but the relative importance of developers of course varies worldwide. For example:

> In the UK, unlike other parts of the world, individuals rarely have the chance to make their own homes – housing is provided by developers as a commodity, not as homes where the customers have control. . . . [T]he majority of new homes built are driven by a developer-led model resulting in conventional housing typologies. Funders also prefer this certainty.
>
> (Dove, 2020:xii)

By contrast, in Singapore and Malaysia, for example, private developers have become much significant over the decades since Lefebvre originally wrote, but their large public sector housing development agencies remain, albeit with different remits (Ling & Almeida, 2016; Ling *et al.* 2017). In Australia, by contrast, developers in the past often confined themselves to land and infrastructure, leaving construction to builders employed by individual homeowners, although apartment development has become increasingly significant (Burke, 2012; Shoory, 2016). These international differences remain important and are likely to continue to do so. But nevertheless, the significance of developers in the production of space demands that they, along with planning institutions and other stakeholders, should be included in decisions regarding existing real estate, one of the most important political battlegrounds worldwide.

So, to complement Lefebvre's contrasting dimensions of space, abstract, and differential, I would therefore now suggest that late-stage capitalism (or at least, less this seem too reminiscent of an earlier Marxist over-optimism, *our* stage of capitalism) has produced an important *process*, which can at least potentially range across both dimensions: that of real estate development, of the actual production of space itself. If there is to be analysis, and politics, it would be highly desirable that both should be of and in real estate development and investment itself. And that if, as Lefebvre says, 'A formula for appropriating urban space remains to be found' (Lefebvre, 1986:169), then it does at least merit consideration as to whether, and if so in what way, developers might themselves find a place in this search, even as institutions that must be engaged with, whether as part of a struggle that creates conflictual space or more optimistically as part of a solution that might create differential space.

The potential role of real estate developers

Traditional Marxist explanations of the urban that have sought to reduce the urban to a mere battleground for class struggle have never been convincing for many, and not only on the political Right, especially where they fail to explain the influence of other factors in the development of cities that cannot be wholly explained by class struggle, whether Islamic theology in Turkey (Karaman, 2013), migration in China (Farrer, 2019), or the intricacies of cultural claims to land in Ghana (Agyemang & Morrison, 2018)). Yet Marxists have faced criticism from the Left as well. The notion of a universal proletariat, it has now been said for many years, including by Lefebvre himself, has seemingly now been largely abandoned, whereas anti-capitalist and anti-war protests have become increasingly diffuse in recent years, reaching well beyond class, to alternative, even anarchist, principles of voluntary association, egalitarianism, direct action, and radical democracy (Springer, 2014:264). Marxism, if one were to be uncharitable, meanwhile skulks in the academy. It is not an entirely fair criticism: much of Marxism has evolved, even if radical geography and urban theory have been reluctant to change along with it. This applies as much to its ontology as to strategies for change. Who acts?

This criticism can be extended. Whilst there has been much debate over the detail, there is widespread agreement that Marx not only had a concept of both individual and collective agency but also believed simultaneously in his principal collective agent of historical change – class and, in particular, the proletariat. By comparison, Lefebvre has a much more nuanced conception of the working class as an agent for change, but one aspect of that refinement is significantly to denude it of that legacy of agency from historical materialism. Yet apart from space itself, Lefebvre does not advance any other, alternative agency. Nor, it seems, do others adopting his perspective (e.g. Gallico, 2016). Who will activate urban revolution, and how, is never made explicit – Lefebvre no doubt sincerely believed that it would close off too many possibilities, and go too far in political prognostication, even to sketch that out. This omission has, however, potentially serious consequences in terms of the application of Lefebvre to organisations and individuals: if we were to 'marry Lefebvre's rhythm analysis to the critiques of neoliberalism and neo-imperialism developed by David Harvey (2005) and Mike Davis (2006)' (Mendieta, 2008:151), then we might ask about the offspring. For although Harvey makes the important admission that 'I don't think we are in a position to define who the agents of change will be' (Harvey, 2009), he then goes on to identify the different elements of a 'co-revolutionary movement' (Harvey, 2010), 'a co-revolutionary dynamic that can replace the present system of compounding accumulation of capital with some other forms of social coordination, exchange and control (Harvey, 2010a), itself a particular kind of concept of political agency' (Das, 2017:607), from which developers will not be surprised to discover themselves having been excluded.

Marxist geographers have wanted to 'upgrade' historical materialism to historical–geographical materialism (Harvey, 1985:xii). And yet there is a sense in which Marxist geography often seems caught between nostalgia for the categories and certainties of historical materialism and a yearning for postmodernist complexity, neither of which are easily translated into a political programme. Such nostalgia, whether for the actual past or missed opportunities, is a luxury in which, as Lefebvre himself recognised, Marxists should be very careful not to over-indulge. *Marxism cannot, must not, degenerate into a nostalgia for a past future lost*. We may therefore be especially interested in what we can glean from Lefebvre as to what ought to be done to affect the production of space, and by whom. We should constantly set this out in urban terms, including those of real estate development. Lefebvre himself largely avoided this challenge for largely justifiable and certainly explicable historical reasons of time and place, but we ourselves now cannot avoid the question of *whose* development praxis, a question that ought perhaps even to have haunted Lefebvre more than it ever did.

Lefebvre inside the developer

By the time Lefebvre theorised the urban, it was in his view already beyond the concepts of traditional proletarian revolution, and in his view continued to recede from it thereafter. Yet the production of space, as with all capitalist production, created a range of poles of antagonism – in Marxist terms, contradictions – for example, between developed and developing countries, as well as between the urban centre and its periphery. As a result, 'the urban is as much an instrument of capitalist production and reproduction as it is a social resource for a different – 'differential' – space' (Stanek, 2011:164). We confront extremes of poverty and wealth, because of the all-conquering power of the market transforms the city into a patchwork of central commercial districts, surrounded by underprivileged ghettos and wealthy inaccessible enclaves (Parker, 2015:21). People cannot be properly human in a capitalist city: their need for creative activity, for the *oeuvre* (not only of products and consumable material goods), of the need for information, symbolism, the imaginary and play, is not, and cannot be met, within the capitalist urban fabric. The historical ties between use value, the material base, and urban life have been torn asunder.

> His hypothesis contains two premises: a) the city and urban reality. The material base and urban life have been historically related to the value of use. The city, he argues, can be interpreted as an oeuvre, as a work of art. created and appropriated by its producers; (b) however, the generalisation of the world of the markets has cracked open the city as a work and, with it, its use value.
>
> (Ahumada, 2015:24)

There is also another potential aspect to the dialectic of space that Lefebvre came closer, at least, to exploring. The material base of capitalism has remained the enterprise, where land, labour, and capital are fused in the pursuit of profit, wholly or in part, and with greater or lesser success. Meanwhile, the notion of the fragmented city that is constantly being reassembled but which has no fixed or historically rooted identity is consistent with many postmodern accounts of contemporary urban life (Parker, 2015:21). Yet the fragmentation of space, both practically and theoretically, is where the reproduction of the relations of production is achieved, through the introduction of multiple contradictions (Lefebvre, 1973 [1976:19]). The conclusion is inescapable: enterprises produce fragmentary space. Might they do more?

There is a long-standing tradition now in political science of trying to separate out agency in relation to the demand for urban development – the State, developers and construction companies, future owners, or various combinations of different agents all jostle for space– within a broader ideological and political agenda (Bardet *et al.*, 2020:205–206). Within this debate, the role and significance of developers has been recognised by more orthodox Marxist geographers: they perform 'the vital function of promoter, coordinator and stabilizer of land-use change' (Harvey,

1985:68). Take them away, Harvey suggests, and the result would be chaos, with finance capital withdrawing its investment from the suburbanisation process, and by extension, real estate development. Real estate developers have become key drivers of the production of space (Robin & Brill, 2018). There is however a better reason, I suggest, to look upon developers with a less jaundiced eye. Lefebvre's criticism of public planning and architecture, of the state as privileged producer of space, can be expanded to include an institutional perspective:

> [T]he state-centred approach to housing supply has precluded a role for other actors and institutions, including drawing on the agency of people themselves, joint actions with community-based organizations and collaboration with the banks, housebuilders and other private sector bodies. The sense of entitlement has encouraged passivity and protest, rather than enabling active citizenship and collective effort.
>
> (Turok & Scheba, 2019:506)

They could also have added the powerful argument that any organisation makes a poor regula of itself. Conflicts of interest between the State acting as developer, whether at local level or more widely, seem inevitable, and are certainly well documented. If Marxists want to see strong regulation of developers, then they may do well to heed the observations made with respect to problems found in respect of local council development activity in Australia:

> [T]here is inherent potential for a conflict of interest for local councils who may be both the owner or proponent of a development, and responsible for regulating and enforcing compliance with applicable laws and regulations. This conflict is not just a hypothetical possibility.
>
> (New South Wales Ombudsman, 2020:1)

If state-centred approaches have been found wanting in this way, which surely have a high chance of persisting in at least some form even when capitalism has been superseded, then the clear challenge for Marxists must be, what kind of organisation should be responsible for real estate development?

Developers and the right to the city

For Lefebvre, and therefore any developer acting with positive regard to his work, "The right to the city' recognizes how places enable or disable various human capabilities and freedoms: economic advancement is the main reason people seek access to the city and resist displacement' (Turok & Scheba, 2019:498). A developer will no doubt immediately want to build on these fine sentiments, much more practically, to suggest that the right to the city involves asking questions like these:

> Do they have a right to equal, and not separate, education for their children, and a right to accessible transportation to jobs and schools? Do people have

> a right to remain in their homes and in their neighborhoods? Do they, along with their neighbors, have a right to decide how their neighborhoods develop and change?
>
> (Smithsonian Museum, 2020)

And many more, different across jurisdictions, age groups, gender, and life experience. For if Marxists recognise along with Lefebvre the importance of individuality, as much as they have always appreciated the value of community, they will also surely agree that people will 'encounter space differently, embodying and enacting its ruptures and contradictions' (Kinkaid, 2020:184). In contemporary capitalism, real estate development is the site, and developers the organisations, through which many of the consequences of that encounter will eventuate. These questions can therefore be asked of developers themselves. So whilst yes,

> if the process of struggle is to achieve substantive change, it has to move beyond opposition . . . to be effective the right to the city, though initiated by social actors, has to be underpinned by legal and regulatory reform.
>
> (Brown, 2013:962)

Even this will be insufficient for the achievement of real change, which will also require the struggle to be taken to the creators of space within the urban fabric, to draw them into the project.

Exerting influence, shifting practice

Differential space may involve very different actual development depending on the cultural, economic, and political context. A space to meet in public, certainly, but perhaps also much improved sleeping quarters with individual privacy where there was none before. Spaces of public performance, again certainly, but also freedom from the impact of drought or flooding. And spaces for citizens to shape urban policy, very definitely as well, but also reliable, safe, environment-friendly public transport. It is perhaps not surprising, therefore, that there have been protagonists for 'more interesting' new spaces (Lehtovuori, 2010:54]), for example, the characterisation of derelict areas when hosting temporary uses as differential spaces (Ambrosino & Andres, 2008). Less vocal, understandably in view of how they have historically been perceived by radical geographers, have been any protagonists for the potential role of developers themselves, especially in the production of less obviously interesting but still vital real estate, housing in particular.

A wholly differential developer would exist *primarily* to create differential space, alongside their other civic responsibilities. Even if they could find a way to avoid compromises with the providers of capital, or in a post-capitalist world, they might have some difficulty in measuring their achievements, and in deciding how to resolve the inevitable trade-offs involved in development, for example between social and environmental goals. In practice, in a capitalist economy, however measured, all of these dimensions of differential space will have differences in mission, proportion, and emphasis within the strategy and project execution of individual developers. Moreover, some of them may be forced upon developers in any event, as a result of legislation and regulation, distorting the extent to which developers themselves have social goals and in any way tried to act in any other way than pure profit maximisation. As research engaging with developers themselves discovered, 'every one of these developers has acknowledged [that], none of them views their existing development process or projects as perfectly embodying the full social impact they'd like to achieve' (Zaccack, 2020:51.

Use value and exchange value

The subordination of use value to exchange value is the core of the reason why Lefebvre originally framed the right to the city primarily as the right of a city's inhabitants, who daily use the city, counterposed to the right of developers, real estate agents, and financiers who perceive the city as a space of opportunities for realising (spatial) exchange values. If the constant generalisation of exchange value relation under capitalism tends to 'destroy the city and urban reality', and 'overwhelms, the 'user', the 'participant', the simple 'inhabitant', then Lefebvre draws the logical conclusion that it is the exchange value relation itself that should be abolished so that the right to the city could meaningfully be realised (Kuymulu, 2014:65). The problem with this formulation, especially viewed from the standpoint of the subsequent century, is that the binary opposition between inhabitants and capital, the moral fable that pits the disadvantaged against the oppressor, is – to be blunt – neither a wholly accurate depiction of reality, nor an especially politically efficacious distinction to make. A revision of Lefebvre should recognise that epistemological and ethical categories are not always perfectly symmetrical.

The objective for those who would take Lefebvre's project for developers seriously remains that 'the prevalence of use-value over exchange-value such that the qualitative significance of place enjoys primacy over the quantitative commodification of space. Therefore, if urban experience and social needs are more than mere conceptual abstractions' (Stevens, 2007:7), 'the streets' are only one aspect: the principal actors that create those streets must also feature in understanding not only spatial practices, but the other elements of Lefebvre's triad as well.

But observing complexity and ambiguity within the production of space leads to the further recognition that use value and exchange value are not – and never have been – separable in this fashion, either ontologically or epistemologically. Under capitalism, they are created in the same process, inhere in the same spaces, and are often confused in the perception of individuals, groups, and even social classes. So far as real estate developers are concerned, this logic implies that they create equally complex space, and what matters is the balance between use and exchange value within the space they create. This balance is an outcome of what all agree is a complex process of real estate development. The next part of the problem, and where developers might, at least under certain circumstances, play a role, is in the delineation, calculation, and perhaps above all the balancing of competing use values for particular space prior to creating the differential space that this decision-making process necessarily entails. In this sense, at least for the foreseeable future, the developer can and must act in lieu of a completely democratic process; and it is not even certain, if one believes that certain forms of alienation will persist even in the absence of capitalism (Schaff, 1965 [1970:128]) that this social function for real estate developers will continue to be required indefinitely, at least in part, given both this and the sheer practical difficulties of implementation for democratic planning adverted to in Chapter 3. It is here that 'Rather than understanding developers solely in terms of their contribution to "making space for capital"' (Searle, 2010), more recent papers ask the crucial questions, of how developers 'actively leverage finance capital to support their own ambitions' (Rouanet & Halbert, 2016:1404). The reality, hiding in plain sight, is that both the exchange and use value of real estate produced by some not-for-profit developers, whether public sector agencies, housing associations, or some other organisational form, is frequently superior in quality to that produced by for-profit developers in other jurisdictions. This is especially the case in making comparisons between social housing in developed economies and lower value private housing elsewhere. Lefebvre himself recognised that the achievement of a world beyond capitalism was a global project, not an event (Lefebvre, 1980:257). From a political standpoint, those taking Lefebvre's project seriously should therefore be able to recognise utopian traces of the future even in the agency of at least some existing developers. The political task is therefore not only to evaluate developers, nor solely to criticise their many failings, but to highlight where developers have 'done the right thing', both as evidence of the possibilities of the future and as encouragement for them to go further. Developers are political battlegrounds where Marxists may find useful allies as well as, no doubt, forceful opponents.

Who can act?

There is a second strand to this attention to what developers do. Lefebvre joined those who envisaged a world in which work, as traditionally conceived, and therefore workers, would be replaced by a far more amorphous, flexible, all-embracing urban fabric. The extent to which the precariat, a redefined working class, or any other constellation of forces can acquire the agency to overcome capitalism is a thoroughly justified preoccupation of the global Left: 'How such disparate groups may become self-organized into a revolutionary force is the big political problem' (Harvey, 2012:xiv).

But in searching for, sculpting, and sanctifying a suitable replacement for the proletariat, it would be perhaps unwise to overlook the warnings that Marx himself gave as to the inevitable lack of agency of a *lumpenproletariat*. For if those taking Lefebvre seriously are now to

> envisage a citizenship conceived as something urban, as something territorial yet one in which territoriality is narrower and broader than both 'city' and 'nationality'; a citizen of the block, of the neighborhood, becomes a citizen

> of the world, a universal citizen rooted in place, encountering fellow citizens across the corridor and at the other end of the planet.
>
> (Merrifield, 2014:9)

Then creating more differential space for citizens will form an important constitutive element, perhaps even the essential grounding, for the creation of that citizenship. The importance of developers at the centre of 'urban life and the everyday' (Lefebvre, 1973 [1976:36]) can therefore only be reinforced when the working class, in which even as he conceived of the production of space Lefebvre was already losing faith as the driving force of revolution (Lefevre, 1973 [1976:37]), can no longer easily be identified, let alone relied upon to act as a class to overcome a capitalism that they had accepted. 'These populations on the edge have been for a long time disinterested in urban politics' (Lefebvre, 1986:172). Put far more bluntly, evidence shows that the *favelas* cannot generate future revolutionary change, and only development can replace them – brick by brick, or increasingly, manufactured house by manufactured house. For if we take the idea of 'the personal is the political' seriously, recognising that the struggle against capitalism is reflected in the soul of every human being, and that *every* exercise of agency provides the opportunity for a contribution to be made to that struggle, then we are no longer trapped in the depressing cycle of successive heralded but ultimately largely unsuccessful sporadic political movements as the principal or even sole location of a politics of resistance (Martinelli *et al.*, 2013:xxiii). Instead, we can and should focus at least as much attention on an internal resistance within the process of planning, development, and investment itself: actual activities where *l'espace veçu* can and is created.

Juxtaposition of abstract and differential space

Part of the problem intrinsic to the traditional radical approach to Lefebvre lies in the stark distinction between abstract and differential space. in one optimistic formula, 'differential space is then developing out of an abstract space and in addition to that opposed to it' (Bauer & Fischer, 2019:11). The central question of how this is to occur, Lefebvre leaves unanswered. For Lefebvre, his two creations cannot coexist in the same *physical* space, all space with the city must be one or the other – to recognise that space can be a medium of both compliance and resistance seems as far as he is prepared to go. This ontological separation, for example between 'spaces of production' and 'spaces of leisure' (Lefebvre, 1974 [1991:58–59]), has now been rendered opaque by technological developments that allow for far easier switching between work and leisure in the same physical location, and across very short spaces of time. The complication of the dialectic through the creation of differential space *within* abstract space is now the complex reality confronting those taking Lefebvre seriously. This has significant practical implications. Whilst Lefebvre certainly recognises the complicity of individuals and groups in the reproduction of abstract space, he looks to 'moments' of alternative local spatialisations that may come into existence, for example in the *favellas*, but the eruptions of resistance through spatialisation to create a 'counter-space' (Shields, 1999:184) is still conceptualised in dialectical terms that were undergoing critical reformulation even last century, for example at the level of individual identity. However, initially appealing from a dialectical perspective, this division therefore ought to be challenged. If, as Marxist humanism now asserts, the individual can be a battlefield between competing ideological forces, and must be, as even institutions to which Marxists have retreated, such as the academy, have been placed under threat from capitalism, then it is scarcely unreasonable to extend the same duel to space itself. The practical importance of this move is considerable, especially in relation to the engagement with real estate of subsequent chapters.

It is easy to see how the Lefebvrian moment has been imprisoned within a narrow conception of political practice that always denies it free rein across even the political spectrum, let alone more widely. 'The political moment is an absolute act of contestation: a street demo or flying picket, a rent strike or a general strike' (Merrifield, 2009:939). Some useful things a general strike may be, but in the involvement of many moving parts, patient organisation, and nuanced strategy, it is in many ways the very antithesis of a 'moment'. Lefebvre himself was hardly the union man, and scarcely even much of a successful participant in political organisations. For Rémi Hess, 'alienation reflects an absence, a dead moment, empty of critical content', the Lefebvrian moment signifies 'a modality of presence', a fullness, a connection, a certain notion of liberty and passion. As he quotes Lefebvre, 'For the old-fashioned romantic . . . the fall of a leaf is a moment as significant as the fall of a state for a revolutionary' (Hess, 2009:173). So 'the moment' is also potentially an artistic and creative one as well as a purely political one. Whilst this emphasis on 'moments' in Lefebvre is a particular characteristic of Hess' presentation of his work, Lefebvre would surely be the first to agree that an inspirational architectural design can be such a 'moment'. *All I seek to add to this is that so might be the vision of a real estate developer*. To coral 'moments' within a narrow political practice is not what Lefebvre either intended, nor even if it were, would it make sense now. As he said of the Situationists in relation to the expulsion of a member whose colleague had worked on the architecture of a church: 'It's rubbish. It was really about keeping oneself in a pure state, like a crystal' (Ross & Lefebvre, 1997:76).

There is both an advantage and a risk in recognising both the wider frame and the ethical ambivalence of 'moments' inside capitalism, rather than positing them reassuringly as almost synonymous with political activity overtly opposed to it. The advantage is that rather than seeing them as inevitably fragmented and subsiding, essentially marginal events, as for example in street protests or festivals, almost all of which – even the Arab Spring – represent no threat to the established order, they can also be seen in the actions of individuals and organisations that traditional Lefebvrian thought has written off as part of the problem, never the solution. The risk is that the easy clarity of identification is no longer available, replaced by difficult, awkward personal judgements about strategy. It will always be thus when the individual is both the site of political controversy and the judge of right and wrong, as those such as Lefebvre, Garaudy, and even eventually Sève felt when they left the PCF. 'Another aspect of intellectual history can be seen in the (non)existent connections between Lefebvre and other leftist philosophers' (Bauer & Fischer, 2019:3).

Developers as producers of differential space

Here then we reach the core of the argument of this book. On the one hand, 'the old prejudices and old-fashioned centralistic beliefs which have always characterised the Marxist mainstream' (De Souza, 2010:321). It would be wrong to assume that only Marxists tend to rely on this approach: even the United Nations New Urban Agenda, although it contains a flurry of policy recommendations, makes not one mention of developers – and therefore indirectly places no requirements on them (United Nations, 2021). On the other hand, there are the possibilities left open by Lefebvre. In his schema, abstract space is the organisation of abstract labour and exchange, the space both created by and critical for abstract labour, money, commodities, and capital (Lefebvre, 1974 [1991:348]). Differential space by contrast represents an inversion of the alienated realities of abstract space – use over exchange, difference over homogeneity, the qualitative over the quantitative, the lived over the conceived, and as such, proponents suggest that it demands the transcendence of productivism and, at least eventually, the flourishing of a postproductivist society (Lefebvre, 1968a [1996:37]; Wilson, 2013:373). This is no doubt true, almost as a point of definition.

But nowhere does Lefebvre specify as to who or what organisations can produce or control all or even some of these – not even what characteristics individuals or organisations might require. Nor does Lefebvre specify whether it is always necessary to pass through a conflictual stage in order to reach differential space: 'Lefebvre is rather vague in his writing on how this postproductivist differential space is realised' (Lennon & Moore, 2019:119). All he does is point an admonishing finger in the general direction of 'geographers, town-planners, sociologists, *et al.*' (Lefebvre, 1974 [1991:94]), from which we might glean that it is unlikely that we should look to them for the production of differential space, especially left to their own devices.

By comparison to the traditional Marxist approach, the implications of taking Lefebvre's approach to the urban seriously can however serve to remind us, as it has already reminded other authors in relation to social housing in Australia (Gilmour & Milligan, 2012) of another Marxist voice from last century in a different context: 'The policy of letting a hundred flowers bloom and a hundred schools of thought contend is designed to promote the flourishing of the arts and the progress of science' (Mao, 1957 [1967:363). Others have now spoken, suggesting in the developing country context that to solve housing problems in particular, the material translation of objectives such as return on investments and profitability, which in many instances do resonate poorly with local needs (Robin, 2022), it will be necessary to 'harness the energy and ideas of different actors in providing solutions, including emerging and established housing developers' (Turok & Scheba,

2018:507). It might be hoped that Lefebvre's influence can result in a more success in the production of space for this policy of diversity and even competition for resources between different potential creators of differential space.

Use value and exchange value in the production of space

This is where, I suggest, work on reinterpreting Lefebvre and applying his theoretical insights to real estate development should begin, not end. I would like to see this work develop in two ways, which one might characterise as the philosophical and the political, or even the theoretical and the practical. The theoretical development concerns what Lefebvre might have called 'the explication of differential space'. If those taking Lefebvre seriously are to motivate, let alone convince, those who are sceptical that the end of capitalism will bring about a highly desirable, substantial change in space, we must explain *what the change will look like*, at least to the extent of presenting a vision that is sufficiently attractive to motivate. For although the traditional interpretation of Lefebvre has been that differential space can only somehow be created and owned ephemerally by the underprivileged, and then only if they follow certain acceptable patterns of rebellion, I argue that there may be advantages in an alternative approach. The reality, hiding in plain sight, is that both the exchange and use value of real estate produced by some not-for-profit developers, whether public sector agencies, housing associations, or some other organisational form, is frequently superior in quality to that produced by for-profit developers in other jurisdictions. This is especially the case in making comparisons between social housing in developed economies and lower value private housing elsewhere.

What matters most to Lefebvre is both how space is known and how it is created, not that it should be created by a unilateral state force, a view with which developers would find it easy to concur. The argument of the contemporary implications of Lefebvre's approach to the production of space is therefore twofold. Firstly, the traditional Marxist geographers argue that

> publically owned, lifetime, rented housing cuts across the ideological foundations of capitalism – private property and profit. Moreover, the restoration of council [public] housing raises the question of control over the urban process and urban space which have largely been ceded to private development interests.
>
> (Robbins, 2020:656)

They ignore Lefebvre's identification of the failure of the state as a developer at national and local developer in both capitalist and socialist economies to create differential space, which should not be allowed to be forgotten. A return to mass public housing does not therefore represent a model of urban development with which those taking Lefebvre seriously can now be completely comfortable. As Lefebvre himself observed, 'after every period of dogmatism comes a period of irony' (Lefebvre, 1962 [1995:10]).

The alternative therefore is to recognise that any post-capitalist future *will* still demand expertise, and will therefore still require developers of some kind, and although in some cases they may be more land and infrastructure developers than housebuilders – that depends on population and density – we will still need more traditional developers to mobilise the resources required to build warehouses and apartment blocks. And second, that glimpses of these future entities – and sometimes more than that – can be obtained from the actions of developers operating within a capitalist economy, to be used politically by Marxists aiming at the supersession of capitalism through the transformation of its own critical infrastructure, the production of space.

Immediately the objections to this hypothesis crowd in. Firstly, from those who would wish to preserve a pure and unsullied Lefebvre, who cannot be co-opted in this fashion, since he insisted on the continuing capacity of critical thought to 'clear a path leading to real rupture' (Lefebvre, 1975:246), insisting on this possibility and qualitative difference at the level of the totality, calling for a maximal right to difference that lay claim to a self-determined urban society that would transcend capitalism (Pinder, 2013:43). These objectors may never be satisfied with any inadequate, partial approach that entails working with and within still-capitalist institutions. It might be said that their objections certainly ought to extend to the planning process under capitalism as well as to developers, although a strong bias in favour of the public sector is often noticeable, notably even if it is a public sector of the capitalist state. It might also be observed that Lefebvre's own work, especially his later work, does not chime with these objections. As has been observed, 'for all this concern with difference, [The] Production [of Space] is marked by a lack of attention to historically concrete forms of difference' (Kinkaid, 2020:169).

Secondly, how can developers actually reduce alienation, critics will demand, let alone build genuinely differential space, in the midst of so many conflicting pressures, most of them directed at exactly the opposite? Critics will point out, with justification, that most developers, at least, are capitalist firms with the interests of their shareholders at their core. Every attempt to create differential space runs the risk of contradicting itself, of falling back into abstract space: Stanek suggests that the concepts coined or shaped by Lefebvre, such as centrality, monuments, urban everyday, even the right to the city, have been 'increasingly incorporated into dominant discourses of architects, planners, administrators, and developers' (Stanek, 2011:2) – with the underlying assumption of redwashing in its broadest sense, that is, not only confined to corporate relations with indigenous peoples (Weaver, 2008).

There are two aspects to a response to this criticism. Firstly, that as Lefebvre himself insisted, reform and revolution are not contradictory. Marxists do not need, and I argue should not, to stand aside from engagement with developers in order to protect a commitment to replace capitalism, any more than they should do so in politics more widely. Secondly, developers, like states and capitalist enterprises more widely, are complex organisations with multiple conflicting objectives and constraints. Opportunities may therefore exist to modify – yes perhaps, even nudge – their behaviour in such a way as to create differential space, either through their funding sources or through other means, even their own internal dynamics.

An imperfect, slow, and frustrating political struggle no doubt beckons, akin in its multidimensionality and incremental approach to the one that Sève identified as characterising 'thinking with Marx' more widely in the contemporary political and economic environment: a combination of 'political clashes, bioethical debates, scientific exchanges' (Sève, 2004:264). But thirdly, if we are to follow Lefebvre in his criticism of the state, it is a struggle in which those taking Lefebvre's project for developers seriously should engage; we should, for example, look to alternative methods of economic organisation such as *autogestion* as models for developers to follow in the production of space. Even if we do not find them in full operation, elements of their form may be found and encouraged.

We might find some resonance with the way in which knowledge of the city, in particular, is valuable. Real estate developers, for whom an interdisciplinary approach is very familiar, may need little encouragement 'to start from their own experiences of cities, to seek out connections between what they have experienced and what they have read, to integrate knowledge with life' (Fraser, 2009:272). We should however not expect the task to be easy, as much of Lefebvre's language has been adopted by organisations that have the preservation of the status quo at the heart of their being, rather than any attempt to transform it. It is curious: no doubt these organisations would very much prefer to envisage themselves as 'black boxes' that do not warrant opening, but those taking Lefebvre seriously should not agree: if contradictions are exposed through their adoption, that may be a progressive or positive force for change.

Spatial differentiation

The prevailing wisdom from Marxist geography has been that urban redevelopment has been largely a culprit in the process of increasing socio-spatial differentiation. Developers have undoubtedly been willing accomplices in a series of adverse political developments, from beginnings with urban renewal in the United States, 'making the poor invisible by driving them out of the city' (Harrington, 1962; Gans, 1967), replicated worldwide, for example, in China (He & Wu, 2007) to neoliberal urban programmes that have further intensified socio-spatial division, within which 'real estate development and property-led redevelopment have been prevalently employed to create the "revanchist city"' (Smith, 1996, 2003).

Two significant counterpoints to this pessimistic narrative should however be advanced at this point. Even staunch critics of redevelopment concede that the housing conditions in China's cities, for example, were 'in need or urgent attention' (Shin, 2007:165). There was a lack of maintenance and management funds. In 1985, more than half the residents did not have a private kitchen and nearly two-thirds had no access to private toilets. Only half had in-house tap water (Fan, 1989). Yet two decades later, despite the huge and undeniable policy mistakes, leading to the failed cities and the collapse of very significant developers, this dismal picture had been radically transformed for the better, and as a direct result of the actions of real estate developers. According to statistics from the Ministry of Construction, the average home area for each urban dweller in Beijing rose from 27 m^2 in 2006, despite a rise in population from 5.14 m to 13.6 m, and then again to 33.4 m^2 by 2021, despite a further rise in population (Zhang, 2022). These represent a fivefold increase since the late 1970s. For Marxist geography, at least as presently constituted, this is not a cause for celebration. Rather, Lefebvre has been used to justify an explicit focus on the marginalised minority rather than the majority (Shin, 2007:163).

Secondly, geography itself. Lefebvre cannot be excused from a largely Western perspective on the city any more than can Marx himself on economics. We may read – in a work that deliberately draws its inspiration primarily from Lefebvre – that in Melbourne, 'These pathways take pedestrians past a rich, fine-grained mix of retail and other uses' (Stevens, 2007:69), but both the extraordinary time dependence and the geographical limitations of this bucolic vision are now clear. We are back in the world of Jane Jacobs (1961) with reference to the argument that

> urban vitality depends on short blocks, which provide a multiplicity of alternative routes and frequent interconnections between them. No longer do we think as Walter Benjamin did of Marseille, Moscow or Naples. These are surpassed in size by the cities of the developing world, where short blocks and alleyways never did have the same positive connotations. Yet one must be careful not to make almost a romantic assumption of the superiority of 'lived space' over conceived and perceived space.
>
> (Kingma *et al.*, 2018:11)

What principally makes the urban now, I suggest a real estate developer would argue, is the mass of residential real estate, and the enormous network of production, distribution, and consumption that is organised through space and time to meet the needs, real and imagined, of that mass. Contemporary real estate can be either well suited to those needs, as high-tech warehouses undoubtedly are, or poorly suited, as with much legacy retail development, or surviving awkwardly in between, as the CBD now is. But whichever real estate a developer examines, it now stands in relation to that mass of residential real estate – in relation to the new urban. If cities are to be constructed – more accurately, *re-constructed*, both literally and in a wider social and political sense, in ways that correspond to human social needs, it is developers who will not only be responsible in significant measure: not only for execution, or simply for working in conjunction with public authorities and according to the requirements of planning, but even also to take the lead in discovering, analysing, and formulating those needs in terms of social space and ultimately real estate development itself. In short, the evolution of 'market research' into a broader concern with differential space rather than simply affordability and economic demand.

It is fortunately not the case that transdisciplinary research on space entirely 'still awaits its development' (Stanek, 2011:xiii). Rather, as might be expected at the current stage of capitalism internationally, it is actually being forged at least to some extent within firms engaged in the production of space. This should scarcely come as a surprise: in their domination of the urban real estate, developers have as their central organisational function the ability to knit together a network of collaborative and conflicting expertise (Robin, 2022), all organised around the central priority of the production of spaces of representation. Insofar as theory has an actual place in real estate development, it is splintered between and within firms, across professions, within individual developments, and as a conflict within the individuals themselves who participate in development. If, as has been suggested, Lefebvre's Right to the City had two main themes: it enfranchised citizens to participate in the use and production of urban space, and to appropriate the city – a right to full involvement in urban life (Brown, 2010:3) – then these individuals are placed at the fulcrum, between a potentially active citizenry and the actual production of space. If what Marxists inspired by Lefebvre intend are 'new processes of reappropriation by human beings, their space and their temporality, from the perspective of urban transition to a more just and democratic city' (Santos Junior, 2014:157), then given their importance in the production of space, it is imperative to understand and engage with developers themselves. Those who work for developers are human beings too.

For if there is any lesson that those taking Lefebvre should accept, and they may do so directly from Marx, it is that the conditions of political change depend on existing social and economic relations. As for Lefebvre himself – his thought was too elusive and even ambiguous, his work was always evolving and responsive to changing conditions, and his Marxism, always of the humanist variety, eventually became shrouded in a democratic mist behind which urban radicals of any stripe can rally. In a world in which developers are the principal producers of space, they too can, and should, understand Lefebvre, especially where they act not to reinforce the real estate economy but to undermine it.

Conclusion: not always villains

If it be true that architecture 'has great difficulty thinking its own thoughts '(Coleman, 2014:15), then this is surely even more true of real estate development. Likewise, if 'Lefebvre actually speaks to architects by showing how they *ought* to speak' (Waterman, 2015:417) and if it is accepted that Lefebvre should (but did not) also 'speak' to real estate developers, how ought *they* to speak? I agree completely that 'Henri Lefebvre wasn't concerned with getting things "right" so much as he was intent upon making good ideas work; good ideas that value history, allow flourishing in the present, and are adaptable, building for the future' (Waterman, 2015:418). No doubt mainly because of the time and circumstances under which he wrote, where real estate development, especially housing, was dominated by the French state, Lefebvre did not speak to developers, let alone indicate what 'good ideas' they should adopt. But if I may then paraphrase remarks to be applied to architects, Lefebvre did not, but must now, under very different global conditions, be employed to voice to derive a properly human mission of real estate developers as a process of becoming in which all people, developers included, play a part – even, in some cases, assuming para-statal responsibilities for the development of entire regions, as has happened in the UK (Harrison, 2014). It is, and of course so long as capitalism prevails, always will be a struggle.

No doubt modern cities are 'diverse spatial constellations of intersecting, contradictory and conflictual practices and experiences' (Prakash, 2008:7). No doubt spatial injustices, for example those associated with migrant labour, can be compared and contrasted with social injustices, even if the conclusion drawn is that the former are less pronounced than the latter (Landy *et al.*, 2020). No doubt too, the detailed empirical studies of individual cities focused on the dynamics of power are underpinned by deep ethical concerns and a commitment to radical politics. But if we are to take Lefebvre seriously, space is produced, not merely consumed – or analysed – so if the relations of production are changed, then so must the production of space – and in a capitalist economy, much of that activity is organised by real estate developers.

Yet as the argument of this chapter seeks to demonstrate, even in the most sophisticated texts, whether from Marxists or fellow travellers on the Left, developers play the role of pantomime villains. Investors and homeowners alike are the developer's accomplices, whilst the role of the proletariat devolves upon a small minority of rebels in a confused alliance with heroic public sector planners. So too then must policies: the campaigns and demands that have been identified in this chapter as characteristic of Marxist geographers (Merrifield & Swyngedouw, 1996:22) not only elide over the important distinction between real estate development, as opposed to investment, they also elevate the politics of urban resistance to a position of centrality in Marxist political strategy. Real estate developers find themselves *wholly* on the opposite side of a line drawn against them, irrespective of their own structure and purpose, what real estate they are developing and for whom, and whatever fissures or factions may emerge within them. It is now time, I suggest, for an alternative: to ask not only how Marxists in general, and geographers in particular, should theorise real estate development, but how they – we – should engage with real estate developers. And to do so, I propose, to borrow an expression from how Garaudy claimed he entered Islam (Garaudy, 1998:126), with Lefebvre (1974 [1991]) under one arm and Graskamp (1981) under the other.

Bibliography

Agyemang, F. S. and Morrison, N. (2018). Recognising the barriers to securing affordable housing through the land use planning system in Sub-Saharan Africa: A perspective from Ghana. *Urban Studies*, 55(12), 2640–2659. https://doi.org/10.1177/0042098017724092

Ahumada, M. P. (2015). Ciudadanía urbana y derecho a la ciudad: hacia una política del habitar. In Gasic, I., Narváez, A. and Quiroz, R. (eds.) *Reapropiaciones de Henri Lefebvre: Crí tica, Espacio y Sociedad Urbana*. Santiago, Editorial Triángulo, 10–39.

Ambrosino, C. and Andres, L. (2008). Friches en ville: du temps de veille aux politiques de l'espace: acteurs informels, planification et mutabilite´ urbaine dans le Quartier Berriata Grenoble. *Espaces et Société 'espace*, 134(3), 37–51.

Bardet, F., Coulondre, A. and Shimbo, L. (2020). Financial natives: Real estate developers at work. *Competition & Change*, 24(3–4), 203–224.

Bauer, J. and Fischer, R. (2019). Introducing Lefebvre. In In Bauer, J. and Fischer, R. (eds.) *Perspectives on Henri Lefebvre. Theory, Practices and (Re)Readings*. Berlin, De Gruyter, 55–76, 1–16.

Behuria, P. and Goodfellow, T. (2019). Leapfrogging manufacturing? Rwanda's attempt to build a services-led 'developmental state'. *The European Journal of Development Research*, 31(3), 581–603.

Berman, M. (1982). *All That Is Solid Melts Into Air*. New York, Simon & Schuster.

Brown, A. (2013). The right to the city: Road to Rio 2010. *International Journal of Urban and Regional Research*, 37(3), 957–971.

Brown-Saracino, J. (2013). *The Gentrification Debates: A Reader*. New York and London, Routledge.

Burke, T. (2012). The Australian residential housing market: Institutions and actors. In Tomlinson, R. (ed.) *Australia's Unintended Cities: The Impact of Housing on Urban Development*. Melbourne, CSIRO Publishing, Melbourne, 35–48.

Coleman, N. (2014). *Lefebvre for Architects*. New York and London, Routledge.

Counter-Information Services. (1973). *The Recurrent Crisis of London*. London, Counter-Information Services.

Das, R. (2017). David Harvey's theory of accumulation by dispossession: A Marxist critique. *World Review of Political Economy*, 8(4), 590–616.

Davis, M. (2006). *Planet of Slums*. London, Verso.

De Souza, M. L. (2010). Which right to which city? In defence of political-strategic clarity. *Interface*, 2(1), 315–333.

Dias, M. (2021). Centralized clientelism, real estate development and economic crisis: The case of postwar Luanda. *African Geographical Review*, 40(3), 309–323.

Dove, C. (2020). *Radical Housing: Designing Multi-Generational and Co-living Housing for All*. London, RIBA Publications.

Fan, Y. (1989). Beijing Chengshi Zhuzhai Wenti de Xiannzhuang he Renwu (Current situation of Beijing's urban housing problems and tasks). *Beijing Guihua Jianshe* (Beijing City Planning and Construction Review), 8, 30–33.

Farrer, J. (2019). *International Migrants in China's global city: The New Shanghailanders*. New York and London, Routledge.

Fraser, B. (2009). The 'kind of problem cities pose': Jane Jacobs at the intersection of philosophy, pedagogy, and urban theory. *Teaching in Higher Education*, 14(3), 265–276.

Gallico, T. (2016). *Urban space interventions, appropriation and the creation of differential space: An analysis of Berlin*. PhD, University of New South Wales. Available at: http://handle.unsw.edu.au/1959.4/57835. [Accessed 5 August 2021].

Gans, H. (1994). Urbanism and Suburbnanism as ways of life: A reevaluation of definitions. In Kasinitz, P. (ed.) *Metropolis. Center and Symbol of our Times*. New York: Doubleday, 170–194.

Gans, H. J. (1967). *Urban Poverty and Social Planning. The Uses of Sociology*. New York, Basic Books, 437–476.

Garaudy, R. (1998). *L'avenir, mode d'emploi*. Paris, Éditions Vent du Large.

Gilmour, T. and Milligan, V. (2012). Let a hundred flowers bloom: Innovation and diversity in Australian not-for-profit housing organisations. *Housing Studies*, 27(4), 476–494.

———. (1981). *The Fundamentals of Real Estate Development*. Washington, DC, Urban Land Institute.

Graskamp, J. (1981). *The Fundamentals of Real Estate Development*. Washington, DC, Urban Land Institute.

Harrington, M. (1962). *The Other America: Poverty in the United States*. New York, Palgrave Macmillan.

Harrison, J. (2014). Rethinking city-regionalism as the production of new non-state spatial strategies: The case of peel holdings Atlantic gateway strategy. *Urban Studies*, 51(11), 2315–2335.

Harvey, D. (1985). *The Urbanization of Capital*. Baltimore, Johns Hopkins University Press.
———. (2005). *A Brief History of Neoliberalism*. Oxford, Oxford University Press.
———. (2006). *The Limits to Capital*. London, Verso.
———. (2009). Is this really the end of neoliberalism? *Counterpunch*, 13–15 March. Available at: www.counterpunch.org/2009/03/13/is-this-really-the-end-of-neoliberalism/. [Accessed 7 August 2021].
———. (2010). *The Enigma of Capital and the Crises of Capitalism*. New York, Oxford University Press.
———. (2010a). *The Enigma of capital and the crisis this time*. Paper prepared for the American Sociological Association Meetings in Atlanta, 16 August. Available at: http://davidharvey.org/2010/08/the-enigma-of-capital-and-the-crisis-this-time/. [Accessed 21 February 2023].
———. (2012). *Rebel Cities: From the Right to the City to the Urban Revolution*. London, Verso.
He, S. and Wu, F. (2007). Neighborhood changes and residential differentiation in Shanghai. In Wu, F. (ed.), *China's Emerging Cities. The Making of New Urbanism*. London, Routledge, 185–209.
Hess, R. (2009). *Henri Lefebvre et la Pensée du Possible*. Paris, Anthropos.
Jacobs, J. (1961). *The Death and Life of American Cities*. New York, Vintage Books.
Jessop, B. (1997). A neo-Gramscian approach to the regulation of urban regimes. In Lauria, M. (ed.) *Reconstructing Urban Regime Theory*. London: Sage, 51–73.
Kaika, M. and Ruggiero, L. (2015). Class meets land: The social mobilization of land as catalyst for urban change. *Antipode*, 47(3), 708–729.
Karaman, O. (2013). Urban neoliberalism with Islamic characteristics. *Urban Studies*, 50(16), 3412–3427.
Kingma, S. F., Dale, K. and Wasserman, V. (2018). *Organisational Space and Beyond: The Significance of Henri Lefebvre for Organisation Studies*. New York and London, Routledge.
Kinkaid, E. (2020). Re-encountering Lefebvre: Toward a critical phenomenology of social space. *Environment and Planning D: Society and Space*, 38(1), 167–186.
Kuymulu, M. B. (2014). *Claiming the Right to the City: Towards the Production of Space from Below*. New York, City University of New York Press.
Lamarche, F. (1976). Property development and the economic foundations of the urban question. In Pickvance, C.G. (ed.) *Urban Sociology: Critical Essays*. New York, St. Martin's, 85–118.
Landy, F., Noûs, C. and Agrawal, K. (2020). *What COVID-19 Tells Us about spatial injustices in India. Justice spatiale-Spatial justice*. Available at: https://hal.parisnanterre.fr/hal-03048380/document. [Accessed 21 February 2023].
Lefebvre, H. (1962 [1995]). *Introduction à Ia modernite*. Paris, Minuit. Translated by J. Moore as *Introduction to Modernity*. London, Verso.
———. (1968 [1996]). *Le Droit à la ville*. Paris, Anthropos. In Kofman, E. and Lebas, E. (eds.) *Henri Lefebvre. Writings on Cities*. Oxford, Blackwells, 63–184.
———. (1968a). Lost in transposition – Time, space and the city. In Kofman, E. and Lebas, E. (eds.) *Henri Lefebvre. Writings on Cities*. Oxford, Blackwells, 3–62.
———. (1973 [1976]). *La Survie du capitalisme: La reproduction des rapports de production*. Paris, Anthropos. Translated by F. Bryant as *The Survival of Capitalism. Reproduction of the Relations of Production*. London, Allison & Busby.
———. (1974 [1991]). *La production de l'espace*. Paris, Anthropos. Translated by D. Nicholson-Smith as *The Production of Space*. Oxford, Blackwell.
———. (1975). *Le temps des méprises: entretiens avec Claude Glayman*. Paris, Stock.

———. (1980). *Une pensée devenue monde: faut-il abandonner Marx?* Paris: Fayard.

———. (1986). *Le retour de la dialectique*. Paris, Messidor.

———. (1989 [2014]). Dissolving city, planetary metamorphosis. [Quand la ville se perd dans une métamorphose planétaire]. *Environment and planning D: Society & Space*, 32(2), 203–205.

Lehtovuori, P. (2010). *Experience and Conflict: The Production of Urban Space*. Farnham, Ashgate.

Lennon, M. and Moore, D. (2019). Planning, 'politics' and the production of space: The formulation and application of a framework for examining the micropolitics of community place-making. *Journal of Environmental policy & Planning*, 21(2), 117–133.

Ling, C. S. and Almeida, S. J. (2016). *Demystifying the affordable housing issue in Malaysia*. Annual Report 2016. Kuala Lumpur, Bank Negara Malaysia, 90–98. Available at: www.bnm.gov.my/documents/20124/6443040/ar2016_en_box5.pdf. [Accessed 21 February 2023].

Ling, C. S., Almeida, S. J. and Wei, H. S. (2017). Affordable housing: Challenges and the way forward. *BNM Quarterly Bulletin*. Fourth Quarter. Kuala Lumpur, Bank Negara Malaysia, 19–26. Available at: www.bnm.gov.my/documents/20124/770512/p3ba1.pdf. [Accessed 21 February 2023].

Lofland, L. H. (2004). The real-estate developer as villain: Notes on a stigmatized occupation. In *Studies in Symbolic Interaction*. Volume 27. Bingley, Emerald, 85–108.

Mao Zedong. (1957 [1967]). Mao Tse-tung on "contradictions". *Current History*, 33(196), 361–368.

Martinelli, F., Moulaert, F. and Novy, A. (eds.) (2013). *Urban and Regional Development Trajectories in Contemporary Capitalism*. London and New York, Routledge.

Mendieta, E. (2008). The production of urban space in the age of transnational mega-urbes: Lefebvre's rhythmanalysis or Henri Lefebvre: The philosopher of May'68. *City*, 12(2), 148–153.

Merrifield, A. (2009). Review essay. The whole and the rest: Remi Hess and les lefebvriens français. *Environment and Planning D: Society and Space*, 27(5), 936–949.

———. (2014). *The New Urban Question*. London, Pluto Press.

Merrifield, A. and Swyngedouw, E. (1996). *The Urbanization of Injustice*. New York, New York University Press.

Molotch, H. (1979). Capital and neighborhood in the United States: Some conceptual links. *Urban Affairs Quarterly*, 14(3), 289–312.

Moulaert, F., Novy, A. and Martinelli, F. (2013). Introduction. Fighting amnesia and recovering the scientific heritage of urban and regional analysis. In Moulaert, F. *et al.* (eds.) *Urban and Regional Development Trajectories in Contemporary Capitalism*. London and New York, Routledge, 1–17.

Mouton, M. and Shatkin, G. (2020). Strategizing the for-profit city: The state, developers, and urban production in Mega Manila. *Environment and Planning A: Economy and Space*, 52(2), 403–422.

New South Wales Ombudsman. (2020). *An Inherent Conflict of Interest: Councils as Developer and Regulator*. Sydney, NSW Ombudsman.

Novy, A., Mehmood, A. and Moulaert, F. (2013). The DEMOLOGOS methodology for analysing urban and regional trajectories. In Moulaert, F. *et al.* (eds.) *Urban and Regional Development Trajectories in Contemporary Capitalism*. London and New York, Routledge, 45–62.

Oosterlynck, S. and Swyngedouw, E. (2013). Brussels – the strange case of disarticulated development and governance: About disjointed scales, institutional fridges and the follies

of urban regime politics. In Moulaert, F. *et al.* (eds.) *Urban and Regional Development Trajectories in Contemporary Capitalism*. London and New York, Routledge, 85–105.
Parker, S. (2015). *Urban theory and the Urban Experience: Encountering the City*. 2nd edition. Abingdon, Routledge.
Pinder, D. (2013). Reconstituting the possible: Lefebvre, utopia and the urban question. *International Journal of Urban and Regional Research*, 39(1), 28–45.
Prakash, G. (2008). Introduction. In Prakash, G. and Kruse, K. (eds.) *The Spaces of the Modern City. Imaginaries, Politics and Everyday Life*. Princeton, Princeton University Press, 1–18.
Preteceille, E. and Briquet, J.-L. (1989). Les marxistes et la question urbaine. *Politix*, 2(7–8), 24–29.
Robbins, G. (2020). Fiddling around the edges: Mainstream policy responses to the housing crisis since 2016. *Critical Social Policy*, 40(4), 649–661.
Robin, E. (2022). Performing real estate value(s): Real estate developers, systems of expertise and the production of space. *Geoforum*, 134, 205–215.
Robin, E. and Brill, F. (2018). The global politics of an urban age: Creating cities for all' in the age of financialisation. *Palgrave Communications*, 4(1), 1–5.
Robinson, J., Wu, F., Harrison, P., Wang, Z., Todes, A., Dittgen, R. and Attuyer, K. (2022). Beyond variegation: The territorialisation of states, communities and developers in large-scale developments in Johannesburg, Shanghai and London. *Urban Studies*, 00420980211064159.
Ross, K. and Lefebvre, H. (1983 [1997]). Lefebvre on the Situationists: An interview. *October* (79), 69–83.
Rouanet, H. and Halbert, L. (2016). Leveraging finance capital: Urban change and self-empowerment of real estate developers in India. *Urban Studies*, 53(7), 1401–1423.
Santos Junior, O. (2014). Urban common space, heterotopia and the right to the city: Reflections on the ideas of Henri Lefebvre and David Harvey. *urbe. Revista Brasileira de Gestão Urbana*, 6(2), 146–157.
Schaff, A. (1965 [1970]). *Marksizm a jednostka ludzka*. Warsaw, PWN. Translated by O. Wojtasiewicz as *Marxism and the Human Individual*. New York, McGraw-Hill.
Schmid, C. (2012). Henri Lefebvre, the right to the city, and the new metropolitan mainstream. In Brenner, N. *et al.* (eds.) *Cities for People, Not for Profit*. Abingdon and New York: Routledge, 42–62.
Searle, L. G. (2010). *Making space for capital: The production of global landscapes in contemporary India*. PhD. University of Pennsylvania. Available at: https://repository.upenn.edu/dissertations/AAI3431173. [Accessed 4 September 2022].
Sève, L. (1968 [1978]). *Marxisme et théorie de la personalitié*. Paris, Éditions Sociales. Translated by J. McGreal as *Man in Marxist Theory and the Psychology of Personality*. Brighton, Harvester.
———. (2004). *Marx et Nous Penser avec Marx aujourd'hui. Volume 1*. Paris, Éditions La Dispute.
Shields, R. (1999). *Lefebvre, Love, and Struggle: Spatial Dialectic*. London, Routledge.
Shin, H. B. (2007). Residential redevelopment and social impacts in Beijing. In Wu, F. (ed.) *China's Emerging Cities. The Making of New Urbanism*. London, Routledge, 163–184.
Shoory, M. (2016). *The Growth of Apartment Construction in Australia*. RBA Bulletin, 19–26 June. Available at: www.rba.gov.au/publications/bulletin/2016/jun/pdf/bu-0616-3.pdf. [Accessed 21 February 2023].
Smith, N. (1996). Of rent gaps and radical idealism: A reply to Steven Bourassa. *Urban Studies*, 33(7), 1199–1203.

———. (2003). Foreward. In *The Urban Revolution*. Minneapolis, University of Minnesota Press, vii–xxiii.

———. (2005). *The New Urban Frontier: Gentrification and the Revanchist City*. Abingdon, Routledge.

Smithsonian Museum. (2020). *A right to the city*, 28 February. Available at: https://storymaps.arcgis.com/stories/a4efe9024ab44f50a86b243d1a2ca9e2. [Accessed 8 August 2021].

Springer, S. (2014). Why a radical geography must be anarchist. *Dialogues in Human Geography*, 4(3), 249–270.

Stanek, L. (2011). *Henri Lefebvre on Space: Architecture, Urban Research, and the Production of Theory*. Minnesota, University of Minnesota Press.

Stevens, Q. (2007). *The Ludic City. Exploring the Potential of Public Spaces*. London, Routledge.

Tian, Y. Y. and Wong, C. (2007). Large urban redevelopment projects and sociospatial differentiation in Shanghai. In Wu, F. (ed.), *China's Emerging Cities. The Making of New Urbanism*. London: Routledge, 186–209.

Turok, I. and Scheba, A. (2019). 'Right to the city' and the New Urban Agenda: Learning from the right to housing. *Territory, Politics, Governance*, 7(4), 494–510.

United Nations. (2021). *Urban regeneration as a tool for inclusive and sustainable recovery*. Available at: https://unhabitat.org/sites/default/files/2022/05/report_egm_urban_regeneration.pdf. [Accessed 6 October 2022].

Waterman, T. (2015). Lefebvre for architects: Book review. *Utopian Studies*, 26(2), 416–418.

Weaver, K. (2008). *First nations: Land rights and environmentalism in British Columbia*. Available at: www.firstnations.de/indian_land/misrepresented-redwashing.htm. [Accessed 2 February 2022].

Williams, P. R. (1976). The role of institutions in the inner London housing market: The case of Islington. *Transactions of the Institute of British Geographers*, 1(1), 72–82.

Wilson, J. (2013). "The devastating conquest of the lived by the conceived" the concept of abstract space in the work of Henri Lefebvre. *Space and Culture*, 16(3), 364–380.

Zaccack, N. N. R. (2020). *How real estate developers define and implement their social impact goals through the real estate development process*. PhD, Massachusetts Institute of Technology.

Zhang, W. (2022). *Per capita living space in urban areas of Beijing, China from 2008 to 2021*, 19 December. Available at: www.statista.com/statistics/1135698/china-per-capita-living-space-in-urban-areas-of-beijing/#:~:text=In%202021%2C%20per%20capita%20living,to%20around%2033.4%20square%20meters. [Accessed 7 November 2022].

Zukin, S. (1987). Gentrification: Culture and capital in the urban core. *Annual Review of Sociology*, 129–147.

6 Lefebvre and the analysis of real estate developers

Real estate developers as organisations

In order to analyse real estate developers as producers of space, those taking Lefebvre seriously will want to understand real estate developers themselves. When we read about 'organisation' in Lefebvre's work, it is in the sense of activity, process, and function, which largely derives from outside the Marxist tradition, principally from management studies. Management studies however also includes theories of an organisation as a bounded group of resources, usually associated with a definite purpose and with which specific individuals are associated in distinction with those who are not (Bedeian, 2018, Chapter 5). It is this use of the term which is noticeably absent in Lefebvre's writing: he along with his contemporaries paid scant attention to the intermediate role that organisations play in society, let alone in the production of space. Yet developers *are* organisations, and so to understand their role in the production of space, it is vitally necessary to engage with organisational theory, as far as possible from a Marxist perspective.

Some research into developers as organisations does exist, but there is no explicit connection made with Lefebvre. For example, one researcher distinguished between 'pioneer', 'pragmatic', and 'sceptical' brownfield developers (Payne, 2009:153–155). Still more so therefore is relevant theory necessary in this area, if it is thought to use that understanding to develop a praxis that whilst recognising the contemporary importance of developers, seeks to engage with them as an integral part of the process of the eventual supersession of capitalism. For if 'ideas, representations or values that fail in making their mark on space . . . lose all pith and become mere signs, resolve themselves into abstract descriptions, or mutate into fantasies (Lefebvre, 1974 [1991:416–417), then it follows that those taking Lefebvre seriously should pay special attention to those organisations that are close, if not closest, to the production of space: real estate developers themselves.

So, what do other Marxists say about organisations? In brief, their main interest has been in charting the impact that changing economic forms have had on organisational structure, role, and performance (Adler, 2011). Van der Pijl (2004) gave an optimistic Marxist portrait of the senior managers in the private and public sectors of global capitalism, and the dual pressures they are under, as agents of both socialisation and exploitation. It seems that when Marxists themselves, or those

DOI: 10.1201/9781003220244-6

following in the tradition, discuss organisations, the language employed is familiar to both institutional critiques and everyday life: they are

> characterized as a complex network of competing and cooperating individuals and coalitions in which conflict is the natural occurrence. The central variable of political model is power, and understanding of its nature and consequences is essential if the mysteries of the organizations are to be unraveled. . . . The neo-Marxist perspective is closely related to the political perspective as the former views organizations as instrument that advances the interests of one group at the expense of another. Those who are able to own, control, and manage organizations are able to exercise domination and power over others.
> (Khan *et al.*, 2007:50)

Marxism as a whole has long moved on from a gladiatorial approach to organisational theory, in particular as a result of nuanced conceptions of class, but also with the recognition that conflict *within* organisations is a frequent, almost inevitable, consequence of the existence not just of capitalism, but of organisations themselves, including the capitalist firm. In the past, such conflicts were almost inevitably expressed as between owners and workers, but many Marxists have gone beyond this narrow perspective to incorporate the challenges posed by different forms of economic organisation, the reality of conflict at numerous levels, including gender and ethnicity, and even the importance of recognising that individuals themselves can be fields of conflict, and in fact usually are. Lefebvre's own view reflected that of Marx himself observed in relation to the opposing pull of consumption and accumulation of capital, 'Generally there are two *or more* contradictory spirits living inside the capitalist' (Lefebvre, 1947 [2014:41–42], my emphasis). From this last point, building on Marx, we may wish to have further reference to Lefebvre. Any connection between Lefebvre's work and organisational theory would be very welcome, especially as Lefebvre himself simply dismissed institutional analysis as unavoidably oscillating between the ratification of current conditions and predictions of catastrophe (Lefebvre, 1973 [1976:56]). We may therefore regret that he did not pay more attention to those ever-present intermediaries, organisations, rather than indulging in observation such as that 'Everything great and splendid is founded on power and wealth. They are the basis of beauty' (Lefebvre, 1947 [2014:252]). However plausible this observation may be, it is far from a helpful basis for understanding how any organisation works, including a real estate developer, and unfortunately, we do not find in his work much that is helpful in studying developers as organisations, with all their potential contradictions: nothing that enables us to relate to the fact that they often employ large amounts of capital but generally have relatively few employees, and certainly little in the way of stratified management, labour unions, industrial confrontation or the critical conflict within developers, as for architects and others, between public purpose and private gain.

There *is* at least one text concerned with precisely the relationship between Lefebvre's work and organisational theory, but the emphasis is unidirectional and in the wrong direction for our purposes: How can Lefebvre's theory of space can be successfully introduced into organisational studies? As for where real estate developers do surface, it is in the usual roles with which Marxists will be extremely familiar: either homogeneous villains (Petani & Mengis, 2018:55) or as passively responding to government initiatives, for example for open park space (Zhang, 2018:252–253). In both cases, the disparity between theoretical rigour and empirical informality is striking – the intention of the authors is not to study real estate developers as agents. Underlying this is an assumption that 'there is a *more or less seamless* collaboration among property capital, the state, retail capital, and financial capital' (Smith, 1996:xxi, quoted by Goonewardena, 2005:70, who added the emphasis, which if he had not already done, I would have). No doubt it is a perennial truth that 'Developers build [or should build] their strategies according to their knowledge of the property sector (local property markets and international property cycles), but also their knowledge of the local socioinstitutional context within which their projects are embedded' (Robin & Brill, 2018:3; Healey, 1992). However, if Lefebvre's theory is to be applied to contemporary urban reality, there is a need for the obverse: How can research into imperfect understanding and very much less than seamless collaboration between and within organisations help us understand the ways in which real estate developers create space, understood in Lefebvrian terms? And potentially provide opportunities to exploit these jagged edges and incomplete sequences to drive a wedge between developers and purely financial goals?

Such opportunities may already exist. There is already empirical evidence for the conflict Lefebvre identified generically to capitalists themselves within real estate developers at an important level, that of financialisation of discourse:

> [T]he vast majority of subordinate employees reject the idea of a financialization of their profession, and their actual practices show a complete separation with financial instruments. These employees on the ground reason with an accounting margin indicator but never with financial formulae such as the IRR and the Net Present Value (NPV), even if they know that their directors pay attention to these calculations.
>
> (Bardet *et al.*, 2020:208)

Consideration of such important issues as financialisation, or the environmental impact of real estate development, does not – or certainly Marxists should not want it to – amount to a mere reformist response that does not aim at the overthrow of capitalism. We must never lose sight of the fact that for Lefebvre:

> [p]ollution or the fight against it, destruction or construction of the environment, zero growth, negative or positive growth, none of these problems has anything beyond a limited, topical interest unless the question of the renewal of the relations is involved.
>
> (Lefebvre, 1973 [1976:13])

It is, however, to recognise the need to avoid painting Lefebvre into a corner alongside occasional, spontaneous, but ineffective resistance to capitalism, and to deny his theory a place in the evaluation of real estate developers, complex organisations that under current conditions are important agents for the production of urban space. The crux of the argument of this book is that under contemporary conditions, developers, public and private, are the institutions that will have to produce that changed space, and that, therefore, those taking Lefebvre seriously for developers will want political strategy to focus on how to make them do so: to try to create a dialectic from two opposing ends of real estate development – the development thesis, the antithesis of insurgent space and then a synthetic response, that can make progress towards the supersession of capitalism.

If this is the goal, it is hard to disagree with the proposition (Lefebvre, 1968 [1996]) that Marxists should understand contemporary patterns of urban restructuring in order to analyse their implications for action, nor with the assertion that the largely – but not exclusively – profit-oriented strategies that drive them are contested amongst different social forces. Where a developer might cavil, however, is the implicit assumption that, at the organisational level at least, these social forces can be neatly divided into two different types of organisation: the one representing exchange value and the other, use value, with developers, regardless of their source of funding or the nature of their output, firmly placed in the former category (Brenner *et al.*, 2012:3). Rather than envisaging developers as wholly, even intrinsically, aligned with the interests of financial players such as banks and pension funds, for example in the creation of hotel-style old-age care facilities (Horton, 2021), there is certainly scope for tension, if not outright conflict, between these two perspectives. The possibility for developers to carve out a very different path to that which would have been chosen by investors alone is especially obvious when the developer themselves are not-for-profit, whilst ironically the universities from whence so much of the criticism of developers has emerged have edged towards objectives of profit and financial return.

Early leaders in the field were found in the United Kingdom, the United States, and the Netherlands, with Australia not far behind (Milligan *et al.*, 2015:2) – the United States now has the largest number of not-for-profit developers: traditionally reliant on tax credits, they have now for several decades embraced joint ventures with for-profit institutions as well as with housing finance agencies (Chung, 2004), notwithstanding the potential tax complexities such arrangements may entail (Warren, 2018). Australia has also seen similar developers (Gilmour & Milligan, 2012), and the pace and scale of their activities have now ramped up. Moreover, many real estate developers are not only a nexus of contracts that draw in the public sector in capitalist economies but are actually either partly or even wholly owned by the public sector. Examples abound worldwide, notably in the Middle East, and in China, where 'the use of metropolitan-scale resources and state-owned development corporations to promote long term economic development and yield a stable tax base' (Robinson *et al.*, 2021:8) is frequently observed.

Developers and the right to the city

What this suggests is that those planning to take Lefebvre seriously for developers would be well advised to exercise caution as to any attempt to insist upon a rigid or even a reliable relationship between the existence of a given corporate form and the behaviour of a developer. Developers following a Lefebvrian path may themselves seek a right to the city, even if they are at least partly privately funded, whilst state-owned enterprises may display a cavalier disregard of the social and environmental consequences of their work. None of this attempt to refocus is meant to deny either the historical diversity of approaches to real estate development, nor in particular the important and largely positive role that has been played by a range of public agencies at different geographical levels and with diverse objectives worldwide. It is however to caution that neither employing Lefebvre to emphasise the importance of political and economic processes in the production of space, nor recognising that these processes inevitably involve 'negotiation, resistance and compromise' (McGee *et al.*, 2007:10) should deter Marxists from the recognition that as capitalism changes, so too do the role and relative importance of different actors. This is especially so as Marxists have come to accept what Lefebvre and others argued, not without opposition, when they wrote that small-scale, human-level developments are probably best produced by agile organisations – a phrase not likely to enthuse radical geographers, cropping up so frequently as it does in management literature – that can operate at the same scale. Because economies of scale and globalisation in the future of development and construction may threaten this, the future of real estate development matters for the extent of possibilities for creating differential space.

This recognition poses awkward problems for those who would want to characterise developers as a homogeneous part of a capitalist *class*, and equally for those Marxist geographers who envisaged them as driven by more or less consistent, explicable, almost universal profit motives. Even profit itself is entwined with public policy: for nominally private sector organisations, 'Developers like to present themselves as tooth and claw, red-blooded capitalists, giving the market what it wants and living on their wits. In fact, throughout the Western world developers rely on public subsidy to make their activities profitable' (Sudjic, 1992:49), a reliance now familiar also in developing countries (Klug, 2013; Schechla, 2015). In such a fashion, ownership by the public sector is by no means the only way in which real estate developers are inextricably connected with social objectives. For all their many deficiencies, public–private partnerships for the production of space – relatively unknown in Lefebvre's time, where the most that could be expected was a construction contact for the private sector to build public housing – bind developers to social objectives in a multitude of complex and not necessarily predictable ways.

It is but a short step from this conclusion to the next question, that of agency.

Developer agency

Agency is a concept fraught with debate, contradictions, and uncertainty. It bids fair for inclusion in any global list of that frequently mentioned term, 'essentially contested concepts' (Gallie, 1955). Yet there is much about the concept to interest Marxists. Notably, in the context of the production of space, extensive claims have been made for the agency of real estate developers – claims that sit awkwardly with their characterisation by traditional Marxist geographers as bereft of agency altogether, merely predictable organisations, collectively responsive to local conditions. Perhaps this characterisation of the motives of a real estate developer may suggest otherwise:

> The developer is like an impresario. He (*sic.*) is the catalyst, the man in the middle who creates nothing himself, maybe has a vague vision, and causes others to create things. His raw material is land, and his aim is to take land and improve it with bricks and mortar so that it becomes more useful to somebody else and thus more valuable to him.
>
> (Marriott, 1967:24)

Both perspectives are caricatures. It is scarcely an exceptional claim to make in response that developers are neither merely responsive to outside pressures nor oblivious to social change. In a capitalist economy, the agency of *any* individual organisation to achieve social transformation is constrained and stymied, and there is no reason to expect real estate developers to be any different. As do all people, they make their own history, not as they please, not under self-selected circumstances, but under circumstances existing already, given and transmitted from the past (Marx, 1852:1). There is no doubt that developers continue to seek to influence local political processes, especially planning at a city and local level, but also taxation and corporate structure at the national or even supra-national level. 'In North America, developers have shaped both federal guidelines and municipal land use planning' (Harris, 2018:274). Equally, however, there is no developer who would not proffer a narrative of constraint and direction imposed on their actions by a multiplicity of other actors, planners and regulators, consultants and funders.

Reinforcing this, and if it be true that political alienation is 'the most serious type of alienation' (Lefebvre, 1947 [1991:85]), and that as Lefebvre claims, the State reigns over all social life, including in the production of space (Lefebvre, 1974 [1991:320–321]), there is surely no doubt of the crucial link between state and territory, of the control exercised by states over their physical territory, and of the fragility of state persistence in the event that it fails to lose control over territory. But to make such a distinction is perhaps a simplification in itself, given the complexity of the interrelationship between the state and real estate market actors. It does not even seem unreasonable to suggest that Lefebvre precisely did not want to amplify conceptions of extra-territoriality, because of the threat that it might pose to his attempt to integrate a theory of space with Marxism. The relevance of this issue is that in the context of the opaque relationship between public and private sector actors that surrounds much real estate development, it should also not now be too far of a stretch to incorporate the actions of quasi-state agents in this formulation. In their subsumption of some of those State powers, in such a vital arena, developers – and not only the giant state-owned conglomerates of the Gulf, but some less obvious examples in other parts of the world as well – are assuming some of these powers themselves.

We may pause to ask ourselves in this context of agency, how alienated, in the traditional Marxist sense of which Lefebvre approved, the real estate developer employee feels from their labour. A very difficult question to answer for any employee, even a director, but like traditional crafters, or even artists, real estate developers do take pride in what they produce, even to the extent of regarding it not just with benevolent eyes, but even with a sense of proprietorship distinct from actual ownership, and hence still in existence long after it has been sold on to investor or owner-occupiers. 'That was *my* development, you know', is a familiar refrain. Perhaps one reason lies in the coordinating function of real estate developers, rendering them less exposed to the issues of division of labour, at least from their own subjective perspective, which may result in their feeling less alienated than others, at least at a personal level, especially when they retain the idea of 'work well done, and of the product as a personal creation and to a certain extent on a par with the object created by a craftsman or an artist' (Lefebvre, 1961 [2014:383]). It may be necessary to revise Lefebvre's conception of the elite that in his mind's eye, he saw leading the struggle for differential space. Are the boundaries confined only to 'critics, theorists and artists' (Conley, 2012:23)? If the boundaries of the urban elite are to be shifted outwards ever so slightly, might not a few of these people, at least, find themselves working for developers, just as others become academics, architects, or urban planners?

Analysing developer performance

What is left open for analysis is the relationship between performance along non-financial axes and organisational and financial structure. Given both his scepticism towards grandiose public planning and his Marxist humanism, Lefebvre might be expected to be more sympathetic to a complex and multidimensional approach to the relationship between the organisational and financial structure of real estate developers and their performance than those attempting to impose a segregation on developers according to whether they are allegedly driven exclusively by a profit motive or not. Given Lefebvre's silence, however, what can usefully be said about the relationship between developer structure and performance – in a Marxist, rather than a purely financial sense?

Work has recently begun to identify the types of real estate developer who try to break free of an entirely profit-driven approach to the production of space and as a result I suggest can and do create differential space. Authors in this emerging tradition do not necessarily identify themselves as Marxists; they do not even now necessarily mention Lefebvre, but they go straight to the point in emphasising the importance of categorisation and evaluation of developers:

> Rosen (2017) identifies different ideal types where the economic rationale is not always the dominant strategy, such as the case of 'socially conscious developers'. Alfasi & Fabian (2008) propose the category of ideological developers that seem to put concerns of the community (and their prestige) over financial consideration. Elsmore (2020) also highlights to importance of building reputational capital, a process of political reinterpretation of

> development contributions. Our research based on the *Economie des Conventions* (Boltanski & Thevenot, 2006) has shown different logical frameworks at work in the decision-making process of developers and often additional concerns for prestige/symbolic, political/influential power or civic concerns converge with the economic rationale.
>
> (Boanada-Fuchs & Boanada-Fuchs, 2022:176)

It is possible, in this context, that developers may be influenced through a combination of subsidies and regulations to act *as if* they were not-for-profits, either wholly or in part. A cynical evaluation is that where these factors are evident, decision-makers within developers are undoubtedly at the very least often significantly influenced by the profit motive in so doing, even if it is not always either immediately obvious to them exactly what they should do to maximise profits:

> Developers have framed their role in these initiatives as altruistic and involving non-economic motivations. . . . The activities of developers in these projects cannot be reduced to economic calculations and instead rely on cultural framings and fictional expectations that work to mystify increases in profit-making through a language of reciprocity and gift-giving.
>
> (Hyde, 2022:194)

But not always, and not in a predictable or linear fashion, and in this case, the developer is thus caught in a critical web from which there would appear to be only one escape – either to work closely with not-for-profits or even to become not-for-profit themselves. This in turn raises important questions about the future of real estate developers as organisations, especially when social and affordable housing are the largest and most important real estate development tasks worldwide.

No doubt there are critical issues within the real estate development process that largely, but not necessarily, militate against developers as utopian visionaries, potential creators of differential space that merit especial concern. Three examples are land banking, zoning, and developer finance.

Land banking

If we should reconceptualise land financialisation as 'a process of embodied political struggle over the production of space' (Ward, 2019:5), as Lefebvre would almost certainly agree we should, then the question arises: Where does that struggle take place? The land banking process certainly encourages developers to visualise space in a more overtly political sense. Marxist geographers have always been scathing of the financialisation of land that this concept implies: 'we wish the von Thunen theory of the urban land market to become not true' (Harvey, 1973:137). They therefore often deplore the strategy of accumulating large portions of inhabited land by buying, at relatively low prices, from inner-city owner-occupiers, and then holding it vacant while passively waiting (or actively lobbying) to get zoning changed and/or building regulations loosened (López-Morales, 2010:147). At the core of this objection lies the complaint that 'The 'mobilisation of land as a financial asset' (Harvey, 2006) denotes an inherent tendency within capitalism for land to be treated as pure interest-bearing capital (Ward, 2019:2). What might the responses of the differential developer be to this criticism? One might be that if managed in a wider interest, land banking – for example by a not-for-profit housing developer – can serve to reduce the extent to which CBD areas are dominated by particular interest groups. Another more purely functional response is that the process of changing zoning regulations is often prolonged and intense, so developers need to own, or least control, the land in order to commence this process. Their only other alternative would be to buy land with the appropriate zoning already in place, either as a result of decisions made by planning authorities – which might usefully apply to brownfield development – or, potentially less satisfactorily, by buying from land assemblers of one kind or another, effectively contracting out the rezoning process to organisations that are much less capable of producing differential space, and perhaps not even interested in doing so at all. There is undoubtedly an argument to be made differentiating developers from those who profit from land without developing it – mere land speculators, sometimes profiting from informal occupation of their own land (Davis, 2006). Saudi Arabia along with many other jurisdictions has introduced a specific measure – the white lands tax – aimed at forcing landowners to develop, or else to sell (Zakaria *et al.*, 2019). There is an argument to be made differentiating developers from those who profit from land without developing it – mere land speculators. Many jurisdictions have introduced specific measures aimed at forcing landowners to develop, or else to sell. The distinction between development and speculation needs careful elucidation.

More widely, those taking Lefebvre seriously for developers will want to watch profits versus purpose carefully, but in a capitalist economy, resources are needed for both, and the land value benefit of rezoning provides the opportunity to cross-subsidise development itself, and often does, even in a purely financially oriented development. Take that away from developers, and their shrunken resource base as a result may limit their capacity to deliver differential space.

Developers and zoning

David Harvey described different perspectives towards real estate:

> [A]n architect . . . may appreciate visual rhythms and historical references. . . . A traffic engineer may think of street design and traffic flow. . . . The historian may contemplate the palimpsest of urban forms. . . . [while] The property developer . . . looks at buildings in terms of rent per square foot, zoning regulations, setbacks and height limitations.
>
> (Harvey, 1989:2)

Although given that 'In the United States, for example, speculator-developers usually realize monopoly rents through the manipulation of zoning decisions' (Harvey, 1985:65), a phenomenon is now observed globally:

In practice,

> [In Florida] speculators used the courts and local governments to force valuable black-owned land onto the market – through such legal devices as eminent domain, partition sales and tax delinquency proceedings. Developers also learned how to manipulate zoning ordinances and land-use regulations to ensure that all of the profits from area real estate markets flowed in one direction – and all of the hazards and liabilities in another. They learned how to turn laws and regulations designed to curb growth and protect the environment into tools of profit and destruction.
>
> (Kahrl, 2017)

A continent away, the complaint was very similar:

> Across the country – and especially in superheated London, where stratospheric land values beget accordingly bloated developments – authorities are allowing planning policies to be continually flouted, affordable housing quotas to be waived, height limits breached, the interests of residents endlessly trampled. Places are becoming ever meaner and more divided, as public assets are relentlessly sold off, entire council estates flattened to make room for silos of luxury safe-deposit boxes in the sky. We are replacing homes with investment units, to be sold overseas and never inhabited, substituting community for vacancy.
>
> (Wainwright, 2014)

Developers will no doubt insist that zoning changes are the prerequisite for development, and with the single exception of a pure redevelopment of an existing site without any alterations to its components, which is rare, they are right. From a Lefebvrian perspective, the issue is not whether developers should seek to alter zoning – clearly they must – but in what way they do so, and what social purpose is achieved, if any, by so doing. A differential developer will be identifiable through not only full compliance with zoning that, for example, demands affordable housing, but actively encourages it.

Financial structure and real estate development

There is little doubt that the organisation of credit in the development industry directly affects the construction of projects (Savini & Aalbers, 2016:879). Within a capitalist economy, development, on a large scale especially, for example, where masterplans are involved, frequently requires the mediation of capital markets, and the creation of mobile investment products funnelling capital into and across the built environment – a concept that is itself a 'gross simplification' (Harvey, 1985:16). These expectations as to future value are highly mediated by state and financial market actors, and this intermediation, it is suggested, breeds speculative bubbles in periods of financial stability (Konings, 2018; Konings *et al.*, 2021).

There have already been frank discussions of financialisation of real estate, especially housing, tracing a connecting line between developers worldwide and the financialisation process itself (Aalbers, 2019; Robin & Brill, 2018; Wu *et al.*, 2020; Robinson, 2022). No doubt that for the majority, this is a fair assessment. Analysis of real estate developers, whether by Marxists or not, must also entail their financial structure and economic implications. Low-rated Chinese real estate developers, for instance, 'have also made heavy use of funding via joint ventures and trust loans, given they have been largely shut out of more conventional funding' (Chow & Liang, 2021). Financial structure influence developer strategy and in turn their production of space. But not always, and not necessarily, and for at least two reasons.

Firstly, the concept of financialisation itself remains nebulous, and may refer to capital markets more narrowly rather than home ownership through mortgages, a much older phenomenon, but one where 'The suppression of housing finance channels has consequently driven developers to find alternative financial resources' (Wu, 2021:7), such as presales and bond issuance, often disguised as equity (Wu, 2021:10). So, whilst much of the literature has suggested tacit alliances between government and real estate developers, there are many examples to the contrary, for example that Government's role as regulator has been highlighted by the adverse incentives of financial structure influencing developers towards off-plan sales (Goodfellow, 2017:794). Ethiopia is far from the only country where the poor regulation of off-plan sales, either exploited by unscrupulous developers or as a result of unfavourable economics beyond the developer's control, has caused financial hardship to purchase. Developers no doubt seek a range of different financing alternatives, and presales certainly have acquired an ugly reputation in the past, especially in the absence of effective escrow regulations, but as well as regulations imposed upon them by government (Chawla & Kumar, 2022), developers may self-regulate in terms of how they employ any of their funding techniques (for reasons of brand value, ethics, or any other reasons). These choices matter: the achievement of differential space for one group should – if at all possible – not come at the expense of disadvantage to another, which applies as much to funding as to development outcomes.

Secondly, Lefebvre tried to use the traditional categories of Marxism, as capital investment, profit, rent, wages, class exploitation, and uneven development in urban analysis, in order to prove that urban development was a direct and inevitable result of capitalism, indeed its most important product: 'in his work on the production of space, he shows how conceiving of land simply as rent is a partial and reductive analysis' (Elden & Morton, 2016:63). But by definition, real estate *developers* do not receive *actual* rents – *investors* do. So, whilst it is true that 'People are paying huge amounts of the incomes that they're making, which are insufficient, to landlords – you can think of it as a pretty direct transfer of capital from employers to building owners' (Stein, 2019), to assign this ethical and practical problem to developers is for Marxists incomplete, for whilst it is certainly the case that in many cases developers retain developed properties and lease them, whether at market or other rents, others benefit only indirectly, as with some exceptions, notably in the Gulf, the overwhelming investment in real estate for leasing is by third parties, not by developers. In many countries, it is Real Estate Investment Trusts (REITs) that receive a growing proportion of rental income: as a tax-exempt form of property investment, REITs are a major repository of real estate capital. Through regulation, REITs are largely excluded from development altogether, and even where they are not, as in the United States, the proportion of their revenues derived from development is relatively small. Marxists and many others may complain about rents, but they are not received directly by developers. Nor is it possible to derive value with any precision from a projection of future rents. Ironically perhaps as well, the market value of real estate, especially in a modern capitalist real estate economy, represents as much if not more a store of value (Chung & Carpenter, 2022) – what the Mayor of London, Sadiq Khan, famously called 'gold bricks for investment' (Booth, 2016), the underlying process of which has also been described as 'zombie urbanism', 'the production of significantly underoccupied secondary homes that function as investment properties' (Soules, 2021:16–17), rather than either a reflection of future income or some concatenation of previous labour.

It has been argued in response that developers have not only internalised investors' expectations (Weber, 2015; Guironnet *et al.*, 2016), but also circulated them to local planning authorities. Indeed, state strategies and practices are restructured in order to facilitate the transformation of 'urban products' such as infrastructure as financial assets (Ashton *et al.*, 2016; Ward, 2019). Developers profit from this, in the same way that gold producers do. But blame for the lucrative gains made by real estate investors should not necessarily always be laid at the door of developers – the regulatory, tax and planning regimes, and much more besides, should bear much of the responsibility. In many other markets, moreover, margins are much tighter, and the relationship between funding and outcomes is therefore always uncertain: it is a mistake to believe that real estate development is inevitably profitable, or even that it is always aimed exclusively at profitability.

What should the differential developer do?

We should recall at this point the distinction between the objectives of Marxism and those of a poststructuralist identity politics. We can find some very candid admissions of the difference:

> Rather than the 'equality politics' espoused by universalizing liberalism, with its call for the homogenizing of difference and unification of identity; or the 'revolutionary politics' of modernist Marxism, which in another way ultimately seeks similar goals; the new cultural politics seems social justice through the assertion and preservation of difference and the maintenance of strategically chosen and non-exclusive individual and collective identities.
>
> (Soja, 1996:190)

He might have added that this cultural politics became so alien to many on the Left that they abandoned politics altogether, either retreating into quietism of one kind or another, or even moving to the political Right. Some, perhaps tempted by liberal dreams but tempered by an awareness of the limitations imposed by capitalism, may have even decided that the celebration of cultural differences should never be regarded as either a substitute for poor housing or the lack of neighbourhood resources, and turned to real estate development as a way to promote greater equality. The differential developer, then – what might be their view of development? If space after capitalism has been superseded and is to be different in certain key aspects, then it is possible to think about ways in which the construction and utilisation of space in the present day can not only point to, but help create, that future after capitalism has been superseded.

The differential developer will also be concerned about their own structure and organisation, including questions of internal democracy as well as the more familiar issues of racial and gender equality. Lefebvre insisted:

> Several well-known but somewhat neglected forms – such as associative life or grassroots democracy (*autogestion*) – must be reinstated as key priorities; they assume new meanings when applied to the urban. The question then is to know if social and political action can be formulated and rearticulated in relation to specific problems that, even if they are concrete, concern all dimensions of everyday life.
>
> (Lefebvre, 1989 [2014:205])

It has even been suggested that what Lefebvre meant was that

> [a]s this awakening grows and spreads, the current managers of the city, specialized professionals like state officials, corporate boards, planners, developers, architects, and so on, become increasingly redundant.
>
> (Purcell, 2014:150)

Two points arise from this contention. Firstly, I am not sure Lefebvre ever meant to suggest that democratic participation in both production and planning would somehow conspire to deprive a future city of expertise or technical skills altogether. It would after all be a curious suggestion. It is, rather, *at whose service these skills should be placed* that is the issue at stake. Certainly, a democratic planning process could be a successful, if potentially unwieldy, complement or even replacement for formal urban planning as it currently exists. Secondly, however, the idea that developers as the coordinators and, yes, managers, of the multiple resources and competing, often conflicting, priorities required to bring complex real estate projects to fruition could hardly be replaced by a loose alliance of multiple interests. Again, it is not that a future right to the city would deny real estate development: rather, it would eventually claim it for the citizens of the city as a whole, and not only for the privileged few, *and as a result of the actions of developers*. Without such actions, after all, the immense inequality in housing quality globally is destined to persist.

The arguments against the wholescale privatisation of rental housing that has proliferated globally over past decades have been made forcefully many times. Individuals within organisations have mounted resistance to neoliberal discourses that have involved a growing orientation towards external private investment in social housing (Power & Bergan, 2019). Lefebvre himself was noticeably silent about the issue of who, exactly, should be producing desirable housing. Caught between dislike of mass-produced public sector delivery and disdain for the inequity of private sector provision, his preferred delivery vehicle was unlikely to be the capitalists state, even at local level; it may well have been some kind of *autogestion*. The central objection to any approach of this kind is the economy of scale that development of real estate on anything other than the most modest scale of an individual dwelling necessarily entails, as whilst self-construction projects have led to excellent outcomes for upgrading neighbourhoods, enshrined in the UN New Urban Agenda (United Nations, 2017), they have remained on a small scale (Montaner, 2020:5), frequently demanding common land tenure arrangements that may also be difficult to recreate through state policy measures (Simonneau *et al.*, 2019:13–14). We are left with the awkward requirement to combine the existence of entities sufficiently well-resourced (which in a capitalist economy implies well-capitalised) to develop apartment blocks, warehouses, etc., with the promotion of construction on a much smaller scale for as much residential development as possible. Whether developers can and do coexist satisfactorily alongside community or even individual construction is therefore a matter of prime importance.

Differential developers operating in a capitalist economy also have the responsibility to survive, both in the immediate interests of their stakeholders and of promoting themselves vis-à-vis developers with diametrically opposite values, objectives, and strategies. Both for this reason and because of wider political issues where developers affect the economy as a whole, as has regularly happened in China but is an increasingly frequent aspect of capitalist economies worldwide, Marxists may wish to comment on, if not attempt to influence, the regulation of developers at a government level. Notable from a regulatory standpoint was the 'three red lines' rule introduced by China, regulations that cap lending to developers that fail to meet thresholds on leverage and liquidity (Kaaresvirta *et al.*, 2021).

Discounting differential space

Distinguishing between different groups in the allocation of resources directed at the creation of differential space is compounded in difficulty by the introduction of a time value of space. The principle of discounting may be found at its capitalist intensity in feasibility studies produced by developers, where, as a veritable mountain of literature has discussed over many decades (e.g. Langston & Lauge-Kristensen, 2002; Gupta, 2019; Moorhead *et al.*, 2022), projected revenues and costs for construction and sale are discounted by the cost of capital of the firm, whether wholly equity financed or supplemented by debt at the firm or project level. There are many technical issues, involved, not least that of how to calculate the discount rate. But discounting is also applied by governments to social and economic benefits (Harrison, 2010), in order to avoid a Stalinist addiction to investment, as after all more or less any project can be made worthwhile provided its benefits are projected sufficiently into the future. On the other hand, conventional discount rates, even those based on government bond rates, reduce the value of the future dramatically over time. At a discount rate of only 2%, for example, the value of a benefit in two centuries is slightly under 2%. In response, some governments have adopted lower discount rates for projects of major environmental significance (Nesticò & Maselli, 2020). Establishing future benefits and costs for large public investment projects is a difficult and complex process.

The differential developer will face no less formidable a set of challenges, which will start to emerge as ESG considerations are taken seriously, but only take centre stage once the developer is able to dedicate themselves to the production of differential space. Quite apart from the issues of balancing different kinds of differential space discussed above, the question of what discount rate to employ will probably have to be addressed somehow. Fortunately, in the same way that government can divorce its social discount rate from its cost of borrowing if there is the political will, there is no need for the kind of benefits implied by differential space to be discounted at anything remotely resembling a commercial cost of capital (Harrison, 2010; Tuen *et al.*, 2023). This is not to suggest that developers will (or indeed necessarily should) have a free hand, however sympathetic they may be to the creation of differential space, as it is likely that there will have to be a relatively close alignment of what we might describe as the time value of differential space of the providers of capital – in a still capitalist economy – and resources more broadly thereafter – with that of the differential developer. We may expect that such discount rates will be much lower than their purely financial forebears, following the lead of environmentally conscious governments, but as to balance between future value and the risks of obsolescence, we can also probably expect that there will be differences of opinion, and therefore different discount rates between institutions.

There is little doubt that where it has existed, the combination of insufficiently vigorous planning and developers propped up by short-term financial capital has been immensely unsatisfactory from a public policy standpoint, let alone virtually ineffective in the creation of differential space. Yet there does exist green, patient capital, some of it from the public sector, which constitute alternative mechanisms for financing developers, that provides them with the opportunity to create just greener developments. The conclusion to be drawn is surely that the financial structure of real estate developers matters, that those taking Lefebvre seriously for developers should be alive to its implications for the production of space, and that every effort ought to be made to ensure that developers are both organised and financed in a way that permits them to create more socially responsible and collective outcomes, as they would be in a post-capitalist economy.

Developer agency again

All of these issues together raise the question of how much agency real estate developers actually do have, especially by comparison to those organisations that plan the urban environment and those that fund them. Those empirical analyses of development that have been undertaken from an avowedly Lefebvrian position do not grant developers agency. For example, in a Turkish context, although the literature is extensive (Ghulyan, 2019), neither the theses Ghulyan cites on urban development nor, for example, a study of ethnicity, social tensions, and production of space in forced migration neighbourhoods (Doğan & Yılmaz, 2011) focus on specific Turkish developers, but rather on the planning process and outcomes in terms of the production of space. Over time, this perspective has begun to change. Whereas in the past it was necessary that to reach an understanding of urban transformation in China, 'we do not want to downgrade the role that is played by Chinese "corporate enterprises" and market entrepreneurs that have increased dramatically in the 1990s' (McGee *et al.*, 2007:15), two decades later the extent to which they could be categorised as only superficially similar to their Western counterparts, concealing their close liaison, has now surely largely dissipated. The troubles of the developer Evergrande (Chow & Liang, 2021) provide a solid example of how the economics and politics of real estate development now rest every bit as much with developers themselves as with public agencies. Lefebvre's urban theory must now be applied to developers and their strategies, and not seen entirely from the perspective of urban planning or urbanisation more widely: by recuperation, Lefebvre does not intend us to understand purely privatisation.

If Lefebvre is to still teach us anything, it is no iron law to suggest that nominally capitalist enterprises *cannot* create differential space, whilst state institutions, even those in a socialist economy, always do, as evidenced by state socialist societies of the Peoples' Democracies. 'It is easy to blame capitalism and the pursuit of profitability and social control. This response seems all the more inadequate since the socialist world has encountered the same difficulties and the same failures in that domain' (Lefebvre, 1989 [2014:204]). Similarly, if 'the right to be different' is to be included within the global project, how will that difference be protected, promoted, enhanced, and even celebrated?

This is not to suggest that real estate developers constitute part of any technocracy; there is ample reason to be entirely sceptical of the actual or even possible existence of

> a layer, caste or even a class of people which is capable of substituting itself for the capitalists and the bourgeoisie – competent, disinterested experts and practitioners, organisers of enterprises, of production and consumption, and ultimately of space.
>
> (Lefebvre, 1973 [1976:24])

Quite the opposite, it is to take seriously the admonition delivered against radical geography that

> for every such concept, there is taken to be a something out there corresponding to it. The disappearance of people and activities is striking once we attend to it. Agency is assigned to conceptually constructed entities that lack determinant referents. It is left to readers to fill in for absence of specified referent or clearly defined meaning.
>
> (Smith, 2005:56)

It is to suggest instead that, because they are created and managed by people, not abstract ideas, and subject to a wide range of forces, real estate developers are internally contradictory. Their impulse to profit is frequently balanced by other factors. Some of these are generated by the external environment; the positive components of these may certainly derive from urban planning, including local community activism. There may however be other factors driving real estate developers away from a single-minded pursuit of profit and an unswerving avoidance of social housing. Potential routes to the creation of differential space may derive from other stakeholders, whether architects with a social and environmental sense of purpose, employees from a range of different social and cultural backgrounds, or even, as with housing associations and other not-for-profit developers, the fundamental mission of the enterprise as envisaged by its Articles of Association or other defining charter. That in doing so, they become gravediggers of their own organisational form may be an irony, but it is scarcely one to which Marxists are strangers, albeit that Marx and Engels' own original formulation may have been only a 'rhetorical flourish' (Vidal, 2018:71). Nor would it come as any surprise to theorists of institutional change, for whom institutions are not only often themselves adapting in response to changes in the external environment, but that 'History has shown that new institutions evolve from old institutions, and that some old institutions survive the growth of the new ones if they can cooperate or avoid conflict with the new institutions' (Cao, 2016:505; Cao & Yu, 2019).

Inside representations of space

Applying Lefebvre, however, should therefore mean much more than simply the recognition of dynamic constraints of space and time in spatial representations alone. It should also involve representations of space as well. We may be interested in not only the concept of representations of space, but in some understanding of its agency and structure. Lefebvre's broad brush does not take us into its crevices, but even otherwise detailed studies mention 'people' as the agents of representations of space (Stevens, 2007:6). Yet as Marxists we can be sure enough that there are not ever simply 'people' – there are socially constructed individuals living and working in the particular socio-economic conditions that prevail in their time and space, participating in widely disparate groups and organisations. It is these 'people' who create representations of space, and they and the social worlds in which they live that are the places in which we should look to find them.

Representational spaces

It is not only 'inhabitants' who create representational spaces. Amongst other creators, real estate developers envisage, establish, promote, and use representational space both within their organisations and in their interaction with other organisations and with individuals. Nor are developers themselves interchangeable, as the radical geographical portrayal of them does tend to imply. There are many reasons why they differ.

Secondly, the suggestion by radical geographers that developers can not only unerringly identify HBU, but equally unerringly follow it, must be challenged. Developers are subject to many external influences, even if they intended to pursue HBU at the expense of other objectives (such as the strategic building of reputation, the pursuit of personal goals).

The result is that their manipulation of land is a more complex and nuanced process than the straightforward appropriation of rent according to HBU principles, or the pursuit of development to the complete exclusion of all other surrounding interests, as the property rights regime theoretically dictates (Purcell, 2014:149). Every development is a battleground of ideas, values, and interests – one in which those following Lefebvrian principles for the creation of differential space should take at least a keen interest. Developers cannot and should not be expected to reject the three components of the traditional framework altogether: demands for differential space will not transcend the physical reality that constrains what type of real estate can be constructed in specific locations, such as how many storeys a residential tower can safely reach. Nor now, or in any post–capitalist future, can the dissolution of planning regulations, zoning, or building control to be expected to disappear. In a capitalist world, financial feasibility will also be required – the third pillar cannot evaporate either. What *can* change, what those taking Lefebvre seriously for developers should be urging on them, is the function of the third pillar of HBU – from the goal of the development to a role similar to that of the first and second pillars, a constraint. The new fourth pillar of a revised HBU that a differential developer will introduce is to maximise social benefit subject to the constraints of the other three pillars. Such a developer, committed to the production of differential space, will shift from purely financial feasibility towards a much more all-embracing, socially oriented process of analysis. We might call it Socially Best Use (SBU).

In the contradictory actions of real estate developers within a global capitalist economy, how should those taking Lefebvre seriously for developers set about evaluating their performance? And what to make of existing very partial tools developed within capitalism, including by developers themselves? Recent research has highlighted a potentially valuable empirical turn that is now required in the battleground for the creation of differential space by developers.

> [A]cknowledging various motives, and trying to distinguish between discourse and reality, [these] fundamental questions are moving into the centre of consideration. What are adequate profit margins, how much margin should a socially conscious developer still be allowed to make and where does exploitation start? While the answers to such questions are deeply context-specific, seeking them will likely challenge current research approaches as in many parts of the world such information are well-guarded secrets (Hyde, 2022). In order to better relate profits to costs and risks, future investigations will have to look in more detail at numbers and business models.
>
> (Boanada-Fuchs & Fuchs, 2022)

Critics, radical geographers no doubt amongst them, will suggest that this is entirely illusory at worst, temporary at best. They will suggest that ESG considerations of this kind cannot and will never be able to transform the objectives and therefore the behaviour of real estate developers. Profit will always be their objective and only

> [a] real 'urban revolution' will take place when the social space becomes action, planning, project of those who dwell in it and who stride on it; when there is the possibility of free production of space, shared, plural, democratic and no more subjected to interests and private profit.
>
> (Biagi, 2020:227)

There are two problems with this response. Firstly, there may be positive as well as negative aspects to developer behaviour under capitalism, for example the assertion that in emerging markets, 'developers hoping to distinguish themselves from their competitors are interested in quality as in the delivery of a finished building to buyers' (Searle, 2010:249). Secondly, even if we agree with the assertion, it omits how such free space will be produced, and leaves us with the same conundrum. What should those taking Lefebvre's project seriously do now? The way out of the conundrum, or least part of the way out, is surely to recognise that developers' actions are not simply reflexive, that the space they produce does not necessarily always run counter in all ways to what would be the result of the production of space beyond capitalism. ESG in itself can never be expected to transcend capitalism, it may even reinforce it – but at the same time it forms the basis of what might be considered as both a set of transitional demands to put to real estate developers and a useful set of standards and guidance by which to judge them on Marxist, rather than capitalist criteria. So, 'although DIY-urbanism projects may not be explicitly anti-capitalist, they can serve as playful and messy experiments in postcapitalism' (Foster, 2020:313), it may be not only possible to see developers themselves as engaged in such experiments, but also necessary to focus on how to measure their likely and actual success.

Measuring the creation of differential space

Even mainstream organisations such as the Royal institute of Chartered Surveyors (RICS) have now pointed to both the potential correlation of real estate development with the UN Sustainable Development Goals and the pitfalls that can also exist in the creation of sustainable space (RICS, 2018), with the many problems associated with balancing an emphasis on environmental goals such as sustainable cities and communities (SDG11), climate action (SDG 13), and affordable and clean energy (SDG7) with social goals, including decent work and economic growth (SDG8), responsible consumption and production (SDG12), clean water and sanitation (SDG6), zero hunger (SDG2), gender equality (SDG5), good health and well-being (SDG3), quality education (SDG4) and perhaps more than any others, reduced inequalities (SDG10), peace, justice and strong institutions (SDG16), and no poverty (SDG1). The Sustainable Development Goals do themselves contain aspirational, utopian glimpses of differential space, a future after capitalism has been superseded. The UN Sustainable Development Goals also reflect an increasing emphasis on 'the role of the business environment in designing and implementing the sustainability objectives. In this respect, entities are encouraged to align their values with those of the community in which they operate' (Ionaşcu *et al.*, 2020:1). Individual 'social' developers have taken up the challenge of refining these goals and placing them into a development context (Shift Capital, 2022). Much more can and of course should be done, but aside from the huge gap between aspiration and reality, however, the SDGs could not be expected to be organised specifically around real estate development. They are too broad to represent anything more than pointers to the potential role of real estate developers in creating differential space – they do not even provide a basis for measurement. But they are not intended to

> [m]easuring of social impact is incredibly complex, as it heavily depends on the project context, asset type, local stakeholders, and dimension of time. . . . [T]he measurement of impact also depends on who is defining what to measure and what the value of the measure is. Whoever becomes the leading agency, will likely define what 'positive' social impact is, and set the parameters as to how to measure it.
>
> (Zaccack, 2020:25)

With these caveats in mind, it is of interest to comment on the most widely used current Standard used by real estate developers to report on their environmental, social, and governance performance (GRESB, 2019). The limitations of the Standard are very evident, especially when it is borne in mind that reporting is not only voluntary, but that the Standards organisation does not have the resources to perform audits on compliance, or even check the adequacy and accuracy of the supporting evidence that entities provide.

Firstly, the measurement of environmental outcomes is both easier, in that it is more readily quantified, and less contentious, than social outcomes. By no means is this intended to minimise the importance of environmental considerations, the massive role of the built environment in the generation of emissions, or the essential future work of developers in reducing it. But it is worth noting in this context that the significance of this role of the public sector may be occluded by the structure of existing (and possibly future) sustainability reporting, which does not stress questions of equality or public access: in the 2019 reporting round, the last before the pandemic, public sector entities recorded a score of only one higher than those of the private sector.

Secondly, GRESB developer reporting is a largely developed country exercise. Many developers elsewhere do not have the financial headroom even to consider social goals, let alone to report on them to a Standards organisation a world away.

Thirdly, and of great significance overall, GRESB generally avoids double materiality criteria, in that it does not focus on overall impacts on communities and society as a whole. There are alternative approaches that do embrace the double materiality criterion, even possibly the new ISSB Standards, influenced by the Global Reporting Initiative, may lean towards it (De Cristofaro & Gulluscio, 2023). When these extend to real estate developers, as they can be expected eventually to do, those taking Lefebvre seriously for developers may be more inclined to use them politically. In the meantime, however, so long as sustainability Standards are focused only on impacts that materially affect the providers of capital, they will find them of very limited use.

Finally, as with any essentially political strategy, an accurate measurement is only possible post hoc, and given the very long-term nature of this strategy, they may only provide the faintest of light as to how to measure 'differentiality'. Developers, like architects, may have to work in the dark, establishing their own values, priorities, and strategies. There is no universal arbiter to oversee them, and Lefebvre would have been the first to decry any such attempt. Nevertheless, as Lefebvre again himself stressed, the reactions of occupiers, whether tenants or even owners, is a crucial post hoc tool to evaluate developer performance. By definition, developers cannot know these in advance, nor unless they remain owners after completion enjoy much influence over them, so the significance of feedback so far development itself is concerned lies principally in the impact they have on future strategy.

For all of these reasons, therefore, to take Lefebvre seriously for developers obviously does entail reliance on sustainability Standards alone, any more than on the generalities of the SDGs. They may help provide background statistics, or provide encouragement to wavering participants in the development process, but they were never designed to measure something as nebulous and difficult to coral as the production of differential space. Marxists will continually seek more ambitious criteria, reflections from the future of how a post-capitalist developer will operate and be judged.

Some provisional criteria

Developers can nevertheless, and on occasion do, produce differential space even in a capitalist economy. They have the capacity to do much more, although exactly how much more, no one is sure, as 'The arena of social impact in general, and specifically in real estate, is a very complex, early-stage, and at times, a subjective topic' (Zaccack, 2020:7). Those taking Lefebvre seriously for developers need to intervene, to create, promote, and lead a debate over how this social impact should be measured, promoted, and reinforced.

Critics have also argued that the production of green spaces within the urban environment is not itself necessarily a universal good. Rather, in this view of

> urban green grabbing residential real estate developers in particular – although there is no reason why they should be unique in this regard – appropriate additional surplus value, extract rent, social capital and/or prestige through locating developments adjacent to new urban greening projects.
>
> (García-Lamarca *et al.*, 2022:2)

What is required, therefore, is the application of a transductive approach: *to formulate the role of a real estate developer in the post-capitalist urban* and then to use that utopian concept of a developer to evaluate existing developers and to help formulate political strategy that seeks to build urban transformation at least in part through the agency of real estate developers themselves. With both that caveat and the objective in mind, some possible values and strategies for such a 'differential developer' – though certainly not an exhaustive list – are as follows:

1. Assuming that greater equality is an essential component of the creation of differential space, there are a range of ways in which real estate developers can help increase that equality. The most obvious way is to reduce the quality gap between housing accessible through purely market means and other housing, whether defined as affordable or social. Developers equally have a range of possible strategies in this direction, depending to a significant degree on what is on offer from planners, including choices about which housing sub-markets to enter and density policies, price caps either absolute or in proportion to the market, and especially, though often controversially, introducing affordable housing as a proportion of each development. Economically, it is cross-subsidisation, whatever policy name it is given.
2. The provision of non-market housing may be the most obvious way in which developers can achieve social goals, including the promotion of greater equality, but it is by no means the only one (RICS, 2018). The creation of more gender-neutral and disability-friendly housing and workspaces, the facilitation of public safety measures that permit safe pedestrian access, and careful design of less expensive housing to provide the maximum opportunity within the space, as well as cultural sensitivity, are all less overt but potentially significant ways that developers can – working in tandem with their architect and planning partners – achieve social goals.
3. So far as developers' involvement in environmental issues is concerned, there are two facets: construction and development projects themselves. The first includes such measurable items as the use of recyclable materials in construction, reducing waste, managing construction efficiently. Much of the direct responsibility for these issues lies with construction companies themselves, rather than developers, but the contractual relationship between the two provides opportunities for leverage. The second also contains many elements, also largely measurable, such as renewable energy production, energy efficiency, modular facilities, recycling, durability, shared spaces, community spaces, and protection of land reserves for indigenous people. No Marxist is likely to judge an entity entirely by its environmental performance, but neither are they oblivious to it, and as Lefebvre pointed out now decades ago, environmental questions are inextricably tied to, and of radical importance for, the production of space.
4. More redevelopment of brownfield, rather than greenfield sites. It is probably unviable to ascribe benchmark percentages to a criterion of this kind, as circumstances vary internationally, regionally, even in cities, as well as across sectors. A trend may be more useful than a specific number.

5. Differential developers seek to work with, not against, local communities. A developer of differential space would be very unlikely to participate in any scheme which involved the forcible eviction of a group of local residents. Where there are clear public benefits for the scheme, such as the need for a public transport hub, and no plausible alternative locations, the developer would be expected to make every effort to ensure the alignment of objectives and values between local groups and the project masterplan, eventually working in consultation with planners to determine the final outcome. More generally, the role of developers in achieving a universal right to the city can be assessed under a number of different criteria. Lefebvre would surely approve of any such list being open-ended and subject to continual change, but access to public transport and contributions by developers to public transport are obvious examples.
6. More architectural experimentation, and a willingness to engage with architects 'from the streets', whose social and environmental goals are more important than their interest in contributing to profitability and conformity, rather than celebrity architects whose selection may owe more to financial than design criteria.
7. Market research that involves studying and understanding what organisations as a whole need, and providing information about how those needs could be/were being met, and less into marketing projects – so a shift in money spent on chartered surveyors, not necessarily less. Commitment of future resources to 'mending fences' (refurbishments and indeed also relations with the community) where required on previous developments. This would no doubt include a greater willingness to share easements with owners and other social groups.
8. Internal issues of the firm. As one ESG consultant recently observed, 'To me, it's understanding that no one size fits all . . . [internally, it's about] how a company functions, its workforce management, health and safety, and its diversity, equality and inclusion' (Day, 2023). Aside from the obvious internal issues such as the relationship between CEO and junior employee pay, the extent of gender equality, indigenous employment, the distribution of dividends, and the extent to which the organisation corresponds to the principles of *autogestion*, developers may also be able to influence similar employment issues within their supply chains, as another professional involved in development also observed (Day, 2023). This is especially relevant in terms of their close working relationships with construction companies, where labour pay and conditions have traditionally lagged norms in other industries, whilst accident rates have been atrociously high, both in an industry that in many jurisdictions remains sparsely unionised. Lefebvre was not only silent on who would create differential space and how they would do so, but on the conditions under which they would work. By comparison, placing the onus of creating differential space at least in part on organisations such as developers and interrogating their internal structure and operation opens a window into the work of those who will create future space, which those seeking to apply Lefebvrian principles to developer actions can seek to widen further.

9. Transparent accounts, including subsidies required, marketing and branding expenditure, and their justification. This would not be new, nor does it represent in itself a transformation – but it is a sine qua non of an effective autogestive institution and a goal to which developers can be urged. Under this heading may also be included a lively appreciation of externalities and a willingness to compensate any group disadvantaged by a development, especially an already less privileged one.
10. Lefebvre himself was never explicit that differential space leans heavily into public space, although both subsequent authors and organisations working in his name have done so. What is clear is that developers have the ability to go beyond what is mandated in terms of the provision of community facilities such as schools, hospitals, sports centres, places of worship, community meeting places, and even – at a time when retail real estate is becoming increasingly difficult to sustain as a purely commercial venture – local retail outlets. All of these are of importance both in diverting resources away from private towards public consumption and in helping to create greater equality as a result of what might be described critically as 'the privatisation of pre-distribution' but which remains a key criterion nonetheless.

What the adoption of some or all of the items in this list – which in accordance with Lefebvrian principles is entirely provisional – of necessity entails is not the dismissal of the HBU concept altogether, but rather its reformulation in more equitable terms, its transformation into Socially Best Use. In practice, in a capitalist society, albeit one that takes ESG considerations with increasing seriousness, this entails incorporating fresh dimensions – environmental, equitable, social – into what was always a process of balancing alternatives with different merits and impediments. Re-envisioned as a methodology for the relative potential contributions of alternative development opportunities of differential space, SBU has a bright future, not only as a real alternative for HBU under capitalism, but as a generalised process in a post-capitalist world where developers will no longer be constrained by the demands of capital but facing immense challenge of reconstructing the urban in the interests of its inhabitants as a whole.

Sourcing differential capital

Under capitalism, the financial structure of real estate developers is central to their capacity to create space of any kind, including differential space. It may be the case that the creation of differential space in any of these ways may require developers operating in a capitalist economy to control and constrain cashflows and capital gains to the providers of capital in favour of social objectives. On the other hand, it may be easier for developers to raise finance, especially from public and quasi-public or green sources, if they are focused on achieving wider social goals as well as, or even to the exclusion of, financial returns to shareholders.

The second available mechanism, gradually growing in importance, is segmented, specialised, or otherwise directed finance. There are several ways in which developers can avail themselves of this.

Firstly, developers can channel their own positive cashflows and capital gains (for example from value capture) into any or all of the social goals listed above, effectively preventing these resources reaching the providers of capital. Given the profitability of much real estate development, this is a real possibility.

Secondly, whilst there is already widespread recognition of the way development can impact in severely negative ways on indigenous peoples, developers have frequently benefitted from the grant of land by public authorities, which can potentially serve as a cushion for their financial returns even if they are pursuing social goals. Under contemporary conditions, where land has become an ever-greater proportion of total development costs, its injection into SPVs by the public sector, often as a long-term lease, can have the effect of empowering the developer to pursue social goals such as affordable housing, either as part of an explicit agreement with the public sector to do so or even covertly. This can be achieved without necessarily preventing the use of market-based financing within the SPV: even a lease of land within an SPV can also be used as the security for raising further finance.

Thirdly, aside from what the public sector can do, developers that prioritise social goals recognise the need for 'patient capital', which is most likely to be made available for social housing but may also in the future extend to neighbourhood retail and local community facilities. Conversely, if within the framework of capitalism there is a need for a decent and well-regulated credit system, providing credit for adequate and appropriate social functions and needs (Harvey, 2020:37) – an observation that would not have found a place in the traditional Marxism of earlier decades (Harvey, 1973) – then such an institution, whether a public utility as Harvey suggests, or not, needs borrowers, a role to which such developers can certainly play.

In addition to these external mechanisms, developers also possess internal financial mechanisms to achieve social goals. The most obvious one at their disposal is cross-subsidisation, which is implicit in the creation of social and affordable housing by developers. The assumption is frequently made that developers will cross-subsidise within individual projects, but this is not necessary: it can equally apply between projects. One very complex part of this calculation lies in the question of developer land banks. Both the UN and the RICS have stressed the importance of effective land governance policies in the context of real estate development. But with growing populations and an urgent need to produce housing worldwide, land governance cannot be reduced to issues of land conservation, forced displacement, or the conservation of historic sites, vitally important as all these are.

Conclusion

The production of space within capitalist society now rests to a very significant extent with real estate developers. Recognising that the state socialist experiment had failed, as much in the arena of the production of space as in any other, Lefebvre implicitly calls on developers, like architects, planners, and us all as inhabitants of the urban to act beyond their function within capitalism, to create differential space themselves. To go further, however, to achieve more than the recognition that developers will significantly control the production of space within capitalist economies worldwide, and that Lefebvre cautions us against rejecting diversification in favour of failed state socialist policies, I would suggest we need answers to at least three questions:

- What would it mean for Lefebvre's theory to be 'adopted' by developers?
- How would we identify whether or not developers had applied Lefebvre's theory?
- What adaptions to Lefebvre's theory would we expect, or seek?

Our problem then is twofold. Firstly, to understand how real estate developers are constituted as organisations, including very much their disparity in form and content internationally, in turn leading to an understanding of what capacity for the creation of differential space real estate developers do have. For example, how this varies between developers according to criteria such as ownership, size, funding, strategy, competition, and the location of individual projects, and how it is affected by their interrelationship with other real estate actors, both public and private sectors, and divisions and struggles within individual developers in the course of their activity. Those seeking to take Lefebvre seriously for developers will want to know how to exploit all of these factors in the interests of the creation of further differential space.

Bibliography

Aalbers, M. B. (2019). Financialization. In *American Association of Geographers, International Encyclopedia of Geography: People, the Earth, Environment and Technology.* New York and London, Taylor & Francis, 1–11.

Adler, P. S. (2011). Marxist philosophy and organization studies: Marxist contributions to the understanding of some important organizational forms. In Tsoukas, H. and Chia, R. (eds.) *Philosophy and Organization Theory (Research in the Sociology of Organizations, Vol. 32)*, Bingley, Emerald, 123–153.

Alfasi, N. and Fabian, R. (2008). Ideological developers and the formation of local development policy: The case of inner-city preservation in Tel Aviv. *Journal of Urban Affairs*, 30(5), 489–505.

Ashton, P., Doussard, M. and Weber, R. (2016). Reconstituting the state: City powers and exposures in Chicago's infrastructure leases. *Urban Studies*, 53(7), 1384–1400.

Bardet, F., Coulondre, A. and Shimbo, L. (2020). Financial natives: Real estate developers at work. *Competition & Change*, 24(3–4), 203–224.

Bedeian, A. G. (2018). *A Standardization of Selected Management Concepts*. New York and London, Routledge.

Biagi, F. (2020). Henri Lefebvre's urban critical theory: Rethinking the city against capitalism. *International Critical Thought*, 10(2), 214–231.

Boanada-Fuchs, A. and Boanada-Fuchs, V. (2022). The role of real estate developers in urban development. *Geoforum*, 134, 173–177.

Boltanski, L. and Thévenot, L. (2006). *On Justification: Economies of Worth*. Princeton, Princeton University Press.

Booth, R. (2016). Sadiq Khan condemns foreign investors' use of London homes as 'gold bricks'. *The Guardian*, 26 May. Available at: www.theguardian.com/society/2016/

may/25/sadiq-khan-condemns-foreign-investors-london-homes-gold-bricks-housing-policy. [Accessed 4 November 2021].
Brenner, N., Marcuse, P. and Mayer, M. (2012). Cities for people, not for profit: An introduction. In Brenner, N. *et al.* (eds.) *Cities for People, Not for Profit*. Abingdon and New York, Routledge, 1–10.
Cao, S. (2016). A win–win path for institutional change. *Time & Society*, 25(3), 493–512.
Cao, S. and Yu, Z. (2019). Seeking the gravediggers of capitalism in China. *Time & Society*, 28(3), 1288–1306.
Chawla, N. and Kumar, B. (2022). Does Indian real estate regulation protect urban homebuyers? policy implications. *Cogent Business & Management*, 9(1), 2117164.
Chow, M. and Liang, A. (2021). *China Property Watch: Strains in the Key Of 'B'*. Standard and Poors. Available at: www.spglobal.com/ratings/en/research/articles/211027-china-property-watch-strains-in-the-key-of-b-12162219. [Accessed 27 September 2022].
Chung, A. (2004). *Bridging Sectors: Partnerships Between Nonprofits and Private Developers*. Neighborhood Reinvestment Corporation. Harvard, Joint Center for Housing Studies at Harvard University. Available at: www.jchs.harvard.edu/sites/default/files/media/imp/w04-8_chung.pdf. [Accessed 9 September 2022].
Chung, J.-Y. and Carpenter, K. (2022). Safe havens: Overseas housing speculation and opportunity zones. *Housing Studies*, 37(8), 1350–1378.
Conley, V. A. (2012). *Spatial Ecologies: Urban Sites, State and World-Space in French Cultural Theory*. Liverpool, Liverpool University Press.
Davis, M. (2006). *Planet of Slums*. London, Verso.
Day, K. (2023). Social climbing: How developers can help build equality. *Modus*, 13 January. Available at: https://ww3.rics.org/uk/en/modus/business-and-skills/ethics/developers-social-equality.html. [Accessed 5 February 2023].
De Cristofaro, T. and Gulluscio, C. (2023). In search of double materiality in non-financial reports: First empirical evidence. *Sustainability*, 15(2), 924.
Doğan, A. E. (2005). *İslamcı belediyelerin on yılı (1994–2004): Kayseri örneğinde sosyo-mekansal bir çözümleme [Ten years of Islamist municipalities: A socio-spatial evaluation of the example of Kayseri] (Yayınlanmamış Doktora Tezi)*. Sosyal Bilimler Enstitüsü, Ankara Üniversitesi. Available at: https://kitaplar.ankara.edu.tr/xmlui/handle/20.500.12575/80833. [Accessed 2 September 2021].
Doğan, A. E. and Yılmaz, B. (2011). Ethnicity, social tensions and production of space in forced migration neighbourhoods of Mersin: Comparing the case of the Demirtaş neighbourhood with newly established ones. *Journal of Balkan and Near Eastern Studies*, 13(4), 475–494.
Elden, S. and Morton, A. D. (2016). Thinking past Henri Lefebvre: Introducing "The theory of ground rent and rural sociology". *Antipode*, 48(1), 57–66.
Elsmore, S. (2020). Strategies of responsibilization: Development contributions and the political role of property developers. *Urban Geography*, 41(3), 389–408.
Foster, N. (2020). Rethinking the right to the city: DIY urbanism and postcapitalist possibilities. *Rethinking Marxism*, 32(3), 310–329.
Gallie, W. B. (1955). Essentially contested concepts. *Proceedings of the Aristotelian Society*, 56, 167–198.
García-Lamarca, M., Anguelovski, I., Cole, H. V., Connolly, J. J., Pérez-del-Pulgar, C., Shokry, G. and Triguero-Mas, M. (2022). Urban green grabbing: Residential real estate developers discourse and practice in gentrifying Global North neighborhoods. *Geoforum*, 128, 1–10.
Ghulyan, H. (2019). Lefebvre's production of space in the context of Turkey: A comprehensive literature survey. *SAGE Open*, 9(3). Available at: https://journals.sagepub.com/doi/10.1177/2158244019870537 [Accessed 2 September 2021].

Gilmour, T. and Milligan, V. (2012). Let a hundred flowers bloom: Innovation and diversity in Australian not-for-profit housing organisations. *Housing Studies*, 27(4), 476–494.
Goodfellow, T. (2017). Urban fortunes and skeleton cityscapes: Real estate and late urbanization in Kigali and Addis Ababa. *International Journal of Urban and Regional Research*, 41(5), 786–803.
Goonewardena, K. (2005). The urban sensorium: Space, ideology and the aestheticization of politics. *Antipode*, 37(1), 46–71.
GRESB. (2019). *2019 Developer scoring document*. Available at: https://gresb.com/wp-content/uploads/resources-2019-developer-scoring-document.pdf. [Accessed 1 December 2022].
Guironnet, A., Attuyer, K. and Halbert, L. (2016). Building cities on financial assets: The financialisation of property markets and its implications for city governments in the Paris city-region. *Urban Studies*, 53(7), 1442–1464.
Gupta, S., Sharma, A., Gupta, S. and Bhargava, R. (2019). *Real estate investment model*. Proceedings of Recent Advances in Interdisciplinary Trends in Engineering & Applications (RAITEA) 2019. Available at: https://papers.ssrn.com/sol3/papers.cfm?abstract_id=3353109. [Accessed 2 August 2022].
Harris, R. (2018). Modes of informal urban development: A global phenomenon. *Journal of Planning Literature*, 33(3), 267–286.
Harrison, M. (2010). *Valuing the Future: The Social Discount Rate in Cost-Benefit Analysis*. Canberra, Australian Government.
Harvey, D. (1973). *Social Justice and the City*. London, Edward Arnold.
———. (1985). *The Urbanization of Capital*. Baltimore, Johns Hopkins University Press.
———. (1989). *The Urban Experience*. Oxford, Blackwell.
———. (2006). *The Limits to Capital*. London, Verso.
———. (2020). *The Anti-Capitalist Chronicles*. London, Pluto.
Healey, P. (1992). An institutional model of the development process. *Journal of Property Research*, 9, 33–44.
Horton, A. (2021). Liquid home? Financialisation of the built environment in the UK's "hotel-style" care homes. *Transactions of the Institute of British Geographers*, 46(1), 179–192.
Hyde, Z. (2022). Giving back to get ahead: Altruism as a developer strategy of accumulation through affordable housing policy in Toronto and Vancouver. *Geoforum*, 134, 187–196.
Ionaşcu, E., Mironiuc, M., Anghel, I. and Huian, M. C. (2020). The involvement of real estate companies in sustainable development – An analysis from the SDGs reporting perspective. *Sustainability*, 12(3), 798.
Kaaresvirta, J., Kerola, E. and Nuutilainen, R. (2021). *China's real estate sector and the impacts of its possible disorder on Chinese economy and the euro area*. BOFIT Policy Brief, No. 13/2021. Helsinki, Bank of Finland. Available at: https://nbn-resolving.de/urn:nbn:fi:bof-202112162156. [Accessed 9 November 2022].
Kahrl, A. (2017). The cost of coastal capitalism: How greedy developers left Miami ripe for destruction. *Washington Post*, 12 September. Available at: www.washingtonpost.com/news/made-by-history/wp/2017/09/12/the-cost-of-coastal-capitalism-how-greedy-developers-left-miami-ripe-for-destruction/. [Accessed 15 September 2022].
Khan, M. Z., Siddique, M. and Qammar, A. (2007). The fight of invisibles in invincible territory: A relative contribution of neo-Marxism to organizational theory. *Journal of Managerial Sciences (Qurtuba University)*, 1(2), 45–56.
Klug, N., Rubin, M. and Todes, A. (2013). Inclusionary housing policy: A tool for re-shaping South Africa's spatial legacy? *Journal of Housing and the Built Environment*, 28(4), 667–678.

Konings, M. (2018). How finance is governed: Reconnecting cultural and political economy. *Distinktion: Journal of Social Theory*, 19(2), 135–151.
Konings, M., Adkins, L. and Rogers, D. (2021). *The Institutional Logic of Property Inflation*. Volume 53. London, Sage, 448–456.
Langston, C. and Lauge-Kristensen, R. (2002). Feasibility studies. In Langston, C. and Lauge-Kristensen, R. (eds.) *Strategic Management of Built Facilities*. London, Routledge, 143–150.
Lefebvre, H. (1947). *Critique de la vie quotidienne. Volume One. Introduction*. Paris: Grasset. Translated by J. Moore (1991 [2014]) as *Critique of Everyday Life. Volume One. Introduction*. London, Verso.
———. (1961). *Critique de la vie quotidienne. Volume Two. Fondements d'une sociologie de la quotidiennetë*. Paris, L'Arche. Translated by J. Moore (1991 [2014]) as *Critique of Everyday Life. Volume Two. Introduction*. London, Verso.
———. (1968 [1996]). *Le Droit à la ville*. Paris, Anthropos. In Kofman, E. and Lebas, E. (eds.) *Henri Lefebvre. Writings on Cities*. Oxford, Blackwells, 63–184.
———. (1973 [1976]). *La Survie du capitalisme: La reproduction des rapports de production*. Paris, Anthropos. Translated by F. Bryant as *The Survival of Capitalism. Reproduction of the Relations of Production*. London, Allison & Busby.
———. (1974 [1991]). *La production de l'espace*. Paris, Anthropos. Translated by D. Nicholson-Smith as *The Production of Space*. Oxford, Blackwell.
———. (1989 [2014]). Dissolving City, Planetary Metamorphosis. [Quand la ville se perd dans une métamorphose planétaire]. *Environment and planning D: Society & Space*, 32(2), 203–205.
López-Morales, E. J. (2010). Real estate market, state-entrepreneurialism and urban policy in the 'gentrification by ground rent dispossession' of Santiago de Chile. *Journal of Latin American Geography*, 9(1), 145–173.
Marriott, O. (1967). *The Property Boom*. London, Hamish Hamilton.
Marx, K. (1852). *The 18th Brumaire of Louis Bonaparte*. Die Revolution. Available at: www.marxists.org/archive/marx/works/download/pdf/18th-Brumaire.pdf. [Accessed 6 September 2022].
McGee, T. G., Lin, G. C. S., Marton, A. M., Wang, M. Y. L. and Wu, J. (2007). *China's Urban Space. Development Under Market Socialism*. London, Routledge.
Milligan, V., Hulse, K., Pawson, H., Flatau, P. and Liu, E. (2015). *Strategies of Australia's Leading Not-for-Profit Housing Providers: A National Study and International Comparison*. AHURI Final Report 237. Melbourne, Australian Housing and Urban Research Institute.
Montaner, J. M. (2020). Remaking slums: International examples of upgrading neighbourhoods. *Buildings*, 10(12), 216.
Moorhead, M., Armitage, L. and Skitmore, M. (2022). Feasibility practices of types of property developers. *Journal of Property Investment & Finance*, 41(1), 92–105.
Nesticò, A. and Maselli, G. (2020). Declining discount rate estimate in the long-term economic evaluation of environmental projects. *Journal of Environmental Accounting and Management*, 8(1), 93–110.
Payne, S. L. (2009). *The institutional capacity of the UK speculative housebuilding industry – responding to the brownfield development policy agenda*. PhD. University of Glasgow. Available at: https://theses.gla.ac.uk/853/1/2009PaynePhD.pdf. [Accessed 3 February 2022].
Petani, F. J. and Mengis, J. (2018). Rhythms of historical disposal: The role of absent spaces in the organizational process of space planning. In Dale, K. *et al*. (eds.) *Organisational Space and Beyond: The Significance of Henri Lefebvre for Organisation Studies*. New York and Abingdon, Routledge, 46–71.

Power, E. R. and Bergan, T. L. (2019). Care and resistance to neoliberal reform in social housing. *Housing, Theory and Society*, 36(4), 426–447.

Purcell, M. (2014). Possible worlds: Henri Lefebvre and the right to the city. *Journal of Urban Affairs*, 36(1), 141–154.

Robin, E. and Brill, F. (2018). The global politics of an urban age: Creating 'cities for all' in the age of financialisation. *Palgrave Communications*, 4(1), 1–5.

Robinson, J., Harrison, P., Shen, J. and Wu, F. (2021). Financing urban development, three business models: Johannesburg, Shanghai and London. *Progress in Planning*, 154, 100513.

Robinson, J., Wu, F., Harrison, P., Wang, Z., Todes, A., Dittgen, R. and Attuyer, K. (2022). Beyond variegation: The territorialisation of states, communities and developers in large-scale developments in Johannesburg, Shanghai and London. *Urban Studies*, 00420980211064159.

Rosen, G. (2017). Toronto's condo-builders: Development approaches and spatial preferences. *Urban Geography*, 38(4), 606–625.

Royal Institute of Chartered Surveyors. (2018). *Implementing UN Sustainable Development Goals – – a common language for land, construction and real estate*. Available at: www.rics.org/globalassets/implementing-un-sustainable-development-goals-rics.pdf. [Accessed 4 December 2022].

Savini, F. and Aalbers, M. B. (2016). The de-contextualisation of land use planning through financialisation: Urban redevelopment in Milan. *European Urban and Regional Studies*, 23(4), 878–894.

Schechla, J. (2015). The right to the city: Cairo. The land and its people. In *Housing and Land Rights Network, the Land and Its People: Civil Society Voices Address the Crisis over Natural Resources in the Middle East/North Africa*. Cairo, Housing and Land Rights Network, 313–326.

Searle, L. G. (2010). *Making space for capital: The production of global landscapes in contemporary India*. PhD, University of Pennsylvania. Available at: https://repository.upenn.edu/dissertations/AAI3431173/ [Accessed 3 October 2022].

Shift Capital. (2022). *We are real estate developers who do things differently*. Available at: http://shiftcapital.us/. [Accessed 6 November 2022].

Simonneau, C., Denis, É. and Valitutto, I. (2019). *Land-based commons for housing and the inclusive city. A comparative approach*. Paper presented at the Lima, IASC Conference "In Defense of the Commons. Available at: https://dlc.dlib.indiana.edu/dlc/handle/10535/10627. [Accessed 9 November 2021].

Smith, N. (1996). *The New Urban Frontier: Gentrification and the Revanchist City*. Abingdon, Routledge.

———. (2005). *The New Urban Frontier: Gentrification and the Revanchist City*. New York, Routledge.

Soja, E. W. (1996). *Thirdspace: Journeys to Los Angeles and Other Real-And-Imagined Places*. Oxford: Basil Blackwell.

Soules, M. (2021). *Icebergs, Zombies, and the Ultra-Thin: Architecture and Capitalism in the 21st Century*. San Francisco, Chronicle Books.

Stein, S. (2019). *Transcript: Real estate capitalism and gentrification with Samuel Stein*, 2 May. Available at: https://thedigradio.com/transcripts/transcript-real-estate-capitalism-and-gentrification-with-samuel-stein/. [Accessed 3 May 2022].

Stevens, Q. (2007). *The Ludic City. Exploring the Potential of Public Spaces*. London, Routledge.

Sudjic, D. (1992). *The 100 Mile City*. London, Andre Deutsch.

Tuen, Y. J., Bulley, A., Palombo, D. J. and O'Connor, B. B. (2023). Social value at a distance: Higher identification with all of humanity is associated with reduced social discounting. *Cognition*, 230, 105283.

United Nations. (2017). *New urban agenda*. Available at: https://habitat3.org/wp-content/uploads/NUA-English.pdf. [Accessed 4 September 2022].

Van der Pijl, K. (2004). Two faces of the transnational cadre under neo-liberalism. *Journal of International Relations and Development*, 7, 177–207.

Vidal, M. (2018). Was Marx wrong about the working class? Reconsidering the gravedigger thesis. *International Socialism*, 158, 65–80.

Wainwright, O. (2014). The truth about property developers: How they are exploiting planning authorities and ruining our cities. *The Guardian*, 17 September. Available at: www.theguardian.com/cities/2014/sep/17/truth-property-developers-builders-exploit-planning-cities. [Accessed 10 December 2022].

Ward, C., Van Loon, J. and Wijburg, G. (2019). Neoliberal Europeanisation, Variegated Financialisation: Common but divergent economic trajectories in the Netherlands, United Kingdom and Germany. *Tijdschrift voor economische en sociale geografie*, 110(2), 123–137.

Warren, J. (2018). *Nonprofit real estate development projects – UBIT and real property tax*. Real Estate Taxation, Q2. Available at: https://cbmslaw.com/wp-content/uploads/2018/06/UBIT-JRET-2Q18-41-Warren-NRED-002.pdf. [Accessed 6 September 2022].

Weber, R. (2015). *From Boom to Bubble How Finance Built the New Chicago*. Chicago, University of Chicago Press.

Wu, F. (2021). The long shadow of the state: Financializing the Chinese city. *Urban Geography*, 44, 37–58.

Wu, F., Chen, J., Pan, F., Gallent, N. and Zhang, F. (2020). Assetization: The Chinese path to housing financialization. *Annals of the American Association of Geographers*, 110(5), 1483–1499.

Zaccack, N. N. R. (2020). *How real estate developers define and implement their social impact goals through the real estate development process*. PhD, Massachusetts Institute of Technology.

Zakaria, N. Ali, Z. and Awang, M. (2019). White Land Tax: Evidence in the Kingdom of Saudi Arabia. *Journal of Accounting and Auditing: Research & Practice* (2019), 1–12.

Zhang, Z. (2018). Exploring the spatial dynamics of the city: A case study in China. In Kingma, S. *et al.* (eds.) *Organisational Space and Beyond: The Significance of Henri Lefebvre for Organisation Studies*. New York and London, Taylor & Francis, 237–260.

7 Living at the centre

Residential real estate development

Introduction

What has been defined as 'the housing problem' was admirably summarised half a century ago that

> there are not enough dwelling units in decent condition, at bearable prices, with required amenities and secure tenure, at accessible locations, in safe and congenial communities with adequate services and facilities.
>
> (Stone, 1978:180)

The problem remains and has moreover undeniably intensified globally, with rapid population increases and the intensification of urbanisation, the inadequacy of existing stock to provide adequate standards evident, and three billion people in urgent need of housing by the end of the decade (Masterson, 2022). It is common knowledge that despite laudable goals from UN agencies, amongst many others, the 'Inclusive City' (United Nations, 2021) remains as far away as ever: housing remains largely unaffordable for many in both the developing and developed world, with over a billion people living in slums and informal settlements lacking basic services and homelessness an ever-increasing problem, even in developed countries such as the United States (Vissing *et al.*, 2019). This will undoubtedly remain the case in subsequent decades, with a continued mismatch between housing requirements and supply. The problem is especially acute in developing countries, for example, Nigeria (Moore, 2019), where the urban crisis is 'manifest in the acute shortage of housing units which has resulted in overcrowding, high rents, and slum settlements' (Godwill *et al.*, 2021:57), a story repeated worldwide, even if there have already been suggestions that population growth will eventually start to taper off, a process that has already begun in some countries and defrayed in others only through the expedient of immigration, both of which bring their own planning problems (Beunen *et al.*, 2020).

In practice, movement towards the achievement of differential space Lefebvre set out has been neither even nor uniformly successful. Progress is undoubtedly excruciatingly slow, there is frequently an excluded underclass, and there have

DOI: 10.1201/9781003220244-7

undoubtedly also been setbacks, which have been characterised as 'undoing the right to the city' (Freitas, 2017:953). Despite the prevailing neoliberal agenda globally, governments are constantly urged that 'any serious effort to confront housing unaffordability demands a more pro-active and socially responsible state that promotes a fairer housing tax and policy regime' (Pawson *et al.*, 2020:341), ultimately one that does not exalt home ownership and end up politically dependent on the trajectory of house prices.

The emphasis in the documents of such public goals is on planning, policy, and the role of government, however, and the process of execution through other stakeholders remains in the background: as if a depiction of industrial capitalism centred only on banks and regulators, without a commensurate focus on industrial firms themselves. There is little doubt that the effects of 'rentier capitalism' – depressed living standards as a result of increasing percentages of disposable income draining out as rent, issues with key worker housing, and a range of others – have posed significant problems for states, institutions, and people worldwide, even fundamentally challenging capitalism itself in the view of some (Collins, 2021). The solution, as is widely recognised – certainly not only by Marxists – lies in the widespread provision of affordable housing – the US definition suggests that affordable (as opposed to social) housing is that which 'the occupant is paying no more than 30 percent of gross income for housing costs, including utilities' (US Department of Housing and Urban Development, 2006).

Where proposals for mass housing have been revived, for example to nationalise the housing market in the UK, the proposed project is accompanied by the creation of a National Housing Body, which would have

> overall responsibility for matching housing demand with supply across the country. It should work with other government departments and take responsibility for surplus government land that could be used for housing rather than it being sold to developers with the funds going to the Treasury. It should take on the role of the national housing developer where the key output is low-cost, high-quality housing.
>
> (Blythe, 2017:99)

What would Lefebvre have made of this statist idea? It is extremely difficult to envisage him offering his support. Marxists, whether of a Lefebvrian stripe or not, are likely to sympathise with the argument that 'claiming back the right for everyone to live in a decent house in a decent living environment can be seen as the first step towards a more comprehensive revolutionary movement' (Harvey, 2012:137). No doubt. But those who want to take Lefebvre's project seriously for developers should also recognise that what made the shift against the public provision of mass housing politically possible worldwide was the widely accepted belief that it had in many cases been an ignominious failure. In developed countries, from its heyday in the years immediately following World War II, it fell over succeeding decades to share the catastrophically low esteem with which housing projects were held in

America (Sudjic, 1992:181), with the claim being made that in many cases, 'public housing has left a grim heritage' (Buckley *et al.*, 2016:199). Of course, there is a continued need for public housing, no Marxist will be ever likely to deny that fundamental political demand. At the same time, however, those taking Lefebvre's project seriously for developers should be sympathetic to Lefebvre's criticisms of the flawed application of the ideas of Le Corbusier and other utopian architects to the mass housing estates of the past, even the new towns in the UK. How can we take Lefebvre seriously in thinking about the future, and yet of course want to be rid of capitalism once and for all?

Residential housing developers

As the previous chapters of this book have sought to show, developers, rather than planners or government, have often been principal targets for Marxist geographers in their criticism of the continuing inability of capitalism to solve global housing problems. The litany of problems with residential real estate developers is long, and the litany of complaints incessant. There can be no doubt that failures to deliver altogether, including absconsions with homebuyer deposits, shoddy construction standards, and inadequate post-construction support for homeowners have been all-too-frequent characteristics of residential real estate development worldwide. This comes on top of the persistent objections from Marxists to the entire industry, that a profit-driven approach to residential development can only ever satisfy the demands of the affluent minority, not the needs of the majority, let alone of those many worldwide who are priced out of homeownership and whose living standards remain atrocious. There is no denying that 'We increasingly live in divided, fragmented, and conflict-prone cities' (Harvey, 2012:15). It necessarily follows that to take Lefebvre seriously for developers entails recognition that the creation of differential space is not simply about architectural variety, nor attractive small-scale developments in desirable locations. It should also include at its core the promotion of equality through access to safe and well-maintained residential real estate for all. But – and this is obviously the most important issue at stake – if not through mass public housing, how is this to be delivered?

Far from all, developers are as willing to accept defeat in the struggle to provide affordable housing without sacrificing quality as the radical paradigm suggests. For example:

> In Rwanda, upgrading to a concrete floor can cost more than two months' wages for the average family. Non-profit startup EarthEnable is using local materials and labour to provide an earthen floor alternative that delivers the same benefits as concrete at a quarter of the price.
>
> (Reckford, 2022)

Another well-known potential opportunity is 3D printing.

Mvule Gardens: 3D Printing of affordable homes in Africa

Kenyan developer 14Trees is a joint venture company between Holcim, which specialises in sustainable construction solutions, and British International Investment plc, the UK Government's impact investor. Its Mvule Gardens project, just off the main Kilifi Highway, is 45 km from Mombasa and 55 km from Malindi, is a gated, low-density development of 52 one-bed, two-bed, and three-bed units on 1,550 m^2 in Kilifi County, the first part of a larger masterplan development (Figure 7.1). At the time of its announcement, Mvule Gardens was the largest 3D printed housing development in Africa (14Trees, 2023).

The development uses Holcim's proprietary ink, TectorPrint, via a local subsidiary, Bamburi Cement; the 3D printed walls have sufficient load-bearing capacity for the house as a whole. It has also been awarded the Edge Advanced Design Certification from the International Finance Corporation (IFC) to reflect the houses' eco-friendly features, such as reduced window to wall ratios, reflective paint for roof and external walls, roof and wall insulation, energy-saving lighting for internal and external spaces, low-flow

Figure 7.1 Rendition of a 3D printed home at Mvule Gardens.

Source: 14Trees.

faucets for wash basins, showerheads, and kitchen sinks, dual flush options for water closets, in situ concrete floor slab for floor, steel sheets on timber rafters for roof, timber weatherboard on timber studs and in situ reinforced wall for external walls, plasterboards on timber studs and in situ reinforced wall for internal walls, finished concrete and ceramic tiles for flooring, and steel window frames (Edge Buildings, 2023).

These are not homes that will directly replace slums, but they are not intended to be. They are, however, potential pointers to the future of low-cost housing, and drastically improve the lives of many middle-income Kenyans.

The efforts of developers like 14Trees are reinforced whenever it is recognised that the housing problem lies mainly in who *pays*, but also partly in who *provides* this housing. So, whilst it is quite predictable that the IFC should argue that 'As Sub-Saharan Africa become more urbanized, the private sector can help governments meet the critical need for housing' (IFC, 2015), those who have been actively involved in practice have also continued to advocate an indirect approach via NGOs and developers (Reckford, 2007, 2022). It is noteworthy that even a strong advocate of enabling mechanisms for mass programmes of affordable housing, where the state is an active agent, stop short of insisting that the state should also be responsible for project management, noting, for example, that under a state-designed but privately delivered programme in China, low-income households are provided housing units at 50–70% of the market value (Sengupta, 2019:511).

Real estate development is also now being undertaken by not-for-profit agencies, further complicating the problematic of the relationship between capitalism, the state, and real estate development. For example, the Australian charity Habitat for Humanity has adapted designs for affordable housing resilient to extreme climate events for a range of developing countries in the Asia-Pacific region (Habitat for Humanity, 2021). Its programmes included the repair and improvement of more than 800 homes damaged during cyclones in Tonga (Habitat for Humanity, 2022:2). In the United States, where public housing programmes have been stymied for lack of funding, charities such as Mercy Housing have stepped forward, with the objective of

> developing affordable, program-enriched housing for low-income families, seniors and people with special needs who lack the economic resources to access quality, safe housing opportunities . . . including supportive housing for the formerly homeless, transitional housing, and permanent rental.
>
> (Mercy Housing, 2023)

In their role as developers, not-for-profit organisations such as Mercy Housing not only partner with local authorities to build much-needed new housing, but also upgrade existing facilities. In so doing, Mercy also aims to employ sustainable development standards for all of its new construction, as well as implementing upgrades and retrofits to save on building energy costs. Their local knowledge and understanding are invaluable tools of production; perhaps Marxists might still be inclined to underestimate them.

For all the difficulties involved, the evidence from Lefebvre's own later views (e.g. Lefebvre, 1990) strongly suggests that he himself would not have done so. He would have favoured disaggregated development, more but on a much smaller individual scale, the active involvement of local communities in each case, and the agency of development itself to reside within specific, local organisations focused on the creation of differential space to the maximum extent possible within the context of an enduring and resilient international capitalism. And to retain hope that that process will, eventually, lead to the supersession of capitalism itself.

The answer to the first question provided so far, that developers should, can, and do create 'differential space', the space of what socialism ought to be, 'a space that doesn't look superficially different but that is different, different to its very core' (Merrifield, 2006:113), is evidently along Lefebvrian lines, but it naturally leads to an attempt to answer the second question: In what would the creation of differential space consist, at this point in the evolution of capitalism? Here Lefebvre can serve developers not only as a guide to actual development, but also in some instances a way of categorising thinking, as he did with the issue of levels.

With his insistence on totality and his suspicions of arithmetical formulae employed by technicians, Lefebvre would no doubt have been sceptical of any attempt to formalise a set of evaluation criteria in order to 'score' an individual development. Certainly, recently developed ESG criteria for real estate, still anyway in their infancy, can only ever be expected to contribute to an overall evaluation, not replace it, and they also run the risk of leaning in the direction of environmental concerns at the potential expense of social issues, even of regarding social issues as matters of regulatory compliance rather than mission. For example, one leading rating agency, venturing into ESG territory, could only bring themselves to issue this tepid observation with respect to social issues for housebuilders:

> Social cohesion risks emerge when developers fail to meet tougher regulations, a development proposal or operation creates community issues, land permits or land conversion rights are viewed to have been prone to lobbying or bribery, or the rising price of property in urban areas is perceived as contributing to income inequality and social instability.
>
> (Standard & Poors, 2019)

Expressed in this way, so far as residential developers are concerned, such criteria can only point to general categories, such as the environmental performance of developments, the proportion of social and affordable housing within a development or a portfolio of development projects, and the lived experience of residents, together with individual, specific achievements of the type highlighted in the examples that follow. Further tentative steps are already being taken by developers on their own initiative, emerging during the course of the writing of this book itself, which those who want developers to take Lefebvre's project seriously should neither disparage nor ignore.

Brent Cross Town – judged by new criteria

Set to be carbon neutral by 2030, the £5 billion Brent Cross Town development will have 6,700 new homes, 50 acres of green spaces, and workspace for 25,000 people. These measurements are part of a bid to ensure the scheme actively contributes to the health and well-being of its new community – so far, the developer has donated to projects as diverse as a women's Farsi group to a children's skateboarding project.

In the UK, there are already frameworks that provide measurement standards for social, including the Social Value Portal, used by Landsec, and the Impact Evaluation Standard. To this can be added the World Green Building Council's Health and Wellbeing Framework on top of which can be layered a subset of locally based research to give it a 'hyper local' view. For example, although an asset in an affluent part of a city may appear to have high employment and good education surrounding it. When local data was layered on top, however, it revealed very high food-bank use on the periphery of the building's area.

For this new development (Figure 7.2), the developer, Related Argent, has proposed what they have called a 'Flourishing Index', building, inter alia, on previous work tying the built environment to physical activity and well-being

Figure 7.2 Brent Cross Town.

Source: Related Argent (2023), https://argentllp.co.uk/2020/10/05/argent-related-unveils-its-vision-for-one-of-the-uks-largest-developments-brent-cross-town.

(Benton *et al.*, 2016) as a part of the social pillar in its environment, social, and governance (ESG) strategy. This is not without self-interest on Argent's part, at least according to Paul Bugust, the head of property standards at the Royal Institute of Chartered Surveyors, who suggested that 'Investors now expect social value to be part of developments and day-to-day building. It's not an add-on anymore and should be a central pillar of a development strategy' (Day, 2023). Those who take seriously Lefebvre's project for developers should be encouraged at the potential political opportunities such expectations may present.

These are surely early days. Marxists may be intensely suspicious of greenwash, even redwash as well in this instance. But ESG measurement may well be refined in future, and it will be an important political question both as to how this happens, what these standards include (and what remains excluded), how they evolve, and what stance those who take Lefebvre's project seriously adopt with regard to how developers perform according to those future measurements and standards.

As to the third question, any revision of Lefebvre, aside from whether he should be chided over the specific question of quantification of measurement, as the aforementioned example would suggest, is the examination of the actual production of differential space provokes the difficult recognition that there is a dialectical tension at its core, which ignoring the specifics of physical real estate or concentrating only on sporadic liberation of space within the urban environment merely evades. We are therefore entitled to ask, how far does this sympathy with *autogestion* run? Especially in a developing country context, where for many years, 'informal processes, which regulate and underpin informal settlements, have evolved to 'undermine, accommodate, complement and reinforce' formal real estate markets (Nkurunziza, 2007:510). Those who would co-opt Lefebvre entirely to a radical cause that owes more to anarchist than Marxist principles urge that the *autogestive* qualities of informal space reveal a challenge to the inevitability of capitalist space and neoliberal development and the global inequality of power that these relationships serve, produce, and reproduce. (Bower, 2016:93). Perhaps so, although the efficacy of that challenge is contestable, as *autogestion* is a way of organising production, not of disrupting it.

Moreover, every piece of future real estate, every owner, every tenant, each development, and each real estate developer can potentially exhibit aspects of differential space, even at the same time as it may be far more part of abstract space. Differential space is not homogeneous or streamlined: far from it, it is and will be for the foreseeable future, perhaps forever, heterogeneous and spiky, even internally contradictory itself. In a residential context, and especially in a capitalist context, achievement in one direction, such as the creation of culturally harmonious space that helps communities to integrate, may come at the expense of another, such as environmental protection or equality in housing provision. Some of this is inescapable: Lefebvre recognised that the form of this society could not be fully defined in advance and could only emerge through actions and struggles by groups and social movements, and this must be of necessity, entail equal uncertainty as to the exact physical forms of differential space and their characteristics. Clearly, the challenge for developers in adopting a Lefebvrian perspective is to shape their developments in such a way as to maximise their overall potential future social benefit, most logically discounted, as discussed in Chapter 6, but there will be no getting away from the need to make difficult choices on occasion.

The existence of these potential contradictions within differential space does explain, however, why the examples cited below are so partial, even weak. They are scarcely likely to excite traditional Marxists, whose ambitions for social justice in housing will rightly always remain much more ambitious and whose inclinations are always to favour mass housing programmes. It is therefore reassuring that Lefebvre will always be there to temper their enthusiasm with the recognition that solving this problem is hard, indeed one of the hardest problems to solve worldwide, that in the past state socialist governments conspicuously failed to solve the problem, and that in solving contemporary urban problems, numerous different types of organisation, including developers, can play useful roles.

Equally important is the financial structure of the entwining of capital with housing to create residential real estate as an asset class of supreme importance in capitalist economies. Critics have laid the blame for many urban problems at the door of 'financialisation', especially of housing. But the meaning of the term itself is not entirely settled, even it has been suggested there has been a debate as to the very meaning of the term, between 'a trend toward a greater reliance on assets and/or debt' (Ward *et al.*, 2019:123) or 'the increasing dominance of financial actors' (Aalbers, 2019:2). Or, specifically in relation to housing:

> A mega-trend across housing markets everywhere, it can be understood as (1) the disproportionate growth of housing finance relative to the underlying housing economy or (2) the turn to Housing as an Asset Class (HAC), captured by the increasing for-profit and financial orientation of actors in housing markets.
>
> (Gabor & Kohl, 2022:2)

Or as 'a process through which otherwise non-tradeable goods become, first, tradeable commodities and, subsequently, investment assets with high liquidity' on the other (Wu *et al.*, 2020:1485). So far as housing is concerned, these approaches are far from exclusive: the former is closer to a definition, whilst the latter encompasses aspects and consequences, respectively. Against this is stacked the public provision of housing as part of a political process, which at least in principle seeks to curb or even reverse the process by which housing, in particular, but potentially other forms of real estate, become privately owned assets. The role of planning is therefore central to the extent to which financialisation takes hold of housing.

On the other hand, adopting a Lefebvrian perspective rules out an appeal to institutional theory as a single method of avoiding the twin quietist traps of positivism and academic Marxist urban analysis. Institutional theorists have suggested that approach to a specific real estate development can be explained by a thorough description of the facts, institutional analysis of the strategies adopted by each of the actors involved – including the developer – and an understanding of urban political economy, both locally and more broadly (Healey, 1992). Such an analysis may well have its uses, and those taking Lefebvre seriously for developers would certainly not seek to disparage the significance of social and broader economic concerns in developer decision-making. But whilst critics of specific applications have suggested that this approach emphasises the social over the economic, the local over the regional or national, and agency over structure (Guy & Henneberry, 2000:2403), for those taking Lefebvre's project for developers seriously, the real problems will always lie elsewhere, in political indifference, and ethical neutrality. So, whilst the investigation of individual projects is surely desirable, outcomes must always be measured in political terms.

What can they expect? Caught in capitalism between the Scylla of private rented accommodation and the Charybdis of home ownership, they must look to what benefits can be extracted from each, even if they both remain unsatisfactory at root. For example, a new generation of purpose-designed private rented accommodation with shared social spaces may prove to be a successful model for different generations to live together. Historically, there are many successful examples of multigenerational and collaborative housing (Dove, 2020:xii).

All the examples in this book come with heavy caveats, of the type with which Marxists will be all too familiar. They are snapshots at one point in time: success at one point can easily be followed by failure at another. They are also very much partial, as inevitable in a capitalist economy, and no doubt also prevalent in real estate development even after capitalism has been superseded, given physical, social, and planning constraints that will inevitably constrain the ability of any development to exhibit purely differential characteristics. A river may necessitate a bridge, for example, dividing two halves of a new community; the requirements of one community may be at odds with the social conceptions of another; and the needs of the community as a whole may necessarily trump those of the residents in any one particular development.

With that proviso, an example that has been cited is the Leuchtturm, or lighthouse, in the Berlin District of Prenzlauer Berg. The design of the building allows for flexible floor plans, so that each individual flat can be adapted to suit changing needs. The residents are a mixed community of young and old, all of whom were actively seeking an improved quality of life by joining forces together. The set-up is not a substitute for nursing care, though some support during short-term illness, for example, is a responsibility of the community (Dove, 2020:28). Europe in particular has examples of such success in several countries – a solution at scale for housing issues, probably not, but welcome, undoubtedly. Another example comes from Denmark.

In the Aarhus Municipality project 'House of Generations', three of Aarhus Municipality's magistrate departments participate: Health and Care, Children and Youth, and Social Conditions and Employment. A public housing association that provides student dorms also participates in the project. The buildings comprise a multi-generational house comprising a mixture of flexible public housing units for students, the elderly, and residents who require care (elderly disabled people and people with acquired brain injuries).

Generationernes Hus ('House of Generations') is one of the most innovative projects of the municipality. Ethnographic researchers agree wholeheartedly with the Lefebvrian recognition of the need to be aware of hermeneutical gaps, and Studio Design and Social Innovation at Aarhus School of Architecture in conjunction with Aarhus Municipality, the architects, used design methods aimed at understanding and describing the needs of the user groups. Their intention was to use the results in the subsequent building programme to be sure that the building and public spaces have the power to transform and improve, as far as possible, how people work, learn, and live – in short, to create differential space. The results of such a process may even make the designer design something for a user instead of acting for themselves, work that has now been undertaken for several decades (Löwgren & Stolterman, 2004; Frich *et al.*, 2021)

It has also been suggested that there may be a more implicit benefit of involving users in the design process: that the user takes ownership of the product (Jensen, 2017); the House of Generations has been claimed to have become a strong dialogue-driven process between the team and the City of Aarhus. As an environmental starting point, the entire project is based on Aarhus Municipality's 360° sustainability model, which is aligned with national Danish green building certification (Rum Architects, 2023). On a rectangular plot with tall buildings and long canals, it has been created as eight closely joined and different building bodies. Diversity, the project architects claim, is the essence of the project – in terms of both the residents, the homes, the functions, but also in the architecture.

Architecturally, it is evident that the building is certainly *different*. The number of floors of the house varies from three to nine, and the facade materials change, creating a scaled and very varied – almost disruptive – effect, which is no doubt no for everyone, but certainly does exhibit a diverse facade with rhythm and clear diversity. The colours employed, textures, and materials all change across the building, just as terraces and openings are placed according to interior needs and not according to some requirement for external perception of conformity or smooth evenness.

Inside, the House of Generations (Figure 7.3) consists of a wide range of different homes that ensure the mixed composition of both generations and people. Within the one development of 27,400 m, there are 100 nursing homes, 100 homes for the elderly, 40 youth homes, 40 family homes, and 24

Figure 7.3 The House of Generations.

Source: RUM Architects (2023).

homes for people with physical disabilities. All the homes conform with the Danish rules for general housing construction, so they vary in size and rent. The aim is that young people, the elderly, single people, and the disabled each must be able to afford their special housing (Ibler, 2021).

There is also a diversity of urban facilities for residents. There are, among other things, kindergartens, cafes, offices, physiotherapy clinics, workshops, studios, health clinic, laundry, sensory garden, balconies, common living areas, all common areas located close to where people live, and which as far as possible also function as resources for the local area, whatever Lefebvre's reservations about the benefits of these facilities within projects.

It would be unrealistic to expect this kind of radical, intergenerational housing to be widely adopted worldwide. There are too many obvious obstacles. But for developers (and their architects) to hold true to Lefebvre's vision for the creation of differential space, they should at least argue for them – and as the House of Generations demonstrates, with the right political will, they *can* become a reality, albeit that this example comes from one of the most sympathetic jurisdictions in the world. It is welcome that even a venerable institution such as the Royal Institute of British Architects (RIBA) has become actively involved in the promotion of such projects (Branson, 2020).

Spaces of representation in residential real estate

We should recall the emphasis within the right to the city on authentic citizen participation in urban governance and its co-option by state institutions (Brenner *et al.*, 2012:6) and its essential connection with curbing, if not transcending, the world of commodities that generates abstract space as another central aspect of Lefebvre's perception of urban reality, but it too has its problematic aspects. Unfortunately, for any politically convenient division between good and evil, citizens do not always conform to the positive stereotypes of radical geography – all too often they can act to create paradoxically conservative spaces of representation, and not only because of the alienation flowing from capitalism, a reality with which Lefebvre would no doubt have been very uncomfortable, although he could hardly have denied its reality even in his own lifetime. It has long been recognised that there is a danger of creating a reactionary politics if rights are to emerge from inhabitance (Purcell, 2003), as the Scarborough Beach example in Chapter 3 sought to demonstrate, and that such an approach 'may collapse into a reactionary and exclusivist defence of locality' (Butler, 2012:134). It is not therefore surprising that it has been asserted that 'Lefebvre's notion of the right to the city, in and of itself, is not helpful in tackling this problem' (Speer, 2015:5). In the midst of potentially contradictory political impulses, moreover, the actions that developers take in accord with a sense of social mission can easily be dismissed as a dead end so far as fundamental socio-economic transformation is concerned – or worse, that such window dressing both obscures the retreat of the public sector from its responsibilities and serves to disguise the failure of developers to provide proper, liveable accommodation for all.

What might therefore a Lefebvrian response be? Certainly, not to argue *against* developers responding to such pressure by withdrawing from financing the construction of women' refuges, providing temporary accommodation for homeless young people, or engaging in any other social project. Rather, surely, to argue that these should sit alongside more mainstream housing projects in their portfolio. For under such circumstances, the would-be creators of differential space are the developers themselves, so perhaps it can be after all, if the right to the city can be interpreted more broadly.

Developer as neighbourhood upgrader: remaking favelas in Brazil

NGOs originally established as social organisations can start as service providers, and then recognise that their next step is to become developers themselves. Such an example is being seen in Favela Marte (Figure 7.4) where Valquírias World and Gerando Falcões, exactly such an organisation (Mari, 2021), negotiated with the São Paulo State Housing and Urban Development Company (CDHU) to employ residents, trained for two years, to participate in the urbanisation process – in the construction of their own future housing. The delivery of the work, with all the infrastructure and the construction of

Figure 7.4 Favela Marte under construction.

Source: diariodaregiao.com.br (2023), https://www.diariodaregiao.com.br/cidades/riopreto/pioneira-ate-no-nome-favela-marte-sera-regularizada-e-vai-virar-bairro-1.1057113.

240 low-income housing by CDHU, is said to be underway at the same time this book has been written. Gerando Falcões claims that since the start of the favela's urbanisation project, undertaken as a result of an urban inclusion pact with dozens of companies in Rio Preto, unemployment among residents has dropped from 70% to 19% in two years.

For the construction of the planned 240 houses, R$58 million will be invested in the project, R$28 million from the State government, R$15 million from the City Hall, and R$15 million raised by the NGO, Gerando Falcões, from the private sector. Favela Marte will be the first such development in Brazil to have solar panels and to be fully self-sustainable in terms of electricity generation. All installation equipment will be funded by the Brazilian private sector firms, Banco BV and Meu Financiamento Solar. The houses will also be delivered to residents with appliances. The project has overcome pride and prejudice, including in how to arrange temporary accommodation for residents whilst construction is underway, to deliver a project of which Lefebvre would surely have approved immensely (Dos Santos, 2022).

Increasing density

The challenges of more affluent parts of the urban fabric are of course very different, a fact that in itself militates in favour of agile organisations acutely aware of local conditions. There, one of the key aspects of any struggle against gentrification are developments that combat sprawl, most obviously by increasing density. New Urbanist architects and developers have long been critical of suburbia, recognising that in-fill is the most responsible form of development, as the infrastructure is already there (St Antoine, 2007:130). High-rise development though is not necessarily a universally attractive solution. Little has dented the very reasonable conclusion that 'Many, but by no means all, residents are more satisfied by low-rise than by high-rise housing. High rises are more satisfactory for residents when they are more expensive, located in better neighbourhoods, and residents chose to live in them' (Gifford, 2007:14), with the equally reasonable suggestion made more recently that 'compact development is not necessarily detrimental to subjective well-being when high densities are accompanied by mixed land uses, public transport, limited car traffic, access to green spaces, and social equity' (Mouratidis, 2019:270).

Developers against sprawl – the logic of high-rise at South Quay Plaza in Central London

Far from all, developers are enthusiastic about sprawl, and many have become highly cognisant of the issues involved, now emphasising what is often described as 'social sustainability' in their proposals for high-rise developments. The developer of South Quay Plaza has set out to demonstrate how the next generation of tall buildings can be friendly and successful places where people from all backgrounds can participate in what the developer views as a potentially high quality of life (Berkeley Group, 2014). If proved true, this would be a significant contribution to the debate over high-rise living in London, with potential implications worldwide.

Designed by Foster & Partners, the development includes 1,284 mixed tenure homes, a nursery and children's play space, a new proposed bridge across South Dock, and a £26.6 million contribution to infrastructure and services (Berkeley Group, 2023).

The developer has provided indoor space for the community which can be used for a nursery, crèche, or to host events. The precise use of the space has been determined through consultation with the social housing providers and residents (not fixed in advance) and the facility will be accessible and affordable to people of every tenure (Berkeley Group, 2014:8). A far-reaching community strategy had been developed for this site, drawing on a detailed review of best practice in high-rise buildings. This strategy has influenced building design, estate management, and public realm treatments, and includes a proactive approach to encouraging links between neighbours. South Quay (Figure 7.5) is set in over two acres of significantly improved, high-quality public realm comprising both open space, where events open to the local community are now held, and playspace – the development won a British Homes Award in 2022 for Best Landscape Design, whilst only half-way through its completion. More broadly, this public space is a rare inclusion in such schemes and is particularly relevant in Canary Wharf where there is a noticeable lack of it generally (Berkeley Group, 2014:12). There has been an awareness on the part of the developer of the importance of local history: a poet, Nikita Gill, was commissioned to write a poem about the

Figure 7.5 Mixed tenure housing at South Quay Plaza.
Source: Berkeley Group (2023).

local area and the transformation taking place – from a historic shipping port to a commercial and business hub to what the developer has described as a new green, lifestyle quarter. The poem was then inscribed into the landscape, creating a trail for people to walk through and follow the poem. There is also employed a Resident Community Officer to manage the building and the many events that are being hosted for residents. The developer also promised a small grants fund for resident-led initiatives and large-scale annual events which establish new traditions for this part of Marsh Wall. The next phase of the development, Harcourt Gardens, is now under construction. It will have homework clubs for children, play areas for small children, and social housing (Berkeley Group, 2023a).

There is also provision for affordable housing – these residents are already living in the building, their homes are tenure blind to the rest of the homes in the building (Berkeley Group, 2023a).

Delivery on all of these aspects of the development is crucial in helping to generate the social and political credibility that has been so lacking in previous developments of a similar kind. Yet even with their delivery, South Quay Plaza is not a significant part of any solution to the endless crisis of housing in London. But then, it does not claim to be, although the scope of the developer's ambitions is already bold. Regaining that traction for high-rise residential development that was squandered by the mass public housing of the mid-20th century that Lefebvre so detested will be a long and difficult process. But if South Quay makes even a small contribution, those who believe that developers can help solve problems of urban sprawl as well as create them should have reason to give quiet thanks.

Technical innovation

Developers may act as trailblazers, taking the lead in coralling resources to introduce technical innovations for residential development. Lower costs can result in a better product, more readily available to lower-income groups, and even reduce disparities in access to facilities between income groups as a result of new developments. Lefebvre himself tended to refer to technology as a social object, risking in so doing a conception of it as in some sense homogeneous. Where he did specify, he concentrated more on information than construction technology (e.g. Lefebvre, 1979 [2009:133]). Even in respect of information technology itself, however, developers – often it must be readily conceded for scarcely less than reasons of self-interest – have taken the lead in providing access to future residents, working closely to follow a lead sometimes set by planners, politicians, or other parts of the private sector, but equally, sometimes not, as the following two examples demonstrate.

Developer following a planning lead: the case of internet provision in Penang

The time will come, and perhaps quite quickly, when fibre-optic cables are no longer required for internet communication. In the meantime, however, planners worldwide have been keen to introduce it for new developments. In the State of Penang, in Malaysia, the State Transport and Infrastructure Committee chairman Zairil Khir Johari said in 2021 that the State would now enforce fibre-optic installation as a basic utility on par with water and electricity supply.

> Penang is the first state in Malaysia to do so. We are now in the process of replacing outdated copper cables and are expecting to complete this process by the end of next year. Fibre is to pave the way for faster internet. So, fibre is our focus. We want to fiberise as soon as possible.

The Minister said it is compulsory for developers of new housing development or buildings to install fibre optics when seeking planning permission from the local council just like the need to provide water and electricity supply, without which the developers could not obtain the Certificate of Completion and Compliance (CCC) for their finished project (Buletin Mutiara, 2021).

In this case, regulators have claimed to take the lead, although without the developments themselves, progress confined to retrofitting would be slow. By contrast, developers in the same country have thought ahead with respect to design, although they may have been too quick off the mark.

Working from Home (WFH)

Wapshott & Mallett (2012) used what they described as an explicitly Lefebvrian framework of dominated and appropriated spaces to illustrate how efforts to demarcate the physical space of WFH within the home entailed new rules and boundaries that alter the representational space beyond these zones. It is instructive to realise that even after a decade, technology and social practice have found ways to batter through the barriers they record as established to resist the intrusion of work throughout the home. As a result, the efforts at resistance they cite (Nansen *et al.*, 2010) now seem quaint, old-fashioned, and futile. Developers, however, have begun to try to use the design of residential real estate to make WFH more tolerable, and ultimately more human.

Developer as expediter: WFH and the design of residential housing in Malaysia

Recent projects from Malaysian developer Eco World Development Group such as Regent Garden Eco-Grandeur (Figure 7.6) have seen the creation of specific work areas within the home. The developer has tried to maximise views and openings for the WFH area. The developer has also tried to introduce as much as adaption and flexibility as possible through four different types of units. Each unit is similar in size but differs in space layout to suit its users' different needs and preferences (Kholid *et al.*, 2021:270–271). The result is a building whose external appearance is undramatic, but whose impact on future residents' lives may be very considerable.

Figure 7.6 Regent Garden Eco-Grandeur.

Source: Eco World Development Group (2023).

The actual impact of technology itself on the physical production of space Lefebvre left untouched, possibly for the good reason that at the time he wrote, construction technology was relatively static by comparison to rapid advances in information technology. Whilst dynamic change has been long heralded, and perhaps exaggerated even in recent times, that may no longer be the case.

Developer as innovator – another British example

In the London Borough of Wandsworth, developer Pocket Living employed architects Metropolitan Workshop and assembly contractor Vision Modular Systems to create Mapleton Crescent, which was completed in 2018 (Figure 7.7). There were 243 modules required, all built in Vision's factory in Bedford using production line techniques that contemporary descriptions characterised as 'reminiscent of car manufacturing' (Vision Modular Systems, 2017).

> Mapleton Crescent provided 56 below-market price one-bedroom apartments intended for first-time buyers in London. The development is just over a 10-minute walk from a train station and a 20-minute walk to an underground tube station, giving residents excellent transport links into central London. The building itself includes shared amenity spaces such as rooftop gardens providing 360-degree views of the area, shared balconies for residents, and a riverside terrace. All the communal spaces were designed specifically to help create a lasting community inside.
>
> The tower is clad in three profiles of turquoise terracotta. Of itself, perhaps only a statement of style. But Metropolitan Workshop collaborated with local artist Loraine Rutt to develop the special glazing and colour. The building itself is arranged around a triangular stair and lift core, and is composed of two wings, one facing east over the River Wandle and one facing south. All circulation spaces are naturally lit and ventilated and provide views in three directions. The residents lounge, entrance foyer, riverside walkway, and striking sawtooth roadside cladding arrangement.
>
> (urbanNext, 2022)

Although Mapleton Crescent was at the time of its construction Europe's tallest modular residential building of 27 storeys, a record that may not itself stand long, the company said that the modules would take less than six weeks to install onsite, arguing that modular construction could provide high-quality, energy-efficient homes at pace, in areas that traditional construction would find difficult. A similar application of off-site construction of apartment units at allowed the San Francisco housing project, 833 Bryant, simultaneously to build units and engage in site work, shortening the development timeline (Decker, 2021).

Figure 7.7 Mapleton Crescent.
Source: Edmund Sumner, 2022.

Developer Pocket Living claims that it wants to be especially innovative affordable housing provider, and its award-winning design specifications that have been endorsed by the Greater London Authority. As the developer of Mapleton Crescent, Pocket was instrumental in helping to ensure that modular homes became both fully insurable and mortgageable, both extremely important to potential residents.

Co-living

Innovations may not only be technical – they can obviously also be social in nature. Whether it is described as co-living, co-housing, shared housing, or in any other way, a substantial literature has emerged on how it has become a decision of choice for those at or nearing the end of their working lives, as well as its more typical historical use for students and work communities. Citing the Joseph Rowntree Foundation in the UK from decades ago (Bennett & Dixon, 2006), Korean research, for example, has suggested that people who live together 'may sacrifice private space, but living in shared housings may reduce the potential risk of social isolation and the psychosocial stressors caused by loneliness, which is one of the problems that those who live in single person households encounter' (Cho & Kim, 2019:30). The authors conceded that shared housing is certainly not for everyone, to which Marxists may add, certainly not given how human personalities struggle to flourish under capitalism, but also most likely thereafter as well. But they also suggested that those who demonstrate a proclivity for shared living may have a greater capacity to resist alienation and may potentially become important human resources for community-building and for leading active community participation (Cho & Kim, 2019:36). From a Marxist perspective, the comment from a co-living resident that co-living is attractive to those who value experiences over materiality is especially telling (Hurst, 2022). There are also economic advantages to co-livers: business models vary.

As to industry structure, property consultants in the United States have already observed that market participants 'span the spectrum of operational models with some serving as just property operators (managers) to others, such as Common, serving as developer, owner and operator' (CBRE, 2020). In the former case, there is still a need for a builder at least to repurpose existing real estate, but of more interest in the context of the production of space are those who develop their own properties, serving as evidence of how developers can produce differential space, and often in a way in which large traditional mass housing programmes are not suited, at least as yet.

With those positive aspects in mind, it is arguably gratifying that the co-living market globally is growing rapidly, even if a significant proportion of this growth has been driven by affordability concerns in major cities worldwide rather than as a result of active choice. By the end of 2020, estimates suggested that there were about 180 co-living operators worldwide with a total number of about 4,000 facilities and more than 250,000 rental units; 99% of them were in three countries – China, India, and Singapore (Min & Ngo, 2019; Becar, 2021). Critics point out the economic reality, that the occupier pays for all services – and this can be 15–20% more expensive than the rental rate for similar housing in the same location. But considering the cost of utilities and WiFi, cleaning apartments, laundry, using the co-working space and fitness centre, Becar's argument that net costs are at least 15–20% cheaper may have merit, quite aside from the potential social benefits of co-living, which would be of at least equal, if not more, interest to those taking Lefebvre's project seriously for developers (Becar, 2021). There are undoubtedly serious problems with the co-living model, some directly attributable to capitalism but also including those that Marxists often find most inconvenient: interpersonal disagreements and resultant concerns with security, noise and sanitation that, though underlaid with economic issues, may also derive from other sources. Allocating responsibility for these failures is not necessarily straightforward: but the developer role is evidently critical – selecting the site, managing design and construction, and eventually securing a sale or moving to operations themselves – in creating space that requires a certain kind of use to become differential. Whilst there are instances of construction failure as there are across the board, it should be recognised that development and facilities management are different real estate roles, and that the raft of negative publicity surrounding co-living in recent years has been principally a result of poor property and facilities management, exacerbated by the occupancy problems brought on by the pandemic that led to the collapse of London market pioneer The Collective, whose founder yet remains optimistic that the sector can not only survive, but will eventually flourish (Hatcher, 2022). It is moreover inevitable that not every co-living development can be expected to succeed, some do but many have not – but there are examples where participants have been able to reflect on benefits, both to them and to others, for example in the United States (Hughes, 2022).

Developer as social integrator and work facilitator – the Awid Aman Digital Nomad Community in Tenerife

Those who moved there cited the advantages of flexible tenure, catering on the premises, and meeting other digital nomads. The community claims also to have a strong environmental focus, relying on a plant-based diet, and also has access to a range of leisure activities in the neighbourhood (Figure 7.8) (Awid Aman, 2022).

Figure 7.8 Awid Awan.

Source: Hurst (2022).

This development is evidently not for the less advantaged. It is neither inexpensive nor typical of the conditions under which migrant workers and even many digital nomads are obliged to work. It is only an example of what developers can achieve, and what in some cases they are already achieving, to create the kind of living space that Lefebvre would have seen as bridging the divisive gap between public and private space that he lamented now dominated the urban landscape.

Self-build and developers

Self-build projects are another aspect of residential development where developers can assist, at least, in breaking down institutional and social barriers and help communities. The tradition of radical support for self-build as a reaction to centralised planning is exemplified by the work of John Turner (1968, 1979), who sought to demonstrate the economic and political potential of alternative models of participatory housing. Turner shared Lefebvre's enthusiasm for autogestion as an organisational route that could contribute, even solve, economic problems, and so actively supported the development of such spaces through, for example, government-sponsored loans to support individual self-builders to buy building materials from community-operated workshops. Turner also advocated the provision by planning authorities of the necessary infrastructure to support new self-build communities, such as the upgrading of community roads, water supplies, and electricity (Bower, 2016:85). Traditional Marxists rejected this approach in its entirety at the time, maintaining that any such relinquishing of collective government responsibility for the provision of social or affordable housing was simply not socialist (Burgess, 1982). Adopting a Lefebvrian perspective, however, neither compels Marxists to accept all of the intellectual antecedents in which Turner found his inspiration, nor to reject such *autogestive* solutions outright. The right way forward may well be a mix of solutions, in which developers can and should play an active part.

What might be relatively easily accepted by Marxists in a developing country context may however be more difficult to raise any enthusiasm for in developed countries, where the increasingly diverse range of approaches to self-build have thrown up a similarly diverse set of terminologies (Heffernan & Wilde, 2020:2). The organisation representing self-build in the UK has defined three routes: independent community collaboration, supported community self-build groups, and developer-led group projects to which they have attached the appellation of 'custom build' (NaCSBA, 2018). This has resulted in the existence of custom-build developers, who can have varied degrees of involvement in the project, often providing a 'menu of custom build options', ranging from only providing a serviced plot, building the home to a watertight stage, or completing the entire construction (Wilson, 2017; Sadler & Shahab, 2021:3). The market is growing, and those who would advocate that developers take Lefebvre's project seriously should also take self-build equally seriously.

Developer as community partner: custom-build in Leicestershire, UK

The Social impact investor Housing Growth Partnership (HGP) has moved into self-build by backing a site in the village of Frisby on the Wreake by Bowbridge Homes with a £2.2 million investment, bringing two-, three-, four-, and five-bedroom 48 homes to the county of Leicestershire (Figure 7.9). The site is split into 32 open market homes with an additional eight affordable and eight custom-build.

Alongside Lloyds Bank and Homes England, the social investors say that they are

> helping to address housing affordability by providing equity investment to the regional residential development community on a site specific basis to increase the number of new homes built in the UK, and we are keen to support all a variety of residential asset classes including self and custom build, an exciting part of the market currently with a lot of potential for future growth.
>
> (NACBSA, 2022).

In developed countries such as the UK, partnership by self-builders with a developer, as in this case, may be especially useful in navigating the complex planning system, which advocates of self-build in the UK anyway want reviewed in order to disrupt the housing market (NACSBSA, 2018).

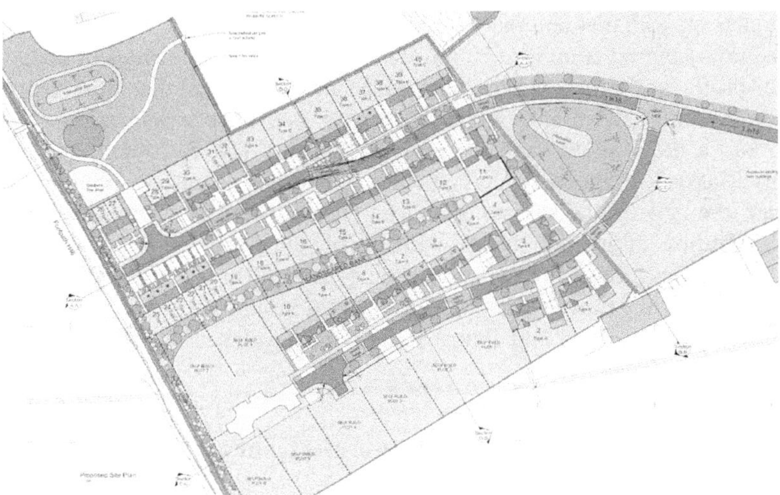

Figure 7.9 Frisby Plan.

Source: Bowbridge Homes, 2022.

Housing for seniors

Self-build may be an attractive option for some, and it certainly does fit relatively easily into a Lefebvrian approach to the creation of differential space, at least in principle. There are large groups within any community, however, that will always lack the administrative or even financial resources to participate in such initiatives. Older members of the community are some of the most obvious examples. For them, housing must be provided collectively. Developers have taken an active role in this area, for example in Australia where not-for-profits have become significant players in the creation of retirement communities, or in the United States where limited equity housing cooperatives have emerged in places across the country: in Vermont, Minnesota's Twin Cities, and the Pacific Northwest. In Los Angeles, co-op evangelist Lois Arkin gathered community donations in the early 1990s to buy and renovate a dilapidated apartment building northwest of downtown. The Los Angeles Eco-Village now includes 47 units spread across three buildings where tenants pay, at most, half the going rent in the surrounding neighborhood (Rainey, 2019).

Admittedly, Marxists are also not likely to believe that simply because an institution is not for-profit, it is inevitably part of a progressive constellation of social forces. Housing associations can behave as unhelpfully as for-profit developers on occasion. The ability for land to be put to different purposes may be inescapable, but even village groups can develop a 'property mind' (Haila, 2016, 2017:502) – essentially internalising the Marxist concept of rent, visualising land as an asset to extract rent, and to use land-based businesses to make profit. Hence, under capitalist conditions where groups may be able to extract land rent, it is what not-for-profit developers *do* with that rent that should matter.

A similar contradiction is to be found in the provision of retirement housing by not-for-profit entities. At least one eminent Marxist suggested that retirement could at least in some sense mimic socialism, at least in the sense that retirement is, or could be, 'a life without capitalist logic at its heart' (Sève, 2008:553), although equally Marxists might be concerned that the vigorous old, especially in the West, are part of a new capitalist class, who lead leisured lives at the expense of both a 'lost generation' of youth in the West and the people elsewhere in the world generally. Such reservations aside, the provision of retirement accommodation without profit is in principle exactly what Marxists should want to see – and it is happening, albeit far too infrequently and almost always in a developed country context.

Developer beyond capitalism – the case of a luxury retirement community in Sydney

Gordon Quarter by Anglicare is a boutique development of 40 upmarket over-60s apartments housed in a combination of low-rise new buildings and the heritage-listed Burnham Thorpe mansion (Figure 7.10). The building

Figure 7.10 Gordon Quarter – the Burnham Thorpe mansion.

Source: Anglicare (2023), https://www.anglicare.org.au/what-we-offer/retirement-living/villages-locations/gordon/.

was later converted into a convalescent home, and since the late 1970s, it has been part of Anglicare's Lady Gowrie Village, a retirement community that includes the Roden Cutler Lodge nursing home and several independent living units. In the redevelopment, new community facilities, including a cinema room, library, and sunroom, are located on the ground floor of the refurbished building. Outside, an oversized terrace overlooks a heated resort-style pool and landscaped grounds.

The pet-friendly community includes a hairdresser, cafe and chapel. Anglicare manages the entire development: an on-site nurse is available during the week for all residents, and at-home domestic support can also be accessed: the development includes not only residential apartments but also residential care. Most of the buyers are aged in their 70s or 80s and live within a 10-km radius. Anglicare suggested that their motivation for buying is to find 'a place to live that keeps them connected to their local community but knowing that ongoing continuing care might be needed in the not-too-distant future' (Murray, 2021).

There are certainly objections to be raised regarding the inability of most citizens, even in Australia, to be able to experience the level of luxury involved in this development. Critics have already noted that 'the broader transformation in social/public housing provision is leading non-profit developers to increasingly act through market logic and thus (wealthier) residents' ability to pay' (García-Lamarca *et al.*, 2022:7), as well as deep-rooted questions as to whether the individualistic lifestyle that it embodies could ever encompass the kind of collective freedom that Lefebvre envisaged and which poses such deep-rooted problems for old age, as a study of residential retirement complexes along Lefebvrian lines demonstrated (Petersen & Minnery, 2013). Even when well-provided with facilities, it is at best a partial and arguably divisive solution to the problem of providing old-age care. Critics suggest that 'Market mechanisms enabled these organizations to address gaps in government care' (Power & Bergan, 2019:437), with the strong implication that these gaps should not exist, that the government should take on responsibility across the whole sector.

Yet such developments by not-for-profits set the high standards by which provision for the old age of an entire population ought to be judged: there can be little doubt that the inhabitants of Gordon Quarter enjoy the right to the city. Anglicare also cross-subsidises its provision of less expensive housing for seniors from developments such as Gordon Quarter. And whatever other criticisms may be levelled against this and other such developments, they are not there because of, or for, shareholders. They constitute part of the social mission of the organisation. If Anglicare does not build more, or provide them at a lower cost, that is a function of much wider social and economic issues, for which they cannot be held responsible.

Fortunately, the role of developers in providing senior housing is however by no means in every case for the more affluent seniors, as this example from the United States demonstrates. With appropriate financial arrangements, much more egalitarian development is certainly possible.

Developer as equaliser: Roseland Place Apartments in Chicago

Roseland Place is an independent senior living facility, part of Chicago's five-year affordable housing plan for seniors (Figure 7.11). It was a built-for-purpose five-storey building with 60 one-bedroom apartments to rent for one or two people, each of approximately 50 m^2. It includes a fitness centre, catering, and laundry. The facility is restricted to for seniors 62 and older *earning 50% or below the area median income.*

Immediately to the north of Roseland Place, there is a small retail development, whilst in the east wing of the building is Chicago Satellite Senior Center, which provides services and activities for all residents of the campus and other seniors in the neighbouring community and is operated by the city (Figure 7.12). The project was developed through a partnership between

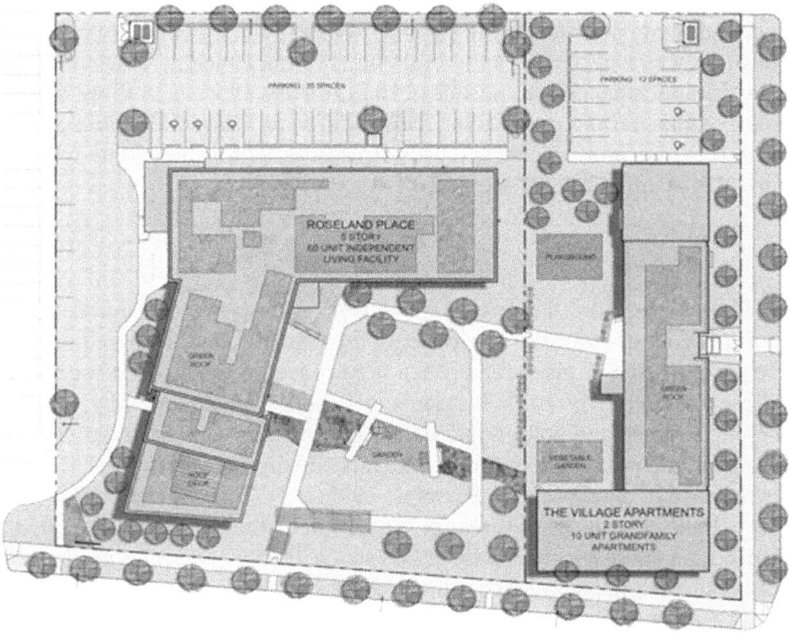

Figure 7.11 Plan of Roseland Place.

Source: LBBA (2023), https://www.lbba.com/work/roseland-place-senior-ilf/.

Figure 7.12 Roseland Place.

Source: LBBA, architects/Ballogg Photography (2023).

Neighborhood Housing Services and Mercy Housing Lakefront. Mercy Housing owns and manages the building (Illinois Housing Council, 2022). From its appearance, nothing out of the ordinary, there is nothing like the House of Generations to shout out 'this is different, this is differential space', but in this case appearances are truly deceptive, as for the people who live there, this is differential space of the first order.

Far from all, seniors however wish to live in purpose-built accommodation. There is a wealth of evidence in support of the contention that where possible, the elderly prefer to age in place rather than in purpose-built residential accommodation (Cerina *et al.*, 2017:207). No doubt it is partially explained by concepts of attachment: 'The idea of home captures much more than a physical dimension; it is a diffuse and complex condition that integrates memories and images, desires and fears, the past and the present' (Pallasmaa, 1995:133). This attachment will not disappear with the creation of differential space, albeit that less alienation may flatten the distribution curve of attachment across space, thereby allowing for the residential spaces of the elderly to be both more ambitious and balanced across the urban fabric. Ageing in place should not therefore be a political target for Marxists – Lefebvre himself was fortunate enough to do so very successfully. Rather, it is the actual conditions under which it takes place that matter and the level of support that is provided by the community which are of importance. In that regard, developers can and do play a part, providing space that empowers seniors by being on a single level, with convenient access and points of communication.

Social and affordable housing

Age-care is but one aspect of the provision of social and affordable housing, the largest and most important issue in the production of space worldwide. The ability of developers operating in a capitalist economy to provide social and affordable housing is obviously circumscribed by their funding model as well as their internal structure, organisation, and the objectives of their management. Where subsidies are available, developers in many jurisdictions have proved both willing and able to create successful communities.

The opportunities for positive change that such subsidies can create has been clearly identified, including in a developing country context, for example in South Africa. Notably, 'One key element to this approach is that the developer controls the entire value chain' (Klug, 2013:674). The company owns the land (which may have been purchased from the municipality), and has in-house planning, marketing, and construction capabilities. Secondly, the developer is also able to draw on government subsidies for low-income and social housing, even aiming at reducing the local level of homelessness. Bulk infrastructure is financed through grants from the National Treasury, enabling cross-subsidisation of the 'gap market' and 'free market' housing components. Thirdly, the developer works in partnership with the municipality, reducing risk. A co-developer agreement with the municipality enables the developer to avoid cash flow problems and to ensure infrastructure implementation and uninterrupted housing roll out (Klug, 2013:674–675). Even under present severe constraints, developers have made significant contributions in a South African context: to take Lefebvre seriously now entails examining these development models as potential positive contributions towards the future of housing provision.

Developer as equaliser: the case of Fleurhof

Fleurhof is a 440-hectare development located on the old buffer strip between Soweto and Florida near developed Johannesburg next to the existing Fleurhof residential township which, on completion, will provide housing for an estimated 83,000 people (Figure 7.13).

The first phase included around 9,000 housing units, including approximately 3,000 fully subsidised BNG housing, 3,000 'gap market' Social, FLISP, and open market rental and rent to purchase/social housing units, and 3,000 free market affordable bonded housing units. The project also included a range of facilities such as business centres, religious sites, community centres, schools, creches, and parks.

Figure 7.13 Fleurhof Views Development.

Source: Madulammoho Housing Association (2023), https://www.mh.org.za/project/fleurhof-views/.

Energy-saving solar water heaters, heat pumps, improved insulation, gas and recycling projects, and a new water reservoir have been installed. The intention was that Fleurhof would obtain electricity from the shared substation the group implemented for the Pennyville project. Importantly from a social inclusion perspective, Fleurhof Drive was intended to be the new dual carriage regional access into Soweto, linking the more affluent neighborhoods of Florida and Roodepoort in the north with the previously disadvantage neighborhoods such as Meadowlands to the south. The City of Johannesburg also planned to utilise the project as a catalyst to drive infrastructure development within the area to unlock future residential developments along Main Reef Road in Roodepoort. The project won several social housing awards in South Africa.

According to the developer, which is involved in a number of similar projects in Johannesburg, the subsidies model is highly profitable, allowing an overall 25–30% return on investment. The economic efficiencies achieved enable them voluntarily to donate community facilities such as creches, schools, and police stations as part of their corporate social investment. It also serves as a strategy to ensure a stable community, thus maintaining or even enhancing the value of the open market units (Klug *et al.*, 2013:275), although from a Marxist perspective the causal chain would be reversed: the importance of open market units is only that they help to create a stable community.

Suppose some transductive thinking along Lefebvrian lines – remove the profit motive from the developer altogether and look at the process again. Developers realise that their actions can in turn affect others. Hence in Saudi Arabia, for example, state-led provision of social housing has begun to incorporate 'designs that keep pace with modernity and move away from traditional housing such as high-density residential buildings' (Al Mulhim *et al.*, 2022:13). Certainly, social housing (including positive effect on the problem of homelessness) will become the main objective of differential development, rather than an add-on, a regulatory requirement, or a response to funding pressure. More Fleurhofs, and a somewhat different balance between social and affordable housing, including the effort to house the homeless, on the one hand, and market property on the other. But it is also necessary to ask the question, should the municipality itself continue to own (or control) the land, and retain all those capabilities – planning, construction, even marketing – in-house themselves? Or would it be a better use of resources for them to continue to be a role for developers, able to specialise and accumulate knowledge and skills, and even advise on priorities across different municipalities? And it is also important to remember – this is an area in which Lefebvre's thinking could usefully be extended – even in the absence of legacy space issues, how in the absence of market mechanisms should differential space be allocated? Removing the market should not from a Lefebvrian perspective entail either drab uniformity, in which joy and festival would always struggle to thrive, or artificial, imposed equalities taking no account of different individual, family, and community needs and achievements.

Cultural diversity in housing

We now venture to tread on more contentious, even dangerous, territory. Marxists have long recognised the extent to which capitalism can cynically harness cultural diversity to pit communities against one another. In the creation of differential space, developers must therefore be held to account for how they approach issues of cultural diversity, and in particular what efforts they make to enhance it. There is no doubt of the difficulty of the task: specific communities wish for, and are frequently in a position to demand, specific aspects of placemaking that other communities neither wish for nor find congenial. Developers must thread their way carefully through this cultural minefield. No more so than in the Middle East, where Lefebvre's antiquated observation that certain Islamic countries have made the choice to 'slow down industrialization so as to preserve their traditional homes, customs and representational spaces from the buffeting of industrial space and industrial representations of space' (Lefebvre, 1974 [1991:122]) has been replaced in many countries with rapid urbanisation and its accompanying cultural challenges and opportunities, especially in the Gulf.

Developer as cultural integrator – the case of a gated community in Qatar

Gated communities are one of the most common and well-known forms of housing developments in the Gulf region. They provide exclusive shared amenities and services, such as swimming pools, children's playgrounds, other recreational facilities, and even roads where it is safe for children to play: resort-style living which residents, though relatively affluent, could not afford otherwise, such as a swimming pool and/or a tennis court. These facilities are marketing opportunities as well as tangible benefits for gated communities in countries such as Qatar that aim at providing expatriate residents with a lifestyle within the compound that resembles, as far as possible, what they have had to leave behind. Restrictions are in place to prevent outsiders from entering, as used to be the case for private estates in London before municipalisation, although in this case the reasons cited are potentially their incongruity between residents' lifestyles and local traditions or laws. Researchers interviewing residents discovered that it was not just a question of security – Gulf countries have low levels of street crime generally – but rather the overall set of benefits that accrued as a result of residence, including, perhaps surprisingly, a sense of community and belonging, better designed urban amenities, as well as those enhanced feelings of safety and security.

The sense of community is perhaps especially surprising: in the research cited here, 80% of the respondents stressed the relatively strong relationships with their neighbours, some of whom they considered their close friends. Just as unexpected, perhaps, for those unfamiliar with the environment, the relationships that are established in gated communities improve the residents' health, especially for female residents. In the same research, 66.6% of the female respondents stated that they started exercising regularly since they have moved to gated community. Similar results were found among children, who elaborated that they have strong friendship with their neighbours as they play, exercise, and study together (El-Ekhteyar & Furlan, 2016).

An example is Al-Rayyan in Doha (Figure 7.14). Rayyan Village is composed of 383 villas in four different types: Villa A, Villa C, Villa E, and Villa R. Villa A has the most villas – 11 units. Each is 549 m^2 with an additional 115 m^2 private garden. The villa is said to be of high-quality construction, finish, and with equipment to match. Its large green areas and private gardens are maintained through advanced automatic irrigation systems. Green spaces, private gardens, and an opulent Club House with swimming pools, squash courts, tennis courts, and saunas, and even a ballet dance and aerobics studio (PrimeLands, 2022).

No doubt, gated communities have severe disadvantages, from both a practical and, of course, a radical perspective. They have represented concentrations of privilege, in particular in a developing country context. In Lefebvrian terms, they are in many respects, indeed, a triumph for abstract

Figure 7.14 Al Rayyan.

space, their gates serving to separate two worlds. In a truly differential space of tolerance and mutual respect, they would surely be unnecessary, and there is some evidence to suggest that in the Middle East at least, reforms may result in their days may be numbered. But equally, as the evidence from Qatar demonstrates, they have also served as schools of tolerance and mutual respect between communities. As a result, integration between communities has been possible within their gates that would not have been possible otherwise. So, if 'Cities at their best are cities where there is a great deal of social autonomy of social groups to do what they want, how they want to do it' (Harvey, 2020:108), then in miniature, and with many caveats, that is nonetheless what has happened within gated communities.

The deduction to be drawn is that no one development can be expected to embed all of the many dimensions of differential space, any more than none of them. They are far more likely to be internally contradictory, fields of struggle in themselves, with some aspects to admire, and others to criticise. Qatar's gated communities are a good example of just such contradictions.

Conclusions

Lefebvre may have wanted to envisage the production of space in its entirety, but the significance of residential real estate as *both* meeting one of the most fundamental human needs and acting as the most important repository of capital is dramatic. This combination should and largely does drive it to the highest possible level in political considerations at all levels, from government to the individual. Marxists must respond by continuing to display the keenest interest in 'the housing question'.

There is no doubt that, as successive generations of researchers have painstakingly elucidated, many using a Lefebvrian framework, there continue to be many urban restructuring projects worldwide that are intensifying the marginalisation, exclusion, displacement, dispowerment, and oppression of urban inhabitants, a stream of research that may now be said to be reaching a crescendo, all replete with implicit and quite justified calls for action (e.g. Mahadevia & Desai, 2019; Frank & Ristic, 2020; Rigon & Broto, 2021). What this chapter has contributed is to ask whether developers are uniformly complicit in these processes. The logic of radical urban geography portrays them as necessarily complicit, their unquenchable thirst for profit driving them to ever-greater exertions towards the production of ever more bloated abstract space, gorging capital, and largely devoid of genuine social use. As the tentative positive examples of this chapter demonstrate, the reality turns out to be more complex than traditional Marxists believed, even more than Marxist geographers have sometimes implied. Lefebvre's struggle to enlist social conservatism in the service of Marxism, for example, remains as vivid a confrontation as ever. Here and there, we find developers worldwide pushing for more affordable housing, better provision for seniors and other disadvantaged groups, acting as cultural integrators, facilitators, technological innovators, and environmental conservators. As their funding demands progressively more social impact, even those whose inclinations veer directly away from the creation of differential space and who seek satisfaction only in complying as closely as possible with the dictates of the market must be increasingly perturbed by a market that is itself evolving, twisting, and turning, embracing social as well as purely financial objectives, returns, and analytics.

The idea that developers have positive contributions to make towards overcoming capitalism may be an equally hard argument for Marxists to accept, but it is vitally necessary if the production of residential real estate is to be included, now and for the foreseeable future, in the political struggles that Marxists can and must wage for the transformation of capitalism. The examples provided in this chapter show that developers have in fact in some cases taken the lead in creating the kind of varied, attractive, sympathetic living space that, in the absence of financial and density constraints, people choose to live – and where all people deserve to live. In Lefebvre's terminology, developers can themselves produce residential differential space. Those seeking to ensure that developers take Lefebvre seriously must strive to ensure that they do.

Bibliography

14Trees. (2023). *Mvule Gardens, the heart of your most treasured memories*. Available at: https://mvulegardens.com/. [Accessed 10 January 2023].

Aalbers, M. B. (2019). Financialization. In *American Association of Geographers, International Encyclopedia of Geography: People, the Earth, Environment and Technology*. Chichester, Wiley, 1–11.

Al Mulhim, K. A. M., Swapan, M. S. H. and Khan, S. (2022). Critical junctures in sustainable social housing policy development in Saudi Arabia: A review. *Sustainability*, 14(5), 2979.

Awid-Aman. (2022). *Slow-living community looking for change-makers*. Available at: www.awidaman-nomadcommunity.com/. [Accessed 30 September 2022].

Becar. (2021). *The global coliving market grows at 30% a year*, 22 June. Available at: https://becar.pro/en/news/?news_id=2048. [Accessed 30 September 2022].

Bennett, J. and Dixon, M. (2006). *Single person households and social policy: Looking forwards*. New York, Joseph Rowntree Foundation.

Benton, J. S., Anderson, J., Hunter, R. F. and French, D. P. (2016). The effect of changing the built environment on physical activity: A quantitative review of the risk of bias in natural experiments. *International journal of Behavioral Nutrition and Physical Activity*, 13(1), 1–18.

Berkeley Group. (2014). *Living in tall buildings*. 2nd edition. Available at: www.berkeleygroup.co.uk/-/media/migration/berkeley-group/about-us/sustainability/communities-and-sustainable-living/berkeley-group-report-living-in-tall-buidlings.ashx?rev=5cb55d3cc95b4e60881c49f0e9e94f8d&hash=DB85A244AF72FB43772D3AEA253D1217. [Accessed 3 September 2022].

———. (2023). *South quay plaza*. Available at: www.berkeleygroup.co.uk/developments/london/canary-wharf/south-quay-plaza. [Accessed 30 September 2022].

———. (2023a). *Correspondence Regarding South Quay Plaza*, 3 February.

Beunen, R., Meijer, M. and De Vries, J. (2020). Planning strategies for dealing with population decline: Experiences from the Netherlands. *Land Use Policy*, 93, 104107.

Blythe, C. (2017). Nationalise the housing market: A radical proposal for an extraordinary crisis. *Construction Research and Innovation*, 8(4), 96–101.

Bower, R. (2016). Who decides and who provides? The anarchistic housing practices of John Turner as realizations of Henri Lefebvre's Autogestive space. *Alternatives*, 41(2), 83–97.

Branson, A. (2020). Is multi-generational living the future of housing? *Modus*, 1 March. Available at: https://ww3.rics.org/uk/en/modus/built-environment/homes-and-communities/all-together-now – mult-igenerational-living.html.

Brenner, N., Marcuse, P. and Mayer, M. (2012). Cities for people, not for profit: An introduction. In Brenner, N. *et al.* (eds.) *Cities for people, not for profit*. Abingdon and New York, Routledge, 1–10.

Buckley, R. M., Kallergis, A. and Wainer, L. (2016). The emergence of large-scale housing programs: Beyond a public finance perspective. *Habitat International*, 54, 199–209.

Buletin Mutiara. (2021). *Penang steps up fiberisation plan*, June 25. Available at: www.buletinmutiara.com/penang-steps-up-fiberisation-plan/. [Accessed 7 September 2022].

Burgess, R. (1982). Self-help housing advocacy: A curious form of radicalism. A critique of the work of John F C Turner. In Ward, P. (ed.) *Self-help Housing: A Critique*. London, Mansell.

Butler, C. (2012). *Henri Lefebvre: Spatial Politics, Everyday Life and the Right to the City*. Abingdon, Routledge.

CBRE. (2020). *High demand, bright future. The rise of co-living*. Available at: www.cbre.us/-/media/cbre/countryunitedstates/media/images/multifamily/innovation-watch/co-living/021420_innovationwatch_january-2020-fw.pdf. [Accessed 6 November 2022].

Cerina, V., Fornara, F. and Manca, S. (2017). Architectural style and green spaces predict older adults' evaluations of residential facilities. *European Journal of Ageing*, 14(3), 207–217.

Cho, G. and Kim, J. (2019). Shared housing as a potential resource for community building. *Cities*, 87, 30–38.

Collins, J. (2021). *Rent*. Cambridge, Polity Press.

Day, K. (2023). Social climbing: How developers can help build equality. Modus, 13 January. Available at: https://ww3.rics.org/uk/en/modus/business-and-skills/ethics/developers-social-equality.html. [Accessed 5 February 2023].

Decker, N. (2021). *Strategies to lower cost and speed housing production: A case study of San Francisco's 833 Bryant street project*. Available at: https://ternercenter.berkeley.edu/research-and-policy/833-bryant-street-sf/. [Accessed 10 October 2022].

Dos Santos, M. A. (2022). *Última família deixa a Favela Marte, em Rio Preto, para início da urbanização*, 6 August 2022. Available at: www.diariodaregiao.com.br/cidades/riopreto/ultima-familia-deixa-a-favela-marte-em-rio-preto-para-inicio-da-urbanizac-o-1.992733. [Accessed 15 September 2022].

Dove, C. (2020). *Radical Housing: Designing Multi-Generational and Co-living Housing for All*. London, RIBA Publications.

Eco World Development Group. (2023). *Correspondence regarding Regent Garden*. Eco-Grandeur 9 February 2023.

Edge Buildings. (2023). *Mvule gardens by 14Trees*. Available at: https://edgebuildings.com/project-studies/mvule-gardens-by-14-trees/. [Accessed 10 January 2023].

El-Ekhteyar, El-S. and Furlan, R. (2016). Sense of community in gated communities in Doha: The case of Al-Ein compound in Ein Khaled neighborhood. *American Journal of Sociological Research*, 6(5), 126–134.

Frank, S. and Ristic, M. (2020). Urban Fallism: Monuments, iconoclasm and activism. *City*, 24(3–4), 552–564.

Freitas, C. F. S. (2017). Undoing the right to the city: World Cup investments and informal settlements in Fortaleza, Brazil. *Journal of Urban Affairs*, 39(7), 953–969.

Frich, J., Mose Biskjaer, M., Remy, C., MacDonald Vermulen, L. and Dalsgaard, P. (2021). User research and design creativity: Three insights for future-studies. *Behaviour & Information Technology*, 40(5), 464–475.

Gabor, D. and Kohl, S. (2022). *The Financialization of Housing in Europe: My Home is an Asset Class*. Greens/EFA. Available at: https://pure.mpg.de/rest/items/item_3364652/component/file_3364653/content. [Accessed 7 January 2023].

García-Lamarca, M., Anguelovski, I., Cole, H. V., Connolly, J. J., Pérez-del-Pulgar, C., Shokry, G. and Triguero-Mas, M. (2022). Urban green grabbing: Residential real estate developers discourse and practice in gentrifying Global North neighborhoods. *Geoforum*, 128, 1–10.

Gifford, R. (2007). The consequences of living in high-rise buildings. *Architectural Science Review*, 50(1), 2–17.

Godwill, I. T., Owei, O. B. and Brown, I. (2021). An analysis of existing housing stock in selected neighbourhoods in Port Harcourt municipality. *European Journal of Environment and Earth Sciences*, 2(3), 57–61.

Guy, S. and Henneberry, J. (2000). Understanding urban development processes: Integrating the economic and the social in property research. *Urban Studies*, 37(13), 2399–2416.

Habitat for Humanity. (2021). *Building Houses that are affordable, sustainable and resilient to climate change*, 13 October. Available at: https://habitat.org.au/building-houses-for-apac/. [Accessed 3 March 2022].

———. (2022). *Habitat and TIST join forces to help Tonga rebuild after disaster*, 10 August. Available at: https://habitat.org.nz/habitat-and-tist-join-forces-to-provide-education-and-hands-on-experience-to-help-tonga-rebuild/. [Accessed 5 March 2022].

Haila, A. (2016). *Urban Land Rent. Singapore as a Property State*. Oxford, Blackwell.

———. (2017). Institutionalization of 'the property mind'. *International Journal of Urban and Regional Research*, 41(3), 500–507.

Harvey, D. (2012). *Rebel Cities: From the Right to the City to the Urban Revolution*. London, Verso Books.

———. (2020). *The Anti-Capitalist Chronicles*. London, Pluto.

Hatcher, D. (2022). Reza Merchant on his return to the market, The Collective's collapse and the future of co-living. *React News*, 24 October. Available at: https://reactnews.com/article/reza-merchant-on-his-return-to-the-market-the-collectives-collapse-and-the-future-of-co-living/ [Accessed 3 November 2022].

Healey, P. (1992). An institutional model of the development process. *Journal of Property Research*, 9, 33–44.

Heffernan, E. and Wilde, P. (2020). Group self-build housing: A bottom-up approach to environmentally and socially sustainable housing. *Journal of Cleaner Production*, 243, 118657.

Hughes, C. J. (2022). As housing costs soar, co-living makes a comeback. *New York Times*, 2 November. Available at: www.nytimes.com/2022/11/02/business/coliving-housing-dorms.html. [Accessed 4 November 2023].

Hurst, L. (2022). *Co-living takes off in Europe amid remote work boom and cost of living crisis*, 8 September. Available at: www.euronews.com/next/2022/09/08/co-living-takes-off-in-europe-amid-remote-work-boom-and-cost-of-living-crisis. [Accessed 8 November 2023].

Ibler, M. (2021). *The house of generations: A new housing experiment in the welfare state's Denmark*, 11 October. Available at: https://ilgiornaledellarchitettura.com/2021/10/11/the-house-of-generations-a-new-housing-experiment-in-the-welfare-states-denmark/ [Accessed 12 December 2021].

Illinois Housing Council. (2022). *Roseland place senior apartments*. Available at: https://ilhousing.org/roseland-place-senior-apartments/. [Accessed 4 September 2022].

International Finance Corporation. (2015). *Affordable housing in Africa*. Available at: www.ifc.org/wps/wcm/connect/news_ext_content/ifc_external_corporate_site/news+and+events/news/trp_featurestory_africahousing. [Accessed 2 August 2022].

Jensen, B. G. (2017). *House of generations*. Paper presented at AMPS Conference: Health: The Design, Planning and Politics of How and Where We Live. University of the West of England. 25–26 January. Available at: http://architecturemps.com/bristol-2018/. [Accessed 4 August 2022].

Kholid, M. F., Zaharin, P. M. B., Kasmuri, K. and Zahari, Y. R. (2021). 'Working from Home'–Recent development trends in terraced housing design in a new suburban township in Malaysia. *Environment-Behaviour Proceedings Journal*, 6(16), 261–272.

Klug, N., Rubin, M. and Todes, A. (2013). Inclusionary housing policy: A tool for re-shaping South Africa's spatial legacy? *Journal of Housing and the Built Environment*, 28(4), 667–678.

Lefebvre, H. (1974 [1991]). *La production de l'espace*. Paris, Anthropos. Translated by D. Nicholson-Smith as *The Production of Space*. Oxford, Blackwell.

———. (1979 [2009]). Comments on a new state form. In Elden, S. and Brenner, N. (eds.) *State, Space, World: Selected Essays*. Translated by G. Moore. Minneapolis, University of Minnesota Press, 124–137.

———. (1990). Du pacte social au contrat du citoyenneté. In Lefebvre, H. and Le Groupe de Navarrenx (eds.) *Du contrat de citoyenneté*. Paris, Editions Syllepse, 15–42.

Löwgren, J. and Stolterman, E. (2004). *Thoughtful Interaction Design: A Design Perspective on Information Technology*. Cambridge, MA, MIT Press.

Mahadevia, D. and Desai, R. (2019). Everyday violence in urban India: Is planning the driver or mitigator? In Salahub, J. *et al.* (eds.) *Reducing Urban Violence in the Global South*. London, Routledge, 177–199.

Mari, G. (2021). Brazil's Gerando Falcões aims to eradicate poverty with smart slums. *Forbes*, 6 January. Available at: www.forbes.com/sites/angelicamarideoliveira/2021/01/06/brazils-gerando-falces-aims-to-eradicate-misery-with-smart-slums/?sh=27148b32c7b3. [Accessed 3 October 2022].

Masterson, V. (2022). What has caused the global housing crisis – and how can we fix it? *World Economic Forum*. Available at: www.weforum.org/agenda/2022/06/how-to-fix-global-housing-crisis/. [Accessed 3 January 2023].

Mercy Housing. (2023). *Affordable housing development*. Available at: www.mercyhousing.org/partner-with-us/housing-development/. [Accessed 5 February 2023].

Merrifield, A. (2006). *Henri Lefebvre: A Critical Introduction*. London, Taylor & Francis.

Min, L. L. and Ngo, K. (2019). Potential impact of sharing economy on Singapore's hospitality industry. *UOB Group*, December. Available at: www.uobgroup.com/web-resources/industry-insights/pdf/real-estate-hospitality/potential-impact-of-sharing-economy.pdf?adobe_mc=MCMID%3D58807668847636526022661862915996130797%7CMCORGID%3D116168F454E6DA2A0A4C98A6%2540AdobeOrg%7CTS%3D1609200000. [Accessed 3 October 2022].

Moore, E. A. (2019). Addressing housing deficit in Nigeria: Issues, challenges and prospects. *Economic and Financial Review*, 57(4), 15.

Mouratidis, K. (2019). Compact city, urban sprawl, and subjective well-being. *Cities*, 92, 261–272.

Murray, E. (2021). *Gordon quarter: The mansion-turned-retirement dream home*, 30 July. Available at: www.domain.com.au/news/gordon-quarter-the-mansion-turned-retirement-dream-home-1073964/ [Accessed 21 October 2022].

Nansen, B., Arnold, M., Gibbs, M. and Davis, H. (2010). Time, space and technology in the working-home: An unsettled nexus. *New Technology, Work and Employment*, 25(2), 136–153.

National Custom and Self-Build Association. (2018). *NACSBA research highlights unequal picture of right to build registers in England*, 30 October. Available at: https://nacsba.org.uk/news/nacsba-maps-of-right-to-build-registers/. [Accessed 30 November 2022].

———. (2022). *Housing growth partnership unlocks Leicestershire site, including eight custom build plots*. Available at: https://nacsba.org.uk/news/hgp-unlocks-custom-builds/. [Accessed 30 November 2022].

Nkurunziza, E. (2007). Informal mechanisms for accessing and securing urban land rights: The case of Kampala, Uganda. *Environment and Urbanization*, 19(2), 509–526.

Pallasmaa, J. (1995). Identity, intimacy and domicile – notes on the phenomenology of home. In Benjamin, N. D. (ed.) *The Home; Words, Interpretations, Meanings and Environments*. Farnham, Ashgate, 131–147.

Pawson, H., Milligan, V. and Yates, J. (2020). Housing policy in Australia: A reform agenda. In Pawson, H., Milligan, V. and Yates, J. (eds.) *Housing Policy in Australia: A Case for System Reform*. Singapore, Springer, 339–358.

Petersen, M. and Minnery, J. (2013). Understanding daily life of older people in a residential complex: The contribution of Lefebvre's social space. *Housing Studies*, 28(6), 822–844.

Power, E. R. and Bergan, T. L. (2019). Care and resistance to neoliberal reform in social housing. *Housing, Theory and Society*, 36(4), 426–447.

PrimeLands. (2022). *Al-Rayyan village*. Available at: https://primelands.qa/alrayyan.html. [Accessed 3 November 2022].

Purcell, M. (2003). Citizenship and the right to the global city: Reimagining the capitalist world order. *International Journal of Urban and Regional Research*, 27(3), 564–590.

Rainey, J. (2019). Burrowing beneath the bottom line. *Providence Journal*, 3 November. Available at: www.providencejournal.com/story/business/real-estate/2019/11/03/in-rapacious-bay-area-market-they-get-beneath-bottom-line/2380618007/. [Accessed 4 September 2022].

Reckford, J. T. (2007). *Creating a Habitat for Humanity: No Hands but Yours*. Minneapolis, Fortress Press.

———. (2022). 3 ways to reinvent affordable housing in a post-pandemic world. *World Economic Forum*, 20 January. Retrieved from www.weforum.org/agenda/2022/01/reinvent-affordable-housing-post-covid19-world-habitat-for-humanity. [Accessed 6 January 2023].

Rigon, A. and Broto, V. C. (2021). *Inclusive Urban Development in the Global South: Intersectionality, Inequalities, and Community*. New York and London, Routledge.

Rum Architects. (2023). *The house of generations. Building diversity and connection*. Available at: www.rum.as/projekter/english-project-2. [Accessed 6 July 2021].

Sadler, G. and Shahab, S. (2021). Self-build and custom housebuilding registers in England: A transaction-cost and effectiveness analysis. *Sustainability*, 13(9), 4912.

Sengupta, U. (2019). State-led housing development in Brazil and India: A machinery for enabling strategy? *International Journal of Housing Policy*, 19(4), 509–535.

Sève, L. (2008). *L'Homme. Penser avec Marx aujourd'hui*. Volume 2. Paris, Editions La Dispute.

Speer, J. (2015). Henri Lefebvre: Spatial politics, everyday life and the right to the city. Book review. *The AAG Review of Books*, 3(1), 4–5.

Standard and Poors. (2019). *ESG industry report card: Real estate and homebuilders/developers*, 3 June. Available at: www.spglobal.com/ratings/en/research/pdf-articles/190603-esg-industry-report-card-real-estate-and-homebuilders-developers. [Accessed 8 November 2021].

St. Antoine, T. J. (2007). Making heaven out of hell: New Urbanism and the refutation of suburban spaces. *Southern Communication Journal*, 72(2), 127–144.

Stone, M. E. (1978). Housing, mortgage lending and the contradictions of capitalism. In Tabb, W. K. and Sawers, L. (eds.) *Marxism and the Metropolis. New Perspectives in Urban Political Economy*. New York, Oxford University Press, 179–207.

Sudjic, D. (1992). *The 100 mile city*. Boston, Mariner Books.

Turner, J. C. (1968). Housing priorities, settlement patterns, and urban development in modernizing countries. *Journal of the American Institute of Planners*, 34(6), 354–363.

Turner, J. F. (1979). Housing in three dimensions: Terms of reference for the housing question redefined. In Bromley, R. (ed.) *The Urban Informal Sector*. Oxford, Pergamon, 1135–1145.

United Nations. (2021). *Urban regeneration as a tool for inclusive and sustainable recovery*. Available at: https://unhabitat.org/sites/default/files/2022/05/report_egm_urban_regeneration.pdf. [Accessed 6 October 2022].

urbanNext. (2022). *Mapleton crescent SW18: A distinctive tower*. Available at: https://urbannext.net/mapleton-crescent/. [Accessed 10 September 2022].

US Department of Housing and Urban Development. (2006). *Glossary of terms to affordable housing*. Available at: https://archives.hud.gov/local/nv/goodstories/2006-04-06glos.cfm. [Accessed 2 November 2022].

Vision Systems. (2017). *Press release*, August. Available at: https://tideconstruction.co.uk/wp-content/uploads/2017/08/NEWS-Press-Release-170727-For-website-Modules-arrive-onsite-at-Mapleton-press-release-draft-CMCA-FD-edits-1.pdf. [Accessed 4 August 2022].

Vissing, Y., Nilan, D. and Hudson, C. (2019). *Changing the Paradigm of Homelessness*. London, Routledge.

Wapshott, R. and Mallett, O. (2012). The spatial implications of homeworking: A Lefebvrian approach to the rewards and challenges of home-based work. *Organization*, 19(1), 63–79.

Ward, C., Van Loon, J. and Wijburg, G. (2019). Neoliberal Europeanisation, Variegated Financialisation: Common but divergent economic trajectories in the Netherlands, United Kingdom and Germany. *Tijdschrift voor economische en sociale geografie*, 110(2), 123–137.

Wilson, W. (2017). *Self-build and Custom Build Housing (England)*. London, House of Commons Library.

Wu, F., Chen, J., Pan, F., Gallent, N. and Zhang, F. (2020). Assetization: The Chinese path to housing financialization. *Annals of the American Association of Geographers*, 110(5), 1483–1499.

8 Swings and roundabouts

Commercial real estate

Introduction

In an attempt to place Lefebvre's insights into the production of space alongside commercial real estate of any kind, let alone to try to provide precepts for real estate developers of commercial real estate, a preliminary question must surely be posted – whether the relationship can ever be anything other than confrontational and hostile. References to commercial real estate in Lefebvre's writings are after all scarcely complementary:

> In the heart of Paris, the tenants of buildings that are very livable despite the absence of so-called 'modern' comfort, are being reproached by competent and well-established people for not paying the 'location rent' because their rents remain low! This justifies, it seems, the destruction of these buildings and their replacement by offices or by high-rent housing.
>
> (Lefebvre, 2000:90)

It does not seem to matter as much to Lefebvre here whether the replacements are residential or commercial: the objection is to the HBU principle, and standing behind that, it would seem, a complaint against change wrought by economies of scale or even non-economic factors. To all of these, the creation of differential space appears to pose a challenge, albeit asymmetrically and not conclusively, and to the subservience of real estate development to the demands of capital. Elsewhere, Lefebvre seems implicitly to suggest that the creation of commercial space specifically has already become excessive, bound up as it had already become – at least and perhaps especially in the French context – with the controlling influence of the State:

> Enormous commercial centers are presently forming, containing service annexes of all varieties and producing a new conception and practice of space; in reality, these new commercial centers are not isolated, but form networks.
>
> (Lefebvre, 1970 [2009:176])

It was always thus, Lefebvre says, painting gigantic modern factories and palaces with the same critical brush (Lefebvre, 1947 [2014:170]). This in turn has led

DOI: 10.1201/9781003220244-8

to Lefebvre's description of the Mediterranean in a particularly noteworthy turn of phrase as 'a nearly *overindustrialized* space' (Lefebvre, 1979 [2009:192], my emphasis). As a reader of Lefebvre would no doubt have come to expect, nowhere is it explained what this term might mean, except perhaps a pointer towards Lefebvre's familiar refrain of the supersession of the industrial by the urban. Of one thing we can be assured: Lefebvre is repelled by the commercial space of capitalism both politically and aesthetically. Politically:

> Constructed space – a transparency of metal and glass – tells aloud of the will to power and all its tricky. It is hardly necessary to add that the 'habitat' too shares in this spatial distribution of domination.
>
> (Lefebvre, 1973 [1976:88])

Aesthetically:

> One must go back towards the centre of Paris to find again, amidst the offices, a little of the beauty and charm that reaches us from other eras.
>
> (Lefebvre, 1947 [2014:53)

The real estate economy, now even more confident, familiar, and all-embracing than in Lefebvre's own time, serves to bring into stark relief, for radical geographers in particular, the problem of the concentration of value in assets that do not contribute in their view to social needs. Or at least, resources that could have been better deployed elsewhere, if meeting social needs were the objective behind their use. Even those experienced real estate commentators recognised in the fact that developers have responded to the demands of markets and created a range of commercial assets – industrial, retail, and offices, those 'Towers of Capital' (Lizieri, 2009) – the objects of Lefebvre's special critical gaze.

In seeking a fundamentally *political* response, radical geographers seeking to co-opt Lefebvre have latched onto 'temporary urbanism' as a counterweight. The movement – which has been growing – has been led by what really might be described as a group of key decision-makers with potentially very different interests, including landowners, local authorities, *and developers* (Andres *et al.*, 2021, my emphasis). Temporary spaces themselves have in fact often been created by real estate developers, at least in part, as in Zurich, for example, it has been suggested that some property owners terminate rent contracts even though they do not already have a building permit or know the date on which they can start reconstructing. The result is that when leases expire, without building permits having yet been issued, there is sometimes a period between dismissal and demolition and then renovation emerges. In this void period, temporary use suddenly becomes potentially profitable. A firm in Zurich, for example, is claimed to have taken advantage of this commercial opportunity, bringing together organisations and people with a wide range of expertise such as technical skills in real-estate management, a good network in Zurich's creative scene, and legal knowledge about local and national regulations regarding temporary use (Debrunner & Gerber, 2021:102998). No doubt that even under these conditions,

> the short-term interests of the property owners and the for-profit mediators get the upper hand over the long-term and stable housing needs of low-income households.
>
> (Debrunner & Gerber, 2021:102998)

This is where the implicit logic of the argument leads, that the political action of Marxists (and others) should be focused on this issue, as it potentially leads to precarious living situations for lower income groups.

But there must surely be more to be said about the relationship between Lefebvre's concept of differential space and commercial real estate than this? Temporary commercial occupation might be acceptable, but unless it be otherwise, residential real estate must always be preferred to commercial, which is incapable of escaping its origins in exchange value and therefore irretrievably destined to remain abstract space, obstinately refusing any attempt to make it behave otherwise. Is this always so? Arguably, at least, no, and for two principal reasons.

Firstly, there are some global dimensions to commercial real estate that have been transformed since Lefebvre wrote, albeit that he anticipated them in principle. Marxist geographers have engaged with the rapid development of commercial property globally, especially in China (de Jong, 2019; Meng & Wu, 2020), but the geopolitical reality has often remained in the shadows. Yet as the global economy has increasingly reflected the dominance of the urban, as Lefebvre both explained and predicted, so the distribution of real estate investment wealth as soft power has altered the global balance of power. In plain words, commercial real estate development in cities such as Shanghai and Dubai – with all their immense social disadvantages in terms of diverting resources away from social needs – has played an undeniable role in creating both a less equal *national* distribution of wealth and power and a more multipolar *global* one, when such new developments are contrasted with traditional real estate reservoirs of capital in the developed countries of the West. This unwelcome method of the global redistribution of power would no doubt have been another painful truth for Lefebvre to add to his honest recognition at the time that if capitalist social relations had not changed, at least part of the explanation had to lie with the tacit complicity of the working class (Lefebvre, 1973 [1976:37]).

Secondly, confronted by this onslaught of what might well appear to them as misplaced, not to add Eurocentric, critical nostalgia, and especially if alighting then on a passage where the observation is made that 'In capitalist society, the space of work consists of production units: businesses, farms, offices' (Lefebvre, 1974 [1991:191]), a real estate developer may then confess themselves not a little bemused, and seek answers to questions of the following sort. In this future society that Lefebvre sketches after capitalism has been superseded, replete with differential space, in which he argues so many Marxist hopes should be founded, what space will there be aside from residential dwellings, leisure and infrastructure? Suppose a world of *autogestion*, and not just for real estate developers themselves, but for all enterprises where it is possible, where 'businesses' will lose their will to profit and serve a wider purpose, and that the collapse of the State, whether gradual or swift, will reduce the need for bureaucracy. Will there not still be a need for *some* kind of office space for the needs of the many organisations that the world after capitalism has been superseded will still require? Production and distribution, too, will still be necessary, as eight billion or more people will still need to be fed, clothed, and supplied with a wide range of goods and services, perhaps even wider than under capitalism in many cases, and certainly different – so there will still need to be factories and warehouses. If in the not-too-distant past it could plausibly be said that 'Foremost among the nonplaces of "supermodernity" and universalizing uniformity is the shopping mall, which is the predominant structure and function of our times' (Coleman, 2013:255), its replacements too will have to be developed – less gaudy, less focused on sales and marketing, for sure, but in turn more directed at meeting practical daily requirements of the active citizen of such a society, and therefore arguably on a global scale more comprehensive. Even after capitalism has been superseded, and granted the enormous effect of the internet on the scope of real estate – including the impact of virtual real estate, leading to the claim that 'the mainstream real estate market is moving towards virtuality' (Soules, 2021:199) – some physical retail real estate will therefore also be required, and the pressures under which it currently operates cannot expect to evaporate with the profit motive. Moreover, a real estate developer may well be tempted to argue, a little provocatively it must be said, any move away from capitalism may well generate not only the need and impetus for a vast amount of residential construction, but also a commensurate requirement for much more 'other' real estate – we should no longer call it commercial, after all, and the distinction between public and private sector real estate will have disappeared. On balance, the prospect of a future society after the supersession of capitalism may lead the commercial real estate developer to feel modestly encouraged about the prospects for their industry, despite the fact that the prospects of deriving profit from the production of space will have evaporated. As Lefebvre himself recognised, outdated spaces are subject to detournement, finding surprising new uses (Lefebvre, 1974 [1991:167]), a process that may be expected to accelerate, rather than slow, once the blocking forces of capitalism are removed.

If so, then it would be imprudent to fail to learn from history, to neglect the experience of commercial development under capitalism. Rather, its most successful elements, those that either are differential in themselves, or at least contain elements of differential space, should be contrasted with its evident excesses and failures, in order to engage in some utopian thinking about Lefebvrian lines: What are some of the positive features of capitalist commercial real estate development that we should want to carry forward into a future beyond capitalism?

Examining individual developments

The three 'moments' expressed within Lefebvre's theory of the production of space – spatial practice, representations of space, and spaces of representation

(Lefebvre, 1974 [1991:33]) – invite the possibility of examining individual developments with each of these concepts of space in turn, notwithstanding their inevitable overlap and other potential difficulties of separating them from each other. One such approach was a study of social equity in a mixed-use development in the United States (Howard, 2008), in which, however, Lefebvre's sequence was inverted, so that spatial practices appeared as the consequence of, first, representations of space, that is, the plans for the development, and second, representational space, the involvement of citizens in the planning and development process. Both triads should no doubt be understood dialectically, each reacting upon the other, but in placing spatial practices first, Lefebvre was one suspects less optimistic about the rationality of development; he envisioned spatial practices as principally those of dominant agents (principally those of capital) and representations of space as similarly largely flowing from those practices and therefore mainly in the interests of the dominant agents of spatial practice. For Lefebvre, it is between representations of space and representational space where the crucial, and possibly revolutionary, step is taken.

Another study of the redevelopment of Hallonbergen in Sweden suggested that what had been produced as abstract space is disguised as differential space (Berg, 2022:182). But because capitalism is not perfect in its ability to control space, induced spatial differentiation can work both ways: what appears abstract can in fact be differential, just as the other way round – though it is worth saying, probably more rarely. Only in a world in which the creation of differential, rather than abstract, space is the norm could therefore Howard's inverted sequence be expected to occur on a frequent basis.

A similar approach was taken in an evaluation of the redevelopment of Cork Docklands using the alternative triad:

> Conceived' space is planned space, the space of planners and architects, the more or less physical or Cartesian space. 'Perceived' space is the ideological or symbolic meanings attached to space. The ways in which 'Conceived' and 'Perceived' space combine then produces [my emphasis] 'Lived' space, space as we all experience it through everyday life.
>
> (O'Callaghan, 2007:14)

There are examples worldwide of the way developers conceive, perceive, and then produce space that is not inimical to the values Lefebvre cherished. Sometimes, even, development outcomes are surprising in the way in which they remedy wrongs and even out inequalities.

Developer as facilitator of the ludic city

In China, for less expensive residential parks, having in place some secluded dancing areas in parks and public green spaces, very much in line with Lefebvre's concept of collective, free, enjoyment, is actually a government mandate. Developers responded to the issue in. 'People need a place to do squaredancing . . . and sometimes we add pavilions and roofed corridors so that they can dance on rainy days'. There is no equivalent requirement for more expensive residential parks, as it was commented that 'If we brag about having dancing areas in our (high-end) parks we'd never be able to sell any house', so it was never done. If residents of the more expensive residential estates want active recreation, they go, or are expected to go, to the park's club. There people can swim, do body-building exercises, and of course, square-dance, allegedly without putting other residents to inconvenience. As for the parks themselves, in these more expensive versions, the entire public space is covered in green in order to prevent people from using it for dancing. But residential clubs charge users membership fees, which may pose a problem of access, for example, for elderly people who live there but either cannot, or do not wish, to afford these fees. They are forced to walk some distance in order to dance (Zhang, 2018:252–4).

The disparity is an interesting example of the way in which private affluence can bring about a diminution of communal benefits, perhaps even reducing peoples' enjoyment overall. Lefebvre would certainly not be surprised, even by the fact that, under capitalism in particular – but perhaps not necessarily, even after it has been superseded, though surely to a much lesser extent – people make choices in favour of the shiny and the new above the functional and the old. The differential developer will be alert to these potential disparities, and on the broad principle of 'do no harm', seek even at the expense of financial return to avoid reducing the quality of life of residents of new estates by comparison to old, and even, as in this case, of more expensive by comparison to less expensive developments, rare as this may be.

Mixed-use developments

One aspect of real estate development that might be held to hold at least the potential of generating differential space is mixed use, albeit that it is a conceptually challenging term, even as the 20th century drew to a close, already said to be 'in danger of becoming an overworked phrase' (Wang, 1996:312), and now encompassing increasing wide multifunctionality, for example, museums, observatories, clinics, and schools (Generalova & Generalov, 2020:4). The social benefits of mixed use have been discussed and recognised by theorists and researchers. These range from those originally identified by Jacobs (1961) that mixed-use development patterns potentially increase pedestrian activity and social interaction, with its attendant health benefits as well as familiar arguments revolving around reductions in automobile dependency, reductions in per capita energy consumption, and lower carbon emissions, to more recent arguments that it can make a contribution to social diversity, at least insofar as mixed-use patterns potentially bring individuals with social, cultural, and demographic differences together and help them become accustomed to, and accept, social and cultural differences (Wickersham, 2000).

Mixed-use development patterns may also promote informal social control of crime (Browning *et al*., 2010), although this has been much debated, along with the claim over many decades that mixed-use planning strategies create synergistic economic benefits, particularly with respect to employment opportunities for a wide range of age groups projected as living within walkable distances to job sites, and that they reduce the elderly and youth's dependence on automobile ownership, ultimately reducing commuting costs (Litman & Colman, 2001). In developed countries, further claims have been made that mixed-use development encourages a greater range of housing market options beyond detached single-family homes, promoting diverse housing types with, perhaps, the potential to increase affordability and equity (Grant, 2002), as 'In most cases, the mixed-use quality evokes different types of land uses which are directly connected with the human needs and ensure active sharing within different stakeholders' (Khan & Tisa, 2019:388), but all now weighed against suggestions that the consequences of mixed-use developments for actual carbon usage are actually rather ambiguous (Zagow, 2020; Li *et al*., 2022). 'Mixed use is not an unquestionable spatial virtue that would solve social problems. To propose so would be physical determinism. Mixed use may have great benefits, but they are not all easy to prove' (Hirt, 2016:145).

On balance probably positive, then, and requiring development to replace much segregated and single-zoned real estate of the past, but complex, requiring expertise and experience to create successfully. It is therefore welcome that, in many cases, it has been developers themselves who have taken the lead to create mixed-use developments that have drawn in local institutions and communities. Without them, the entire initiative would simply never have happened.

Transit-oriented development (TOD)

Another requirement for redevelopment, TOD has been held to assist gentrification and accentuate spatial discrimination, for example a critical analysis of the Culture Casbah of the Swedish city of Rosengård querying whether it could achieve any of the broad range of local and regional objectives for which TOD has been advocated – improving mobility, expanding ridership, attracting investment, reducing urban poverty, improving quality of life, making affordable housing, and fostering urban integration (Derakhti & Baeten, 2020:1). In specific cases, such criticism may be justified: but it is equally so that individual examples of TOD may indeed achieve one or more of these objectives, and where that is the case, those taking Lefebvre seriously for developers might be cautiously supportive of what has been achieved.

Developer as care provider: Mercy Care in Chamblee, Georgia

Mercy Park is a transit-oriented development located near a Metropolitan Atlanta Rapid Transit Authority station, the Chamblee Rail Trail, and historic downtown Chamblee (Figure 8.1).

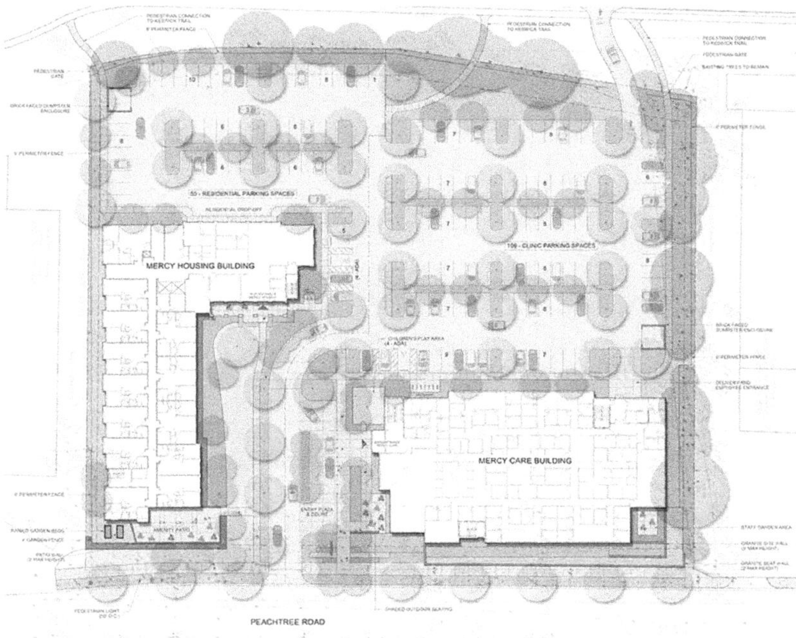

Figure 8.1 Mercy Park Plan.

Source: LBBA, https://www.lbba.com/work/roseland-place-senior-ilf/.

The developer was a partnership between Mercy Care, a not-for-profit healthcare organisation serving the Atlanta area for over three decades, and Mercy Housing, a separate not-for-profit organisation providing service-affordable housing to low-income families throughout the United States. The 4-acre site on Peachtree Road had sat vacant for years, and the community was interested in and welcoming of new development there.

There were several challenges to be overcome. One was funding. Eventually, the project's LEED Certification, as well as its location near public transportation, and healthcare partnership all assisted in obtaining tax credits. As developer, Mercy also coordinated successful concurrent grant applications at Federal, State and County levels. The second set of challenges concerned construction – the need for a vapour barrier to protect residents from any residual brownfield contamination, and complex negotiations over sewage treatment with the local authority. Both were resolved satisfactorily, but they did impact the project timeline, and caused temporary funding concerns (Figure 8.2). 'Yet the development team was able to adapt quickly, navigating environmental tests and negotiating patiently and in good faith with the County, to ultimately overcome these barriers to completion' (House ATL & ULI, 2020).

Figure 8.2 Mercy Park.

Source: Sylvatica Studio (2023), http://www.sylvaticastudio.com/mercy-park/.

Developer social responsibility – a mechanism for the creation of differential space

Developers have also taken the lead with respect to social responsibility. Whilst their efforts can only ever be partially successful until their funding is based entirely on social outcomes, there are examples of initiatives by individual developers that clearly indicate their interest in creating differential space above and beyond pure financial returns.

The developer as conservation leader

In Huntington, Indiana, developer Jon Anderson embarked on a mixed-use redevelopment of a large historic block on the downtown courthouse square in 2017. According to Anderson, he could have leased the completed ground-floor commercial space to a market-rate business enterprise without much difficulty, but he wanted instead to create a place that had value for people in the community. His solution was to collaborate with a local not-for-profit, Pathfinder Services. What emerged from the collaboration was a plan to restore the historic Odd Fellows Block, connected buildings at 48 E. Franklin St, built in 1889 and 1915, into upper-level apartments with ground-floor space for Pathfinder's Creative Abilities Arts Center, serving artists with and without disabilities, and Huntington University's Center for Entrepreneurship, a small business incubator (Figure 8.3) (Harris, 2022). Originally, the buildings were scheduled for demolition. Indiana Landmarks worked with Huntington Alert to prevent that from happening. Using funds from Indiana Landmarks' Efroymson Family Endangered Places Fund and matching funds from the City of Huntington, Indiana Landmarks repaired leaky roofs, commissioned a structural and reuse assessment, and marketed the redevelopment. The restoration was led by Anderson Partners, contracting out to an affiliated company for the construction. Anderson was experienced, having worked with more than 60 not-for-profits in the development of housing and community facilities. The plan was successful, and the building was saved.

Renamed as UB Lofts, the building now contains 37 apartments across the buildings. UB Lofts' is close to the landmark Huntington County Courthouse, as well as downtown restaurants and shops, and the new Huntington Arts and Entrepreneurial Center, a collaboration between Pathfinder Services and Huntington University. Commentary surrounding the development whilst it was in progress suggested that Pathfinder's portion of the centre was to be dedicated to fine arts and culinary arts. The fine arts were to be placed on display in a community art gallery, along with spaces devoted to ceramics, mixed-media art, and photography, with classes offered. The culinary arts were to be practised in a commercial-grade kitchen on the premises. The kitchen was also to serve as a classroom, as well as a space that can be rented by entrepreneurs, such as food truck operators, in need of a commissary kitchen for their business. The gallery was to be located on the ground floor of the building.

Figure 8.3 The Odd Fellows Block.

Source: Indiana Landmarks Association (2017).

The University's part of the centre will, it was suggested, be geared toward supporting entrepreneurs. The university will offer a space that boasts office furniture, a professional meeting area, high-speed internet, and a business mailing address, all of which will be available to entrepreneurs for a nominal fee. Entrepreneurs will also, it is claimed, have access to a chapter of SCORE, a not-for-profit that provides free business mentorship, and the Huntington County Chamber of Commerce, which was planned to relocate to the first floor of the second IOOF building (Gruske, 2019; Clark, 2020; Harris, 2022).

Jon Anderson's example in the United States is not without parallels elsewhere. There now exist developers whose original purpose and continued mission is defined socially, rather than financially. They do not, as yet at least, exist at scale, and traditional Marxists may well query whether in a capitalist economy they ever can, but to take Lefebvre for developers seriously is surely to hope that they will set a precedent for others to follow.

A developer driven by social purpose: Miss Miyagi

This social enterprise sprang out of a group of seven entrepreneurs who were looking for an office building and ended up forming a social enterprise to renovate an old brewery building, De Hoorn in Leuven, Belgium (Figure 8.4).

After the success of this project, the developer was formed, specialising in the development of innovative real estate projects with added social value. The Miss Miyagi team of committed city makers and project managers has developed an ecosystem of services to assist owners of special properties, policymakers, and citizens or organisations with a space requirement at every stage of the development process.

Miss Miyagi has been very transparent about its financial structure and funding. The De Hoorn project was relatively conventionally funded:

> [A]a combination of seed money invested by each of the seven entrepreneurs (both for purchasing the building and developing it), the bank mortgage, investments in return of shares by local investors from the seven entrepreneurs' network, and grants made ends meet.
>
> (Saleh, 2022)

After the formation of Miss Miyagi, however, people and organisations can invest in a Miss Miyagi Development Fund, which in turn invests in projects, aiming at a 3% return – a far cry from the suggestion of a much higher figure with which this book began, and a return that is much more consistent with social returns. The Fund has four criteria for development projects:

Figure 8.4 De Hoorn, before and after.

Source: Saleh (2022).

contribute to the identity of the built environment; cater for vulnerable target groups; induce the transition to a more local and circular economy; and make space for self-development, social interaction, and urban dynamics.

It is of note that the story of Miss Miyagi to date has now been published as an academic case study (Saleh, 2022), from which the summary above has been drawn – an indication, surely, of how valuable the lessons learned and the example it provides are now considered to be, but also how academic scholarship is now open to the study of individual organisations themselves, real estate developers very much included.

Performance measurement

In the early-to-mid-21st century, these perceived advantages are being gradually squeezed into ESG categories, with varying degrees of success. As a step in the right direction, towards a more holistic assessment of commercial real estate, this might be said to be in line with Lefebvrian precepts, even though he would certainly say that it is still quite insufficient, and desperately close to the kind of quantification of which he was always the most suspicious – Lefebvre was always understandably uncomfortable with measurement. Yet we must measure, if criteria for the assessment of individual developments and a balanced critique of individual developers are to be undertaken. Hard choices usually benefit from reliable data to be made well. Fortunately, as observed earlier from the standpoint of architects, there is a large existing literature from which to draw to make at least a starting point with respect to criteria (e.g. Brower, 2022). More can be expected, and those taking Lefebvre's project seriously for developers will welcome the political battles ahead that will likely ensue from the course of their emergence: the conflicts, the compromises, and the creation of differential space that can potentially emerge from them.

What has also changed since the studies of the early part of the century is that no longer are the buildings themselves being treated as inert, independent objects outside their social context. The Gensler metrics are evidently heavily weighted towards environmental issues; although the balance of such metrics is slowly changing, it could not be swiftly enough for Lefebvre, who would surely want every commercial development assessed not only against standards, but in relation to social norms and needs. An immaculately constructed, highly environmentally sensitive office development that houses a money laundering scam or a sales boiler room is no ESG success, a point that Islamic finance has always taken for granted (Perdana *et al.*, 2021). Conversely, the provision of affordable workspace must represent a positive aspect of real estate development; there is evidence that 'developers who instigated the affordable workspace proposals themselves are more likely to perceive affordable workspace as an "opportunity", and see the wider benefits, acknowledging the contribution of affordable workspace to the success of the development as a whole' (Ferm, 2014:12).

Taking a wider perspective, could the resources devoted to office construction be better allocated to affordable housing, is the constant question that not only differential developers must ask themselves, or that planners must think seriously about when determining the balance of types within a mixed-use development, for example, or even that funders must challenge themselves, but that society as a whole must ask of the entire real estate development industry.

A similar, but slightly different, point is about the balance of power in commercial real estate. Lefebvre himself tacitly accepted the power of capital as occupier of commercial real estate, without investigating any potential conflicts or upsides to be gained from the conflict of interest, and potentially the creative tension, between developer and occupier. For centuries, some corporate occupiers have been able to exert significant power – their requirements are uppermost in developers' minds, their cashflows fuel commercial development, their negotiations over rent feed through DCF models into the profitability or otherwise of individual developments and developers themselves. 'Consequently, the power afforded to traditional actors of urban power – developers, planners, landlords – is now rivalled by the rise of new informational monopolies such as Alphabet Inc.'s Google' (Shaw & Graham, 2017:908). The creation of differential space may not be well served by a dramatic imbalance of power between organisations such as these and the entire array of those on the other side of the fence, participating in the development process itself.

The developer as placemaker

Lefebvre contrasted abstract space with traditional places, 'characterized by blurred borders and qualitatively defined by identity, national peculiarities, topography, authority, religion, tradition, and history' (Stanek, 2011:152). Places must have genesis, evolve, and gradually assume their identity – not best, perhaps, be planned and executed by a single organisation, but Lefebvre's closely argued texts must not allow us to believe that all can, or should, hark back to an especially European version of the pre-industrial world. If creating places that include differential space involves an effort to face up to the simultaneous homogenisation and fragmentation of space, then mixed-use development does represent an effort to bring back together what capitalism has separated: work, travel and leisure, production, distribution and consumption. Creating, maintaining, and proving this kind of place is undoubtedly a huge challenge, and there are probably more examples of failure than success.

It is perhaps reasonable to make some exceptions for early mixed-use developments that attempted to tackle the problem of green building and carbon neutrality head-on. Their success may be challenged, the issue of the quantity of resources allocated to them undeniable, but the intention to blaze a trail was also undeniable, and if for that reason alone, Marxists may be tempted to give them a temporary free pass at least.

Developer as sustainability pioneer – Masdar City

Masdar City is the flagship sustainable city project in Abu Dhabi, one of the Emirates of the United Arab Republics, well known like its neighbour Dubai for innovative and often expensive real estate developments (Figure 8.5). The developer is the eponymous Masdar itself, now positioned as both as a master developer and a developer/operator in its own right, responding to government and private sector requests (Griffiths & Sovacool, 2020:5).

> The soul of Masdar City is strictly connected to the soul of its developers: the Masdar Initiative. Here we are in front of a state-owned, commercially driven enterprise, and the fact that attracting capital and making money are its main goals should not surprise. However, Masdar is not a simple enterprise. It is an enterprise committed to sustainable development.
>
> (Cugurullo, 2013:29)

Originally designed by the star architectural firm Foster and Partners, the plans for Masdar City have changed multiple times since the project commenced in earnest in 2008. The Global Financial Crisis hit Masdar City especially hard, with the timeline for full development pushed out progressively, now to around 2030, and many of the original innovative, bold, sustainability targets for the city have been reduced, for example, from zero carbon towards carbon neutrality (Griffiths & Sovacool, 2020:2).

Yet there is much still to admire in what is still in the 2020s a project underway. The city does source energy from solar and other renewable energy sources. It does host the headquarters of the International Renewable Energy Agency (IRENA). It embraces pedestrianisation, as Bloomberg described it positively:

> [N]arrow streets in a traditional grid of short blocks and low-rise buildings packed in close together – a pocket of Greenwich Village-style urbanism amid low-slung gated mansions, superblocks, and tall buildings on podiums. Withering desert heat is countered via natural ventilation and misting; a cooling wind tower, a feature of the early Bedouin encampments in the area, rises up from the central public square, which is festooned with the work of local artists.
>
> (Flint, 2020)

Figure 8.5 Masdar City.

Source: Foster & Partners, 2023, https://www.fosterandpartners.com/projects/masdar-city.

But equally, Bloomberg was critical of the fact that there were, when they took a view, few pedestrians around, it was only possible to reach Masdar City by automobile, and the original ambitious driverless personal rapid transit system was on the verge of significant scaling back. Bloomberg concluded that Masdar was an 'unfinished Utopia', though also conceded that it would be necessary to wait until at least 2030 to make a proper evaluation, when Masdar City is planned to be built out. Lefebvre would no doubt have reminded them that all utopias worth envisioning always remain unfinished, but even finishing the existing scaled-back plans successfully, in the eyes of the world, ten years later than the current target, or even longer, in an historical perspective, would be a significant achievement: Marxists have waited much longer for revolutions that never came at all. 'Finishing it would send a big signal'. (Flint, 2020).

Lefebvre's doubt, which would surely be shared by Marxists of almost every description, and which has been expressed forcefully now for over a decade (Cugurullo, 2013), is that the environmental benefits of Masdar have come at the expense of any particular social goal, and that

> how this marriage between environmentalism and technology-driven capitalism could lead to a consistent equal allocation of goods is still under debate, and Masdar's example confirms how the social aspects of sustainable development orbit its core without really being part of it.
> (Cugurullo, 2013:32)

From the point of view of Lefebvre's 'totality', Masdar could never fully succeed, and was never really intended to. The response of the differential developer must be, as with the gated communities of Qatar and many others, but unlike the slow advance and compromise that typifies a development such as Brent Cross Town, that Masdar is a prototype, and a partial one at that, and one that has not been constructed for reasons of profit, or even along capitalist lines at all. If for that reason alone, all those who look forward to more environmentally sensitive development in the future should give Masdar their support. As Bloomberg conceded, 'There's no shame in starting small to demonstrate feasibility: Chicago's Columbian Exposition of 1893 showed millions the wonders of electricity, and a way of life changed' (Flint, 2020). The issue is how to replicate at scale, and for that, the experience of the developer must be widely circulated, not only in the Gulf but worldwide.

The towers of capital are shaking

Radical theorists of organisations have advanced the concept of hyper-organisation, in which the production of space is aimed at the creation, preservation, and development of hierarchies of status and control, for example that manipulating the boundaries between home and work has shown how both the physical configuration of space and its lived experience are entwined with relations of power (Zhang *et al.*, 2008:893). Such 'hyper-organizational spaces will also produce practices of resistance and struggle amongst those subjected to them, disrupting and even ultimately completely unbalancing the original intentions of architects and planners' (Zhang *et al.*, 2008:891).

Granted the validity of this Lefebvrian perspective, does this entail any conclusion about how *changes* in those boundaries can affect relations of power; in particular, is there anything that can usefully be said about the way in which the parallel (and to some extent directly competing) paradigms of WFH, on the one hand, and residentialised workspaces, on the other hand, can influence those relations? Hyper-organisational spaces will only succeed in contributing to the need of capital to lock in status and control, after all, if their power can actually be maintained for more than a brief period of dominance. In this context, at least one line of traditional Marxist criticism, that employers and consumers are confined to certain kinds of uses and activity patterns for the lifetime of physical real estate investments if rapid devaluation is to be avoided (Harvey, 1985:145), has proved an economic determinism too far. That devaluation is now running riot through commercial space, and, as a result, real estate developers are being forced to examine what often appears like a diminishing range of opportunities to profit from commercial space.

Evidently, this does not apply to *all* types of building, and it acts as an incentive for even the most devotedly capitalist of developers to continue to strive to avoid that obsolescence, because as soon as it is perceived, it will drive down value (both social and financial, use and exchange), and if that happens before the real estate is sold, it will drive down developer returns with it. Such is the nature of DCF valuations. Developers therefore have a vested interest in heading off obsolescence, which ESG considerations redouble.

The quest for excellence

This in turn sometimes pushes them towards technical excellence. Although Lefebvre would probably be inclined still to side with those Marxists who would doubt whether there would ever be much of a trickle-down effect to smaller-scale developments, he might be willing to grant that 21st-century vertical mixed-use developments do more than just serve the immediate needs of capital, albeit that they can often do that very well indeed.

Developer as efficient technical reuser of space: the Shard, London

Built in 2013, on the former territory of the Southwark Towers office complex, the famous Shard is located next to a train station and near the traditional office centre of the City of London, now itself transforming into a large mixed-use neighbourhood (Figure 8.6). In this tall mixed-use building,

Figure 8.6 The Shard.

Source: The Shard (2023), https://www.pexels.com/search/the%20shard/.

lower floors hold offices, whilst ascending there are restaurants, a hotel, and then apartments. A public observation deck sits atop the building. The construction of this tall building next to a major transportation hub, in London, a city with ample historical heritage, introduced several innovations. The construction team had to reconsider basic principles of construction and make use of entirely new methods. Thus, while constructing the concrete core, a top-down construction technology was used for the first time. Because of this technology the first 23 floors of the concrete core and much of the surrounding tower had been built before the basement was fully excavated. Besides, a special drilling rig, which allowed to place piles in underground communications of the Victorian era with an extremely high precision, was specially designed for the construction.

The Shard did not enjoy an easy gestation. More than 300 meetings with the public were held before the building was constructed (Sellar, 2015:139). Nor is the Shard an advertisement for equality or affordable housing. But it is not meant to be; and as 'this is a building that will last for two or three centuries' (Sellar, 2015:140), a longer perspective might view the Shard quite differently.

Already, despite the controversy over its construction, the Shard is at least sometimes now seen as a new symbol of London, a key link in a strategy to cling on to its international status as a thriving, dynamic, forward-looking urban hub, even in the face of WFH and the diminution of commercial activity in what was once the 'City of London' (Generalova *et al.*, 2018:122). Cities may still need monuments after all, not just to the past, but to the future. Even iconic buildings of a kind may play the role, as they do in Paris (Lefebvre, 2000:209), if they themselves are to exhibit difference, and the gap between difference and competition is not as wide as Marxists would perhaps like it to be. But Lefebvre would be the last to want a drab uniformity in the name of justice. Would not London be the poorer without the Shard?

The slow death of the shopping mall that commenced in developed countries and is now wending its way around the world in varying degrees may yet provide opportunities for developers to escape their dismal portrayal by their critics as enablers, enclosers, and even enforcers a process of enclosing what was previously public space. The shopping mall has long been envisaged as the replacement of public with a private space that performs the same, or similar functions, but with very different consequences in terms of social contact and what Lefebvre may have described as '*jouissance*' within the city (Edwards, 2006). The slide of the mall towards obsolescence has given the opportunity for developers to recover for retail something of the lost past that Lefebvre so cherished, albeit that in many cases, concerted efforts by planning authorities and a certain degree of freedom from the strict demands of the market is still actually required in order to generate outcomes that can be almost instantly recognisable as capable of providing the kind of freedom that Lefebvre always believed lay close to the surface in cities, requiring only the right combination of conditions for a developer to bring to the surface.

Ecological perspectives

A persistent drumbeat of social concern should not obviate the need for a Marxist perspective that is ecological, as well as social. Thanks to the work of Kohoe Saito (2017) in particular, we know how focused Marx himself was towards the end of his life on environmental issues, whilst Lefebvre's own commitment to the ecological cause was persistent, his analysis perspicacious (Foster *et al.*, 2020). The differential developer of commercial real estate will strive for both, but eyeing the fact that whilst environmental achievements are usually difficult compromises with capitalism, they should not come at the expense of social gain. In many cases, however, they need not.

Developer as environmental innovator – the case of wooden skyscrapers

Timber towers have been built for centuries, some of the most successful designs being seen in Japan (Buffi & Angelini, 2019). In the 21st century, some developers have also decided to adopt innovative building techniques based around timber construction. For example, in Milwaukee in the United States, an unusual apartment tower, the $80 million Ascent, was developed at 700 E. Kilbourn Ave. by New Land Enterprises LLP and Wiechmann Enterprises (Figure 8.7). The 25-storey, 259-unit high-rise, the tallest timber building in the world upon completion at 87 m, was constructed with a technique known as mass timber or cross-laminated timber (CLT). Part of a larger group of materials known as mass timber, it is produced by gluing strips of laminated wood together at 90° angles to one another, before they are compressed into huge beams, columns, or panels under extreme pressure.

Figure 8.7 The Ascent Building.
Source: Thornton Tomasetti (2023).

An ocean away, and surrounded by farmland and with a population of under 10,000 people, in the Norwegian town of Brumunddal, standing tall beside the neighbouring Mjøsa Lake, more than 100 km north of Oslo, is another record-breaking timber high-rise (Figure 8.8). The 18-storey structure contains apartments, office space, and the aptly named Wood Hotel. And beyond putting a small town on the world map, it has added to a growing body of evidence that timber can provide a sustainable alternative to concrete and steel. What is certain is that the development risk places high-rise timber construction, as of the early 21st century, firmly in the remit of developers with the necessary skills, resources, and financing. As Moelven themselves said, 'Mjøstårnet is a solid proof on what's possible to create when you combine world class engineering skills with high quality glulam structures and of course add a bit of creativity and vision' (Moelven, 2023).

The construction and environmental case (as carbon sequestration) for mass timber is strong, but not necessarily conclusive, at least not yet. Regulations invariably lag behind technology, with each completed tower helping to ease concerns around efficacy and safety. In general, 'the outcomes of the LCA [life cycle assessment] studies show a reduced carbon footprint associated with CLT construction compared to conventional construction solutions'

Figure 8.8 The Mjøstårnet building.

Source: Moelven (2023).

(Younis & Dodoo, 2022). There are however also long-term environmental challenges such as the need to source trees from sustainable forests which raise questions surrounding forest monocultures, and what happens to the sequestered carbon when the site is eventually redeveloped (Kwok *et al.*, 2020).

The overall environmental view, however, from our current standpoint – which we must take – must be positive. In their combination of architectural boldness, environmental advantage, and social utility, the new generation of wooden skyscrapers could hardly fail to earn the approbation of even a sceptical innovator such as Lefebvre, were he to have the opportunity to judge their contribution now.

Yet Lefebvre would not be satisfied only with the environmental aspect of any building. He would also want to judge its social qualities.

Hotels – irredeemably abstract?

Some sectors start at a pronounced disadvantage in that regard, and therefore now also potentially in respect of funding, hotels being one of them. Developers in any commercial real estate subsector will only be able to pursue laudable social objectives if they are able to access funding that is tolerant, sympathetic, and aligned. If returns can be structured in such a way as to match social objectives, then a funding structure might be achieved and akin to the allocation of resources, it might be expected to prevail in a future society where capitalism has been superseded. The hotel industry might be considered an unlikely opportunity for green financing, but that shows signs of changing. The environmental aspects of hotel development, such as predetermined energy targets, are relatively clear; it is possible to evaluate

> the environmental friendliness of a hotel by using rating systems like Tripadvisor's GreenLeaders, Green Key Global, Green Seal, Green Tourism Active, Audubon Green Lodging Program, Travelife, or Earth Check, and LEED or Energy Star Certification provide information about the sustainability of a property.
>
> (CBRE, 2022)

But evaluating the social aspects of hotels are much less easy to evaluate, as there are fundamental issues at stake that have certainly not been satisfactorily resolved. Lefebvre himself referred dismissively to 'the enormous leisure industry, with its hotel chains and air transport on a world scale' (Lefebvre, 1980 [2009:218]). He did not choose to prognosticate on its future in a world in which capitalism has been superseded, and to take his words out of the context in which he placed them – a general assault on the production of space under capitalism – would undoubtedly leave developers in the hotel sector asking about their own future, in such a world. But in fact, Lefebvre was a staunch supporter of leisure, especially where it could be provided as a collective good (Lefebvre, 1973a [2014]). So providing the environmental and social issues involved in tourism can be properly addressed, there may even eventually be more of it than before, albeit that it might look very different if

> [r]Rethinking tourism from the perspective of degrowth might therefore further imply questioning fast speed/long-distance/short-term travel for personal pleasure *en toto*, as part of a deeper level transformation of livelihoods and lifestyles in line with post-capitalist principles.
>
> (Fletcher *et al.*, 2021:17)

How this might transpire in practice remains moot, and so long as it does, differential developers wanting to tackle hotel development may find themselves stymied.

Conclusion

More widely, and despite these examples of dead ends and confrontations in certain types of real estate, bold and often not-for-profit developers have sought to create mixed-use, carbon-neutral developments worldwide. One example is Vauban, 'a dense yet car-free ecovillage, which allows for much open space but short distances to urban activities' (Newman & Jennings, 2008:140). Another well-known example is BedZED in London, developed by the Peabody Trust, of which it has been said that

> the development avoids compromising greenbelts while providing community facilities, open space, and private roof gardens. Energy, water, and

> some food systems, along with biodiversity, are integrated onsite. There is an emphasis on sourcing materials and energy from the local bioregion. Mixed tenure and affordable housing, along with a wide range of public facilities and onsite workspaces, provide the basis for a diverse local community and economy. Networking with local supplies is promoted for economic sustainability, including bulk deliveries of groceries and links with local organic food growers.
>
> (Newman & Jennings, 2008:134)

The list of such developments is not as long as Lefebvre would have liked. Traditional designs, often sought after by equally traditionally oriented clients, including the funds that will own and outsource the management of commercial buildings, still dominate commercial real estate development. Only if, and as, differential developers are able to express their social and environmental ambitions can more of the kind of examples presented so far in this chapter be created.

It will not be easy. Commercial real estate is, quite simply, a much tougher sell for a developer ever to portray accurately as differential. Its umbilical connection with capitalism in terms of much of its occupancy, its long history of providing opportunities for capital to nestle comfortably within as an essential component of the real estate economy, its demands on people to travel and generally uncomfortable relationship with environmental considerations, and the persistent doubt that has arisen in the 21st century that much of it – office and retail in particular – is actually necessary at all, together present a high bar to overcome for a differential developer to justify.

And yet – that coffee shop from the past in which we can espy Henri Lefebvre engaged in animated debate with someone who was once a stranger, but no longer is – was that not commercial space? The design studio where local people can intermingle, presenting their ideas to the entrepreneurs who have been provided with the space they need to interact – is that not commercial space as well? An inspiring, tall mixed-use building that features in so many presentations, that represents the cutting edge of environment-friendly construction materials, and where industrial production proceeds apace in safe conditions on its lower floors, will that too not also be commercial space? The future of commercial real estate in a future where capitalism has been superseded may be very different, but it still seems assured – it will be the role of differential developers deliver it in the future, and their responsibility to try to deliver it even now.

Bibliography

Andres, L., Bakare, H., Bryson, J. R., Khaemba, W., Melgaço, L. and Mwaniki, G. R. (2021). Planning, temporary urbanism and citizen-led alternative-substitute place-making in the Global South. *Regional Studies*, 55(1), 29–39.

Berg, C. (2022). *Public planning, neoliberal hybridity and local activism in Sundbyberg. Epochal reconfiguration of urban development in greater Stockholm*. PhD, Department of Sociology, Uppsala University.

Brower, A., Handelman, A. and Olson, S. (2022). The future of ESG in architecture. *Gensler* [blog]. Available at: www.gensler.com/blog/measurable-impact-the-future-of-esg-in-architecture-design. [Accessed 5 October 2022[.

Browning, C. R., Byron, R. A., Calder, C. A., Krivo, L. J., Kwan, M.-P., Lee, J.-Y. and Peterson, R. D. (2010). Commercial density, residential concentration, and crime: Land use patterns and violence in neighborhood context. *Journal of Research in Crime and Delinquency*, 47(3), 329–357.

Buffi, A. and Angelini, G. M. (2019). Adaptive timber towers. An evolutionary prototype for the 21st century skyscraper. In Bianconi, F. and Filippucci, M. (eds.) *Digital Wood Design: Innovative Techniques of Representation in Architectural Design*. Cham, Springer, 971–987.

CBRE. (2022). A check-in on the Hotel Sector's ESG initiatives, July 26. Available at: www.cbre.com/insights/reports/a-check-in-on-the-hotel-sectors-esg-initiatives. [Accessed 4 December 2022].

Clark, S. (2020). UB Block rehab is one step closer as apartments open in district. *Huntingdon County TAB*, April 6. Available at: www.huntingtoncountytab.com/feature/56625/ub-block-rehab-one-step-closer-apartments-open-district. [Accessed 6 November 2022].

Coleman, N. (2013). Utopian prospect of Henri Lefebvre. *Space and Culture*, 16(3), 349–363.

Cugurullo, F. (2013). How to build a sandcastle: An analysis of the genesis and development of Masdar City. *Journal of Urban Technology*, 20(1), 23–37.

Debrunner, G. and Gerber, J.-D. (2021). The commodification of temporary housing. *Cities*, 108, 102998.

Derakhti, L. and Baeten, G. (2020). Contradictions of transit-oriented development in low-income neighborhoods: The case study of Rosengård in Malmö, Sweden. *Urban Science*, 4(2), 20.

Edwards, P. (2006). Citizenship Inc.: Negotiating civic spaces in post-urban America. *Critical Survey*, 18(3), 19–36.

Ferm, J. (2014). Delivering affordable workspace: Perspectives of developers and workspace providers in London. *Progress in Planning*, 93, 1–49.

Fletcher, R., Blanco-Romero, A., Blázquez-Salom, M., Cañada, E., Murray Mas, I. and Sekulova, F. (2021). Pathways to post-capitalist tourism. *Tourism Geographies*, 1–22.

Flint, A. (2020). What Abu Dhabi's city of the future looks like now. *Bloomberg*, 15 February. Available at: www.bloomberg.com/news/articles/2020-02-14/the-reality-of-abu-dhabi-s-unfinished-utopia. [Accessed 11 January 2023].

Foster, J. B., Napoletano, B. M., Clark, B. and Urquijo, P. S. (2020). Henri Lefebvre's Marxian ecological critique: Recovering a foundational contribution to environmental sociology. *Environmental Sociology*, 6(1), 31–41.

Generalova, E. M. and Generalov, V. P. (2020). Mixed-use high-rise buildings: A typology of the future. *IOP Conference Series: Materials Science and Engineering*, 753(2), 022062.

Generalova, E. M., Generalov, V. P., Kuznetsova, A. A. and Bobkova, O. N. (2018). *Mixed-use development in a high-rise context*. Paper presented at the E3S Web of Conferences 33, High-Rise Construction 2017 (HRC 2017), 01021 (2018). Available at: www.e3s-conferences.org/articles/e3sconf/abs/2018/08/e3sconf_hrc2018_01021/e3sconf_hrc2018_01021.html. [Accessed 7 November 2022].

Grant, J. (2002). Mixed use in theory and practice: Canadian experience with implementing a planning principle. *Journal of the American Planning Association*, 68(1), 71–84.

Griffiths, S. and Sovacool, B. K. (2020). Rethinking the future low-carbon city: Carbon neutrality, green design, and sustainability tensions in the making of Masdar City. *Energy Research & Social Science*, 62, 101368.

Gruske, C. (2019). Historic block redeveloped. *Indiana Construction News*, 19 August. Available at: www.indianaconstructionnews.com/2019/08/16/historic-block-redeveloped/. [Accessed 4 October 2022].

Harris, S. F. (2022). *Joint venturing for nonprofits: The benefits, the common pitfalls and how to navigate them.* Available at: www.lisc.org/our-resources/resource/joint-venturing-non profits-benefits-common-pitfalls-and-how-navigate-them/. [Accessed 16 October 2022].

Harvey, D. (1985). *The Urbanization of Capital.* Baltimore, Johns Hopkins University Press.

Hirt, S. A. (2016). Rooting out mixed use: Revisiting the original rationales. *Land Use Policy*, 50, 134–147.

HouseATL and Urban Land Institute Atlanta. (2020). *Case study mercy park.* Available at https://ulidigitalmarketing.blob.core.windows.net/ulidcnc/sites/40/2020/10/5f9aeeed 46384-5f9aeeed46385HouseATL-Case-Study-Mercy-Park-10.15.20.pdf.pdf. [Accessed 7 November 2022].

Howard, S. L. (2008). *Urban mixed use development: The socially responsible allocation of space*. PhD, University of Colorado at Denver.

Jacobs, J. (1961). *The Death and Life of Great American Cities.* New York, Random House.

de Jong, M. (2019). From eco-civilization to city branding: A neo-Marxist perspective of sustainable urbanization in China. *Sustainability*, 11(20), 5608.

Khan, M. R. and Tisa, S. A. (2019). Multifaceted dimensions of urban form to revitalizing human interaction in dense cities. In Samarawickrama, S. *et al.* (eds.) *Re-evaluating Space Across Disciplines: Proceedings of the 12th International Conference of Faculty of Architecture Research Unit (FARU).* University of Moratuwa, Sri Lanka, 3 December, Colombo, 385–393.

Kwok, A., Zalusky, H., Rivera, M. I., Rasmussen, L. and McKay, H. (2020). Seeing the forest and the trees: Environmental impacts of cross-laminated timber. *Technology| Architecture+ Design*, 4(2), 144–150.

Lefebvre, H. (1947). *Critique de la vie quotidienne. Volume One. Introduction.* Paris: Grasset. Translated by J. Moore (1991 [2014]) as *Critique of Everyday Life.* Volume One. Introduction. London, Verso.

———. (1970). Reflections on the politics of space. In Elden, S. and Brenner, N. (eds.) *State, Space, World: Selected Essays.* Translated by G. Moore. Minneapolis, University of Minnesota Press, 167–184.

———. (1970a [2009]). Reflections on the politics of space. In Elden, S. and Brenner, N. (eds.) *State, Space, World: Selected Essays.* Translated by G. Moore. Minneapolis, University of Minnesota Press, 176.

———. (1973 [1976]). *La Survie du capitalisme: La reproduction des rapports de production.* Paris, Anthropos. Translated by F. Bryant as *The Survival of Capitalism. Reproduction of the Relations of Production.* London, Allison & Busby.

———. (1973a [2014]). *Vers une architecture de la jouissance.* Translated by R. Bononno as *Toward an architecture of enjoyment.* Minnesota, University of Minnesota Press.

———. (1974 [1991]). *La production de l'espace.* Paris, Anthropos. Translated by D. Nicholson-Smith as *The Production of Space.* Oxford, Blackwell.

———. (1979 [2009]). Space: Social Product and Use Value. In Elden, S. and Brenner, N. (eds.) *State, Space, World: Selected Essays.* Translated by G. Moore. Minneapolis, University of Minnesota Press, 185–195.

———. (1980 [2009]). Space and Mode of Production. In Elden, S. and Brenner, N. (eds.) *State, Space, World: Selected Essays.* Translated by G. Moore. Minneapolis, University of Minnesota Press, 201–222.

———. (2000). *Espace et politique: le droit à la ville II.* Paris, Anthropos.

———. (2000) *Writings on Cities*. Edited by E. Kofman and E. Lebas. Oxford, Blackwell.

Li, Q., Chen, X., Jiao, S., Song, W., Zong, W. and Niu, Y. (2022). Can mixed land use reduce CO2 emissions? A case study of 268 Chinese cities. *Sustainability*, 14(22), 15117.

Litman, T. and Colman, S. B. (2001). Generated traffic: Implications for transport planning. *ITE Journal*, 71(4), 38–46.

Lizieri, C. (2009). *Towers of Capital: Office Markets and International Financial Services*. London, Wiley.

Meng, J. and Wu, F. (2020). Institution-monopoly rent and competition amongst China's local governments: A Marxist analytical framework. *China Political Economy*, 3(2), 303–327.

Newman, P. and Jennings, I. (2008). *Cities as Sustainable Ecosystems: Principles and Practices*. Washington, DC, Island Press.

O'Callahgan, C. (2007). Just add water: (re) Producing Cork Docklands. *Progress in Irish Urban Studies*, 3, 13–24.

Perdana, A., Setijanti, P. and Cahyadini, S. (2021). Evaluation of real estate development process in sharia housing based on the application of the ideal Islamic housing concept. *IPTEK Journal of Proceedings Series* (6), 156–160.

Saito, K. (2017). *Karl Marx's Ecosocialism*. New York, Monthly Review Press.

Saleh, R. (2022). Collaborative ecosystems connecting people and heritage the journey of Miss Miyagi, a positive impact real estate developer in Belgium. *City, Culture and Society*, 29, 100447.

Sellar, I. (2015). *Developing an icon – the story of the shard*. Paper presented at the Proceedings of the CTBUH 2015 International Conference "Global Interchanges: Resurgence of the Skyscraper City" 26–30 October, 138–145. Available at: https://global.ctbuh.org/resources/papers/download/2450-developing-an-icon-the-story-of-the-shard.pdf. [Accessed 4 September 2022].

Shaw, J. and Graham, M. (2017). An informational right to the city? Code, content, control, and the urbanization of information. *Antipode*, 49(4), 907–927.

Soules, M. (2021). *Icebergs, Zombies, and the Ultra-Thin: Architecture and Capitalism in the 21st Century*. San Francisco, Chronicle Books.

Stanek, L. (2011). *Henri Lefebvre on Space: Architecture, Urban Research, and the Production of Theory*. Minnesota, University of Minnesota Press.

Stryker, B. and Nagati, O. (2016). Cairo downtown passageways: A framework for urban regeneration. In Stryker, B. and Nagati, O. (eds.) *Creative Cities: Re-Framing Downtown Cairo*. Cairo, Cluster, 177–187.

Wang, V. (1996). Mixed use: The answer to the successful urban environment. *Built Environment*, 22(4), 312–314.

Wickersham, J. (2000). Jane Jacob's critique of zoning: From Euclid to Portland and beyond. *Boston College Environmental. Affairs Law Review*, 28(4), 547–563.

Younis, A. and Dodoo, A. (2022). Cross-laminated timber for building construction: A life-cycle-assessment overview. *Journal of Building Engineering*, 52, 104482.

Zagow, M. (2020). Does mixed-use development in the metropolis lead to less carbon emissions? *Urban Climate*, 34, 100682.

Zhang, Z. (2018). Exploring the spatial dynamics of the city: A case study in China. In Kingma, S. *et al.* (eds.) *Organisational Space and Beyond: The Significance of Henri Lefebvre for Organisation Studies*. New York and London, Taylor & Francis, 237–260.

Zhang, Z., Spicer, A. and Hancock, P. (2008). Hyper-organizational space in the work of JG Ballard. *Organization*, 15(6), 889–910.

9 In the way of public buildings

Rights for everyone?

Marxist and radical geographers have focused significantly on *access* to public space and directed their anger at *exclusion* from it. With Lefebvre's tacit encouragement, their taxonomy can be envisaged as classifying public space on a spectrum on a different dimension to functional use. An alternative division into quadrants has been proposed (Mehta & Palazzo, 2020), with similar intent (Figure 9.1).

At one end of such a spectrum are public spaces where, in principle, the right to free access and movement guaranteed to everybody remains broadly true, such as streets, public parks and forests, and parts of the seashore, the top right quadrant in Figure 9.1, although even in these cases there are restrictions and increasing discrimination, 'parks, sidewalks, and notionally public buildings such as libraries, from which the poor are excluded through a variety of means, including state force and social norms' (Pierce, 2022:21), the forcible eviction of the homeless from the US parks (Goodling, 2020), a space that is inaccessible for the disabled, for example, insufficiently well-lit or hard to access through public transport, or even redolent of past racial or other forms of injustice and culturally insensitive.

Lefebvre himself was keen to stress that the power of abstract space – the dimension of control in the alternative formulation above – means that such exclusion can and does also operate in a much more subtle fashion, social norms indeed, even on those who would normally be considered (and is considered) far from poor, socially excluded, or discriminated against:

> The meanings conveyed by abstract space are more often prohibitions than solicitations or stimuli (except when it comes to consumption). Prohibition – the negative basis, so to speak, of the social order – is what dominates here. The symbol of this constitutive repression is an object offered up to the gaze yet barred from any possible use, whether this occurs in a museum or in a shop window. It is impossible to say how often one pauses uncomfortably for a moment on some threshold: the entrance of a church, office or 'public'

DOI: 10.1201/9781003220244-9

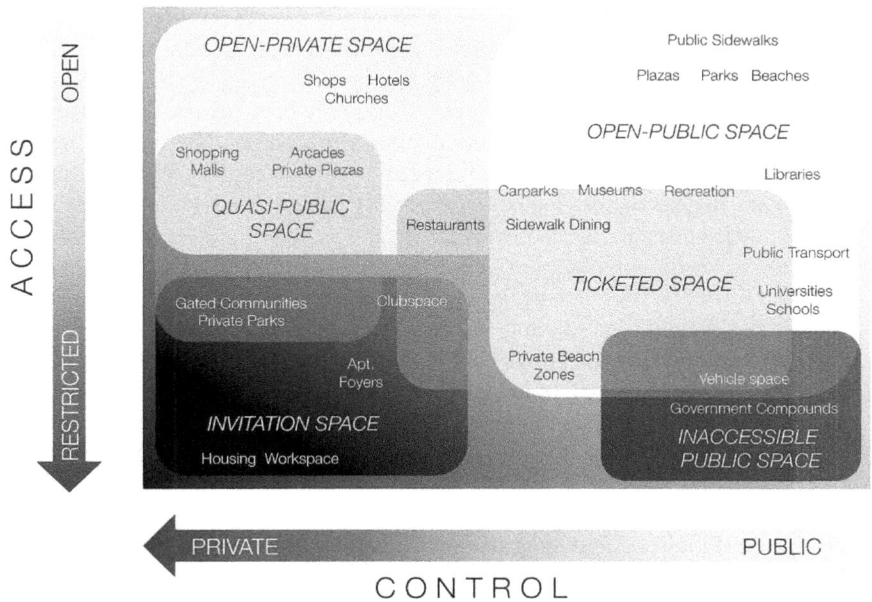

Figure 9.1 Dividing up public space.

Source: Mehta and Palazzo (2020).

> building, or the point of access to a 'foreign' place – while passively, and usually 'unconsciously', accepting a prohibition of some kind.
>
> (Lefebvre, 1974 [1991:319])

Such space may therefore be *formally* public space; but in practice it can often be used to a greater extent, dominated, *appropriated* by particular sections of the community, usually – but not always – the more privileged, at the expense of others. Lefebvre was consistent across the decades in arguing that enacting the right to public space for those who were otherwise 'alienated from the spaces of everyday life' (Mitchell & Villanueva, 2010:667) would always be essential to the right to the city, alongside other fundamental rights such as housing, culture, and work (Lefebvre, 1970, 1974 [1991]).

Lefebvre's examples may have been carefully chosen, but there is surely some truth in the suggestion that the creation of difference, even of sheer variety, in social and cultural forms must almost inevitably bring some measure of prohibition in its wake. For example, the supersession of capitalism is unlikely to bring out anything like the coalescence of all global religions, and nor do Marxists suggest that it will. Developers of 'religious space', a counterpoint to 'military space' (Eves, 2014:12), in a taxonomy that explicitly derives from Lefebvre, can take some credit for achievements in this direction.

Developer as promoter of tolerance – a Hindu temple in Abu Dhabi

Marxists – including Lefebvre – have traditionally been critical of religion, although some have discovered more tolerance in the Founding Fathers than the mere 'opium of the people' that has been quoted so frequently. In addition to its many negatives, religion has a potentially positive social role; however, it is a matter of historical record. Even Lenin was prepared to accept believers into the Communist Party.

For the Hindu religion to promote social identity and a sense of collective justice in a Muslim jurisdiction far from India would however require the construction of a Hindu temple. That is exactly what is being delivered. The Hindu temple that is being built in Abu is the first traditional stone temple to be built in the United Arab Emirates (UAE). It was announced by the UAE government in 2015 during a visit by Indian Prime Minister. He returned three years later to lay the foundation stone of the temple, albeit via video conferencing from the opera house there. The location of the new temple in Abu Dhabi will be approximately 30 minutes away from the main island by car, and around 40 minutes from Jebel Ali, Dubai, so very accessible throughout the Emirates.

Figure 9.2 The BAPS Hindu Mandir.

Source: Siasat.com (2021), https://www.siasat.com/abu-dhabis-first-hindu-temple-will-last-over-1000-years-2198307/.

The development of the temple is being led by a religious organisation known as BAPS Swaminarayan Sanstha, a group which has developed (in the sense of instigated the project, raised the finance, and managed the construction process) more than 1,100 Hindu temples across the globe (Figure 9.2). The Abu Dhabi temple is being constructed under the guidance of Sanskrit scriptures on architecture and design. With the foundation work of the temple completed over its 27 acre area, Rajasthan pink stone and Italian Macedonian marble will be used by artisans from Rajasthan and Gujarat in India to build the seven spires and five domes of the temple itself. Inside, the temple will be designs of nature and stories from ancient Hindu scriptures. The temple complex will also have a meeting centre, prayer hall, library, classroom, community center, halls, amphitheatre, play area, gardens, books and gift shops, food court, and other facilities (Fatima, 2021). An iconic development indeed. And built to last: BAPS project members claim that the temple will stand for a thousand years.

As the first Hindu temple in Abu Dhabi, the BAPS Hindu Mandir is claimed to be a reflection of the UAE's religious tolerance and multicultural population. In September 2019, the temple became the first Hindu place of worship to receive an official license in Abu Dhabi.

Across the spectrum, there are however also public spaces on which different degrees of access and circulation restrictions have been placed on a quite different, purportedly exclusively technical basis, such as employment or participation in educational programmes, or family relationships, such as official and administrative buildings, educational and health institutions, and cultural centres. Most obviously, hospitals and schools set access, use, and circulation rules for their spaces. No doubt the basis of exclusion even in these cases is not entirely without a social dimension – employment is inherently discriminatory in a society with private schooling, inheritance, and the whole panoply of social tools at the service of inequality in a capitalist society – but even in a future society where capitalism has been superseded, it is surely inevitable that many of this kind of exclusion will continue to be necessary. It is the purpose for which exclusion is enacted and its consequences that matter, not its formal existence as a set of rules and representations of space.

Finally, under conditions of capitalist urban development, it is also more likely than not that public spaces will be placed under a range of pressures to be 'privatised by stealth'. These include public health facilities, such as gymnasia, swimming pools, and public meeting halls that have increasingly been forced into acting as quasi-businesses, as well as many of the panoply of assets to which the financial techniques of the 'user pays' type of public–private partnerships (PPP) have been applied. Not all pay-as-you-go facilities are necessarily socially exclusionary, however: the question revolves around empirical questions of charges and incomes amongst existing and potential users, as the following example demonstrates.

Neoliberalism at work 1? The case of a public swimming pool in Singapore

Pasir Ris is a suburb of Singapore, mainly consisting of publicly constructed and freehold owner but privately owned Housing Development Board (HDB) apartments, as is typical of the majority of Singapore suburbs in the 21st century (Figure 9.3). The suburb is served by a leisure resort, originally constructed in the early 1990s along with the majority of Pasir Ris HDB apartments. At that time, the Olympic-sized open-air swimming pool in what was named Downtown East was the only sports facility there, complementing a range of public chalets in what in many respects resembled Lefebvre's ideal of a publicly available leisure space: at a time when international level was still relatively rare, rents were very low, and all Singaporeans could afford not only to visit, but once in a while to stay there. By the standards of the mid-21st century, however, the whole resort was relatively spartan, and it is surely doubtful that had nothing been done, it would continue to enjoy the same kind of patronage as it did in the latter part of the previous century.

Two decades later, Downtown East leisure resort was reconstructed (Figure 9.4). It now houses a swimming complex which again includes an Olympic-length (but no longer width) lane pool, as well as other pools for junior and less able swimmers, but also a sports hall with a seating capacity of 2,000, a gymnasium offering pool views, a dance studio, and a much larger F&B and retail area. By comparison to its predecessor, built without 21st century considerations of equity, the centre is accessible to the visually

Figure 9.3 The original Pasir Ris pool.

Source: FourSquare.com (2023), https://foursquare.com/v/downtown-east-swimming-pool/4c53aa834623be9ab6917bf1/photos.

Figure 9.4 The new Pasir Ris pool.

Source: ActiveSG (2023), https://www.myactivesg.com/Facilities/pasir-ris-swimming-complex.

disabled, with many braille markings and tactile warning strips. There is also a ramp and slip-resistant tiles in the pool which make the pool accessible to wheelchair users. The facility has also incorporated several green features, including vertical green walls. The design of its landscape helps cut down ambient heat. It also makes use of a rainwater harvesting system which adds to its sustainability by reusing rainwater to meet irrigation needs (Design Curial, 2011).

The transformation of the facility has not excluded Singaporeans or visitors – far from it. Visitor numbers to the redeveloped facility are high, it is important to note partly on account of very low entry fees, which are not aimed at reflecting construction and maintenance costs. Pasir Ris Sports Centre is in fact one of the top five most visited sports venues in Singapore, with the swimming pools alone recorded as attracting a monthly visitorship of 25,000–30,000 people (Kung & Pang, 2015:110).

But it no longer serves quite the same function as its predecessor. Lefebvre might just have to accept, times have changed – even leisure cannot be expected to remain as it was in the mid-20th century.

Restrictions on access may not only be based on payment, however. In fact, no matter how free the public spaces may be, it is necessary to ask, in each context, who appropriates them, and on what basis (Santos Junior, 2014:147). Lefebvre insisted on not only the physical appearance, structure, and nominal function of public spaces, but also the way in which they have been increasingly co-opted into abstract space.

Public–private partnerships

The PPP model has been much criticised, as placing an unnecessary, profit-oriented intermediary between the public sector and the construction company, although much-publicised examples of cost overruns by PPP projects did obscure other cases where PPP delivered projects at lower cost, at least by comparison to benchmarks. Globally, the model has now been radically extended to include participation by developers in a wide range of projects, from housing to healthcare, and often on a joint venture basis in which the local authority plays only a role as enabler, and sometimes the donor of land, rather than as a customer.

The Guangzhou R&F International Hospital

The Guangzhou hospital is the result of a consortium, including the developer R&F Group, UCLA Health, and Medpoint Health Partners (Figure 9.5). It has 100,000 m^2 of floor space over 15 storeys, and 277 private rooms, with the capacity to expand to 500 beds as the hospital grows. Medically, the hospital provides secondary and tertiary care services, including intensive care complex surgical services, obstetrical and newborn care, adult and paediatric medical and surgical care, including subspecialties, and traditional Chinese medicine services. So far as the campus itself is concerned, the consortium emphasised that the planning and details of public spaces and inclusion of amenities is intended to facilitate the lives of patient families and visitors, with naturally lit, comfortable waiting areas, natural landscape zones for reflection and privacy, and an open, inviting dining area with views of the city. The nursing home, senior housing, and rehab center, with several hundred apartments and 24/7 care, although separate buildings, are integrated into the design of the hospital, with a bridge connection to the hospital and landscaped paths that point to a unified healthcare campus.

Private healthcare is hardly an activity in itself with which Marxists can be comfortable. Nevertheless, a gradual end to the dominance of Western developed countries in respect of advanced healthcare facilities is as welcome as the international levelling of wealth effect from commercial development in cities like Shanghai and Dubai mentioned in the previous chapter. Insofar as they do participate in any such process, capital is directed towards

Figure 9.5 Guangzhou R&F International Hospital Campus.

broadly positive social goals, which is clearly preferable to 'Towers of Capital'. In the case of the Guangzhou hospital, R&F Properties bid for the land itself was ¥529 million, with an mandated total investment of ¥3 billion yuan in this project, of which one-third was designated for medical equipment. By any standards, this is a considerable resource commitment (Guangzhou China, 2018).

Expenditure is one metric, but there are others. Lefebvre's admonitions, as well as concerns over payment, may yet serve as a warning to developers involved in the PPP process, especially those who rely upon 'user pays' PPP such as toll roads and airports for a significant proportion of their income: these are politically dangerous waters, and always will be. It is worth recalling, however, that PPP does not have to come in this potentially regressive form. The original PPP model as developed in the UK intended to utilise the experience of private sector developers in project management in order to deliver public buildings which were intended for use by institutions such as the UK's National Health Service, which is free of charge at the point of use. Modifications of the original system of a single unitary charge have divided payments into construction and operation (Shi *et al.*, 2020) and the mechanism remains available to governments in a range of forms. Developers who take Lefebvre seriously, who are keen to create differential space that embodies concepts of justice and even equality, will note carefully the difference between the two types of PPP model, prefer the original model, and if they are caught in the requirements of 'user-pays', will be determined to engage to the fullest extent possible in contributing to the design and operation of these arrangements.

The PPP example leads to the reflection that no developer can take responsibility for their building indefinitely: locational obsolescence, public policy changes, even surreptitious subletting can all jeopardise a building's 'ethical standpoint'. Equally, however, their responsibility is not confined merely to contractual obligations in terms of the performance of the intended structure. What the differential developer can and should do is negotiate to ensure that just as the building has been built to high standards of safety and is thoroughly fit for purpose, the initial user arrangements put in place will not be onerous, inequitable, or unjust.

Extending the value capture model

Conversely, value capture by the public sector can also be directed at creating public services in mixed-use, privately owned, buildings. Through the planning process,

> municipalities and public planning agencies may require a developer or a property owner, who builds on their plot, to designate floorspace for public functions and transfer ownership of these floors to the local government. At times this would be done for free, or alternatively while paying compensation to the developer or by granting owners extensive rights to develop.
>
> (Mualam *et al.*, 2019:131)

What is however largely missing in the increasing use of this process is any form of systemisation, so that although there have been attempts to do so, as in Tel-Aviv, 'the exact size of the allocated space, however, appears is some cases to be quite random, as it is the result of several factors' (Mualam *et al.*, 2021:12). Likewise, the extent of the compensation paid to the developer is not consistent at national level, let alone internationally. Nevertheless, the idea shows promise and is one that can with sufficient transparency form the basis of community pressure and political campaigning.

Public space is not always disruptive

At the same time as these reformist initiatives, the politics of resistance can frequently also be found most active in public space, where it may meet fewer immediate obstacles. Those who identify Lefebvre with such resistance argue:

> Spaces in the city gain new meanings through these practices: squares, streets, collectively occupied buildings, museums, theatres, parks, rivers, beaches, abandoned sheds, trains, buses, steps, bridges, and schools, among others. No public space escapes from the new possibilities created such that all of these can be reappropriated in a creative fashion through collective action.
>
> (Santos Junior, 2014:152)

Such an approach elides, however, over the fact that for Marxists, what really matters in relation to museums, to take one example, is what is exhibited, how, when, and to whom, the management of visitors, funding (and where they apply, pricing), structures, and internal management. In short, how the museum fits between abstract and differential space. The physical arrangement of space, to which developers and their advisers contribute their expertise, plays a significant, sometimes decisive, role in each of these politically important aspects of a museum, and at a more granular level, here are a large number of technical aspects of construction that bear on a building's social use, for example, in relation to the design of a school in the Middle East:

The size and shape of courtyards – a cause for concern?

There is widespread recognition that building and open spaces interact in relation to indoor temperatures. A study using Design Builder software benchmarked against actual data from the New Assiut city school sought to analyse the effect of the height/width ratio for internal school courtyards on interior temperature (Figure 9.6).

> The results showed that better thermal conditions are achieved by reducing courtyard width and increasing building height. Thus, a deep courtyard (more than 10 m width) is more effective and provides better thermal conditions than shallow courtyard. Also, it is concluded that the more the courtyard width and building height, the higher the annual school energy consumption especially when the courtyard width exceeds 10 m due to excessive facades exposure to solar radiation.
>
> (El-Samea *et al.*, 2020:130)

The environmental logic is impeccable. Any social disadvantages might well be overshadowed by the internal comfort benefits, but there is no calculus to determine the trade-off, and the social impact of high, deep courtyards is not considered.

Figure 9.6 The New Assiut City School.

Source: El-Samea *et al.* (2020).

True, there has been a tremendous variety of analysis, Marxist, critical, and otherwise, expanding on the purely physical aspect of common spaces to include their purposes, cultural significance, position within the commodity value chain, and a host of other material, technical, and symbolic aspects of public space that seek to explain the various functions of public space, in particular now in an urban context and in a capitalist economy. This multidimensional approach is evidently sensible at a practical level, as public real estate, much of it clearly a public good in the sense economists mean, would probably be the easiest aspects of legacy space to integrate into a world in which capitalism has been superseded. As Lefebvre himself speaks of them with respect:

> Castles, palaces, cathedrals, fortresses, all speak in their various ways of the greatness and the strength of the people who built them and against whom they were built. This real greatness shines through the fake grandeur of rulers and endows those buildings with a lasting 'beauty'.
>
> (Lefebvre, 1947 [2014:252])

Such public buildings have always escaped much of the ire Marxists have directed at real estate developers – even though, in many cases, their construction has been undertaken by developers, or specialist project managers who come close in form and function.

The centre and the periphery

Lefebvre thought and wrote at a time when the distinction between the administrative centre of most cities, together with in many cases the business district (the CBD), and core elements of affluent residential space, and the periphery of the city spread out beyond it, were still relatively clear. This distinction has become embedded in analysis that has followed in the Lefebvrian tradition:

> City space is, therefore, the expression of the 'great social oppositions objectivized in the physical space', in the form, for example, of division between a city's center and its periphery, and it tends to be reproduced in the forms of representation.
>
> (Santos Junior, 2014:150)

The rise of online administration, WFH, decentralised local government, big box out-of-centre stores, and a number of other pressures towards the strengthening of the role of the suburbs by comparison to the CBD may all give pause for thought in this historical emphasis. There are still, for example, spaces of political representation in the heart of the city, and this 'political space' can still very much matter, as examples as far apart geographically and politically as the Arab Spring (Riphagen *et al.*, 2018) and the wave of demonstrations across Australia against historical racial injustices demonstrated (Ciccarelli & Slade, 2023). However, they are now by no means the only spaces where collective aspirations for political freedom can be expressed, or where collective action can advance the condition of equality or reflect the democratic formation of opinion and public will (Santos Junior, 2014). Online space may well matter almost or even as much, as many activists and analysts alike have pointed out in relation to the Arab Spring (e.g. Jamali, 2014; Chiovaro *et al*., 2021), especially in view of the potentially more egalitarian aspects of line communication and discourse by comparison to traditional male dominance of physical space (Newsom & Lengel, 2012).

Of critical importance to the way in which Lefebvre should now be interpreted and applied is the evident fact that the internet has already achieved that for which, using the technology of the time, unitary urbanism, already discarded as a result of the rise of the suburbs, had only the palest blueprint – to enable different parts of the city to communicate with one another rapidly and on a basis of equality or near-equality, as Lefebvre himself had anticipated (Ross & Lefebvre, 1997:73). This places into question the assertion that 'It is primarily in urban public spaces that individuals can act publicly, communicate with the public' (Stevens, 2007:11), and, in turn, enables us at least to question whether the importance of urban public spaces is as great as in the traditional interpretation of Lefebvre. For example, although no doubt it remains true that 'Where gambling is located is never a choice without consequences' (Järvinen-Tassopoulos, 2020:1), the attempt to apply a traditional Lefebvrian theoretical framework to regulation of this space is complicated by the fact that control of traditional physical space is now simply insufficient, an issue beyond let alone city limits, if not in many cases to a significant degree beyond the reach of state power (Warf, 2021:316).

The importance of the Lefebvrian distinction between centre and periphery remains – but it can perhaps be now regarded as less important, or at least profoundly changed, by comparison to the relative quality of access to public facilities across different socio-economic localities within the urban, an issue in which differential developers ought to be expected to take a close interest, as the creation of new facilities in disadvantaged localities in order to provide better service chimes not only with their social purpose, but also under capitalism with their financial objectives.

Who develops public buildings?

The implicit assumption that runs through Lefebvre's comments on public space (e.g. Lefebvre, 1973 [2014], 1974 [1991] has often been that the public sector has itself acted as developer, commissioning architects, construction companies, and, where necessary, advisers; in so doing they can avoid the opprobrium attached to private sector developers. In many cases, this has been entirely correct. The construction of university buildings, leisure centres, civic offices, and the plethora of other public buildings has frequently been project managed directly by the public sector end user acting as developer (Perry & Wiewel, 2005). In other cases, development has been undertaken by government-owned developers, as in the case of Masdar presented earlier, and many others.

Neoliberalism at work 2? The case of Lafrowda Buildings, Exeter University

That UK universities have for many decades now been driven down a budget-conscious, increasingly economically driven route is scarcely up for dispute. Critics have suggested that the destruction of town houses as a result of the expansion, upgrading, landmarking, and rebranding of university campuses entails the loss of everyday urban life and local traditions (Troiani & Carless, 2021), whilst also suggesting that capitalism has succeeded in privatising Lefebvre's public space, 'the space of representation, [which] "spontaneously" becomes a place of promenades, encounters, intrigues, diplomacy, trade and negotiations, theatricalising itself' (Lefebvre, 1986 [1996:237]), converting teaching and learning spaces into facsimiles of contemporary workplaces that aim at rendering home and work spaces interchangeable. 'Work becomes play, and the marketing of these new, casual university architectures is used to maximize returns' (Troiani & Carless, 2021:8).

Specifically, however, they also suggested that what is described as the extreme makeovers of university buildings from the 1990s were enacted particularly by former polytechnics, and focused on those that were deemed ugly, cheaply built, and generally unsuitable, 'a form of university-building genocide or superficial facade refurbishment for marketing and advertising' (Troiani & Carless, 2021:7).

Strong words and clear objections. But where is the boundary between actions taken purely to create abstract space and those aimed at modernising the lived environment and enhancing the lives of students, arguably completely the opposite? What happens when the brutalist concrete buildings – ironically often the targets of Lefebvre's own vitriol – which can be seen as an architectural style that carries the university brand, become themselves part objects of affection, but part also alienating, hostile, abstract objects that deter, rather than promote, the experience of the university? When, for example, a shared bathroom, once taken for granted as normal for student accommodation (to declare an interest, I was once happily resident in what was then just 'Lafrowda'), becomes a throwback to a bygone age, and accommodation can be described as 'simple, communal living in its purest form – no one can accuse you of being pampered' (Evans, 2015). The benefit to residents now is that Old Lafrowda is less expensive than its younger sibling, but this comes with its own issues (Figure 9.7).

The University – the prestigious Russell Group member Exeter in this case, far from a former polytechnic – then has a problem. It is virtually forced to consider redevelopment, and has done so by progressively rebuilding. This creates an unmistakable and scarcely desirable inequality between new and old, so the eventual solution will no doubt be to replace the remainder of Old Lafrowda. The effect will be to reduce inequality between residents and

Figure 9.7 New Lafrowda viewed from old Lafrowda.

Source: Evans (2015).

improve student living standards from an original level which, as in the case of Pasir Ris Leisure Centre, could not be supported indefinitely. It is hard to recognise in this process the increase of alienation that redevelopment can often bring. Rather, if differential space is characterised by an absence of the kind of inequality represented by the disparity between Old and New Lafrowda, and as it is of course impossible to go back, it must be welcomed.

Marxist concern will no doubt be focused on the resultant increase in rents and the inequality between those at University in the first place and those not, an exclusionary quality which is definitely not a characteristic of differential space, but that is not the immediate concern either of Lefebvre's original critique of Nanterre, nor of those of his successors.

The idea that the public sector should establish 'bespoke single-minded central government development agencies based on the New Town Development Corporation model' (Leary, 2013:16), which would then act as master planner and developer, is not new, but it has been persistent since its origination, amongst other places in the post-war new towns of the UK, such as Milton Keynes (Roche, 1977). It is therefore of little surprise to find that the public sector is still responsible for initiating, and in many cases also managing, a significant proportion of global real estate, especially in the housing sector, and even under the economic and political conditions that would normally be characterised as neoliberal. The public sector is also actively engaged in a large range of real estate development projects that reflect, or ought to reflect, the responsibility of planners to create (and to protect) what Lefebvre describes as 'hétérotropies' – palaces, temples, but also cemeteries, prisons, and museums. In some cases, these development corporations, such as Development WA in Western Australia, which acts as a master developer as well as developing itself (Wilkinson *et al.*, 2022), operate on an accounting and financial basis extremely akin to a private sector developer: the old boundaries between public and private sectors are fraying, and no more so than in respect of real estate development, with all the attendant risks of conflicted interest between the role of developer and that of regulator that were adverted to in Chapter 3.

In some cases, however, including but by no means limited to PPP, and in a manner rather different to the relatively straightforward contractual relationships of Lefebvre's own era, developers have been retained essentially as intermediaries between the public sector end user and the process of construction. Their skill sets as project managers, introducing, utilising, and sharing across borders their expertise, for example, the use of GIS to monitor and evaluate the use of public space, have worked in the public interest. So, whilst it may indeed be that, in many cases of purely private sector development,

> The relationship between the public and private sectors of the economy is, therefore, not an antagonistic structure as crude economic theory may lead one to believe. In fact, the formation of these dual sectors can be seen as a product of the internal contradictions of capital accumulation, requiring public funding mechanisms to 'socialise' the costs of production.
>
> (Moreno, 2014:266n)

Equally, a product of the same internal contradictions of capital accumulation is that the expertise of real estate developers is put to work in the public interest.

The example of transport

An entire theoretical coalition has now coalesced in relation to transport, drawing parallels in significant measure with Lefebvre's analysis of space, with mobility theorists arguing that 'bodies and objects shape cities, and in turn are shaped through their rhythms of movement, their pace and synchrony' (Sheller, 2015:15) Equally importantly, 'Just as the social philosopher Henri Lefebvre (1974 [1991]) theorized that the character and nature of urban space reflected dominant modes of production and social relations (and power) within a given society, so, too, does mobility contain embedded social relations' (Henderson, 2015:e318). For radical mobility theorists, it is then but a short step to interrogating space to ask how transportation is experienced, represented, and contested within networked urban places (Sheller, 2015:30). No doubt this is an entirely valid political practice for Marxists, but there are also questions to be asked in the production of space, in which the role of the developer may not always be as negative as it is frequently portrayed. Developers have much to gain from the creation of efficient public transport networks, frequently contribute to their construction, some even volunteering to do so, and may even be found contesting in favour of public transport where others, even those in government, fail to do so, either out of ideological conviction or as a result of a failure of political courage. Conversely, transport organisations may create their own development arms in order to maximise their own synergies between real estate development and transportation. In some cases, they may adopt public transport as the underlying motivation for their creation of developments that push the boundaries of planning and even social norms.

Developer as public transport advocate in Arizona: the case of Tempe

The developer's stated aim was to produce communities prioritising biking, walking, and transit over cars and parking. They partnered with leading mobility companies to deliver convenient and affordable transportation services, in order 'to create a vibrant urban lifestyle without the need for a private vehicle' (Culdesac, 2022). Culdesac Tempe is a neighbourhood of 16 acres designed for 1,000 people, and intended to provide 636 low-rise living spaces, with 4,460 m^2, in a configuration where no cars will be permitted beyond of a small parking lot in the mixed-use commercial area designed for visitors. The developer's contractual removal of cars allows for a porous, fine-grained urban pattern with a network of narrow, shaded, pedestrian-only paseos, intimate courtyards, and a central plaza activated by restaurants, a small grocery, a co-working space, and a coffee shop (Steuteville, 2022). Instead of covering the neighborhood in pavement, more than half of the land area is planned to be covered in landscaping, public courtyards, and greenery – a very high ratio for an urban development, if it turns out to be correct.

The developer claims that the small 1,000-person scale of the neighbourhood allows them to think holistically, which would come as no surprise to Lefebvre. So, for example, instead of people having private guest rooms (which do not actually get used that often), residents can put up friends in bookable guest suites sprinkled throughout the neighborhood.

The developer also sought to partner with leading mobility companies in order to provide residents with shared, on-demand mobility, again a policy decision which Lefebvre would support, and to reduce thereby their demand for private automobile use. Culdesac Tempe, they claim, will be a welcoming home for shared bikes and scooters, providing them with dedicated parking spaces and charging infrastructure (Figure 9.8). Our one small mini-lot will be stocked with hourly rentable car-sharing. Dedicated rideshare pickup zones are placed around the perimeter of the neighborhood. It was also planned that residents would receive complimentary access to a Lyft Pink subscription, preferred pricing for a fleet of Bird scooters, an Envoy car share membership, and free unlimited passes on the Valley Metro transit system (Bliss, 2021). In addition, Culdesac Tempe is to be designed for walkability, something that not only Lefebvre would have welcomed, but Jane Jacobs too (Sung & Lee, 2015:320).

Figure 9.8 Culdesac Tempe.

Source: Culdesac (2022).

For Tempe to happen, the developer needed to invest time and resources into negotiating a development agreement with the city of Tempe. The developer reported that it was the first development agreement between a developer and the city to build a neighbourhood-scale development with zero residential parking (Lutz, 2019). The developer also needed venture capital funding, of which by 2022, it had received US$40 million in four rounds, en route to it hoped to much larger real estate funding (Crunchbase, 2022).

As with many other innovative, risky attempts to create differential space in the midst of a capitalist economy, the ambition may be laudable, but there is no certainty that the project will succeed. In many cases of previous technical and well as social development, there have been failures, sometimes many failures, before success – think of the history of flight, for example, or the creation of pedestrian zones in cities. Those favouring the adoption of Lefebvre's project by developers will want to support such actual initiatives in the 21st century, just as Lefebvre promoted and supported theoretical innovations by radical architects in his own. Just as now, Culdesac Tempe owes much to the utopian visionaries of the past, so in the future, no doubt developers will look back at Culdesac Tempe and explain how it could have been designed, funded, and managed in a superior fashion. If they are honest, they will however also admit that without pioneers such as Culdesac Tempe, they would not have the expertise to pass judgement.

The example of surveillance

For Marxist geographers, Lefebvre's disdain for an automobile-based culture – he mainly lived and worked in the centre of Paris, we should recall, where public transport served him well for many decades – chimes well with their own inclinations to support public transport in as many different forms as possible. The question of surveillance, however, is a radically opposite case. The working assumption of Marxist geographers has been that surveillance promulgated by the state is evidence of a denial of the right to the city (Harvey, 2008), tied indissolubly with control, hierarchy, and oppression within the urban environment (Parker, 2015). Examples where this chimes with the actual use and abuse of video surveillance abound. The result has been a call for a 'political geography of surveillance' (Klauser, 2012:4), based around Lefebvre's conception of the intricate but undeniable relationship between space and power.

By all means, however, the fact that 'CCTV is associated with a modest and significant reduction in crime' (Piza *et al.*, 2019:26), especially when it is recognised that CCTV has roles outside the policing sphere, such as accident prevention and detection, traffic flow measurement (Elharrouss *et al.*, 2021), ought to give pause for thought in making a presupposition against it in *all* cases, still less to identify wholeheartedly with the liberal standpoint that there is some inherent evil in CCTV with which those of a radical disposition should never have any patience. Perhaps, alternatively, 'There is no clear distinction between the 'watchers' and the 'watched' (Klauser, 2012:24). Might it indeed not be, that radical and conservative, beneficial and negative, can coexist within the phenomenon of surveillance, as they do with Lefebvrian space in general? Although historically the bias of the Left was always hostile, a small but steadily growing literature attesting CCTV surveillance of neighbourhoods provides evidence that when created as a result of a neighbourhood initiative (Hong & Cho, 2018), and used appropriately, for example, that the cameras are actively monitored, and when they are combined with other interventions such as police patrols, lighting, or community outreach (Piza *et al.*, 2019), surveillance can provide tangible benefits, even in poor communities. Where it forms part of a process in which crime control is decentralised, it can be considered as a neoliberal strategy (Trebilcock & Luneke, 2019), but to suggest that it is *always* so is surely contentious, especially if conjoined with the complaint that surveillance is often greater in more affluent communities and districts. Therefore, the role of the Marxist is not to object *in principle* to surveillance, as for example one might expect from positions held in principle by campaigning civil liberties organisations in the past (American Civil Liberties Union, 2002), but to investigate empirically its use, to ask *who benefits*, to determine its role on a case-by-case basis, and even on occasion to support it, where the beneficiaries are those at the margin who Lefebvre wished to protect.

Public buildings and sustainability

One key and very obvious area where developments can make a contribution to public space is sustainability. There are clear examples where they have done so; in some of these cases, the developer has been a consortium, perhaps led by an architect as in the following example, cross-subsidising, raiding the exchange value they have in order to create use value elsewhere, often the best possible way in a capitalist economy for even the most socially conscious developer to create differential space.

Developer as teacher: the Reggio school of Madrid

The developer in this case has been the combination of a group of Reggio school supporters and the Spanish architect Andrés Jaque, whose practice, the Office for Political Innovation, has carved out a niche over the last two decades for what Oliver Wainwright described as provocative, mischievous research projects, often taking the form of videos and installations, alongside a series of quirky private projects. In this case, however, it is a school, built on a tight construction budget of US$9.1 million. The building itself is located on the northern outskirts of Madrid, in the suburb of Encinar de los Reyes, close to a network of parks running up the Castellana, Madrid's main north–south axis. The building is in the form of a compact five-storey block, with playgrounds in simple rammed earth out, front and back.

Media reporting on the Reggio school has tended towards the lyrical, as Wainwright's own description aptly demonstrates (Figure 9.9).

> [T]he Reggio school's lumpy, yellowish, room-sized blocks appear to be stacked up on a frame of concrete shelves, with rows of beady bubble windows bursting through their gungey surfaces, like eyes

Figure 9.9 The Reggio school.

Source: Jose Hevia Blach.

> emerging from the gloop. The blocks leave gaps where lush gardens sprout, while polished metal ducts poke up from the zigzag rooftop, like the chimneys of a cartoon factory. Down below, the concrete base is sliced open with gaping arches, stretched wide and squeezed tight, as if the building is flexing its muscles.
>
> (Wainwright, 2023)

There are so many radical, different aspects to the design that observers report that they crowd upon one another. The envelope is in lightweight perforated brick, while the upper levels are constructed from a steel frame with thin concrete floor slabs, designed so as to try to village feel these areas of the school. Yellow cork insulation is sprayed onto the external envelope, a sustainable technique that encourages biodiversity, as it is intended to weather like the tree bark it once was, gathering moss, lichen, and other forms of non-human life. Likewise, tiny recessed gardens set into the school's facades are intended to attract birds, butterflies, and bats, increasing the building's 'third teacher' potential. Generous glazing panels allow abundant light into the building, whilst polycarbonate bubble porthole windows add to the building's unconventional appearance, to its natural ventilation – and to its charm.

As children come to the school very young and stay until they leave in their late teens, a decision was made to stratify the building, with the youngest pupils on the ground floor, their classrooms opening on to the front playground, and also the dining room that can be shared with parents and carers. The school's main entrance and common spaces – the library and the double-height sports/assembly hall – are on level two, looking out over the trees, connecting the viewer to the wider ecosystem. As in a castle, the main entrance is gained via a footbridge (the land slopes down from the street). This part of the building, in concrete, is perched high on pilotis, and engineered as thinly as possible, thanks to an impressive series of structural arches that, the architects say, reduced the need for steel reinforcement. On the same level, the library opens on a terrace from which the rear playground can be reached. while the sports/assembly hall enjoys a generous open-air loggia. Middle-school children occupy part of level two and all of level three, while the oldest are up on the top levels, their two floors organised around a double-height tree-filled atrium. Finally, looking out toward the towers of Madrid's business district on level five, three interconnecting laboratories – chemistry, physics, and biology – symbolically place senior students in the wider context of science, economics, society, and the world at large.

The developer, as radical architects, also use unusual materials, for example, surplus supplies, items that have little or no alternative use, out of fashion in the fast-moving world of abstract space, where subtle distinctions give away the difference between this year's design and last. The bubble windows, for example, were originally manufactured as roof lights for trailers, for which there is now little demand. The developer insists that it is the design that must adapt to the availability of materials, not the other way round. In very much a nod to Lefebvre, the chief designer observed, 'it's like mining new materials – and celebrating the potential of quotidian things' (Wainwright, 2023). The result is of the design, Wainwright suggested, with the parts lovingly assembled with meticulous care and childlike imagination, which have created one of the most extraordinary schools in Spain, perhaps in the world.

There are critics: though it is clearly deliberate – an informal aesthetic of raw truth whose unintimidating mess can stand whatever is thrown at it – one wonders what design lessons children will take away. Anything goes? A reactionary retreat into hyper-minimalism? (Ayers, 2023). What might the differential developer say in response? Fortunately, the developer can speak for himself:

> If schools are places where children and teenagers learn to live in society, the standardization of these buildings transmits an idea of order typical of a disciplinary society. This project, on the contrary, dismantles order and replaces it with a space in which girls and boys interact with the building, water, plants, earth, and a series of elements with whom they coexist while, incidentally, learn to face the complexities of a world that is not at all orderly.
>
> (Jaque, 2020:48)

Even if we might worry that not every pupil will necessarily thrive in such an unstructured learning environment, Lefebvre himself would surely have approved, and there must be elements, at least, of designs of this kind that developers can usefully incorporate into more conventional responses to traditional school Requests for Proposals (RFPs). We cannot after all wish for schools of this kind to remain as unusual oddities in a world of conformity – they have lessons to teach other developers, as well as the children who learn within them.

Conclusion

The balance so far as public space is concerned between the egalitarian access that preoccupied Lefebvre so much, on the one hand, and the functional efficiency of space, on the other hand, is of obvious and permanent importance, as well as of great political importance. Restrictions and control on access based on financial capacity may be of special concern to Marxists, both for their threat to public provision in general and for the risks they pose to equality of access to public services.

But access is not the only issue that defines public space. So far as real estate developers are concerned, aside from providing maximum access possibilities at the physical level, their influence over decision-making in this area may be minimal. All that they may be able to do is influence both the choice and the content of RFPs from urban planners and governments, and to ensure that their own internal codes of governance disallow them from participating in forms of PPP, for instance, that may discriminate against the poor or other disadvantaged sections of the community.

Where developers may have much more positive to offer is in relation to the functionality of public space: its design, efficiency of operation, and its capacity, at least, to provide ease of access to all.

Bibliography

American Civil Liberties Union. (2002). *What's wrong with public video surveillance?* Available at: www.aclu.org/other/whats-wrong-public-video-surveillance. [Accessed 3 August 2022].

Ayers, A. (2023). Andrés Jaque takes an unconventional approach to design and construction at Madrid's Colegio Reggio Explora. *Architectural Record*, 7 January. Available at: www.architecturalrecord.com/articles/15989-andres-jaque-takes-an-unconventional-approach-to-design-and-construction-at-madrids-colegio-reggio-explora. [Accessed 21 January 2023].

Bliss, L. (2021). Developers offer mobility services to lure car-free renters. *Bloomberg*, 8 September. Available at: www.bloomberg.com/news/articles/2021-09-08/paying-rent-will-get-you-wheels-in-new-car-free-complex. [Accessed 2 November 2022].

Chiovaro, M., Windsor, L. C., Windsor, A. and Paxton, A. (2021). Online social cohesion reflects real-world group action in Syria during the Arab Spring. *PLoS One*, 16(7), e0254087.

Ciccarellim, R. and Slade, L. (2023). 'Invasion day' protests across the country draw huge crowds. *9 News*, 26 January. Available at: www.9news.com.au/national/australia-day-2023-invasion-day-protesters-pack-streets-as-country-remains-divided-over-january-26/4d10632a-d179–4855–8cef-69b24e5eef88. [Accessed 29 January 2023].

Crunchbase. (2022). *Culdesac*. Available at: www.crunchbase.com/organization/culdesac-f070. [Accessed 16 January 2023].

Culdesac. (2022). *Welcome to Culdesac Tempe*. Available at: https://culdesac.com/. [Accessed 14 January 2023].

Design Curial. (2011). The $40 million Pasir Ris sports complex has opened in Singapore. *Design Curial*, 9 November. Available at: www.designcurial.com/news/pasir-ris-sports-complex-opens-in-singapore375363 [Accessed 7 November 2022].

Elharrouss, O., Almaadeed, N. and Al-Maadeed, S. (2021). A review of video surveillance systems. *Journal of Visual Communication and Image Representation*, 77, 103116.

El-Samea, A. M. A., Hassan, N. M. and Abdallah, A. S. H. (2020). The effect of courtyard ratio on energy consumption and thermal comfort in a primary governmental school in new Assiut city, Egypt. In Kamel, S. *et al.* (eds.) *Architecture and Urbanism: A Smart Outlook*. Cham, Springer, 121–131.

Evans, I. (2015). Old Lafrowda is a loveable shithole. *The Tab*, 26 November. Available at: https://thetab.com/uk/exeter/2015/11/26/old-lafrowda-is-a-loveable-shithole-28896. [Accessed 5 August 2022].

Eves, R. C. (2014). Finding place to speak: Sarah Winnemucca's rhetorical practices in disciplinary spaces. *Legacy: A Journal of American Women Writers*, 31(1), 1–22.

Fatima, S. (2021). Abu Dhabi's first Hindu temple will last over 1,000 years. *Siasat*, 27 September. Available at: www.siasat.com/abu-dhabis-first-hindu-temple-will-last-over-1000-years-2198307/. [Accessed 13 October 2022].

Goodling, E. (2020). Intersecting hazards, intersectional identities: A baseline critical environmental justice analysis of US homelessness. *Environment and Planning E: Nature and Space*, 3(3), 833–856.

Guangzhou China. (2018). *Construction of UCLA health and R&F properties hospital begins*, 24 July. Available at: www.eguangzhou.gov.cn/2018-07/24/c_257896.htm. [Accessed 25 February 2023].

Harvey, D. (2008). The right to the city. *New Left Review*, 53(1), 23–40. Available at: https://newleftreview.org/issues/ii53/articles/david-harvey-the-right-to-the-city. [Accessed 21 October 2021].

Henderson, J. (2015). From climate fight to street fight: The politics of mobility and the right to the city. In Cidell, J. and Prytherch, D. (eds.) *Transport, Mobility, and the Production of Urban Space*. New York, Routledge, 101–116.

Hong, S. and Cho, B. S. (2018). Citizen participation and the redistribution of public goods. *Public Administration*, 96(3), 481–496.

Jamali, R. (2014). *Online Arab Spring: Social Media and Fundamental Change*. Hull, Chandos Publishing.

Jaque, A. (2020). Colegio Reggio. Encinar de los Reyes, Madrid, España, 2019. *ARQ (Santiago)*, 106, 48–59.

Järvinen-Tassopoulos, J. (2020). Les espaces de jeux d'argent: une analyse sociologique de la production de l'espace, du risque et de la prévention du jeu problématique. *Sciences du jeu*, 13, 1–17. Available at: https://journals.openedition.org/sdj/2552. [Accessed 23 January 2022].

Klauser, F. (2012). *Espaces, pouvoirs et régulations: vers une géographie politique de la surveillance*. MAPS Working Paper No 4–2012/F. Université de Neuchâtel. Available at: www.unine.ch/maps/home/publications/workingpapersmaps.html. [Accessed 6 June 2022].

Kung, J. and Pang, L. (eds.) (2015). Pasir Ris Sports Centre. Sports for Everyone. *Citygreen*, 10, 108–117.

Leary, M. E. (2013). A Lefebvrian analysis of the production of glorious, gruesome public space in Manchester. *Progress in Planning*, 85, 1–52.

Lefebvre, H. (1947). *Critique de la vie quotidienne. Volume One. Introduction*. Paris: Grasset. Translated by J. Moore (1991 [2014]) as *Critique of Everyday Life. Volume One. Introduction*. London, Verso.

———. (1970). *Du rural à l'urbain*. Paris, Anthropos.

———. (1973 [2014]). *Vers une architecture de la jouissance*. Translated by R. Bononno as *Toward an architecture of enjoyment*. Minnesota, University of Minnesota Press.

———. (1974 [1991]). *La production de l'espace*. Paris, Anthropos. Translated by D. Nicholson-Smith as *The Production of Space*. Oxford, Blackwell.

———. (1986 [1996]). Rhythmanalysis of mediterranean cities. In Kofman, E. and Lebas, E. (eds.) *Writings on Cities*. Oxford, Blackwell, 228–240.

Lutz, S. (2019). Post-car real estate developer, Culdesac, announces first car-free neighborhood built from scratch in the U.S. *Business Wire*, 19 November. Available at: www.businesswire.com/news/home/20191119005568/en/Post-Car-Real-Estate-Developer-Culdesac-Announces-First-Car-Free-Neighborhood-Built-From-Scratch-in-the-U.S. [Accessed 2 November 2022].

Mehta, V. and Palazzo, D. (eds.) (2020). *Companion to Public Space*. New York and London, Routledge.

Mitchell, D. and Villanueva, J. (2010). Right to the city. In Hutchinson, R. *et al.* (eds.) *Encyclopedia of urban studies*. Thousand Oaks, Sage, 667–671.

Moreno, L. (2012). A review of "Henri Lefebvre on space: Architecture, urban research and the production of theory". *Annals of the Association of American Geographers*, 102(4), 885–890.

———. (2014). The urban process under financialised capitalism. *City*, 18(3), 244–268.

Mualam, N., Hendricks, A., Maliene, V. and Salinger, E. (2021). Value capture and vertical allocations of public amenities. *Sustainability*, 13(7), 3952.

Mualam, N., Salinger, E. and Max, D. (2019). Increasing the urban mix through vertical allocations: Public floorspace in mixed use development. *Cities*, 87, 131–141.

Newsom, V. A. and Lengel, L. (2012). Arab women, social media, and the Arab spring: Applying the framework of digital reflexivity to analyze gender and online activism. *Journal of International Women's Studies*, 13(5), 31–45.

Parker, S. (2015). *Urban Theory and the Urban Experience: Encountering the City*. 2nd edition. New Ork and London, Routledge.

Perry, D. and Wiewel, W. (2005). *From Campus to City: The University as a Developer*. New York, Routledge.

Pierce, J. (2022). How can we share space? Ontologies of spatial pluralism in Lefebvre, Butler, and Massey. *Space and Culture*, 25(1), 20–32.

Piza, E. L., Welsh, B. C., Farrington, D. P. and Thomas, A. L. (2019). CCTV surveillance for crime prevention: A 40-year systematic review with meta-analysis. *Criminology & Public Policy*, 18(1), 135–159.

Riphagen, W. and Woltering, R. A. (2018). Tales of a square: The production and transformation of political space in the Egyptian (counter) revolution. *Arab Studies Quarterly*, 40(2), 117–133.

Roche, F. L. (1977). New towns' contribution to inner areas. *Town and Country Planning*, 45(4).

Ross, K. and Lefebvre, H. (1983 [1997]). Lefebvre on the Situationists: An interview. *October*, 79, 69–83.

Santos Junior, O. A. D. (2014). Urban common space, heterotopia and the right to the city: Reflections on the ideas of Henri Lefebvre and David Harvey. *urbe. Revista Brasileira de Gestão Urbana*, 6(2), 146–157.

Sheller, M. (2015). Foreword 2: Mobilizing transportation, transporting mobilities. In Cidell, J. and Prytherch, D. (eds.) *Transport, Mobility, and the Production of Urban Space*. New York and Abingdon, Routledge, 12–18.

Shi, L. Li, W. and He, Y. (2020). An incentive analysis of availability payment mechanism in PPP projects. *IEEE Access*, 8, 106046–106058.

Steuteville, R. (2022). 'Car-free' development substantially built. *Public Square*, 2 September. Available at: www.cnu.org/publicsquare/2022/09/02/car-free-development-substantially-built. [Accessed 4 November 2022].

Stevens, Q. (2007). *The Ludic City. Exploring the Potential of Public Spaces*. London, Routledge.

Sung, H. and Lee, S. (2015). Residential built environment and walking activity: Empirical evidence of Jane Jacobs' urban vitality. *Transportation Research Part D*, 41, 318–329.

Trebilcock, M. P. and Luneke, A. (2019). Crime prevention and the coproduction of security: Outcomes of citizen participation at the neighborhood level in Neoliberal Chile. *Latin American Perspectives*, 46(6), 56–72.

Troiani, I. S. and Carless, T. (2021). The death and life of UK universities and the cultural spaces they consume. *Architecture MPS*, 19(1), 1–12.

Wainwright, O. (2023). Rainforest? Turn left after the drawbridge! Inside Madrid's eye-popping living school. *Guardian*. Available at: www.theguardian.com/artanddesign/2023/jan/17/reggio-school-andres-jaque-madrid-rainforest-zig-zag. [Accessed 6 November 2022].

Warf, B. (2021). Place, space, and cyberlaw. In Bartel, R. and Carter, J. (eds.) *Handbook on Space, Place and Law*. Cheltenham, Edward Elgar Publishing, 316–326.

Wilkinson, G. S., Haslam McKenzie, F. and Bolleter, J. (2022). Why does Perth stand alone? Interviews with subject matter experts about the drivers of settlement in Western Australia. *Australian Geographer*, 53(2), 183–200.

10 Conclusion

Lessons learned

Where we began

It is easier to research, analyse, and sketch than to plan, compromise, and deliver, so whilst radical geographers, including Marxists, have delivered a series of uncompromising denunciations of the activities of real estate developers, they have been much less vocal in suggesting how developers should behave and how they should be evaluated in a capitalist society. The consequence of this disparity, however, has been an increasingly wide divergence between radical theory and real estate practice, with many radical geographers looking to the capitalist state to provide housing, whilst standing back from attempting to guide developers themselves, except to criticise behaviour is so egregiously unethical as to represent an unmissable poster opportunity for an attack on capitalism itself.

Equally of concern, and no doubt partially because of the widespread absence of the kind of state involvement in real estate development for which they have called for so long, some Marxists themselves have begun to spend more time looking backwards towards historical space rather than engaging with the present and contributing to the future of differential space. For sustained criticisms by radical and Marxist geographers of the production of space within capitalism do have echoes of the past, in terms of both the identification of those adversely affected by real estate development in class terms and in the advocacy of public sector solutions:

> Defending what Lefebvre termed 'the right to the city' political economists have for decades criticised schemes that enhance capital accumulation to the detriment of ordinary residents. With varying hopefulness concerning the possibilities for meaningful social action, they endorse community movements that oppose large-scale economic development projects and gentrification. They support construction of housing for low income people, especially in the form of co-ops or public ownership, criticize 'right-to-buy' schemes that withdraw housing from the low-income rental stock, favour rent control, and stand up for the rights of tenants, squatters, and homeless people to housing security, even when their interests come into conflict with those of working-class neighbours seeking to protect their own interests in neighbourhood stability.
>
> (Fainstein, 1996:22)

DOI: 10.1201/9781003220244-10

They continue to do so (Vives-Miró, 2022). But the problem remains that what has been said of possibly the most famous urbanist of all, Jane Jacobs, could equally well be said of Lefebvre and his successors, that 'many have found her to be a beckoning screen on which to project their ideologies. Jane Jacobs has had a lasting power for many reasons, but one of them certainly is that she offers something for everyone' (Page, 2017:4).

So, we are entitled to ask:

> What, then, are the present prospects for his [Lefebvre's] critique of alienation, and his call for the right to the city and self-management? Lefebvre will not protest if we leave the last word on this question to those engaged in radical praxis – the struggle to wrest a properly human world from the inhuman Planet of Slums in the Age of Empire, which may yet stretch his work to new frontiers, just as he did Marx's.
>
> (Goonewardena, 2011:60)

Applying Lefebvre: revising the critical narrative

This book has been an attempt in at least one area to invoke the thought and work of Henri Lefebvre to reverse what could be seen as a dangerous trend, and to suggest instead why developers should take Lefebvre seriously, and how they can. And for Marxists to focus on what developers can offer that is positive, how they may form part of a contribution to the supersession of capitalism, and even, if they wish to think with Lefebvre in a utopian way, what they may be able to offer after it has been superseded.

To do so involves challenging the critical narrative dominant in radical geography that has suggested that there is a set of homogeneous 'universalizing ideologies of the city' – all undesirable, whether positivist, technoscientific, entrepreneurial, eco-managerial, and/or neoliberal variants – irrevocably embedded in mapping policy and practice both in international organisations, such as the World Bank, the United Nations SDGs, the New Urban Agenda, and the Paris Agreement, and in

> a range of corporate actors and property developers for whom the construction of 'global cities', 'smart cities', 'creative cities', 'sustainable cities', 'eco-cities', and the like is seen as the optimal pathway for ensuring continued economic growth without disrupting the currently hegemonic formation of neoliberalized, financialized accumulation by dispossession.
>
> (Brenner, 2018:571–572)

According to this narrative, any disruption to these ideologies must necessarily derive from actors placed in a politically privileged – if largely economically disadvantaged – position located firmly outside this distinct, prevailing global nexus of power. This operates specifically over the development and control of urban space, which corals entire organisations at the same time as excluding others, executing the same divisive distinctions between individuals, though as always with the traditional difficulties Marxists have always had with managerial functions by comparison to the relative clarity over capitalist ownership. Challenging and seeking to disrupt this prevailing narrative requires, amongst many others, the contention that the term 'neoliberal' has been made to serve too many masters. There is no such single set of universalising ideologies, if there ever was. On the one hand, the vision of the SDGs is only very partially aligned with the objectives of many developers who have concentrated precisely on the process of accumulation by dispossession, whilst, on the other hand, there are developers worldwide who have made every effort to create differential space, working with (and in some cases against) parts of the state, community groups, and many others who do not feature within the social ontology of the critical narrative.

Urban protest

The analysis is sharp and penetrating, in the best tradition of Marxism. Yet, on the other hand, Marxists have long been forced to confront the failure of revolutionary politics based on conceptions of 'the dictatorship of the proletariat' and a 'vanguard political party' that will direct the working class towards socialism, as conceived by the Leninist founders of the Soviet Union. Many have reformulated their approach altogether, illustrated by the approach to defining Marxism taken by the renowned French Marxist Lucien Sève, who towards the end of his long life enjoined us to 'think with Marx' rather than being Marxists (Sève, 2004). Sève, amongst many others, readily conceded that the failed Leninist experiment was responsible for the creation of bureaucratic state socialist states in a world where capitalism was still both vibrant and more than willing to confront its opponents, and that a future Marxism must never repeat its mistakes. True, the legacy of the debates amongst Marxists in previous centuries does remain, notably in the continued nostalgia that some Marxists, often affiliated with fringe political parties, still demonstrate for the raw class conflict so often manifested in that century (e.g. Arseneau, 2021). But for many Marxists, including Sève and many other former Communist Party members worldwide, the Frankfurt School, New Marxists and Marxist humanists, Lefebvre included, the adoption of the precepts of 'Critical' Marxism entails their no longer being trapped, as were their 'Scientific' predecessors in the past, into insisting on the existence of rigidly defined, traditionally conceived social classes based around the capitalist system of production, distribution, and exchange, the raw concepts of base and superstructure, the necessity of violent revolution, or the requirement for a vanguard party to lead it. In their view, whilst all of these may have once been appropriate to propel strategy, they are now no longer fit for purpose. Rather, Sève argued – as this book also began – that the core of Marxism has always been recognition of the essentially transient nature of capitalism (Sève, 2004:8) and the uplifting vision of humanity in a world that has transcended the alienation that capitalism and its conquest of political power has wrought upon humanity (Sève, 2012). At the same time, a revolutionary concept of citizenship (Lefebvre, 1989 [2014:205]) is required in order 'to struggle for the right of the city' (Misoczky & Oliveira, 2018:1028). If the result is that Marxists end up with 'a rather eclectic mix of concepts – a Marxism without the law of value, a Marxism privileging competition and exchange rather than class and production, for example, or simply a concern for unequal outcomes' (Cox, 2005:3), and an active, campaigning citizenship rather than a dutiful proletariat led by a revolutionary party, then the later Lefebvre, at least, might not be unhappy with the result, if – and only if – it leads to an active political engagement, at the forefront of which lies the production of space.

The evidence of this transformation within Marxism is hardly elusive: although such Marxists are still therefore to be found proclaiming that 'Democratic socialism is the humanist alternative to the divisionist pathways of war, fascism, and destruction' (Fuchs, 2021:23), Marxism has now added two important strands to this assertion.

Firstly, although Marxists have always recognised that 'social justice is not decided by a system of absolute and eternal values and principles, rather, it depends on the social processes operating in a society as a whole' (Liu, 2018:513), there are now prominent writers – to cite just five examples, Paul Blackledge (2012), Kohie Saito (2017), Shahrzad Mojab (2015), Cornel West (Fuchs, 2021), and Stuart Hall (2016) – who have highlighted the rich hinterland in the work of Marx of ethical, environmental, gender, race, and cultural thinking, respectively, and reinvigorated Marxism as a result (Stetsenko, 2020). Lefebvre would surely find himself very much at home in their company and in this rejuvenated Marxism, reconfigured so that the purpose of superseding capitalism is clearly identified as the flourishing of human freedom. Lefebvre's project, to be enacted as a global *oeuvre*, suggests only that economic growth should be limited and directed towards social needs, that the centre and periphery of cities – and by extension, societies – should be joined up, and that *autogestion* should be given the largest possible role, notwithstanding its problems (Lefebvre, 1973 [1976:119]). Lefebvre's direction for the supersession of capitalism was conceived many decades ago – it certainly enjoys close similarities with another proposed global project of Marxist origin conceived around the same time (Garaudy, 1976:217). But the urgency of climate change – of which Lefebvre himself was well aware – and the continuation of spatial injustice both reinforce the necessity of change being at least conceived at a global scale, if not enacted so, and the vitality and contemporary relevance of his approach.

Secondly, Sartre's clarion call to fill the gap where a theory of the individual should be within Marxism (Sartre, 1963:82), surely never adequately refuted by Lefebvre or any other PCF theorist, led over many years to a profound, often painful, recognition by the majority of Marxists that not only was he right, but also eventually to the reluctant acceptance that the transformation of society would rely more on the efforts of individuals and small groups and organisations than on the collective concepts, revolutionary parties in particular, that had demonstrated their failure in practice. What has this profound change meant for Marxists themselves? We no longer find Marxists almost exclusively within the closed confines of ever-smaller minority political parties, or even in an exclusively political entryism, trades unions, or the public sector, but rather, 'out' as individuals in their communities, participating actively in a wide range of different types of organisations with many different economic forms. In summary, Marxists are no longer stereotypes: entryism has gone mainstream.

The combination of these strands has been perhaps best encapsulated in the pejorative term 'cultural Marxism', which has become the focus of those strident critics on the political Right who perhaps preferred Marxists, along with black, gay, and trans people and any other potentially counter-hegemonic group, to remain collectively on the fringe of politics, and certainly not emerge individually at the centre of society and its forms of social organisation (Jamin, 2018). There are, as a result, few Marxists outside minority political parties who would not agree that Marx never welcomed poverty and exploitation (Kolakowski, 1978:302) and who would not therefore reject the Trotskyist mantra of 'the worse the better' as encouraging the collapse of capitalism (Elster, 1981:637; Noys, 2010:5).

In recognising the transience of capitalism, however, contemporary Marxists are keen to avoid the mistakes of their 'Scientific' predecessors in holding too sanguine a belief in regard to the timeframe for its demise. They must recognise that 'seeing the beginning of radical change in every symbolic action or organized protest such as the movement of Indignados in Spain, the Occupy Movement in London or the striking workers in Greece is, at least, overly optimistic' (Frantzanas, 2014:1078). Notwithstanding notable contemporary political movements at odds with at least some, perhaps much, of capitalism, such as the rise from the Civil Rights Movement of Black Lives Matter (Robinson, 2021:15), the climate change movement, and arguably also developments in academic work now dating back decades, such as transgender studies (Stryker, 1994, 2015; Gleeson & O'Rourke, 2021), with which they can often make common cause where the opportunity arises, Marxists now recognise that the overcoming of capitalism will surely be the work of many generations. The utopian enthusiasm of the Occupy movement should neither be forgotten nor be celebrated, as the questions it raised are left as yet unanswered (Pinder, 2013:29). So likewise the liberation of society from work itself has been repeatedly and evidently prematurely forecast, not least by the utopian architects with whom Lefebvre kept company midway through the 20th century (Ross & Lefebvre, 1983 [1997:75]). As, after their initial euphoria evaporated, Christians have patiently explained for almost 2,000 years, it is too greedy to expect to live to see the parousia, but that is no excuse not to hope, nor not strive for it (Bauckham, 1980:6).

Confronted by this unwelcome but undeniable background, Marxists face a choice in how to engage with Lefebvre. One route simultaneously cocoons Lefebvre in the academy, where even the architecture of a lost future past can be cherished, associating his work exclusively with disruptive space, a perpetual series of sparks, never a conflagration. In this world view, much in evidence throughout this book, only Lefebvre's voice is required, a perpetual herald calling for a new conceptualisation of the urban that privileges complementarity and complexity, collectivity and solidarity, diversity and communion over consumption, accumulation, and production (Monte-Mór, 2018). Any revised 'Right to the City' in this view runs the risk of merely creating 'minimal differences', which repeat extant forms, and which do not contribute to changing the relations of production, rather than maximal differences, which do (Lefebvre, 1974 [1991:372]).

The other route, which I hope will be taken, visualises his work also as a theoretical understanding entwined with a call to engage and act to architects, planners, and certainly developers who *can* potentially change the relations of production as well. Underlying the choice is the underlying hope that 'by pushing back against the status quo of the state and global capital – through actions ranging from overt protests to everyday subversions of the system – the dialectics between reality and envisioned utopias can lead to social transformation' (Howe, 2022:393). The evident distance between the two approaches is stark.

If they are to choose the latter route, Marxists must ask, who can carry out these everyday subversions of capitalism? People can. Yet even Lefebvre himself, who broke with the PCF and remained largely independent thereafter, has been criticised on this score: 'One of the remarkable things about his whole discussion of these fundamental geopolitical issues is that people never get a mention' (Unwin, 2000:23). It might be appropriate to admit criticism of the Political Economy approach to urban studies more widely, which focuses on its failure to incorporate the agency of individuals and the organisations to which they belong (Wu *et al.*, 2019:1491). That is, that any Political Economy approach, including Marxism, tends towards 'a top-down, universalistic, single view of the world that cannot explain the local and the particular' (Ribera-Fumaz, 2009:45). No Marxist can be comfortable with such potential weakness in an approach to the urban any more than to politics or philosophy as a whole, which if it is to be resolved, suggests, at least a need to revise Lefebvre's approach to the urban to place people, and the organisations in which they serve, at the centre of analysis – and of political engagement.

Real estate developers now and in the future

What therefore should Marxists make of real estate developers? Do they have any place at all in this campaign, except as the sworn enemy? The evidence of the empirical chapters above has at least hopefully permitted the tentative conclusion that developers are in reality much more complex organisations than the unmitigated purveyors of evil that radical geography has frequently portrayed them. They are often, as with any organisation operating in a capitalist society, beset by contradictory forces both internal and external. On close examination, some not only have the capacity, but have actually succeeded, in creating differential space – in precisely the partial and contradictory sense of which Lefebvre would surely have recognised – such as the turn to affordable housing, the piecemeal advance of ESG within developers themselves, in part driven by the confused requirements of capital itself, and the rise of not-for-profit developers. The upshot is that although they are certainly capable of creating great evil in the service of capitalism, for which there is ample evidence, developers can point to a series of positive achievements and useful roles that Marxists should recognise, encourage, and promote. None of this is however meant to suggest that all the many criticisms that radical geographers have levelled against developers should be thrown overboard in favour of an uncritical admiration for their work: Marxists can safely leave that to others, and anyway, those with no criticism whatever are very few.

There is moreover an opportunity for those taking Lefebvre seriously for developers: a theoretical void within real estate developers exists, even if developers themselves refuse to admit that it does. If 'Architects have often looked to thinkers in philosophy and theory to find design ideas or in search of a critical framework for practice' (Scharr, 2014:xiii), the same can hardly be said for developers. Perhaps it is partly a question of supply, as much as demand: for example, the series in which *Lefebvre for Architects* (Coleman, 2014) appears includes, inter alia, Latour (Yaneva, 2022), Freud (Abell, 2020), and Kant (Morgan, 2017), along with Lefebvre (whose application might seem more obvious), is not yet matched with a similar series of applications of thinkers to real estate development, despite the fact that it is developers who generally employ architects, not vice versa. And if developers do not find material written for them, then like architects (at least if the presupposition for the series is anything to go by) it is less likely that they will act in accordance with the ideas expressed by those thinkers. That is, provided they agree with them, so those taking Lefebvre seriously for developers should seek to fill that void – but in a way that developers will understand, appreciate, and act on.

The importance of this engagement may be decisive, for two reasons. Firstly, if Lefebvre is right that capitalism has been able to survive only by means of 'occupying space, by producing a space' (Lefebvre, 1973 [1976:21], then there can be little doubt that in a real estate economy, what space is created and how it is created both will play a central role in the future of capitalism, and therefore likewise in its downfall. For now, the examples successful developments set can be dangerous. They can often reinforce inequality and widen cultural, racial, and class divisions. They can help lure capital into devastating crises, from which the State extricates it at heavy cost, often to those least able to bear it. On the other hand, the very best of developers even under current economic pressures can and do deliver real estate that is both sensitive to local community requirements and environmentally sustainable. As the examples in the chapters of this book have sought to demonstrate, whilst, as with architecture, the mainstream may be underpinned by the requirements of urban capitalism and the ideology of neoliberalism, individual developments can be the most surprising places, coexisting with profoundly capitalist trends and space, yet acting as beacons of the future for those who hope for better things, whilst individual developers may sometimes or even always act without a profit motive, even in the midst of rampant global capitalism and even at a time when real estate has become the primary investment asset, rendering what was secondary primary.

Secondly, in transductive reasoning regarding the future, Marxists can now use the experience of real estate development under capitalism, together with analysis of real estate developers themselves to sketch out how it might look in its absence. We no longer look forward, as Lefebvre already did not look forward, to a reincarnation of development through central planning, executed exclusively by the State, through either central or local government, with outsourcing, if at all, confined to construction itself. Rather, it is to a future where real estate development will still be enacted by specialist institutions, developers, co-ordinating land, construction materials, management, and other resources as they do now, but no longer constrained by the need to execute developments in the interests of shareholders or profitability. Instead, their developments will be the outcome of the same kind of multi-stakeholder engagement, negotiation, and compromise that are already evident in embryo even within a capitalist development framework, but severely circumscribed by it. They can therefore set positive precedents, as developers' utopianism can be decidedly of the Lefebvrian transductive kind, and in that case, we need more of it, not less. A post-capitalist society would wish to conserve, even enhance, many of these developments, ranging from public infrastructure through to affordable housing. Beyond capitalism, many more could be expected. Until such time, however, Marxist engagement with real estate developers is a combination of criticism and encouragement.

Evaluating developers

As with any Marxist worth reading, Lefebvre should not be reserved solely for radical urban theorists in the academy to cite, and still less only for them to applaud when the streets become temporarily unsafe for capital, however uplifting the occasional sight of capitalism under threat may be. Nor should Lefebvre be monopolised by the public sector more widely, to be admired only by urban planners and regulators. Nor even by architects, welcome as their role in helping to create differential space undoubtedly is. Rather, Lefebvre's work also deserves to be taken seriously by real estate developers and investors. They have a unique capacity to create, maintain, and exchange places that reach beyond capitalism to create differential space themselves – to help shape places that can become an important part of the solution to the most important global problems, rather than to contribute to them, and ultimately to overcome capitalism.

Marxists should argue that the *primary function* of developers, the reason for their existence, should be to produce differential space, in all its myriad forms. None of this is to suggest that differential space is likely to be easy to create: developers will not need to work with different types of organisations, as suggested that Lefebvre should not be read – certainly not read now, with the benefit of many decades of hindsight – as implying that the creation of differential space will entirely remove the need for mediation amongst contrasting – and yes, maybe even competing – uses for space within a post-capitalist society. Even the very concept of differential space may need to be reconsidered, in the way that Marxists have already reformed conceptions of socialism and communism. In this process, which may include the resolution of differences between individuals and groups in regard to differential space, it might be suggested, *a range of intermediate organisations will be needed*; some of these may well exist, again in embryo, even in capitalist society, such as Aboriginal Rights groups in Australia, representatives of immigrants in Europe, local community associations in the Brazilian favelas, and so on. And as and when the State itself becomes redundant, such organisations would take on roles of increasing importance. Marxists should participate in that process, one brick, one organisation, one person at a time.

For if developers are excluded from this movement entirely, as this conventional radical geography framework requires, then in a curious and disturbing way developers are also exonerated from moral responsibility in the process. Characterised as mere tools of a capitalist system beyond their control, they cannot from this standpoint help but deliver socially undesirable outcomes that will never benefit the majority, let alone the dispossessed. Examples of appalling behaviour by developers are more useful than any of the kind of positive examples of real estate development that I have provided as examples of what developers can achieve, even to the extent of producing differential space, as they fit the traditional narrative. My contention throughout this book has been the reverse: that developers should be held to account alongside architects and planners. If they are to be judged as to whether they take Lefebvre seriously, it will be through their commitment to an achievable Utopia, and the results of their endeavours.

Final words

I have tried to make two arguments in this book. The first, aimed at Marxists, is that above all in creating its physical component, reading Lefebvre in the contemporary capitalist environment demands recognition of the fact that real estate developers are both decisive agents of the creation of the future urban and battlegrounds over which its future shape will be decided. For Marxists, therefore, the significance of real estate developers in the production of space within capitalism is now so substantial, and virtually universal, that a theoretical reappraisal of their role and a practical engagement with them is unavoidable. It has been my contention in this book that such an engagement may be of benefit to both Marxists and real estate developers themselves.

Secondly, I have argued that not only can the *oeuvres* produced by developers be usefully analysed using the categories and theory developed by Lefebvre, but that the understanding of space that he brought to Marxism and the project he advocated for the creation of differential space is one that every real estate developer should embrace. The central concern of analysing practice, then, is to understand the balance between domination and appropriation, between abstract and differential space, in the actions and processes of real estate development. Challenged by Marxists, differential developers will find both themselves and what they achieve fragile, incomplete, challenged, and criticised. But in responding positively, humanly, they will stand at the boundary between abstract and differential space: they will find it both an uncertain and an exciting place to be.

Two points emerge so far as developers are concerned, one long-term and utopian in a Lefebvrian sense, the other short-term and responsive to current economic and political conditions.

In the long term, taking Lefebvre seriously entails the recognition of the need for real estate developers as organisations separate from yet entwined with the state, most certainly the current state but even a future more democratic state in a post-capitalist world. But the same approach urges that these real estate developers should be funded differently, organised differently, and have different objectives, whilst remaining nevertheless unlike the cumbersome and insensitive public agencies of the past. In such a utopia, developers would be mostly small, certainly agile, and always responsive to, if not always accepting of, local needs, preferences, and cultural, racial, social, and economic differences. *Autogestion* for developers, in a nutshell, as Lefebvre argued, should be a goal for every enterprise.

In the short term, which may unfortunately endure for a very long time, the suggestion is for Marxists to take two steps. Firstly, to adopt some kind of scalar criticism for developers, a kind of 'social rating', which would evaluate them, not on the glossiness of their brochures, the luxury of their top-end products, and still less on their returns to shareholders, whether family or even pension fund, but on their social and environmental performance, above all their contribution to the creation or retention of differential urban space – to their role not to create abstract private space, but to challenge it, even to surpass it. Existing ESG tools are far from ideal, but it would at least be a coherent way for Marxists to start to structure criticisms of developer behaviour, to build on, and even praise them when they do the right thing. Secondly, to engage in organisational study of developers aimed at providing more specific, local, and individual contexts for the internal and external processes of developers that encourage and support their production of differential space, and likewise discourage them from generating more abstract space in support of capitalist ventures that lead to further inequality, empty space, and other adverse social consequences. In this way, developers may appear as the complex organisations they really are, pulled in many contradictory directions at once as Lefebvre implied and generating equally complex and contradictory space. Perhaps most important of all, the individuals who work within them might then no longer appear as pantomime villains, but as the real human beings that they too really are.

In undertaking such work, Marxists wish that the Founding Fathers had been possessed of an infinite amount of time to extend their research across many subjects that they left largely untouched. One is the whole question of organisational theory, which when combined with traditional Marxist focus on the political party as the principal organisation to achieve political change resulted in a view of other organisations that understandably focused on their comparative organisational structures, class composition, and monochromatic economic role within capitalist or socialist society. In a different world, bereft of political party commitment to the replacement of capitalism, let alone of socialist governments, fresh focus on the role of organisations as agents of change and potential midwives of a post-capitalist future is surely required.

Real estate developers may initially seem the most unlikely of candidates for this role, but the importance of the urban as a political battlefield, the inability of the capitalist state to solve the global housing crisis, the increasing demands placed on developers to take account of interests far wider than those of their shareholders, and their very complexity and power demands that Marxists at the very least engage with them. For it is surely now a principal challenge for Marxists and developers alike: how best to use development to create differential, not abstract, space. Pointing to the most egregious and obvious failures of developers may be necessary, but it is not sufficient: the need is for recommendations for action and structure flowing from the right to the city, understood in its widest sense, reinforced by recognition of developer achievements in the creation of differential space that can and should be used as both inspiration and political leverage with developers. It is appropriate to finish this book by reminding ourselves of the injunction at the outset: the need for relevance, for practical application. To pull the two ends of the chain together – this is the challenge that Lefebvre's work still sets Marxists: our world, and our challenge.

Bibliography

Abell, J. (2020). *Freud for Architects*. London, Routledge.

Arseneau, J. (2021). *The class, the party and the leadership: How to organize revolution*. Available at: www.marxist.com/the-class-the-party-and-the-leadership-how-to-organize-revolution.htm. [Accessed 2 January 2023].

Bauckham, R. J. (1980). The delay of the Parousia. *Tyndale Bulletin*, 31, 3–36.

Blackledge, P. (2012). *Marxism and Ethics: Freedom, Desire, and Revolution*. New York, State University of New York Press.

Brenner, N. (2018). Debating planetary urbanization: For an engaged pluralism. *Environment and Planning D: Society and Space*, *36*(3), 570–590.

Coleman, N. (2014). *Lefebvre for Architects*. London, Taylor & Francis.

Cox, K. (2005). *From Marxist Geography to Critical Geography and Back Again*. Working Paper. Department of Geography, The Ohio State University, 28 October.

Elster, J. (1981). Clearing the decks. *Ethics*, 91(4), 634–644.

Fainstein, D. (1996). Justice, politics and the creation of urban space. In Merrifield, A. and Swyndegouw, E. (eds.) *The Urbanization of Injustice*. New York, New York University Press.

Frantzanas, S. (2014). The right to the city as an anti-capitalist struggle. *ephemera*, 14(4), 1073.

Fuchs, C. (2021). Cornel West and Marxist humanism. In Fuchs, C. *Foundations of Critical Theory*. New York and London, Routledge, 191–226.

Garaudy, R. (1976). *Le projet espérance*. Paris, Éditions Robert Laffont.

Gleeson, J. J. and O'Rourke, E. (2021). *Transgender Marxism*: London, Pluto Press.

Goonewardena, K. (2011). Henri Lefebvre. In Ritzer, G. and Stepnisky, J. (eds.) *The Wiley-Blackwell Companion to Major Social Theorists*. Volume 1. London, Wiley-Blackwell, 44–64.

Hall, S. (2016). *Cultural Studies 1983: A Theoretical History*. Durham, NC, Duke University Press.

Howe, L. B. (2022). Towards a cooperative urbanism? An alternative conceptualization of urban development for Johannesburg's mining belt. *Environment and Urbanization*, 34(2), 391–412.

Jamin, J. (2018). Cultural Marxism: A survey. *Religion Compass*, 12(1–2), e12258.

Kolakowski, L. (1978). *Main Currents of Marxism. Vol. 1. The Founders*. Oxford, Oxford University Press.

Lefebvre, H. (1970). *Du rural à l'urbain*. Paris, Anthropos.

———. (1973 [1976]). *La Survie du capitalisme: La reproduction des rapports de production*. Paris, Anthropos. Translated by F. Bryant as *The Survival of Capitalism. Reproduction of the Relations of Production*. London, Allison & Busby.

———. (1974 [1991]). *La production de l'espace*. Paris, Anthropos. Translated by D. Nicholson-Smith as *The Production of Space*. Oxford, Blackwell.

———. (1989 [2014]). Dissolving City, Planetary Metamorphosis. [Quand la ville se perd dans une métamorphose planétaire]. *Environment and Planning D: Society & Space*, 32(2), 203–205.

Liu, Z. (2018). *On the origins of Marxist geography – a recount of David Harvey's turn to urban studies*. Proceedings of the 2018 International Conference on Management,

Economics, Education and Social Sciences (MEESS 2018). Available at: www.atlantis-press.com/proceedings/meess-18/25900575. [Accessed 7 August 2021].
Misoczky, M. C. and Oliveira, C. M. D. (2018). The city and the urban as spaces of capital and social struggle: Notes on Henri Lefebvre's enduring contributions. *Revista de Administração Pública*, 52(6), 1015–1031.
Mojab, S. (2015). *Marxism and Feminism*. London, Bloomsbury Publishing.
Monte-Mór, R. L. (2018). Urbanisation, sustainability and development: Contemporary complexities and diversities in the production of urban space. In Horn, P. *et al*. (eds.) *Emerging Urban Spaces. A Planetary Perspective*. Cham, Springer, 201–215.
Morgan, D. (2017). *Kant for Architects*. London, Routledge.
Noys, B. (2010). *Persistence of the Negative: A Critique of Contemporary Continental Theory*. Edinburgh, Edinburgh University Press.
Page, M. (2017). Introduction: More than meets the eye. In Page, M. and Mennel, T. (eds.) *Reconsidering Jane Jacobs*. New York, Routledge, 1–14.
Pinder, D. (2013). Reconstituting the possible: Lefebvre, utopia and the urban question. *International Journal of Urban and Regional Research*, 39(1), 28–45.
Ribera-Fumaz, R. (2009). From urban political economy to cultural political economy: Rethinking culture and economy in and beyond the urban. *Progress in Human Geography*, 33(4), 447–465.
Robinson, C. J. (2021). *Black Marxism: The Making of the Black Radical Tradition*. Harmondswoth, Penguin.
Ross, K. and Lefebvre, H. (1983 [1997]). Lefebvre on the Situationists: An interview. *October* (79), 69–83.
Saito, K. (2017). *Karl Marx's Ecosocialism*. New York, Monthly Review Press.
Sartre, J.-P. (1957 [1963]). *Questions de méthode*. Paris, Gallimard. Translated by H. E. Barnes as *Search for a Method*. New York, Knopf.
Scharr, A. (2014). Series editor's preface. In Coleman, N. *Lefebvre for Architects*. London, Routledge, xiii–xiv.
Sève, L. (2004). *Marx et Nous. Penser avec Marx aujourd'hui*. Volume 1. Paris, Éditions La Dispute.
———. (2012). *Aliénation et émancipation. Précédé de" Urgence de communisme", Suivi de" Karl Marx: 82 textes du" Capital" sur l'aliénation*". Paris, La Dispute.
Stetsenko, A. (2020). Hope, political imagination, and agency in Marxism and beyond: Explicating the transformative worldview and ethico-ontoepistemology. *Educational Philosophy and Theory*, 52(7), 726–737.
Stryker, S. (1994). My words to victor Frankenstein above the village of Chamounix: Performing transgender rage. *GLQ: A Journal of Lesbian and Gay Studies*, 1, 237–254.
———. (2015). Transing the queer (in) human. *GLQ: A Journal of Lesbian and Gay Studies*, 21(2), 227–230.
Unwin, T. (2000). A waste of space? Towards a critique of the social production of space. *Transactions of the Institute of British Geographers*, 25(1), 11–29.
Vives-Miró, S. (2022). The urbanization of poverty: Rethinking the production of unjust geographies. *Fennia-International Journal of Geography*, 200(1), 41–51.
Wu, C., Wilkes, R., Silver, D. and Clark, T. N. (2019). Current debates in urban theory from a scale perspective: Introducing a scenes approach. *Urban Studies*, 56(8), 1487–1497.
Yaneva, A. (2022). *Latour for Architects*. London, Routledge.

Index

Note: Page numbers in *italic* indicate a figure on the corresponding page.

For Product Safety Concerns and Information please contact our EU
representative GPSR@taylorandfrancis.com
Taylor & Francis Verlag GmbH, Kaufingerstraße 24, 80331 München, Germany

www.ingramcontent.com/pod-product-compliance
Ingram Content Group UK Ltd.
Pitfield, Milton Keynes, MK11 3LW, UK
UKHW020154200926
475702UK00016B/2698

* 9 7 8 1 0 3 2 1 1 5 1 4 6 *